ADVANCED VIDEO PROCESSING PROJECTS WITH PYTHON AND TKINTER

VIVIAN SIAHAAN
RISMON HASIHOLAN SIANIPAR

Copyright © 2024 BALIGE Publishing

All rights reserved. No part of this book may be reproduced, stored in a retrieval system, or transmitted in any form or by any means, without the prior written permission of the publisher, except in the case of brief quotations embedded in critical articles or reviews. Every effort has been made in the preparation of this book to ensure the accuracy of the information presented. However, the information contained in this book is sold without warranty, either express or implied. Neither the authors, nor BALIGE Publishing or its dealers and distributors, will be held liable for any damages caused or alleged to have been caused directly or indirectly by this book. BALIGE Publishing has endeavored to provide trademark information about all of the companies and products mentioned in this book by the appropriate use of capitals. However, BALIGE Publishing cannot guarantee the accuracy of this information.

Published: MAY 2024
Production reference: 0700524
Published by BALIGE Publishing Ltd.
BALIGE, North Sumatera

ABOUT THE AUTHOR

Vivian Siahaan is a highly motivated individual with a passion for continuous learning and exploring new areas. Born and raised in Hinalang Bagasan, Balige, situated on the picturesque banks of Lake Toba, she completed her high school education at SMAN 1 Balige. Vivian's journey into the world of programming began with a deep dive into various languages such as Java, Android, JavaScript, CSS, C++, Python, R, Visual Basic, Visual C#, MATLAB, Mathematica, PHP, JSP, MySQL, SQL Server, Oracle, Access, and more. Starting from scratch, Vivian diligently studied programming, focusing on mastering the fundamental syntax and logic. She honed her skills by creating practical GUI applications, gradually building her expertise. One particular area of interest for Vivian is animation and game development, where she aspires to make significant contributions. Alongside her programming and mathematical pursuits, she also finds joy in indulging in novels, nurturing her love for literature. Vivian Siahaan's passion for programming and her extensive knowledge are reflected in the numerous ebooks she has authored. Her works, published by Sparta Publisher, cover a wide range of topics, including "Data Structure with Java," "Java Programming: Cookbook," "C++ Programming: Cookbook," "C Programming For High Schools/Vocational Schools and Students," "Java Programming for SMA/SMK," "Java Tutorial: GUI, Graphics and Animation," "Visual Basic Programming: From A to Z," "Java Programming for Animation and Games," "C# Programming for SMA/SMK and Students," "MATLAB For Students and Researchers," "Graphics in JavaScript: Quick Learning Series," "JavaScript Image Processing Methods: From A to Z," "Java GUI Case Study: AWT & Swing," "Basic CSS and JavaScript," "PHP/MySQL Programming: Cookbook," "Visual Basic: Cookbook," "C++ Programming for High Schools/Vocational Schools and Students," "Concepts and Practices of C++," "PHP/MySQL For Students," "C# Programming: From A to Z," "Visual Basic for SMA/SMK and Students," and "C# .NET and SQL Server for High School/Vocational School and Students." Furthermore, at the ANDI Yogyakarta publisher, Vivian Siahaan has contributed to several notable books, including "Python Programming Theory and Practice," "Python GUI Programming," "Python GUI and Database," "Build From Zero School Database Management System In Python/MySQL," "Database Management System in Python/MySQL," "Python/MySQL For Management Systems of Criminal Track Record Database," "Java/MySQL For Management Systems of Criminal Track Records Database," "Database and Cryptography Using Java/MySQL," and "Build From Zero School Database Management System With Java/MySQL." Vivian's diverse range of expertise in programming languages, combined with her passion for exploring new horizons, makes her a dynamic and versatile individual in the field of technology. Her dedication to learning, coupled with her strong analytical and problem-solving skills, positions her as a valuable asset in any programming endeavor. Vivian Siahaan's contributions to the world of programming and literature continue to inspire and empower aspiring programmers and readers alike.

Rismon Hasiholan Sianipar, born in Pematang Siantar in 1994, is a distinguished researcher and expert in the field of electrical engineering. After completing his education at SMAN 3 Pematang Siantar, Rismon ventured to the city of Jogjakarta to pursue his academic journey. He obtained his Bachelor of Engineering (S.T) and Master of Engineering (M.T) degrees in Electrical Engineering from Gadjah Mada University in 1998 and 2001, respectively, under the guidance of esteemed professors, Dr. Adhi Soesanto and Dr. Thomas Sri Widodo. During his studies, Rismon focused on researching non-stationary signals and their energy analysis using time-frequency maps. He explored the dynamic nature of signal energy distribution on time-frequency maps and developed innovative techniques using discrete wavelet transformations to design non-linear filters for data pattern analysis. His research showcased the application of these techniques in various fields. In recognition of his academic prowess, Rismon was awarded the prestigious Monbukagakusho scholarship by the Japanese Government in 2003. He went on to pursue his Master of Engineering (M.Eng) and Doctor of Engineering (Dr.Eng) degrees at Yamaguchi University, supervised by Prof. Dr. Hidetoshi Miike. Rismon's master's and doctoral theses revolved around combining the SR-FHN (Stochastic Resonance Fitzhugh-Nagumo) filter strength with the cryptosystem ECC (elliptic curve cryptography) 4096-bit. This innovative approach effectively suppressed noise in digital images and videos while ensuring their authenticity. Rismon's research findings have been published in renowned international scientific journals, and his patents have been officially registered in Japan. Notably, one of his patents, with registration number 2008-009549, gained recognition. He actively collaborates with several universities and research institutions in Japan, specializing in cryptography, cryptanalysis, and digital forensics, particularly in the areas of audio, image, and video analysis. With a passion for knowledge sharing, Rismon has authored numerous national and international scientific articles and authored several national books. He has also actively participated in workshops related to cryptography, cryptanalysis, digital watermarking, and digital forensics. During these workshops, Rismon has assisted Prof. Hidetoshi Miike in developing applications related to digital image and video processing, steganography, cryptography, watermarking, and more, which serve as valuable training materials. Rismon's field of interest encompasses multimedia security, signal processing, digital image and video analysis, cryptography, digital communication, digital forensics, and data compression. He continues to advance his research by developing applications using programming languages such as Python, MATLAB, C++, C, VB.NET, C#.NET, R, and Java. These applications serve both research and commercial purposes, further contributing to the advancement of signal and image analysis. Rismon Hasiholan Sianipar is a dedicated researcher and expert in the field of electrical engineering, particularly in the areas of signal processing, cryptography, and digital forensics. His academic achievements, patented inventions, and extensive publications demonstrate his commitment to advancing knowledge in these fields. Rismon's contributions to academia and his collaborations with prestigious institutions in Japan have solidified his position as a respected figure in the scientific community. Through his ongoing research and development of innovative applications, Rismon continues to make significant contributions to the field of electrical engineering.

ABOUT THE BOOK

The book focuses on developing Python-based GUI applications for video processing and analysis, catering to various needs such as object tracking, motion detection, and frame analysis. These applications utilize libraries like Tkinter for GUI development and OpenCV for video processing, offering user-friendly interfaces with interactive controls. They provide functionalities like video playback, frame navigation, ROI selection, filtering, and histogram analysis, empowering users to perform detailed analysis and manipulation of video content.

Each project tackles specific aspects of video analysis, from simplifying video processing tasks through a graphical interface to implementing advanced algorithms like Lucas-Kanade, Kalman filter, and Gaussian pyramid optical flow for optical flow computation and object tracking. Moreover, they integrate features like MD5 hashing for video integrity verification and filtering techniques such as bilateral filtering, anisotropic diffusion, and denoising for enhancing video quality and analysis accuracy. Overall, these projects demonstrate the versatility and effectiveness of Python in developing comprehensive tools for video analysis, catering to diverse user needs in fields like computer vision, multimedia processing, forensic analysis, and content verification.

The first project aims to simplify video processing tasks through a user-friendly graphical interface, allowing users to execute various operations like filtering, edge detection, hashing, motion analysis, and object tracking effortlessly. The process involves setting up the GUI framework using tkinter, adding descriptive titles and containers for buttons, defining button actions to execute Python scripts, and dynamically generating buttons for organized presentation. Functionalities cover a wide range of video processing tasks, including frame operations, motion analysis, and object tracking. Users interact by launching the application, selecting an operation, and viewing results. Advantages include ease of use, organized access to functionalities, and extensibility for adding new tasks. Overall, this project bridges Python scripting with a user-friendly interface, democratizing advanced video processing for a broader audience.

The second project aims to develop a video player application with advanced frame analysis functionalities, allowing users to open video files, navigate frames, and analyze them extensively. The application, built using tkinter, features a canvas for video display with zoom and drag capabilities, playback controls, and frame extraction options. Users can jump to specific times, extract frames for analysis, and visualize RGB histograms while calculating MD5 hash values for integrity verification. Additionally, users can open multiple instances of the player for parallel analysis. Overall, this tool caters to professionals in forensic analysis, video editing, and educational fields, facilitating comprehensive frame-by-frame examination and evaluation.

The third project is a robust Python tool tailored for video frame analysis and filtering, employing Tkinter for the GUI. Users can effortlessly load, play, and dissect video files frame by frame, with options to extract frames, implement diverse filtering techniques, and visualize color channel histograms. Additionally, it computes and exhibits hash values for extracted frames, facilitating frame comparison and verification. With an array of functionalities, including OpenCV integration for image processing and filtering, alongside features like wavelet transform and denoising algorithms, this application is a comprehensive solution for users requiring intricate video frame scrutiny and manipulation.

The fourth project is a robust application designed for edge detection on video frames, featuring a Tkinter-based GUI for user interaction. It facilitates video loading, frame navigation, and application of various edge detection algorithms, alongside offering analyses like histograms and hash values. With functionalities for frame extraction, edge detection selection, and interactive zooming, the project provides a comprehensive solution for users in fields requiring detailed video frame analysis and processing, such as computer vision and multimedia processing.

The fifth project presents a sophisticated graphical application tailored for video frame processing and MD5 hashing. It offers users a streamlined interface to load videos, inspect individual frames, and compute hash values, crucial for tasks like video forensics and integrity verification. Utilizing Python libraries such as Tkinter, PIL, and moviepy, the project ensures efficient video handling, metadata extraction, and histogram visualization, providing a robust solution for diverse video analysis needs. With its focus on frame-level hashing and extensible architecture, the project stands as a versatile tool adaptable to various applications in video analysis and content verification.

The sixth project presents a robust graphical tool designed for video analysis and frame extraction. By leveraging Python and key libraries like Tkinter, PIL, and imageio, users can effortlessly open videos, visualize frames, and extract specific frames for analysis. Notably, the application computes hash values using eight different algorithms, including MD5, SHA-1, and SHA-256, enhancing its utility for tasks such as video forensics and integrity verification. With features like frame zooming, navigation controls, and support for multiple instances, this project offers a versatile platform for comprehensive video analysis, catering to diverse user needs in fields like content authentication and forensic investigation.

The seventh project offers a graphical user interface (GUI) for computing hash values of video files, ensuring their integrity and authenticity through multiple hashing algorithms. Key features include video playback controls, hash computation using algorithms like MD5, SHA-1, and SHA-256, and displaying and saving hash values for reference. Users can open multiple instances to handle different videos simultaneously. The tool is particularly useful in digital forensics, data verification, and content security, providing a user-friendly interface and robust functionalities for reliable video content verification.

The eighth project aims to develop a GUI application that lets users interact with video files through various controls, including play, pause, stop, frame navigation, and time-specific jumps. It also offers features like zooming, noise reduction via a mean filter, and the ability to open multiple instances. Users can load videos, adjust playback, apply filters, and handle video frames dynamically, enhancing video viewing and manipulation.

The ninth project aims to develop a GUI application for filtering video frames using anisotropic diffusion, allowing users to load videos, apply the filter, and interact with the frames. The core component, AnisotropicDiffusion, handles video processing and GUI interactions. Users can control playback, zoom, and navigate frames, with the ability to apply the filter dynamically. The GUI features panels for video display, control buttons, and supports multiple instances. Event handlers enable smooth interaction, and real-time updates reflect changes in playback and filtering. The application is designed for efficient memory use, intuitive controls, and a responsive user experience.

The tenth project involves creating a GUI application that allows users to filter video frames using a bilateral filter. Users can load video files, apply the filter, and interact with the filtered frames. The BilateralFilter class handles video processing and GUI interactions, initializing attributes like the video source and GUI elements. The GUI includes panels for displaying video frames and control buttons for opening files, playback, zoom, and navigation. Users can control playback, zoom, pan, and apply the filter dynamically. The application supports multiple instances, efficient rendering, and real-time updates, ensuring a responsive and user-friendly experience.

The twelfth project involves creating a GUI application for filtering video frames using the Non-Local Means Denoising technique. The NonLocalMeansDenoising class manages video processing and GUI interactions, initializing attributes like video source, frame index, and GUI elements. Users can load video files, apply the denoising filter, and interact with frames through controls for playback, zoom, and navigation. The GUI supports multiple instances, allowing users to compare videos. Efficient rendering ensures smooth playback, while adjustable parameters fine-tune the filter's performance. The application maintains aspect ratios, handles errors, and provides feedback, prioritizing a seamless user experience.

The thirteenth performs Canny edge detection on video frames. It allows users to load video files, view original frames, and see Canny edge-detected results side by side. The VideoCanny class handles video processing and GUI interactions, initializing necessary attributes. The interface includes panels for video display and control buttons for loading videos, adjusting zoom, jumping to specific times, and controlling playback. Users can also open multiple instances for comparing videos. The application ensures smooth playback and real-time edge detection with efficient rendering and robust error handling.

The fourteenth project is a GUI application built with Tkinter and OpenCV for real-time edge detection in video streams using the Kirsch algorithm. The main class, VideoKirsch, initializes the GUI components, providing features like video loading, frame display, zoom control, playback control, and Kirsch edge detection. The interface displays original and edge-detected frames side by side, with control buttons for loading videos, adjusting zoom, jumping to specific times, and controlling playback. Users can play, pause, stop, and navigate through video frames, with real-time edge detection and dynamic frame updates. The application supports multiple instances for comparing videos, employs efficient rendering for smooth playback, and includes robust error handling. Overall, it offers a user-friendly tool for real-time edge detection in videos.

The fifteenth project is a Python-based GUI application for computing and visualizing optical flow in video streams using the Lucas-Kanade method. Utilizing tkinter, PIL, imageio, OpenCV, and numpy, it features panels for original and optical flow-processed frames, control buttons, and adjustable parameters. The VideoOpticalFlow class handles video loading, playback, optical flow computation, and error handling. The GUI allows smooth video playback, zooming, time jumping, and panning. Optical flow is visualized in real-time, showing motion vectors. Users can open multiple instances to analyze various videos simultaneously, making this tool valuable for computer vision and video analysis tasks.

The sixteenth project is a Python application designed to analyze optical flow in video streams using the Kalman filter method. It utilizes libraries such as tkinter, PIL, imageio, OpenCV, and numpy to create a GUI, process video frames, and implement the Kalman filter algorithm. The VideoKalmanOpticalFlow class manages video loading, playback control, optical flow computation, canvas interactions, and Kalman filter implementation. The GUI layout features panels for original and optical flow-processed frames, along with control buttons and widgets for adjusting parameters. Users can open video files, control playback, and visualize optical flow in real-time, with the Kalman filter improving accuracy by incorporating temporal dynamics and reducing noise. Error handling ensures a robust experience, and multiple instances can be opened for simultaneous video analysis, making this tool valuable for computer vision and video analysis tasks.

The seventeenth project is a Python application designed to analyze optical flow in video streams using the Gaussian pyramid method. It utilizes libraries such as tkinter, PIL, imageio, OpenCV, and numpy to create a GUI, process video frames, and implement optical flow computation. The VideoGaussianPyramidOpticalFlow class manages video loading, playback control, optical flow computation, canvas interactions, and GUI creation. The GUI layout features panels for original and optical flow-processed frames, along with control buttons and widgets for adjusting parameters. Users can open video files, control playback, and visualize optical flow in real-time, providing insights into motion patterns within the video stream. Error handling ensures a robust user experience, and multiple instances can be opened for simultaneous video analysis.

The eighteenth project is a Python application developed for tracking objects in video streams using the Lucas-Kanade optical flow algorithm. It utilizes libraries like tkinter, PIL, imageio, OpenCV, and numpy to create a GUI, process video frames, and implement tracking functionalities. The ObjectTrackingLucasKanade class manages video loading, playback control, object tracking, GUI creation, and event handling. The GUI layout includes a video display panel with a canvas widget for showing video frames and a list box for displaying tracked object coordinates. Users interact with the video by defining bounding boxes around objects for tracking. The application provides buttons for opening video files, adjusting zoom, controlling playback, and clearing object tracking data. Error handling ensures a smooth user experience, making it suitable for various computer vision and video analysis tasks.

The nineteenth project is a Python application utilizing Tkinter to create a GUI for analyzing RGB histograms of video frames. It features the Filter_CroppedFrame class, initializing GUI elements like buttons and canvas for video display. Users can open videos, control playback, and navigate frames. Zooming is enabled, and users can draw bounding boxes for RGB histogram analysis. Filters like Gaussian, Mean, and Bilateral Filtering can be applied, with histograms displayed for the filtered image. Multiple instances of the GUI can be opened simultaneously. The project offers a user-friendly interface for image analysis and enhancement.

The twentieth project creates a graphical user interface (GUI) for motion analysis using the Block-based Gradient Descent Search (BGDS) optical flow algorithm. It initializes the VideoBGDSOpticalFlow class, setting up attributes and methods for video display, control buttons, and parameter input fields. Users can open videos, control playback, specify parameters, and analyze optical flow motion vectors between consecutive frames. The GUI provides an intuitive interface for efficient motion analysis tasks, enhancing user interaction with video playback controls and optical flow visualization tools.

The twenty first project is a Python project that constructs a graphical user interface (GUI) for optical flow analysis using the Diamond Search Algorithm (DSA). It initializes a VideoFSBM_DSAOpticalFlow class, setting up attributes for video display, control buttons, and parameter input fields. Users can open videos, control playback, specify algorithm parameters, and visualize optical flow motion vectors efficiently. The GUI layout includes canvas widgets for displaying the original video and optical flow result, with interactive functionalities such as zooming and navigating between frames. The script provides an intuitive interface for optical flow analysis tasks, enhancing user interaction and visualization capabilities.

The twenty second project "Object Tracking with Block-based Gradient Descent Search (BGDS)" demonstrates object tracking in videos using a block-based gradient descent search algorithm. It utilizes tkinter for GUI development, PIL for image processing, imageio for video file handling, and OpenCV for computer vision tasks. The main class, ObjectTracking_BGDS, initializes the GUI window and implements functionalities such as video playback control, frame navigation, and object tracking using the BGDS algorithm. Users can interactively select a bounding box around the object of interest for tracking, and the application provides parameter inputs for algorithm adjustment. Overall, it offers a user-friendly interface for motion analysis tasks, showcasing the application of computer vision techniques in object tracking.

The tenty third project "Object Tracking with AGAST (Adaptive and Generic Accelerated Segment Test)" is a Python application tailored for object tracking in videos via the AGAST algorithm. It harnesses libraries like tkinter, PIL, imageio, and OpenCV for GUI, image processing, video handling, and computer vision tasks respectively. The main class, ObjectTracking_AGAST, orchestrates the GUI setup, featuring buttons for video control, a combobox for zoom selection, and a canvas for displaying frames. The pivotal agast_vectors method employs OpenCV's AGAST feature detector to compute motion vectors between frames. The track_object method utilizes AGAST for object tracking within specified bounding boxes. Users can interactively select objects for tracking, making it a user-friendly tool for motion analysis tasks.

The twenty fourth project "Object Tracking with AKAZE (Accelerated-KAZE)" offers a user-friendly Python application for real-time object tracking within videos, leveraging the efficient AKAZE algorithm. Its tkinter-based graphical interface features a Video Display Panel for live frame viewing, Control Buttons Panel for playback management, and Zoom Scale Combobox for precise zoom adjustment. With the ObjectTracking_AKAZE class at its core, the app facilitates seamless video playback, AKAZE-based object tracking, and interactive bounding box selection. Users benefit from comprehensive tracking insights provided by the Center Coordinates Listbox, ensuring accurate and efficient object monitoring. Overall, it presents a robust solution for dynamic object tracking, integrating advanced computer vision techniques with user-centric design.

The twenty fifth project "Object Tracking with BRISK (Binary Robust Invariant Scalable Keypoints)" delivers a sophisticated Python application tailored for real-time object tracking in videos. Featuring a tkinter-based GUI, it offers intuitive controls and visualizations to enhance user experience. Key elements include a Video Display Panel for live frame viewing, a Control Buttons Panel for playback management, and a Center Coordinates Listbox for tracking insights. Powered by the ObjectTracking_BRISK class, the application employs the BRISK algorithm for precise tracking, leveraging features like zoom adjustment and interactive bounding box selection. With robust functionalities like frame navigation and playback control, coupled with a clear interface design, it provides users with a versatile tool for analyzing object movements in videos effectively.

The twenty sixth project "Object Tracking with GLOH" is a Python application designed for video object tracking using the Gradient Location-Orientation Histogram (GLOH) method. Featuring a Tkinter-based GUI, users can load videos, navigate frames, and visualize tracking outcomes seamlessly. Key functionalities include video playback control, bounding box initialization via mouse events, and dynamic zoom scaling. With OpenCV handling computer vision tasks, the project offers precise object tracking and real-time visualization, demonstrating the effective integration of advanced techniques with an intuitive user interface for enhanced usability and analysis.

The twenty seventh project "boosting_tracker.py" is a Python-based application utilizing Tkinter for its GUI, designed for object tracking in videos via the Boosting Tracker algorithm. Its interface, titled "Object Tracking with Boosting Tracker," allows users to load videos, navigate frames, define tracking regions, apply filters, and visualize histograms. The core class, "BoostingTracker," manages video operations, object tracking, and filtering. The GUI features controls like play/pause buttons, zoom scale selection, and filter options. Object tracking begins with user-defined bounding boxes, and the application supports various filters for enhancing video regions. Histogram analysis provides insights into pixel value distributions. Error handling ensures smooth functionality, and advanced filters like Haar Wavelet Transform are available. Overall, "boosting_tracker.py" integrates computer vision and GUI components effectively, offering a versatile tool for video analysis with user-friendly interaction and comprehensive functionalities.

The twenty eighth project "csrt_tracker.py" offers a comprehensive GUI for object tracking using the CSRT algorithm. Leveraging tkinter, imageio, OpenCV (cv2), and PIL, it facilitates video handling, tracking, and image processing. The CSRTTracker class manages tracking functionalities, while create_widgets sets up GUI components like video display, control buttons, and filters. Methods like open_video, play_video, and stop_video handle video playback, while initialize_tracker and track_object manage CSRT tracking. User interaction, including mouse event handlers for zooming and ROI selection, is supported. Filtering options like Wiener filter and adaptive thresholding enhance image processing. Overall, the script provides a versatile and interactive tool for object tracking and analysis, showcasing effective integration of various libraries for enhanced functionality and user experience.

The twenty ninth project, KCFTracker, is a robust object tracking application with a Tkinter-based GUI. The KCFTracker class orchestrates video handling, user interaction, and tracking functionalities. It sets up GUI elements like video display and control buttons, enabling tasks such as video playback, bounding box definition, and filter application. Methods like open_video and play_video handle video loading and playback, while toggle_play_pause manages playback control. User interaction for defining bounding boxes is facilitated through mouse event handlers. The analyze_histogram method processes selected regions for histogram analysis. Various filters, including Gaussian and Median filtering, enhance image processing. Overall, the project offers a comprehensive tool for real-time object tracking and video analysis.

The thirtieth project, MedianFlow Tracker, is a Python application built with Tkinter for the GUI and OpenCV for object tracking. It provides users with interactive video manipulation tools, including playback controls and object tracking functionalities. The main class, MedianFlowTracker, initializes the interface and handles video loading, playback, and object tracking using OpenCV's MedianFlow tracker. Users can define bounding boxes for object tracking directly on the canvas, with real-time updates of the tracked object's center coordinates. Additionally, the project offers various image processing filters, parameter controls for fine-tuning tracking, and histogram analysis of the tracked object's region. Overall, it demonstrates a comprehensive approach to video analysis and object tracking, leveraging Python's capabilities in multimedia applications.

The thirty first project, MILTracker, is a Python application that implements object tracking using the Multiple Instance Learning (MIL) algorithm. Built with Tkinter for the GUI and OpenCV for video processing, it offers a range of features for video analysis and tracking. Users can open video files, select regions of interest (ROI) for tracking, and apply various filters to enhance tracking performance. The GUI includes controls for video playback, navigation, and zoom, while mouse interactions allow for interactive ROI selection. Advanced features include histogram analysis of the ROI and error handling for smooth operation. Overall, MILTracker provides a comprehensive tool for video tracking and analysis, demonstrating the integration of multiple technologies for efficient object tracking.

The thirty second project, MOSSE Tracker, implemented in the mosse_tracker.py script, offers advanced object tracking capabilities within video files. Utilizing Tkinter for the GUI and OpenCV for video processing, it provides a user-friendly interface for video playback, object tracking, and image analysis. The application allows users to open videos, control playback, select regions of interest for tracking, and apply various filters. It supports zooming, mouse interactions for ROI selection, and histogram analysis of the selected areas. With methods for navigating frames, clearing data, and updating visuals, the MOSSE Tracker project stands as a robust tool for video analysis and object tracking tasks.

The thirty third project, TLDTracker, offers a versatile and powerful tool for object tracking using the TLD algorithm. Built with Tkinter, it provides an intuitive interface for video playback, frame navigation, and object selection. Key features include zoom functionality, interactive ROI selection, and real-time tracking with OpenCV's TLD implementation. Users can apply various filters, analyze histograms, and utilize advanced techniques like wavelet transforms. The tool ensures efficient processing, robust error handling, and extensibility for future enhancements. Overall, TLDTracker stands as a valuable asset for both research and practical video analysis tasks, offering a seamless user experience and advanced image processing capabilities.

The thirty fourth project, motion detection application based on the K-Nearest Neighbors (KNN) background subtraction method, offers a user-friendly interface for video processing and analysis. Utilizing Tkinter, it provides controls for video playback, frame navigation, and object detection. The MixtureofGaussiansWithFilter class orchestrates video handling, applying filters like Gaussian blur and background subtraction for motion detection. Users can interactively draw bounding boxes to select regions of interest (ROIs), triggering histogram analysis and various image filters. The application excels in its modular design, facilitating easy extension for custom research or application needs, and empowers users to explore video data effectively.

The thirty fifth project, "Mixture of Gaussians with Filtering", is a Python script tailored for motion detection in videos using the MOG algorithm alongside diverse filtering methods. Leveraging tkinter for GUI and OpenCV for image processing, it facilitates interactive video playback, frame navigation, and object tracking. With features like adjustable motion detection thresholds and a wide range of filtering options including Gaussian blur, mean blur, and more, users can fine-tune analysis parameters. Object detection, highlighted by bounding boxes and centroid display, coupled with histogram analysis of selected regions, enhances the tool's utility for in-depth video examination.

The thirty sixth project, "running_gaussian_average_with_filtering.py", implements motion detection using the Running Gaussian Average algorithm and offers a range of filtering techniques. It employs Tkinter for GUI creation and integrates OpenCV, PIL, imageio, matplotlib, pywt, and numpy modules. The core component, the RunningGaussianAverage class, orchestrates GUI setup, video processing, frame differencing, contour detection, and filtering. The GUI features a canvas for video display, a listbox for object center display, and control buttons for playback, navigation, and threshold adjustment. Mouse events handle zooming and object selection, while histogram analysis and filtering options enrich the analysis capabilities. Overall, it offers a comprehensive tool for motion detection and object tracking with user-friendly interaction and versatile filtering methods.

The thirty seventh project, "kernel_density_estimation_with_filtering.py", implements motion detection using Kernel Density Estimation (KDE) alongside diverse filtering techniques, all wrapped in a Tkinter-based GUI for video file interaction and motion visualization. The main class, KDEWithFilter, orchestrates GUI setup, video frame processing, and interaction functionalities. Leveraging libraries like OpenCV, imageio, Matplotlib, PyWavelets, and NumPy, it handles tasks such as video I/O, background subtraction, contour detection, and filtering. Users can open, play/pause/stop videos, navigate frames, adjust thresholds, and apply filters. Mouse-driven ROI selection enables histogram analysis and filter application, while interactive parameter adjustments enhance flexibility. Overall, the script offers a comprehensive tool for motion detection and image filtering, catering to diverse computer vision needs.

CONTENT

MAIN PROGRAM	**1**
DESCRIPTION	1
SOURCE CODE	3
RUNNING PROGRAM	8
FRAME HISTOGRAM	**9**
DESCRIPTION	9
SOURCE CODE	11
RUNNING PROGRAM	16
FRAME FILTERING	**17**
DESCRIPTION	17
SOURCE CODE	20
RUNNING PROGRAM	24
FRAME EDGES DETECTION	**27**
DESCRIPTION	27
SOURCE CODE	29
RUNNING PROGRAM	41
FRAME HASHING	**44**
DESCRIPTION	44
SOURCE CODE	46
RUNNING PROGRAM	50

FRAME HASHING WITH EIGHT HASH FUNCTIONS — 53
DESCRIPTION — 53
SOURCE CODE — 55
RUNNING PROGRAM — 60

HASHING THE WHOLE VIDEO — 63
DESCRIPTION — 63
SOURCE CODE — 65
RUNNING PROGRAM — 67

MEAN FILTERING OF VIDEO — 69
DESCRIPTION — 69
SOURCE CODE — 72
RUNNING PROGRAM — 77

ANISOTROPIC DIFFUSING OF VIDEO — 80
DESCRIPTION — 80
SOURCE CODE — 81
RUNNING PROGRAM — 87

BILATERAL FILTERING OF VIDEO — 88
DESCRIPTION — 88
SOURCE CODE — 90
RUNNING PROGRAM — 96

NON-LOCAL MEANS DENOISING OF VIDEO — 97
DESCRIPTION — 97
SOURCE CODE — 99
RUNNING PROGRAM — 105

DETECTING CANNY EDGES OF VIDEO — 106
DESCRIPTION — 106
SOURCE CODE — 108
RUNNING PROGRAM — 112

DETECTING KIRSCH EDGES OF VIDEO — 114
DESCRIPTION — 114
SOURCE CODE — 115
RUNNING PROGRAM — 120

LUCAS-KANADE OPTICAL FLOW — 121
DESCRIPTION — 121
SOURCE CODE — 123
RUNNING PROGRAM — 128

KALMAN FILTER OPTICAL FLOW — 129
DESCRIPTION — 129
SOURCE CODE — 131
RUNNING PROGRAM — 136

GAUSSIAN PYRAMID OPTICAL FLOW — 137
DESCRIPTION — 137
SOURCE CODE — 138
RUNNING PROGRAM — 144

OBJECT TRACKING WITH LUCAS-KANADE — 145
DESCRIPTION — 145
SOURCE CODE — 147
RUNNING PROGRAM — 151

CROPPED FRAME FILTERING — 153
DESCRIPTION — 153
SOURCE CODE — 154
RUNNING PROGRAM — 163

MOTION ANALYSIS WITH BLOCK-BASED GRADIENT DESCENT SEARCH (BGDS) — 165
DESCRIPTION — 165
SOURCE CODE — 166

RUNNING PROGRAM 173

MOTION ANALYSIS WITH DIAMOND SEARCH ALGORITHM (DSA) 174
DESCRIPTION 174
SOURCE CODE 176
RUNNING PROGRAM 182

OBJECT TRACKING WITH BLOCK-BASED GRADIENT DESCENT SEARCH (BGDS) 183
DESCRIPTION 183
SOURCE CODE 184
RUNNING PROGRAM 191

OBJECT TRACKING WITH AGAST (ADAPTIVE AND GENERIC ACCELERATED SEGMENT TEST) 192
DESCRIPTION 192
SOURCE CODE 193
RUNNING PROGRAM 199

OBJECT TRACKING WITH AKAZE (ACCELERATED-KAZE) 200
DESCRIPTION 200
SOURCE CODE 202
RUNNING PROGRAM 207

OBJECT TRACKING WITH BRISK (BINARY ROBUST INVARIANT SCALABLE KEYPOINTS) 208
DESCRIPTION 208
SOURCE CODE 211
RUNNING PROGRAM 216

OBJECT TRACKING WITH GLOH (GRADIENT LOCATION-ORIENTATION HISTOGRAM) 218

DESCRIPTION	218
SOURCE CODE	221
RUNNING PROGRAM	227

OBJECT TRACKING WITH BOOSTING TRACKER — 229

DESCRIPTION	229
SOURCE CODE	232
RUNNING PROGRAM	242

OBJECT TRACKING WITH CSRT (CHANNEL AND SPATIAL RELIABILITY TRACKER) — 244

DESCRIPTION	244
SOURCE CODE	246
RUNNING PROGRAM	257

OBJECT TRACKING WITH KCF (KERNELIZED CORRELATION FILTERS) TRACKER — 259

DESCRIPTION	259
SOURCE CODE	262
RUNNING PROGRAM	273

OBJECT TRACKING WITH MEDIAN FLOW TRACKER — 275

DESCRIPTION	275
SOURCE CODE	277
RUNNING PROGRAM	289

OBJECT TRACKING WITH MIL (MULTIPLE INSTANCE LEARNING) TRACKER — 291

DESCRIPTION	291
SOURCE CODE	294
RUNNING PROGRAM	304

OBJECT TRACKING WITH MOSSE (MINIMUM OUTPUT SUM OF SQUARED ERROR) TRACKER — 306

DESCRIPTION	306
SOURCE CODE	308
RUNNING PROGRAM	319

OBJECT TRACKING WITH TLD (TRACKING, LEARNING, AND DETECTION) TRACKER — 321

DESCRIPTION	321
SOURCE CODE	324
RUNNING PROGRAM	334

MOTION DETECTION WITH K-NEAREST NEIGHBORS (KNN) — 336

DESCRIPTION	336
SOURCE CODE	339
RUNNING PROGRAM	348

MOTION DETECTION WITH MIXTURE OF GAUSSIANS (MOG) — 349

DESCRIPTION	349
SOURCE CODE	350
RUNNING PROGRAM	360

MOTION DETECTION WITH RUNNING GAUSSIAN AVERAGE — 362

DESCRIPTION	362
SOURCE CODE	364
RUNNING PROGRAM	373

MOTION DETECTION WITH KERNEL DENSITY ESTIMATION — 375

DESCRIPTION	375
SOURCE CODE	376
RUNNING PROGRAM	386

Bibliography — **388**

MAIN PROGRAM

DESCRIPTION

The purpose of this project is to create a user-friendly graphical user interface (GUI) for executing various video processing tasks. The GUI allows users to perform different operations on video frames, such as filtering, edge detection, hashing, motion analysis, and object tracking, by simply clicking on buttons. This makes it easier for users, especially those who may not be comfortable with command-line interfaces, to run complex video processing scripts.

Steps of the Project

1. Set Up the GUI Framework:
   - Initialize the Main Window: Create the main application window using tkinter. Set its title and configure its properties.
   - Create a Font Object: Define the font style to be used for the title and other text elements in the GUI.
2. Add a Title to the GUI:

   Create a Title Label: Add a label at the top of the window with a descriptive title that explains the purpose of the application.
3. Create a Container for Buttons:

Create a Frame: Use a frame to hold all the buttons in a structured layout, making it easier to manage their positions and alignments.
4. Define Button Actions:
Implement Command Functions: Write functions that will be called when each button is clicked. These functions will execute different Python scripts using the subprocess.Popen method.
5. Create Buttons:
    - Define Button Information: Prepare a list of button labels and their associated command functions.
    - Generate Buttons Dynamically: Loop through the list and create buttons, assigning each button its label and command. Place these buttons in the frame in a grid layout for organized presentation.
6. Run the Main Loop:
Start the GUI Loop: Invoke the mainloop() method of tkinter to start the GUI event loop, which keeps the window open and responsive to user interactions.

Functionalities Included

The GUI provides buttons for the following types of video processing tasks:
1. Frame Operations:
    - RGB histogram analysis
    - Filtering (mean, median, Gaussian)
    - Edge detection (Canny, Sobel, Prewitt, etc.)
    - Hashing (various methods)
    - Thresholding (adaptive)
    - Diffusion and denoising techniques
2. Motion Analysis:
    - Background subtraction and motion analysis using different algorithms
    - Optical flow analysis with methods like Lucas-Kanade and Kalman filter
    - Analysis using feature detectors and descriptors (ORB, SIFT, etc.)
3. Object Tracking:
    - Tracking using algorithms such as mean shift, CamShift, Lucas-Kanade, Kalman filter, and others
    - Advanced tracking techniques incorporating Gaussian pyramids, adaptive methods, and various feature detectors

User Interaction

Users interact with the GUI by:
1. Launching the Application: Running the main script to open the GUI window.
2. Selecting an Operation: Clicking on one of the buttons to execute the corresponding video processing script.
3. Viewing Results: The selected script runs, processes the video frames, and typically produces output in the form of processed videos or visual results, which can be viewed separately.

Advantages

1. Ease of Use: Users can run complex video processing tasks without needing to understand or modify the underlying scripts.
2. Organized Access: The GUI neatly organizes all available video processing tasks, making it easy to find and execute the desired operation.
3. Extensibility: New video processing tasks can be added by creating new scripts and corresponding buttons without significantly altering the GUI structure.

This project effectively combines the power of Python scripting for video processing with a user-friendly GUI, making advanced video processing accessible to a broader audience.

SOURCE CODE

```python
import tkinter as tk
from subprocess import Popen
from tkinter import font

def run_frame_rgb_histogram():
    Popen(["python", "histogram_rgb_each_frame.py"])

def run_frame_edge_detection():
    Popen(["python", "edge_detection_each_frame.py"])

def run_frame_filtering():
    Popen(["python", "filtering_each_frame.py"])

def run_frame_hashing():
    Popen(["python", "hashing_each_frame.py"])

def run_frame_eight_hashing():
    Popen(["python", "eight_hash_functions_each_frame.py"])

def run_hashing_whole_video():
    Popen(["python", "hash_functions_whole_video.py"])

def run_video_mean_filtering():
```

```python
    Popen(["python", "mean_filter_frame.py"])

def run_video_median_filtering():
    Popen(["python", "median_filter_frame.py"])

def run_video_gaussian_filtering():
    Popen(["python", "gaussian_filter_frame.py"])

def run_video_adaptive_thresholding():
    Popen(["python", "adaptive_thresholding_frame.py"])

def run_video_anisotropic_diffusion():
    Popen(["python", "anisotopic_diffusion_frame.py"])

def run_video_bilateral_filtering():
    Popen(["python", "bilateral_filter_frame.py"])

def run_video_nonlocal_denoising():
    Popen(["python", "non_local_denoising_frame.py"])

def run_video_canny_detector():
    Popen(["python", "canny__edge_detection_frame.py"])

def run_video_sobel_detector():
    Popen(["python", "sobel__edge_detection_frame.py"])

def run_video_prewitt_detector():
    Popen(["python", "prewitt__edge_detection_frame.py"])

def run_video_scharr_detector():
    Popen(["python", "scharr__edge_detection_frame.py"])

def run_video_kirsch_detector():
    Popen(["python", "kirsch__edge_detection_frame.py"])

def run_video_freichen_detector():
    Popen(["python", "freichen__edge_detection_frame.py"])

def run_video_lucas_kanade_optical_flow():
    Popen(["python", "gui_optical_flow_lucas_kanade.py"])

def run_video_kalman_filter_optical_flow():
    Popen(["python", "gui_optical_flow_kalman_filter.py"])

def run_video_gaussian_pyramid_optical_flow():
    Popen(["python", "gui_optical_flow_gaussian_pyramid.py"])

def run_video_object_tracking_mean_shift():
    Popen(["python", "object_tracking_mean_shift_new.py"])

def run_video_object_tracking_cam_shift():
    Popen(["python", "object_tracking_camshift_new.py"])

def run_video_object_tracking_lucas_kanade():
    Popen(["python", "object_tracking_lucas_kanade_new.py"])

def run_video_object_tracking_kalman_filter():
    Popen(["python", "object_tracking_kalman_filter_new.py"])

def run_video_object_tracking_gaussian_pyramid():
    Popen(["python", "object_tracking_lucas_kanade_gaussian_pyramid_new.py"])

def run_video_cropped_filter():
    Popen(["python", "rgb_cropped_filtered_frame.py"])
```

```python
def run_motion_analysis_bgds():
    Popen(["python", "gui_motion_analysis_bgds.py"])

def run_motion_analysis_fsbm():
    Popen(["python", "gui_motion_analysis_fsbm.py"])

def run_motion_analysis_dsa():
    Popen(["python", "gui_motion_analysis_fsbm_dsa.py"])

def run_object_tracking_bgds():
    Popen(["python", "object_tracking_bgds.py"])

def run_object_tracking_fsbm():
    Popen(["python", "object_tracking_fsbm.py"])

def run_object_tracking_dsa():
    Popen(["python", "object_tracking_fsbm_dsa.py"])

def run_object_tracking_tss():
    Popen(["python", "object_tracking_fsbm_tss.py"])

def run_motion_analysis_gbbm():
    Popen(["python", "gui_motion_analysis_gbbm.py"])

def run_motion_analysis_adaptive_gbbm():
    Popen(["python", "gui_motion_analysis_gbbm_adaptive.py"])

def run_motion_analysis_gbbm_lucas_kanade():
    Popen(["python", "gui_motion_analysis_gbbm_lucas_kanade.py"])

def run_motion_analysis_gbbm_orb():
    Popen(["python", "gui_motion_analysis_gbbm_orb.py"])

def run_motion_analysis_gbbm_gaussian_pyramid():
    Popen(["python", "gui_motion_analysis_gbbm_pyramid.py"])

def run_motion_analysis_gbbm_sift():
    Popen(["python", "gui_motion_analysis_gbbm_sift.py"])

def run_object_tracking_gbbm():
    Popen(["python", "object_tracking_gbbm.py"])

def run_object_tracking_adaptive_gbbm():
    Popen(["python", "object_tracking_gbbm_adaptive.py"])

def run_object_tracking_gbbm_pyramid():
    Popen(["python", "object_tracking_gbbm_pyramid.py"])

def run_object_tracking_gbbm_orb():
    Popen(["python", "object_tracking_orb.py"])

def run_object_tracking_gbbm_sift():
    Popen(["python", "object_tracking_sift.py"])

def run_motion_analysis_gbbm_agast():
    Popen(["python", "gui_motion_analysis_gbbm_agast.py"])

def run_motion_analysis_gbbm_kaze():
    Popen(["python", "gui_motion_analysis_gbbm_akaze.py"])

def run_motion_analysis_gbbm_brisk():
    Popen(["python", "gui_motion_analysis_gbbm_brisk.py"])
```

```python
def run_motion_analysis_gbbm_fast():
    Popen(["python", "gui_motion_analysis_gbbm_fast.py"])

def run_motion_analysis_gbbm_gloh():
    Popen(["python", "gui_motion_analysis_gbbm_gloh.py"])

def run_object_tracking_agast():
    Popen(["python", "object_tracking_agast.py"])

def run_object_tracking_akaze():
    Popen(["python", "object_tracking_akaze.py"])

def run_object_tracking_brisk():
    Popen(["python", "object_tracking_brisk.py"])

def run_object_tracking_gloh():
    Popen(["python", "object_tracking_gloh.py"])

def run_object_tracking_boost():
    Popen(["python", "boosting_tracker_NEW.py"])

def run_object_tracking_csrt():
    Popen(["python", "csrt_tracker.py"])

def run_object_tracking_kcf():
    Popen(["python", "kcf_tracker.py"])

def run_object_tracking_median_flow():
    Popen(["python", "medianflow_tracker.py"])

def run_object_tracking_MIL():
    Popen(["python", "mil_tracker.py"])

def run_object_tracking_MOSSE():
    Popen(["python", "mosse_tracker.py"])

def run_object_tracking_TLD():
    Popen(["python", "tld_tracker.py"])

def run_frame_differencing():
    Popen(["python", "frame_differencing_with_filtering.py"])

def run_median_frame_differencing():
    Popen(["python", "median_filtering_with_filtering.py"])

def run_knn_frame_differencing():
    Popen(["python", "knn_with_filtering.py"])

def run_mog_frame_differencing():
    Popen(["python", "mixture_of_gaussian_with_filtering.py"])

def run_rga_frame_differencing():
    Popen(["python", "running_gaussian_average_with_filtering.py"])

def run_kernel_density_frame_differencing():
    Popen(["python", "kernel_density_estimation_with_filtering.py"])

def create_gui():
    root = tk.Tk()
    label_title = "ADVANCED VIDEO PROCESSING PROJECTS WITH PYTHON AND TKINTER --- VIVIAN SIAHAAN AND RISMON HASIHOLAN SIANIPAR"
    root.title(label_title)

    # Create a font object with desired properties
```

```python
bold_font = font.Font(family="Helvetica", size=16, weight="bold")

# Create a label with the specified text and font
title_label = tk.Label(root, text=label_title, font=bold_font)

# Place the label in the window
title_label.pack(pady=20)  # You can adjust the padding as needed

# Create a frame to hold the buttons
frame = tk.Frame(root)
frame.pack(padx=10, pady=10)

# Button texts and their associated commands
button_info = [
    ("Frame RGB Histogram", run_frame_rgb_histogram),
    ("Frame Filtering", run_frame_filtering),
    ("Frame Edge Detection", run_frame_edge_detection),
    ("Hashing Frame", run_frame_hashing),
    ("Eight Hashing Frame", run_frame_eight_hashing),
    ("Hashing Whole Video", run_hashing_whole_video),
    ("Video Mean Filtering", run_video_mean_filtering),
    ("Video Median Filtering", run_video_median_filtering),
    ("Video Gaussian Filtering", run_video_gaussian_filtering),
    ("Video Adaptive Thresholding", run_video_adaptive_thresholding),
    ("Video Anisotropic Diffusion", run_video_anisotropic_diffusion),
    ("Video Bilateral Filtering", run_video_bilateral_filtering),
    ("Video Non-Local Denoising", run_video_nonlocal_denoising),
    ("Video Canny Edge Detection", run_video_canny_detector),
    ("Video Sobel Edge Detection", run_video_sobel_detector),
    ("Video Prewitt Edge Detection", run_video_prewitt_detector),
    ("Video Scharr Edge Detection", run_video_scharr_detector),
    ("Video Kirsch Edge Detection", run_video_kirsch_detector),
    ("Video Frei-Chen Edge Detection", run_video_freichen_detector),
    ("Video Lucas Kanade Optical Flow", run_video_lucas_kanade_optical_flow),
    ("Video Kalman Filter Optical Flow", run_video_kalman_filter_optical_flow),
    ("Video Gaussian Pyramid Optical Flow", run_video_gaussian_pyramid_optical_flow),
    ("Object Tracking Mean Shift", run_video_object_tracking_mean_shift),
    ("Object Tracking Cam Shift", run_video_object_tracking_cam_shift),
    ("Object Tracking Lucas Kanade", run_video_object_tracking_lucas_kanade),
    ("Object Tracking Kalman Filter", run_video_object_tracking_kalman_filter),
    ("Object Tracking Gaussian Pyramid", run_video_object_tracking_gaussian_pyramid),
    ("Frame Cropped Filtering", run_video_cropped_filter),
    ("BGDS Motion Analysis", run_motion_analysis_bgds),
    ("FSBM Motion Analysis", run_motion_analysis_fsbm),
    ("DSA Motion Analysis", run_motion_analysis_dsa),
    ("Object Tracking BGDS", run_object_tracking_bgds),
    ("Object Tracking FSBM", run_object_tracking_fsbm),
    ("Object Tracking DSA", run_object_tracking_dsa),
    ("Object Tracking TSS", run_object_tracking_tss),
    ("Motion Analysis GBBM", run_motion_analysis_gbbm),
    ("Motion Analysis Adaptive GBBM", run_motion_analysis_adaptive_gbbm),
    ("Motion Analysis GBBM Lucas-Kanade", run_motion_analysis_gbbm_lucas_kanade),
    ("Motion Analysis GBBM ORB", run_motion_analysis_gbbm_orb),
    ("Motion Analysis GBBM Gaussian Pyramid", run_motion_analysis_gbbm_gaussian_pyramid),
    ("Motion Analysis GBBM SIFT", run_motion_analysis_gbbm_sift),
    ("Object Tracking GBBM", run_object_tracking_gbbm),
    ("Object Tracking Adaptive GBBM", run_object_tracking_adaptive_gbbm),
    ("Object Tracking GBBM Pyramid", run_object_tracking_gbbm_pyramid),
    ("Object Tracking GBBM ORB", run_object_tracking_gbbm_orb),
    ("Object Tracking GBBM SIFT", run_object_tracking_gbbm_sift),
    ("Motion Analysis GBBM AGAST", run_motion_analysis_gbbm_agast),
    ("Motion Analysis GBBM AKAZE", run_motion_analysis_gbbm_kaze),
    ("Motion Analysis GBBM BRISK", run_motion_analysis_gbbm_brisk),
    ("Motion Analysis GBBM FAST", run_motion_analysis_gbbm_fast),
```

```python
        ("Motion Analysis GBBM GLOH", run_motion_analysis_gbbm_gloh),
        ("Object Tracking AGAST", run_object_tracking_agast),
        ("Object Tracking AKAZE", run_object_tracking_akaze),
        ("Object Tracking BRISK", run_object_tracking_brisk),
        ("Object Tracking GLOH", run_object_tracking_gloh),
        ("Object Tracking BOOST", run_object_tracking_boost),
        ("Object Tracking CSRT", run_object_tracking_csrt),
        ("Object Tracking KCF", run_object_tracking_kcf),
        ("Object Tracking Median Flow", run_object_tracking_median_flow),
        ("Object Tracking MIL", run_object_tracking_MIL),
        ("Object Tracking MOSSE", run_object_tracking_MOSSE),
        ("Object Tracking TLD", run_object_tracking_TLD),
        ("Frame Differencing", run_frame_differencing),
        ("Median Frame Differencing", run_median_frame_differencing),
        ("KNN Frame Differencing", run_knn_frame_differencing),
        ("MOG Frame Differencing", run_mog_frame_differencing),
        ("RGA Frame Differencing", run_rga_frame_differencing),
        ("Kernel Density Frame Differencing", run_kernel_density_frame_differencing)
    ]

    # Create and place buttons in a grid (6 columns)
    for i, (text, command) in enumerate(button_info):
        if command:
            button = tk.Button(frame, text=text, command=command)
        else:
            button = tk.Button(frame, text=text)

        button.grid(row=i//6, column=i%6, padx=20, pady=8, sticky="w")

    root.mainloop()

if __name__ == "__main__":
    create_gui()
```

RUNNING PROGRAM

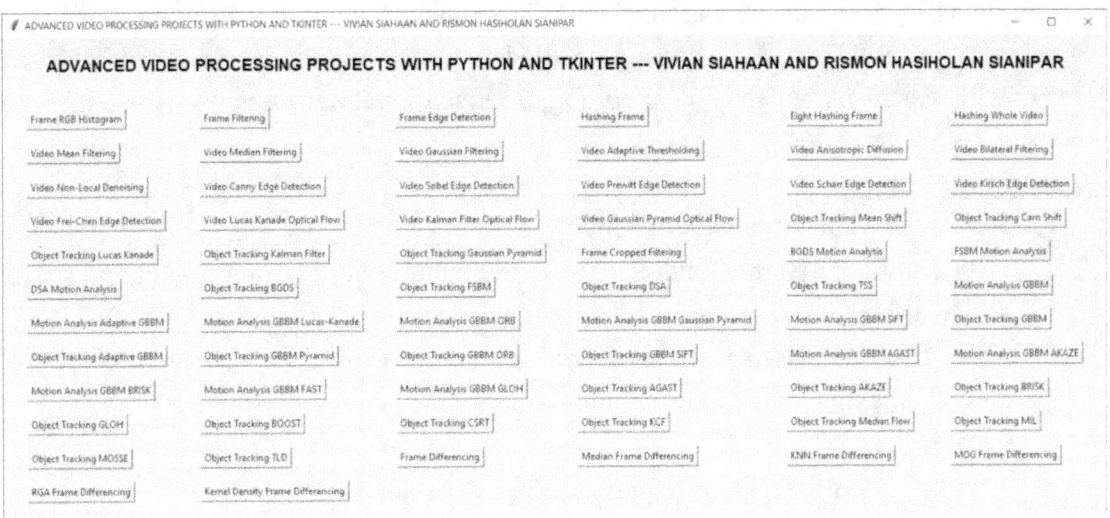

FRAME HISTOGRAM

DESCRIPTION

The purpose of this project is to create a video player application with additional functionalities to analyze video frames. Specifically, the application allows users to open video files, navigate through the frames, and perform analysis such as extracting frames, calculating MD5 hash values, and displaying RGB histograms for each frame. This tool is particularly useful for tasks requiring detailed frame-by-frame video analysis, such as forensic video analysis, video content editing, or educational purposes.

Steps of the Project

1. Set Up the Main Application Window
   - Initialize Main Window: Create the main window using tkinter and set its title.
   - Define Class Attributes: Initialize variables for video management, frame indexing, and zoom scaling.
2. Create GUI Widgets
   - Canvas for Video Display:
     - Create a canvas to display video frames.
     - Bind mouse events for interaction (zooming and dragging).
   - Scrollbar:

- Add a horizontal scrollbar to manage frame navigation.
- Bind scrollbar movement to the canvas.
- Control Buttons:
  - Open Video Button: Allow users to open video files using a file dialog.
  - Zoom Combobox: Provide zoom scaling options.
  - Jump to Time Controls: Include an entry field and button for jumping to a specific time in the video.
  - Playback Controls: Add buttons to play/pause, stop, and extract frames.
  - Additional Functionality: Include a button to open another instance of the video player.

3. Implement Video Playback Functionality
   - Open Video File: Use imageio to read video files and initialize video playback.
   - Play Video:
     - Loop through video frames and display them on the canvas.
     - Handle play/pause functionality and frame indexing.
   - Stop Video: Reset playback and frame position to the beginning.
   - Toggle Play/Pause: Switch between playing and pausing the video.
   - Update Zoom: Adjust the display size of video frames based on the zoom scale.

4. Implement Frame Navigation and Interaction
   - Show Frame: Display the current frame on the canvas, adjusting for zoom and position.
   - Mousewheel Zoom: Adjust zoom level based on mouse wheel input.
   - Drag Frame: Allow users to drag the displayed frame within the canvas.
   - Scroll Navigation: Update frame position based on scrollbar movement.

5. Jump to Specific Time

   Jump to Time: Parse user input to calculate the corresponding frame index and display the frame.

6. Extract and Analyze Frame
   - Extract Frame:
     - Extract a specific frame based on user input.

- Open a new window to display the extracted frame and perform analysis.
    - Display Extracted Frame:
        - Show the extracted frame in a new tkinter window.
        - Plot RGB histograms for the frame using matplotlib.
        - Calculate and display the MD5 hash of the frame.
7. Open Another Instance

    Open Another Video Player: Allow users to open another instance of the video player for parallel analysis.

Detailed Functionality Description
Video Playback and Navigation
- Open Video: The user can select a video file (e.g., .mp4, .avi, .mkv) which is then loaded into the application using imageio.
- Play/Pause/Stop: The application supports basic playback controls, allowing users to start, pause, and stop the video. When playing, the application displays each frame sequentially on the canvas.
- Zoom and Pan: Users can zoom in and out of the video frames and drag the frame to view different parts of it. This is particularly useful for closely inspecting specific areas of the frame.
- Jump to Time: Users can enter a specific time (in seconds) to jump directly to the corresponding frame.

Frame Extraction and Analysis
- Extract Frame: Users can extract a specific frame by entering its frame number. The application then displays the extracted frame in a new window.
- RGB Histogram: For the extracted frame, the application calculates and plots the RGB histogram for each color channel. This provides a visual representation of the color distribution in the frame.
- MD5 Hash Calculation: The application calculates the MD5 hash of the extracted frame, which can be used for integrity verification or to uniquely identify the frame.

Summary

This project enhances a basic video player by adding sophisticated frame analysis tools. Users can interactively explore video content, extract frames for detailed analysis, and utilize visual tools like histograms and hash values for comprehensive frame evaluation. This makes the application valuable for professionals in video analysis, content editing, and educational sectors.

SOURCE CODE

```python
#histogram_rgb_each_frame.py
import tkinter as tk
from tkinter import ttk
from tkinter import filedialog
from PIL import Image, ImageTk
import imageio
import matplotlib.pyplot as plt
from matplotlib.backends.backend_tkagg import FigureCanvasTkAgg
import hashlib

class VideoPlayerApp:
    def __init__(self, master):
        self.master = master
        self.master.title("FRAME HASHING AND HISTOGRAM---VIVIAN SIAHAAN & RISMON HASIHOLAN SIANIPAR")

        self.video = None
        self.video_path = None
        self.paused = False
        self.zoom_scale = tk.IntVar(value=1)
        self.frame_index = 0
        self.start_x = None
        self.start_y = None
        self.current_x = 0
        self.current_y = 0
        self.photo = None  # Save object reference to PhotoImage globally

        self.create_widgets()

    def create_widgets(self):
        # Canvas to display the video
        canvas_width = 800
        canvas_height = 600
        self.canvas = tk.Canvas(self.master, width=canvas_width, height=canvas_height)
        self.canvas.grid(row=0, column=0, padx=10, pady=10, sticky="nsew")
        self.canvas.bind("<MouseWheel>", self.on_mousewheel)
        self.canvas.bind("<ButtonPress-1>", self.on_press)
        self.canvas.bind("<B1-Motion>", self.on_drag)

        # Scrollbar
        self.scrollbar = tk.Scrollbar(self.master, orient="horizontal", command=self.on_scroll)
        self.scrollbar.grid(row=1, column=0, sticky="ew")

        self.canvas.configure(xscrollcommand=self.scrollbar.set)

        # Button to open a video file
        self.open_button = tk.Button(self.master, text="Open Video", command=self.open_video)
        self.open_button.grid(row=2, column=0, padx=10, pady=5)
```

```python
        # Combobox for selecting zoom scale
        self.zoom_combobox = ttk.Combobox(self.master, textvariable=self.zoom_scale, values=list(range(1, 11)))
        self.zoom_combobox.grid(row=2, column=1, padx=10, pady=5)
        self.zoom_combobox.bind("<<ComboboxSelected>>", self.update_zoom)

        # Label and entry for specifying time
        self.time_label = tk.Label(self.master, text="Jump to Time (s):")
        self.time_label.grid(row=0, column=1, padx=10, pady=5, sticky="e")
        self.time_entry = ttk.Entry(self.master)
        self.time_entry.grid(row=0, column=2, padx=10, pady=5, sticky="w")
        self.time_entry.bind("<Return>", lambda event: self.jump_to_time())

        # Button to jump to specified time
        self.jump_button = tk.Button(self.master, text="Jump to Time", command=self.jump_to_time)
        self.jump_button.grid(row=0, column=3, padx=10, pady=5)

        # Button to play/pause the video
        self.play_button = tk.Button(self.master, text="Play/Pause", command=self.toggle_play_pause)
        self.play_button.grid(row=2, column=2, padx=10, pady=5)

        # Button to stop the video
        self.stop_button = tk.Button(self.master, text="Stop", command=self.stop_video)
        self.stop_button.grid(row=2, column=3, padx=10, pady=5)

        # Button to extract frame
        self.extract_button = tk.Button(self.master, text="Extract Frame", command=self.extract_frame)
        self.extract_button.grid(row=1, column=1, padx=10, pady=5)

        # Label and entry for frame number
        self.frame_label = tk.Label(self.master, text="Frame Number:")
        self.frame_label.grid(row=1, column=0, padx=10, pady=5, sticky="e")
        self.frame_entry = ttk.Entry(self.master)
        self.frame_entry.grid(row=1, column=2, padx=10, pady=5, sticky="w")
        self.frame_entry.bind("<Return>", lambda event: self.extract_frame())

        # Button to open another instance of the application
        self.open_another_button = tk.Button(self.master, text="Open Another Video Player", command=self.open_another_player)
        self.open_another_button.grid(row=3, column=0, columnspan=4, padx=10, pady=5)

    def open_video(self):
        self.video_path = filedialog.askopenfilename(filetypes=[("Video files", "*.mp4;*.avi;*.mkv")])
        if self.video_path:
            self.video = imageio.get_reader(self.video_path)
            self.play_video()

    def play_video(self):
        if self.video:
            self.paused = False
            self.show_frame()

    def stop_video(self):
        self.paused = True
        self.frame_index = 0
        self.current_x = 0
        self.current_y = 0  # Reset the current position
        self.show_frame()
```

```python
    def toggle_play_pause(self):
        self.paused = not self.paused
        if not self.paused:
            self.play_video()

    def update_zoom(self, event=None):
        self.show_frame()

    def show_frame(self):
        if self.video:
            if not self.paused:
                self.frame_index += 1
                if self.frame_index >= len(self.video):
                    self.frame_index = 0
            if self.frame_index < len(self.video):  # Tambahkan pengecekan di sini
                frame = self.video.get_data(self.frame_index)
                frame = Image.fromarray(frame)
                frame = frame.resize((frame.width * self.zoom_scale.get(), frame.height * self.zoom_scale.get()))
                photo = ImageTk.PhotoImage(frame)
                self.photo = photo  # Simpan referensi objek PhotoImage secara global
                self.canvas.delete("video")  # Hapus gambar sebelumnya
                self.canvas.create_image(self.current_x, self.current_y, anchor="nw", image=photo, tags="video")
                if not self.paused:
                    self.canvas.after(30, self.show_frame)

    def on_mousewheel(self, event):
        direction = event.delta // 120
        current_value = int(self.zoom_scale.get())
        if direction == 1 and current_value < 10:
            current_value += 1
        elif direction == -1 and current_value > 1:
            current_value -= 1
        self.zoom_scale.set(current_value)
        self.update_zoom()

    def on_press(self, event):
        self.start_x = event.x
        self.start_y = event.y

    def on_drag(self, event):
        if self.start_x and self.start_y:
            x_offset = event.x - self.start_x
            y_offset = event.y - self.start_y
            self.current_x += x_offset  # Update current position
            self.current_y += y_offset  # Update current position
            self.canvas.move("video", x_offset, y_offset)
            self.start_x = event.x
            self.start_y = event.y

    def on_scroll(self, *args):
        scroll_pos = self.scrollbar.get()
        self.current_x = -scroll_pos * self.canvas.winfo_width()
        self.canvas.xview_moveto(scroll_pos)
        self.frame_index = int(scroll_pos * len(self.video))  # Update frame index
        self.show_frame()

    def jump_to_time(self):
        time_str = self.time_entry.get()
        try:
            time_seconds = float(time_str)
            if 0 <= time_seconds:
```

```python
            self.frame_index = int(time_seconds * self.video.get_meta_data()['fps'])
            self.show_frame()
        except ValueError:
            pass

    def extract_frame(self):
        frame_number_str = self.frame_entry.get()
        try:
            frame_number = int(frame_number_str)
            if 0 <= frame_number < len(self.video):
                frame = self.video.get_data(frame_number)
                self.show_extracted_frame(frame, frame_number)
        except ValueError:
            pass

    def show_extracted_frame(self, frame, frame_number):
        extracted_frame_window = tk.Toplevel(self.master)
        extracted_frame_window.title(f"Frame yang Diekstraksi (Frame {frame_number}) --- RISMON HASIHOLAN SIANIPAR")

        extracted_frame_label = tk.Label(extracted_frame_window, text=f"Frame yang Diekstraksi (Frame {frame_number})")
        extracted_frame_label.pack()

        height, width, _ = frame.shape  # Get dimensions of the frame
        extracted_photo = ImageTk.PhotoImage(image=Image.fromarray(frame))

        extracted_frame_canvas = tk.Canvas(extracted_frame_window, width=width, height=height)
        extracted_frame_canvas.pack()
        extracted_frame_canvas.create_image(0, 0, anchor="nw", image=extracted_photo)
        extracted_frame_canvas.image = extracted_photo

        # Plot histogram for each RGB channel
        fig, axs = plt.subplots(1, 3, figsize=(18, 4))
        for i, color in enumerate(['r', 'g', 'b']):
            axs[i].hist(frame[:,:,i].ravel(), bins=64, range=(0, 255), color=color, alpha=0.7)
            axs[i].set_title(f"Histogram Kanal {color.upper()} (Frame {frame_number})")
            axs[i].set_xlabel("Nilai Piksel")
            axs[i].set_ylabel("Frekuensi")
        plt.tight_layout()

        # Calculate MD5 hash value of the frame
        md5_hash = hashlib.md5(frame).hexdigest()

        # Display MD5 hash value
        md5_label = tk.Label(extracted_frame_window, text=f"Nilai Hash MD5: {md5_hash}", font=("Arial", 20))
        md5_label.pack()

        hist_canvas = FigureCanvasTkAgg(fig, master=extracted_frame_window)
        hist_canvas.draw()
        hist_canvas.get_tk_widget().pack()

    def open_another_player(self):
        # Open another instance of the application
        root = tk.Toplevel(self.master)
        app = VideoPlayerApp(root)

def main():
    root = tk.Tk()
    app = VideoPlayerApp(root)
    root.mainloop()

if __name__ == "__main__":
```

    main()

RUNNING PROGRAM

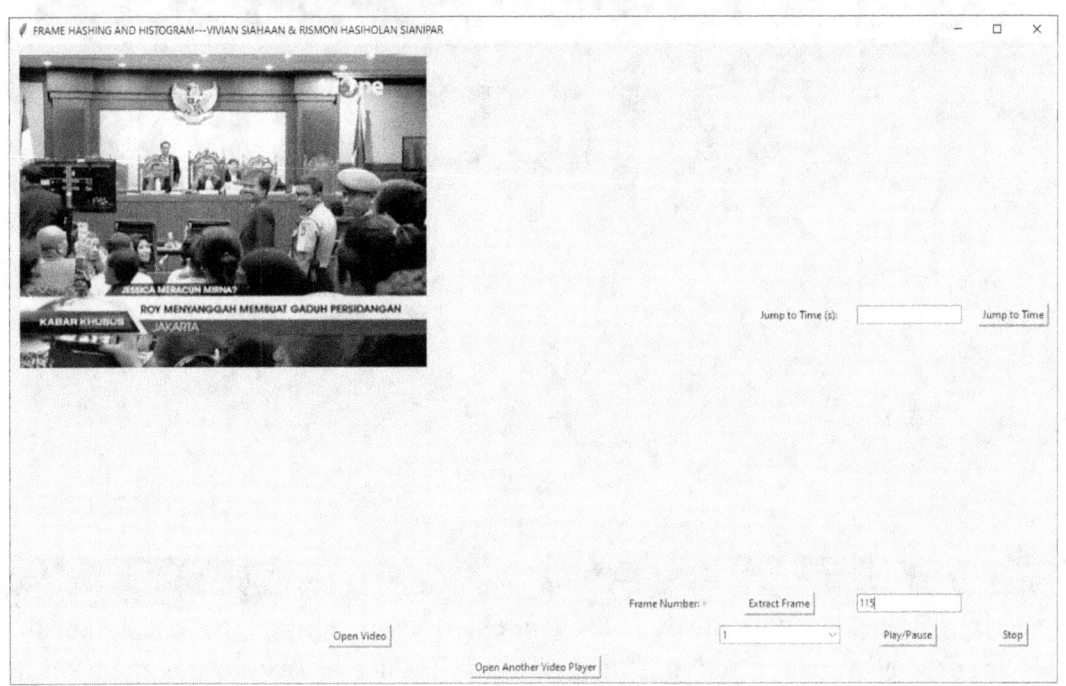

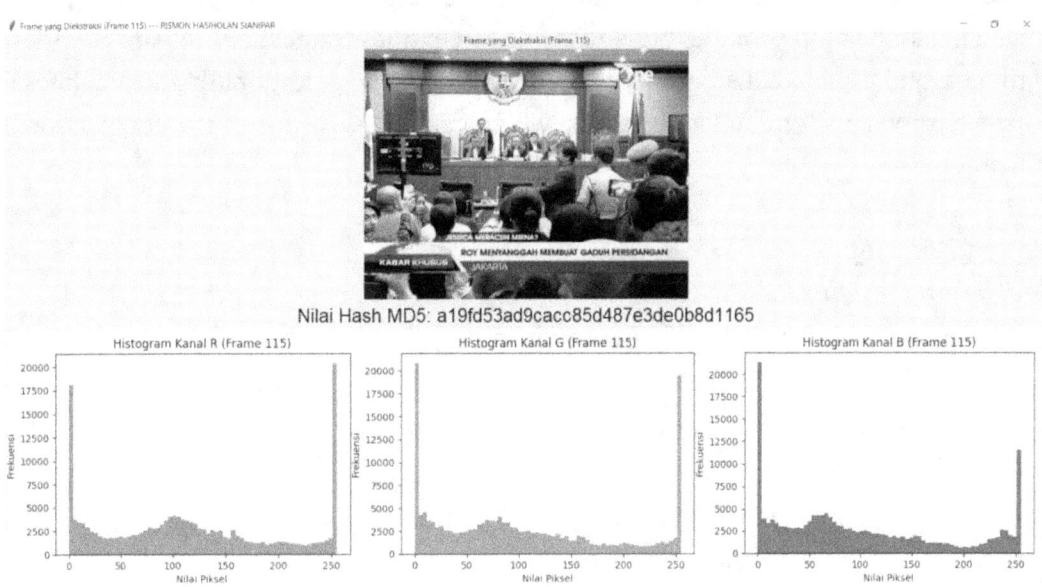

FRAME FILTERING

DESCRIPTION

The script filtering_each_frame.py is a comprehensive Python application designed for video frame analysis and filtering. It leverages the Tkinter library for the graphical user interface (GUI), allowing users to load, play, pause, and analyze video files frame by frame. The application provides functionalities to extract frames, apply various filtering techniques, and visualize histograms of the color channels. Additionally, it calculates and displays hash values for extracted frames, which can be useful for frame comparison and verification.

Detailed Description
Libraries and Modules
- tkinter: For creating the GUI components.
- PIL (Pillow): For image processing and handling within the GUI.
- imageio: For reading video files.
- matplotlib: For plotting histograms.
- hashlib: For generating hash values of frames.
- numpy: For numerical operations.
- cv2 (OpenCV): For image processing and filtering.

- pywt: For wavelet transform.
- skimage.restoration: For image denoising.

Class: FrameFiltering
The main class FrameFiltering encapsulates all the functionalities related to video frame processing and filtering.

Initialization (__init__ method)
GUI Components Initialization: Initializes the main window, video parameters, and zoom scale. Calls create_widgets to set up the GUI elements.

Creating Widgets (create_widgets method)
- Video Panel: A frame containing a canvas for video display and a horizontal scrollbar for navigation.
- Control Panel: A frame with buttons for video operations (open, play/pause, stop, jump to time, extract frame) and a combobox for zoom scale selection.
- Additional Controls: Allows opening another instance of the video player.

Video Handling Methods
- open_video: Opens a file dialog to select a video file and loads it using imageio.
- play_video: Starts or resumes video playback.
- stop_video: Stops video playback and resets the frame index.
- toggle_play_pause: Toggles between play and pause states.
- show_frame: Displays the current frame on the canvas. Handles resizing based on zoom level and updates frames during playback.
- jump_to_time: Jumps to a specific time in the video based on user input.
- extract_frame: Extracts a specific frame by number and opens a new window to display it.

Frame Display and Interaction
- Mouse Events: Handles mouse wheel for zooming, mouse press, and drag for moving the frame within the canvas.
- Scrollbar: Syncs with the canvas to navigate through frames.

Frame Extraction and Analysis
- show_extracted_frame: Displays the extracted frame in a new window, along with histograms of the RGB channels and hash values.
- apply_filtering: Applies the selected filtering method to the extracted frame.

Filtering Methods
Each filtering method processes the frame and applies a specific type of image filter. Here are a few examples:
- apply_gaussian_blur: Applies Gaussian blur to each color channel.
- apply_mean_blur: Applies mean blur.
- apply_median_blur: Applies median blur.
- apply_bilateral_filtering: Applies bilateral filtering.
- apply_non_local_means_denoising: Applies non-local means denoising.
- apply_anisotropic_diffusion: Applies anisotropic diffusion.
- apply_total_variation_denoising: Applies total variation denoising.
- apply_wiener_filter: Applies Wiener filter.
- apply_adaptive_thresholding: Applies adaptive thresholding.
- apply_wavelet_transform: Applies wavelet transform.

Usage
- Open Video: Click the "Open Video" button to load a video file.
- Playback Control: Use "Play/Pause" and "Stop" buttons to control video playback.
- Zoom: Select a zoom level from the combobox or use the mouse wheel.
- Navigation: Use the scrollbar or enter a time in seconds to jump to a specific point in the video.
- Frame Extraction: Extract a specific frame by entering its number and clicking "Extract Frame".
- Frame Analysis: In the extracted frame window, view histograms, hash values, and apply various filtering methods using the combobox.

This application is designed for users who need to analyze video frames in detail, apply various filters, and visualize the results effectively.

SOURCE CODE

```python
#histogram_rgb_each_frame.py
import tkinter as tk
from tkinter import ttk
from tkinter import filedialog
from PIL import Image, ImageTk
import imageio
import matplotlib.pyplot as plt
from matplotlib.backends.backend_tkagg import FigureCanvasTkAgg
import hashlib

class VideoPlayerApp:
    def __init__(self, master):
        self.master = master
        self.master.title("FRAME HASHING AND HISTOGRAM---VIVIAN SIAHAAN & RISMON HASIHOLAN SIANIPAR")

        self.video = None
        self.video_path = None
        self.paused = False
        self.zoom_scale = tk.IntVar(value=1)
        self.frame_index = 0
        self.start_x = None
        self.start_y = None
        self.current_x = 0
        self.current_y = 0
        self.photo = None  # Save object reference to PhotoImage globally

        self.create_widgets()

    def create_widgets(self):
        # Canvas to display the video
        canvas_width = 800
        canvas_height = 600
        self.canvas = tk.Canvas(self.master, width=canvas_width, height=canvas_height)
        self.canvas.grid(row=0, column=0, padx=10, pady=10, sticky="nsew")
        self.canvas.bind("<MouseWheel>", self.on_mousewheel)
        self.canvas.bind("<ButtonPress-1>", self.on_press)
        self.canvas.bind("<B1-Motion>", self.on_drag)

        # Scrollbar
        self.scrollbar = tk.Scrollbar(self.master, orient="horizontal", command=self.on_scroll)
        self.scrollbar.grid(row=1, column=0, sticky="ew")

        self.canvas.configure(xscrollcommand=self.scrollbar.set)

        # Button to open a video file
        self.open_button = tk.Button(self.master, text="Open Video", command=self.open_video)
        self.open_button.grid(row=2, column=0, padx=10, pady=5)

        # Combobox for selecting zoom scale
        self.zoom_combobox = ttk.Combobox(self.master, textvariable=self.zoom_scale, values=list(range(1, 11)))
        self.zoom_combobox.grid(row=2, column=1, padx=10, pady=5)
        self.zoom_combobox.bind("<<ComboboxSelected>>", self.update_zoom)

        # Label and entry for specifying time
        self.time_label = tk.Label(self.master, text="Jump to Time (s):")
        self.time_label.grid(row=0, column=1, padx=10, pady=5, sticky="e")
```

```python
        self.time_entry = ttk.Entry(self.master)
        self.time_entry.grid(row=0, column=2, padx=10, pady=5, sticky="w")
        self.time_entry.bind("<Return>", lambda event: self.jump_to_time())

        # Button to jump to specified time
        self.jump_button = tk.Button(self.master, text="Jump to Time", command=self.jump_to_time)
        self.jump_button.grid(row=0, column=3, padx=10, pady=5)

        # Button to play/pause the video
        self.play_button = tk.Button(self.master, text="Play/Pause", command=self.toggle_play_pause)
        self.play_button.grid(row=2, column=2, padx=10, pady=5)

        # Button to stop the video
        self.stop_button = tk.Button(self.master, text="Stop", command=self.stop_video)
        self.stop_button.grid(row=2, column=3, padx=10, pady=5)

        # Button to extract frame
        self.extract_button = tk.Button(self.master, text="Extract Frame", command=self.extract_frame)
        self.extract_button.grid(row=1, column=1, padx=10, pady=5)

        # Label and entry for frame number
        self.frame_label = tk.Label(self.master, text="Frame Number:")
        self.frame_label.grid(row=1, column=0, padx=10, pady=5, sticky="e")
        self.frame_entry = ttk.Entry(self.master)
        self.frame_entry.grid(row=1, column=2, padx=10, pady=5, sticky="w")
        self.frame_entry.bind("<Return>", lambda event: self.extract_frame())

        # Button to open another instance of the application
        self.open_another_button = tk.Button(self.master, text="Open Another Video Player", command=self.open_another_player)
        self.open_another_button.grid(row=3, column=0, columnspan=4, padx=10, pady=5)

    def open_video(self):
        self.video_path = filedialog.askopenfilename(filetypes=[("Video files", "*.mp4;*.avi;*.mkv")])
        if self.video_path:
            self.video = imageio.get_reader(self.video_path)
            self.play_video()

    def play_video(self):
        if self.video:
            self.paused = False
            self.show_frame()

    def stop_video(self):
        self.paused = True
        self.frame_index = 0
        self.current_x = 0
        self.current_y = 0  # Reset the current position
        self.show_frame()

    def toggle_play_pause(self):
        self.paused = not self.paused
        if not self.paused:
            self.play_video()

    def update_zoom(self, event=None):
        self.show_frame()

    def show_frame(self):
        if self.video:
```

```python
            if not self.paused:
                self.frame_index += 1
                if self.frame_index >= len(self.video):
                    self.frame_index = 0
            if self.frame_index < len(self.video):  # Tambahkan pengecekan di sini
                frame = self.video.get_data(self.frame_index)
                frame = Image.fromarray(frame)
                frame = frame.resize((frame.width * self.zoom_scale.get(), frame.height * self.zoom_scale.get()))
                photo = ImageTk.PhotoImage(frame)
                self.photo = photo  # Simpan referensi objek PhotoImage secara global
                self.canvas.delete("video")  # Hapus gambar sebelumnya
                self.canvas.create_image(self.current_x, self.current_y, anchor="nw", image=photo, tags="video")
                if not self.paused:
                    self.canvas.after(30, self.show_frame)

    def on_mousewheel(self, event):
        direction = event.delta // 120
        current_value = int(self.zoom_scale.get())
        if direction == 1 and current_value < 10:
            current_value += 1
        elif direction == -1 and current_value > 1:
            current_value -= 1
        self.zoom_scale.set(current_value)
        self.update_zoom()

    def on_press(self, self, event):
        self.start_x = event.x
        self.start_y = event.y

    def on_drag(self, event):
        if self.start_x and self.start_y:
            x_offset = event.x - self.start_x
            y_offset = event.y - self.start_y
            self.current_x += x_offset  # Update current position
            self.current_y += y_offset  # Update current position
            self.canvas.move("video", x_offset, y_offset)
            self.start_x = event.x
            self.start_y = event.y

    def on_scroll(self, *args):
        scroll_pos = self.scrollbar.get()
        self.current_x = -scroll_pos * self.canvas.winfo_width()
        self.canvas.xview_moveto(scroll_pos)
        self.frame_index = int(scroll_pos * len(self.video))  # Update frame index
        self.show_frame()

    def jump_to_time(self):
        time_str = self.time_entry.get()
        try:
            time_seconds = float(time_str)
            if 0 <= time_seconds:
                self.frame_index = int(time_seconds * self.video.get_meta_data()['fps'])
                self.show_frame()
        except ValueError:
            pass

    def extract_frame(self):
        frame_number_str = self.frame_entry.get()
        try:
            frame_number = int(frame_number_str)
            if 0 <= frame_number < len(self.video):
```

```python
                frame = self.video.get_data(frame_number)
                self.show_extracted_frame(frame, frame_number)
        except ValueError:
            pass

    def show_extracted_frame(self, frame, frame_number):
        extracted_frame_window = tk.Toplevel(self.master)
        extracted_frame_window.title(f"Frame yang Diekstraksi (Frame {frame_number}) --- RISMON HASIHOLAN SIANIPAR")

        extracted_frame_label = tk.Label(extracted_frame_window, text=f"Frame yang Diekstraksi (Frame {frame_number})")
        extracted_frame_label.pack()

        height, width, _ = frame.shape  # Get dimensions of the frame
        extracted_photo = ImageTk.PhotoImage(image=Image.fromarray(frame))

        extracted_frame_canvas = tk.Canvas(extracted_frame_window, width=width, height=height)
        extracted_frame_canvas.pack()
        extracted_frame_canvas.create_image(0, 0, anchor="nw", image=extracted_photo)
        extracted_frame_canvas.image = extracted_photo

        # Plot histogram for each RGB channel
        fig, axs = plt.subplots(1, 3, figsize=(18, 4))
        for i, color in enumerate(['r', 'g', 'b']):
            axs[i].hist(frame[:,:,i].ravel(), bins=64, range=(0, 255), color=color, alpha=0.7)
            axs[i].set_title(f"Histogram Kanal {color.upper()} (Frame {frame_number})")
            axs[i].set_xlabel("Nilai Piksel")
            axs[i].set_ylabel("Frekuensi")
        plt.tight_layout()

        # Calculate MD5 hash value of the frame
        md5_hash = hashlib.md5(frame).hexdigest()

        # Display MD5 hash value
        md5_label = tk.Label(extracted_frame_window, text=f"Nilai Hash MD5: {md5_hash}", font=("Arial", 20))
        md5_label.pack()

        hist_canvas = FigureCanvasTkAgg(fig, master=extracted_frame_window)
        hist_canvas.draw()
        hist_canvas.get_tk_widget().pack()

    def open_another_player(self):
        # Open another instance of the application
        root = tk.Toplevel(self.master)
        app = VideoPlayerApp(root)

def main():
    root = tk.Tk()
    app = VideoPlayerApp(root)
    root.mainloop()

if __name__ == "__main__":
    main()
```

RUNNING PROGRAM

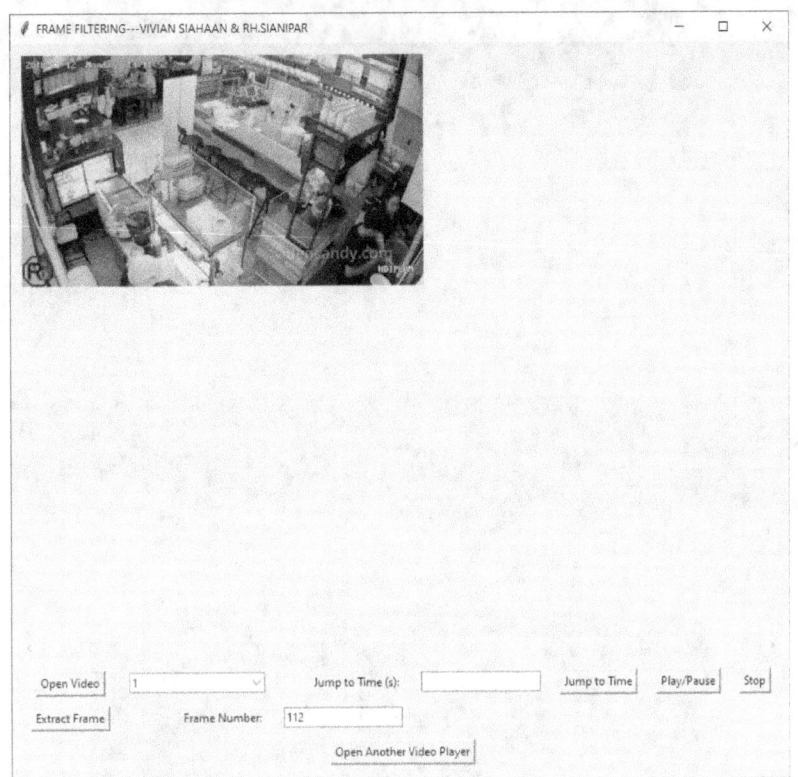

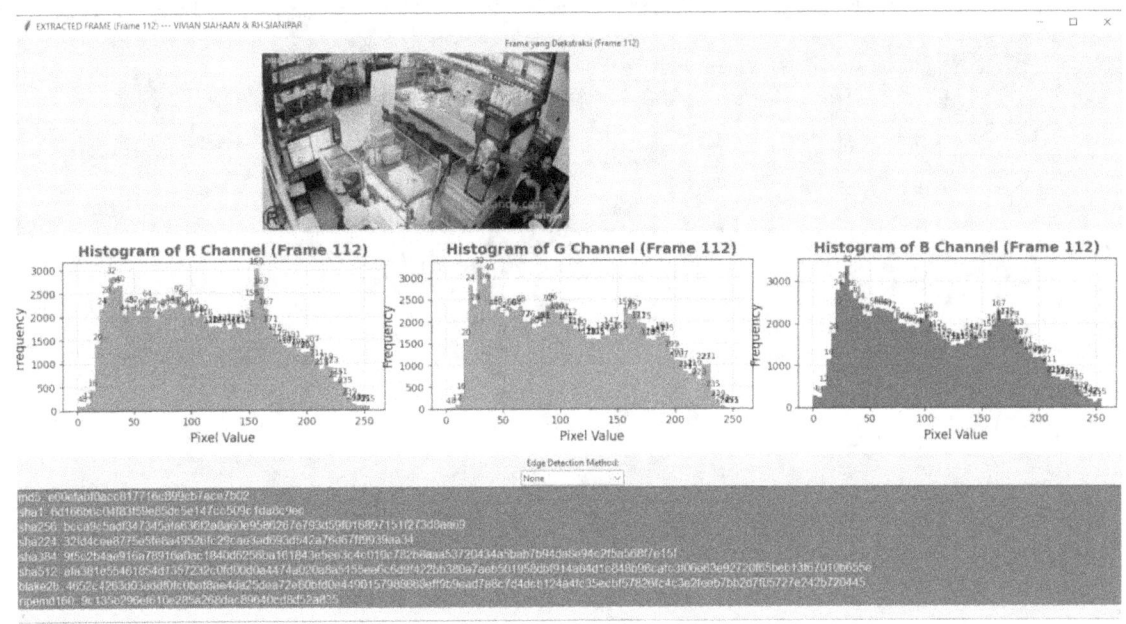

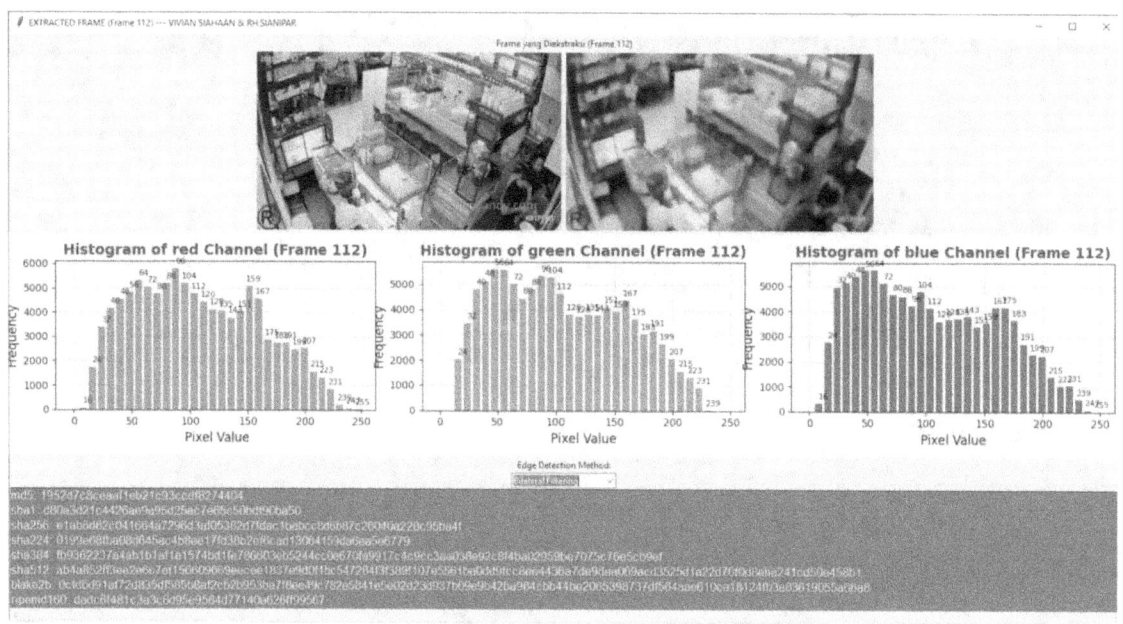

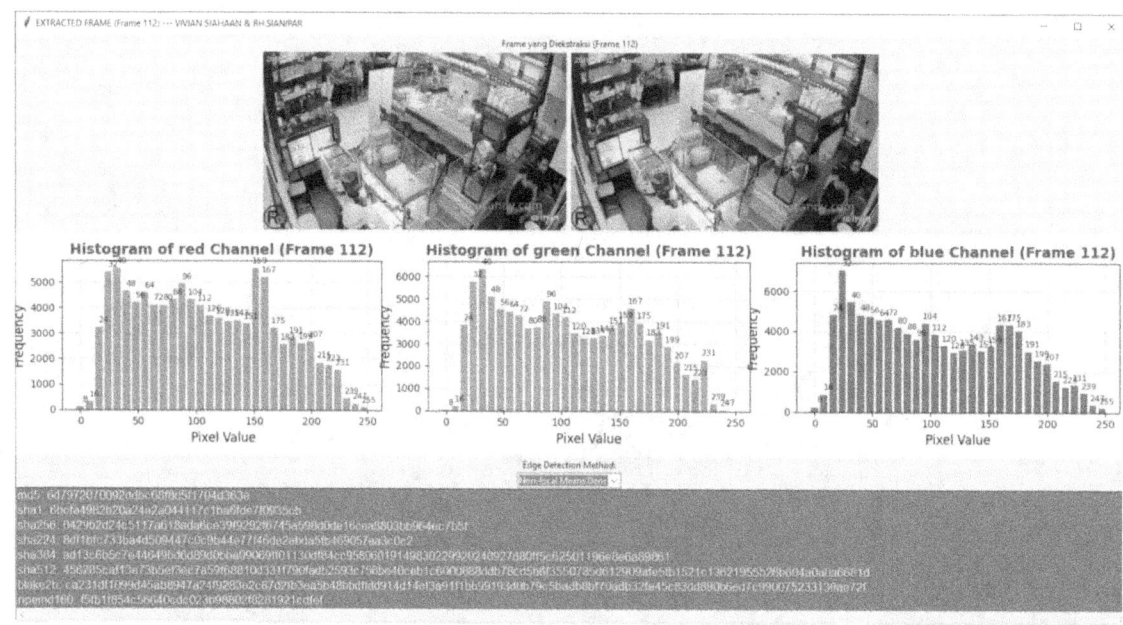

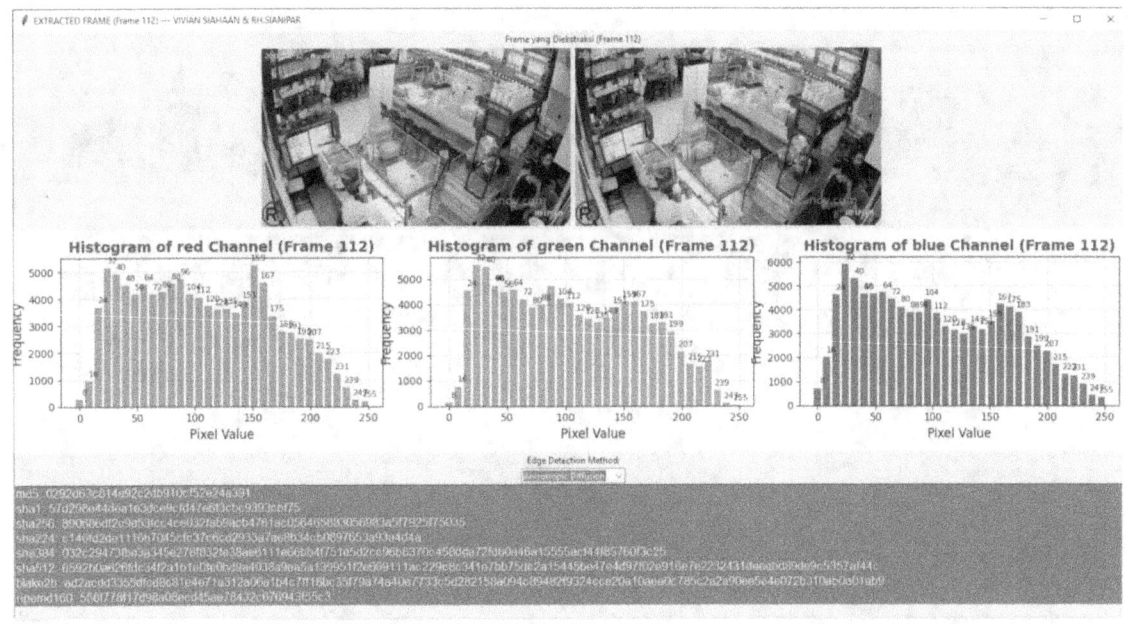

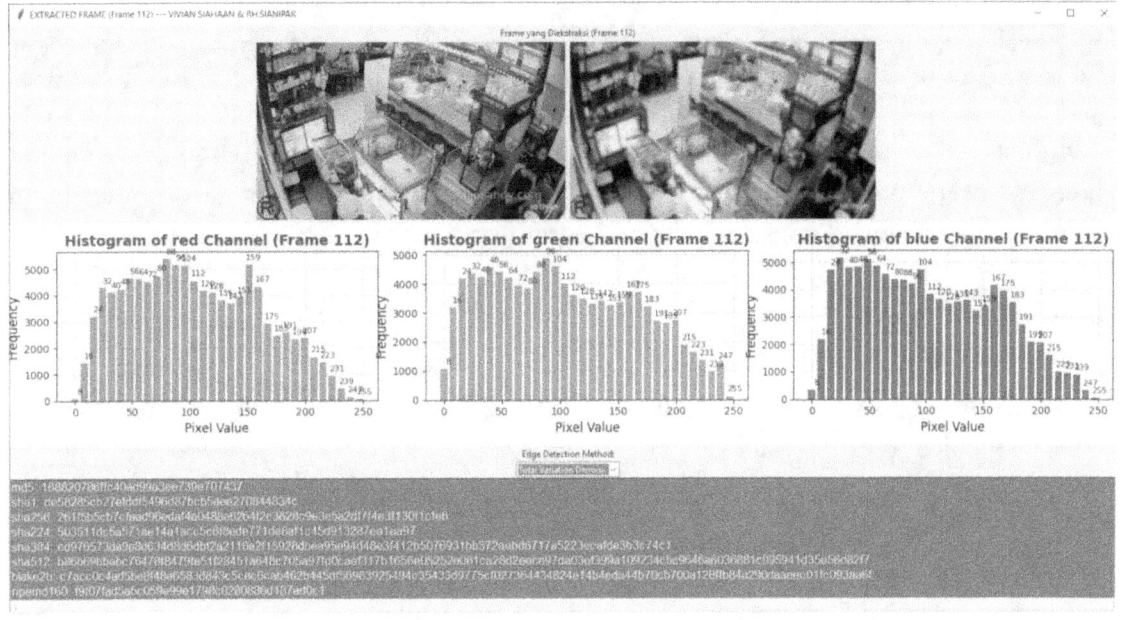

FRAME EDGES DETECTION

DESCRIPTION

The project is a comprehensive application designed to perform edge detection on individual frames of a video. It utilizes a graphical user interface (GUI) built with Tkinter to enable users to load videos, navigate through frames, apply different edge detection algorithms, and view various analyses of the frames including histograms and hash values.

Detailed Description

1. User Interface and Core Functionality:
- Tkinter GUI: The application is built using Tkinter, a Python library for creating graphical user interfaces.
    - Video Panel: A canvas to display video frames, with mouse interaction for zooming and dragging.
    - Control Panel: Buttons and widgets for opening videos, playing/pausing, stopping, jumping to specific times, extracting frames, and opening additional instances of the application.
- Video Handling:
    - Open Video: Uses filedialog to select and open video files in various formats (e.g., MP4, AVI, MKV).
    - Play/Pause/Stop: Controls to manage video playback.

- Frame Navigation: Allows jumping to specific times and frames within the video.

2. Frame Extraction and Edge Detection:
- Frame Extraction:
    - Extracts and displays specific frames from the video.
    - Shows the frame along with its RGB channel histograms and hash values.
- Edge Detection:
    - Provides a variety of edge detection algorithms (e.g., Canny, Sobel, Prewitt, Laplacian, Scharr, Roberts, FreiChen, Kirsch, Robinson, Gaussian).
    - Displays the results of edge detection on the extracted frame.

3. Additional Analyses:
- Histograms:
    - Plots histograms for the RGB channels of the extracted frame.
    - Updates histograms after applying edge detection to visualize the distribution of pixel values.
- Hash Values:
    - Computes and displays hash values using different algorithms (e.g., MD5, SHA1, SHA256) for the original and edge-detected frames.
    - Helps in verifying the integrity and uniqueness of frames.

4. User Interactions:
- Zooming and Dragging:
    - Supports zooming in/out on the video frames using mouse wheel.
    - Allows dragging the video frame to explore different parts when zoomed in.
- Edge Detection Selection:
    - Combobox to select different edge detection methods and apply them on the extracted frame.

Technical Details:
Image and Video Processing:
- Uses imageio for reading video files.
- Employs OpenCV (cv2) for various image processing tasks including edge detection and resizing frames.

- Utilizes PIL (Pillow) for handling image conversions and creating images compatible with Tkinter.

Data Visualization:
- Uses matplotlib for plotting histograms of the RGB channels.
- Embeds matplotlib plots within the Tkinter application using FigureCanvasTkAgg.

Hashing:
- Utilizes Python's hashlib to compute various hash values for frames, aiding in the verification and analysis of frames.

Example Use Case:
A user loads a video file, navigates to a specific frame, and applies different edge detection algorithms to analyze the edges within the frame. The user can view histograms for the RGB channels of the frame and see hash values to ensure frame integrity. This tool can be useful for video analysis in fields such as computer vision, security, and multimedia processing.

Conclusion
The edge_detection_each_frame.py project provides a powerful and user-friendly tool for analyzing and processing video frames through edge detection, making it a valuable asset for both educational and professional purposes in fields involving image and video processing.

SOURCE CODE

```
#filtering_each_frame.py
import tkinter as tk
from tkinter import ttk
from tkinter import filedialog
from PIL import Image, ImageTk
import imageio
import matplotlib.pyplot as plt
from matplotlib.backends.backend_tkagg import FigureCanvasTkAgg
import hashlib
import numpy as np
import cv2
```

```python
import re
import pywt
from skimage.restoration import denoise_tv_chambolle

class FrameFiltering:
    def __init__(self, master):
        self.master = master
        self.master.title("FRAME FILTERING---VIVIAN SIAHAAN & RH.SIANIPAR")

        self.video = None
        self.video_path = None
        self.paused = False
        self.zoom_scale = tk.IntVar(value=1)
        self.frame_index = 0
        self.start_x = None
        self.start_y = None
        self.current_x = 0
        self.current_y = 0
        self.photo = None  # Save object reference to PhotoImage globally

        self.create_widgets()

    def create_widgets(self):
        # Panel for video display
        video_panel = tk.Frame(self.master)
        video_panel.grid(row=0, column=0, padx=10, pady=10, sticky="nsew")

        # Canvas to display the video
        canvas_width = 800
        canvas_height = 600
        self.canvas = tk.Canvas(video_panel, width=canvas_width, height=canvas_height)
        self.canvas.pack(side="top", fill="both", expand=True)
        self.canvas.bind("<MouseWheel>", self.on_mousewheel)
        self.canvas.bind("<ButtonPress-1>", self.on_press)
        self.canvas.bind("<B1-Motion>", self.on_drag)

        # Scrollbar
        self.scrollbar = tk.Scrollbar(video_panel, orient="horizontal", command=self.on_scroll)
        self.scrollbar.pack(side="bottom", fill="x")

        self.canvas.configure(xscrollcommand=self.scrollbar.set)

        # Panel for control buttons
        control_panel = tk.Frame(self.master)
        control_panel.grid(row=1, column=0, padx=10, pady=(0, 10), sticky="ew")

        # Button to open a video file
        self.open_button = tk.Button(control_panel, text="Open Video", command=self.open_video)
        self.open_button.grid(row=0, column=0, padx=10, pady=5)

        # Combobox for selecting zoom scale
        self.zoom_combobox = ttk.Combobox(control_panel, textvariable=self.zoom_scale, values=list(range(1, 11)))
        self.zoom_combobox.grid(row=0, column=1, padx=10, pady=5)
        self.zoom_combobox.bind("<<ComboboxSelected>>", self.update_zoom)

        # Label and entry for specifying time
        self.time_label = tk.Label(control_panel, text="Jump to Time (s):")
        self.time_label.grid(row=0, column=2, padx=10, pady=5, sticky="e")
        self.time_entry = ttk.Entry(control_panel)
        self.time_entry.grid(row=0, column=3, padx=10, pady=5, sticky="w")
        self.time_entry.bind("<Return>", lambda event: self.jump_to_time())

        # Button to jump to specified time
```

```python
        self.jump_button = tk.Button(control_panel, text="Jump to Time", command=self.jump_to_time)
        self.jump_button.grid(row=0, column=4, padx=10, pady=5)

        # Button to play/pause the video
        self.play_button = tk.Button(control_panel, text="Play/Pause", command=self.toggle_play_pause)
        self.play_button.grid(row=0, column=5, padx=10, pady=5)

        # Button to stop the video
        self.stop_button = tk.Button(control_panel, text="Stop", command=self.stop_video)
        self.stop_button.grid(row=0, column=6, padx=10, pady=5)

        # Button to extract frame
        self.extract_button = tk.Button(control_panel, text="Extract Frame", command=self.extract_frame)
        self.extract_button.grid(row=1, column=0, padx=10, pady=5)

        # Label and entry for frame number
        self.frame_label = tk.Label(control_panel, text="Frame Number:")
        self.frame_label.grid(row=1, column=1, padx=10, pady=5, sticky="e")
        self.frame_entry = ttk.Entry(control_panel)
        self.frame_entry.grid(row=1, column=2, padx=10, pady=5, sticky="w")
        self.frame_entry.bind("<Return>", lambda event: self.extract_frame())

        # Button to open another instance of the application
        self.open_another_button = tk.Button(control_panel, text="Open Another Video Player", command=self.open_another_player)
        self.open_another_button.grid(row=2, column=0, columnspan=7, padx=10, pady=5)

    def open_video(self):
        self.video_path = filedialog.askopenfilename(filetypes=[("Video files", "*.mp4;*.avi;*.mkv")])
        if self.video_path:
            self.video = imageio.get_reader(self.video_path)
            self.play_video()

    def play_video(self):
        if self.video:
            self.paused = False
            self.show_frame()

    def stop_video(self):
        self.paused = True
        self.frame_index = 0
        self.current_x = 0
        self.current_y = 0  # Reset the current position
        self.show_frame()

    def toggle_play_pause(self):
        self.paused = not self.paused
        if not self.paused:
            self.play_video()

    def update_zoom(self, event=None):
        self.show_frame()

    def show_frame(self):
        if self.video:
            if not self.paused:
                self.frame_index += 1
                if self.frame_index >= len(self.video):
                    self.frame_index = 0  # Reset frame index if it exceeds the maximum index
```

```python
            if 0 <= self.frame_index < len(self.video):  # Check if frame index is within range
                try:
                    frame = self.video.get_data(self.frame_index)
                    frame = Image.fromarray(frame)
                    frame = frame.resize((frame.width * self.zoom_scale.get(), frame.height * self.zoom_scale.get()))
                    photo = ImageTk.PhotoImage(frame)
                    self.photo = photo  # Save object reference to PhotoImage globally
                    self.canvas.delete("video")  # Delete previous image
                    self.canvas.create_image(self.current_x, self.current_y, anchor="nw", image=photo, tags="video")
                    if not self.paused:
                        self.canvas.after(30, self.show_frame)
                except Exception as e:
                    print("Error:", e)

    def on_mousewheel(self, event):
        direction = event.delta // 120
        current_value = int(self.zoom_scale.get())
        if direction == 1 and current_value < 10:
            current_value += 1
        elif direction == -1 and current_value > 1:
            current_value -= 1
        self.zoom_scale.set(current_value)
        self.update_zoom()

    def on_press(self, event):
        self.start_x = event.x
        self.start_y = event.y

    def on_drag(self, event):
        if self.start_x and self.start_y:
            x_offset = event.x - self.start_x
            y_offset = event.y - self.start_y
            self.current_x += x_offset  # Update current position
            self.current_y += y_offset  # Update current position
            self.canvas.move("video", x_offset, y_offset)
            self.start_x = event.x
            self.start_y = event.y

    def on_scroll(self, *args):
        scroll_pos = self.scrollbar.get()
        self.current_x = -scroll_pos * self.canvas.winfo_width()
        self.canvas.xview_moveto(scroll_pos)
        self.frame_index = int(scroll_pos * len(self.video))  # Update frame index
        self.show_frame()

    def jump_to_time(self):
        time_str = self.time_entry.get()
        try:
            time_seconds = float(time_str)
            if 0 <= time_seconds:
                self.frame_index = int(time_seconds * self.video.get_meta_data()['fps'])
                self.show_frame()
        except ValueError:
            pass

    def extract_frame(self):
        frame_number_str = self.frame_entry.get()
        try:
            frame_number = int(frame_number_str)
            if 0 <= frame_number < len(self.video):
                frame = self.video.get_data(frame_number)
```

```python
                self.show_extracted_frame(frame, frame_number)
        except ValueError:
            pass

    def show_extracted_frame(self, frame, frame_number):
        self.extracted_frame_window = tk.Toplevel(self.master)
        self.extracted_frame_window.title(f"EXTRACTED FRAME (Frame {frame_number}) --- VIVIAN SIAHAAN & RH.SIANIPAR")

        extracted_frame_label = tk.Label(self.extracted_frame_window, text=f"Frame yang Diekstraksi (Frame {frame_number})")
        extracted_frame_label.pack()

        height, width, _ = frame.shape  # Get dimensions of the frame
        extracted_photo = ImageTk.PhotoImage(image=Image.fromarray(frame))

        # Create a panel for the frame and edge detection canvas
        frame_panel = tk.Frame(self.extracted_frame_window)
        frame_panel.pack(side="top")

        extracted_frame_canvas = tk.Canvas(frame_panel, width=width, height=height)
        extracted_frame_canvas.pack(side="left")
        extracted_frame_canvas.create_image(0, 0, anchor="nw", image=extracted_photo)
        extracted_frame_canvas.image = extracted_photo

        # Canvas for edge detection result
        self.edge_canvas = tk.Canvas(frame_panel, width=width, height=height)
        self.edge_canvas.pack(side="right")

        # Create a panel for histogram plots and hash values
        hist_hash_panel = tk.Frame(self.extracted_frame_window)
        hist_hash_panel.pack(side="bottom", fill="both", expand=True)

        # Plot histogram for each RGB channel
        fig, axs = plt.subplots(1, 3, figsize=(20, 3))
        colors = ['red', 'green', 'blue']
        for i, color in enumerate(['R', 'G', 'B']):
            hist, bins, _ = axs[i].hist(frame[:,:,i].ravel(), bins=64, range=(0, 255), color=colors[i], alpha=0.7)
            axs[i].set_title(f"Histogram of {color} Channel (Frame {frame_number})", fontsize=14, fontweight='bold', color='blue')
            axs[i].set_xlabel("Pixel Value", fontsize=12)
            axs[i].set_ylabel("Frequency", fontsize=12)
            axs[i].grid(True, linestyle='--', linewidth=0.5, color='gray', alpha=0.5)
            axs[i].tick_params(axis='both', which='major', labelsize=10)

            # Add frequency values above each bar
            for bar, frequency in zip(hist, bins[1:]):
                if bar > 0:
                    axs[i].annotate(f'{frequency:.0f}', xy=(bins[np.where(hist == bar)[0][0]] + (bins[1] - bins[0]) / 2, bar),
                                    xytext=(0, 3), textcoords='offset points', ha='center', va='bottom', fontsize=8)

        # Ensure the canvas is updated to display the histogram plots
        plt.tight_layout()
        fig.canvas.draw()

        # Display the histogram plots on a Tkinter canvas
        self.histogram_canvas = FigureCanvasTkAgg(fig, master=hist_hash_panel)
        self.histogram_canvas.get_tk_widget().pack(side=tk.TOP, fill=tk.BOTH, expand=True)
        self.histogram_canvas.draw()

        # Calculate multiple hash values of the frame
```

```python
            hash_algorithms = ['md5', 'sha1', 'sha256', 'sha224', 'sha384', 'sha512', 'blake2b', 'ripemd160']
            hash_values = {}
            for algorithm in hash_algorithms:
                hash_obj = hashlib.new(algorithm)
                hash_obj.update(frame.tobytes())
                hash_value = hash_obj.hexdigest()
                hash_values[algorithm] = hash_value

            # Edge detection combobox
            edge_detection_label = tk.Label(hist_hash_panel, text="Edge Detection Method:")
            edge_detection_label.pack()

            self.filtering_method = ttk.Combobox(hist_hash_panel, values=["None", "Gaussian", "Mean",
                "Median", "Bilateral Filtering", "Non-local Means Denoising", "Anisotropic Diffusion",
                "Total Variation Denoising", "Wiener Filter", "Adaptive Thresholding", "Wavelet Transform"])
            self.filtering_method.pack()
            self.filtering_method.current(0)  # Set default method
            self.filtering_method.bind("<<ComboboxSelected>>", self.apply_filtering)

            # Display hash values
            self.hash_listbox = tk.Listbox(hist_hash_panel, height=8, width=40, font=("Arial", 13), bg="crimson", fg="white")
            self.hash_listbox.pack(fill=tk.BOTH, expand=True)

            # Add horizontal scrollbar if needed
            scrollbar = tk.Scrollbar(hist_hash_panel, orient=tk.HORIZONTAL, command=self.hash_listbox.xview)
            scrollbar.pack(side=tk.BOTTOM, fill=tk.X)
            self.hash_listbox.config(xscrollcommand=scrollbar.set)

            for algorithm, value in hash_values.items():
                self.hash_listbox.insert(tk.END, f"{algorithm}: {value}")

    # Define functions for filtering methods
    def apply_gaussian_blur(self, frame, kernel_size=(5, 5), sigma_x=0, sigma_y=0):
        """
        Apply Gaussian blur to each channel of the input frame.

        Args:
            frame: Input image frame.
            kernel_size: Size of the Gaussian kernel. Default is (5, 5).
            sigma_x: Standard deviation in X direction. Default is 0.
            sigma_y: Standard deviation in Y direction. Default is 0.

        Returns:
            List of blurred images for each channel.
        """
        blurred_frames = []
        for i in range(3):  # Iterate over each color channel
            blurred_frame = cv2.GaussianBlur(frame[:,:,i], kernel_size, sigma_x, sigma_y)
            blurred_frames.append(blurred_frame)
        return blurred_frames

    def apply_mean_blur(self, frame, kernel_size=(5, 5)):
        """
        Apply mean blur to each channel of the input frame.

        Args:
            frame: Input image frame.
            kernel_size: Size of the kernel. Default is (5, 5).
```

```python
    Returns:
        List of blurred images for each channel.
    """
    blurred_frames = []
    for i in range(3):  # Iterate over each color channel
        blurred_frame = cv2.blur(frame[:,:,i], kernel_size)
        blurred_frames.append(blurred_frame)
    return blurred_frames

def apply_median_blur(self, frame, kernel_size=5):
    """
    Apply median blur to each channel of the input frame.

    Args:
        frame: Input image frame.
        kernel_size: Size of the kernel. Default is 5.

    Returns:
        List of blurred images for each channel.
    """
    blurred_frames = []
    for i in range(3):  # Iterate over each color channel
        blurred_frame = cv2.medianBlur(frame[:,:,i], kernel_size)
        blurred_frames.append(blurred_frame)
    return blurred_frames

def apply_bilateral_filtering(self, frame, d=9, sigma_color=75, sigma_space=75):
    """
    Apply bilateral filtering to each channel of the input frame.

    Args:
        frame: Input image frame.
        d: Diameter of each pixel neighborhood. Default is 9.
        sigma_color: Filter sigma in the color space. Default is 75.
        sigma_space: Filter sigma in the coordinate space. Default is 75.

    Returns:
        List of filtered images for each channel.
    """
    filtered_frames = []
    for i in range(3):  # Iterate over each color channel
        filtered_frame = cv2.bilateralFilter(frame[:,:,i], d, sigma_color, sigma_space)
        filtered_frames.append(filtered_frame)
    return filtered_frames

def apply_non_local_means_denoising(self, frame, h=10, templateWindowSize=7, searchWindowSize=21):
    """
    Apply Non-local Means Denoising to each channel of the input frame.

    Args:
        frame: Input image frame.
        h: Parameter regulating filter strength. Larger 'h' value removes noise effectively but removes details of image also.
            Smaller 'h' value preserves details but also preserves noise. Default is 10.
        templateWindowSize: Size in pixels of the template patch. Recommended value is 7. Default is 7.
        searchWindowSize: Size in pixels of the window for the search. Recommended value is 21. Default is 21.

    Returns:
        List of denoised images for each channel.
    """
```

```python
        denoised_frames = []
        for i in range(3):  # Iterate over each color channel
            denoised_frame = cv2.fastNlMeansDenoising(frame[:,:,i], None, h=h, 
templateWindowSize=templateWindowSize, searchWindowSize=searchWindowSize)
            denoised_frames.append(denoised_frame)
        return denoised_frames

    def apply_anisotropic_diffusion(self, frame, iterations=1, delta_t=0.25, kappa=10):
        """
        Apply Anisotropic Diffusion to each channel of the input frame.

        Args:
            frame: Input image frame.
            iterations: Number of iterations for diffusion. Default is 1.
            delta_t: Time step. Default is 0.25.
            kappa: Perona-Malik diffusion coefficient. Default is 10.

        Returns:
            List of processed frames after applying Anisotropic Diffusion to each channel.
        """
        diffusion_frames = []
        for i in range(3):  # Iterate over each color channel
            # Copy the input frame channel to avoid modifying the original frame
            img = frame[:,:,i].astype(float)

            # Define the 4-neighbour mask
            mask = np.array([[0, 1, 0],
                             [1, 0, 1],
                             [0, 1, 0]], dtype=np.float32)

            # Perform Anisotropic Diffusion for the specified number of iterations
            for _ in range(iterations):
                # Add padding to the image
                img_padded = cv2.copyMakeBorder(img, 1, 1, 1, 1, cv2.BORDER_REFLECT)

                # Compute gradients using central differences
                dx = cv2.filter2D(img_padded, -1, np.array([[-1, 0, 1]]))
                dy = cv2.filter2D(img_padded, -1, np.array([[-1], [0], [1]]))

                # Resize gradients to match the size of the image
                dx = cv2.resize(dx, img.shape[::-1])
                dy = cv2.resize(dy, img.shape[::-1])

                # Compute gradient magnitude squared
                mag = np.square(dx) + np.square(dy)

                # Compute diffusion coefficients
                c = 1 / (1 + (mag / kappa ** 2))

                # Update image using the diffusion equation
                img += delta_t * (c * cv2.filter2D(dx, -1, mask) + 
                                  c * cv2.filter2D(dy, -1, mask))

            # Append the processed channel to the list of diffusion frames
            diffusion_frames.append(np.clip(img, 0, 255).astype(np.uint8))

        return diffusion_frames

    def apply_total_variation_denoising(self, frame, weight=0.7, eps=0.05):
        """
        Apply Total Variation Denoising to each channel of the input frame.

        Args:
            frame: Input image frame.
```

```
        weight: Denoising weight. Default is 0.7.
        eps: Denoising regularization parameter. Default is 0.05.

    Returns:
        List of denoised frames for each channel.
    """
    denoised_frames = []
    for i in range(3):  # Iterate over each color channel
        denoised_frame = denoise_tv_chambolle(frame[:,:,i], weight=weight, eps=eps)
        # Scale the result to the range 0 to 255
        scaled_denoised_frame = ((denoised_frame - denoised_frame.min()) * (255 / (denoised_frame.max() - denoised_frame.min()))).astype(np.uint8)
        denoised_frames.append(scaled_denoised_frame)
    return denoised_frames

def apply_wiener_filter(self, frame, kernel_size=(3, 3), noise_variance=0.1):
    """
    Apply Wiener Filter to each channel of the input frame.

    Args:
        frame: Input image frame.
        kernel_size: Size of the Gaussian kernel for blurring. Default is (3, 3).
        noise_variance: Variance of the noise. Default is 0.1.

    Returns:
        List of images after applying Wiener Filter to each channel.
    """
    filtered_frames = []
    for i in range(3):  # Iterate over each color channel
        blurred_frame = cv2.GaussianBlur(frame[:,:,i], kernel_size, 0)
        filtered_frame = cv2.fastNlMeansDenoising(blurred_frame, None, h=noise_variance)
        filtered_frames.append(filtered_frame)
    return filtered_frames

def apply_adaptive_thresholding(self, frame, max_value=255, adaptive_method=cv2.ADAPTIVE_THRESH_GAUSSIAN_C, threshold_type=cv2.THRESH_BINARY, block_size=11, constant=2):
    """
    Apply Adaptive Thresholding to each channel of the input frame.

    Args:
        frame: Input image frame.
        max_value: Maximum intensity value. Default is 255.
        adaptive_method: Adaptive thresholding method. Default is cv2.ADAPTIVE_THRESH_GAUSSIAN_C.
        threshold_type: Thresholding type. Default is cv2.THRESH_BINARY.
        block_size: Size of the local region. Default is 11.
        constant: Constant subtracted from the mean. Default is 2.

    Returns:
        List of images after applying Adaptive Thresholding to each channel.
    """
    thresholded_frames = []
    for i in range(3):  # Iterate over each color channel
        thresholded_frame = cv2.adaptiveThreshold(frame[:,:,i], max_value, adaptive_method, threshold_type, block_size, constant)
        thresholded_frames.append(thresholded_frame)
    return thresholded_frames

def apply_wavelet_transform(self, frame, wavelet='haar', level=1):
    """
    Apply Wavelet Transform to each channel of the input frame.

    Args:
```

```python
            frame: Input image frame.
            wavelet: Type of wavelet. Default is 'haar'.
            level: Decomposition level. Default is 1.

        Returns:
            List of images after applying Wavelet Transform to each channel.
        """
        transformed_frames = []
        for i in range(3):  # Iterate over each color channel
            coeffs = pywt.wavedec2(frame[:,:,i], wavelet, level=level)
            # Reconstruct the image from the coefficients
            reconstructed_img = pywt.waverec2(coeffs, wavelet)
            transformed_frames.append(reconstructed_img)

        return transformed_frames

    def apply_filtering(self, event=None):
        # Get selected method from combobox
        method = self.filtering_method.get()

        # Get the current frame number from the title of the tkinter window
        title = self.extracted_frame_window.title()
        frame_numbers = re.findall(r'\d+', title)
        if frame_numbers:
            self.frame_number = int(frame_numbers[-1])  # Extract the last numerical value
        else:
            self.frame_number = 0  # Default frame number if no numerical value is found

        frame = self.video.get_data(self.frame_number)

        # Initialize filtered to None
        filtered = None

        # Apply edge detection method based on selected method
        if method == "Gaussian":
            filtered = self.apply_gaussian_blur(frame)
        elif method == "Mean":
            filtered = self.apply_mean_blur(frame)
        elif method == "Median":
            filtered = self.apply_median_blur(frame)
        elif method == "None":
            filtered = [frame[:,:,i].copy() for i in range(3)]
        elif method == "Bilateral Filtering":
            filtered = self.apply_bilateral_filtering(frame)
        elif method == "Non-local Means Denoising":
            filtered = self.apply_non_local_means_denoising(frame)
        elif method == "Anisotropic Diffusion":
            filtered = self.apply_anisotropic_diffusion(frame)
        elif method == "Total Variation Denoising":
            filtered = self.apply_total_variation_denoising(frame)
        elif method == "Wiener Filter":
            filtered = self.apply_wiener_filter(frame)
        elif method == "Adaptive Thresholding":
            filtered = self.apply_adaptive_thresholding(frame)
        elif method == "Wavelet Transform":
            filtered = self.apply_wavelet_transform(frame)

        # Display edge detection result
        if filtered is not None:
            # Combine channels into a single image
            combined_image = self.combine_channels_to_image(filtered)

            # Convert the combined image to a PIL Image
            pil_image = Image.fromarray(np.uint8(combined_image))
```

```python
            # Convert PIL Image to Tkinter PhotoImage
            edge_photo = ImageTk.PhotoImage(image=pil_image)

            # Display the image in the canvas
            self.edge_canvas.create_image(0, 0, anchor="nw", image=edge_photo)
            self.edge_canvas.image = edge_photo

        # Update histogram and hash values
        self.update_histogram_and_hashes(frame, filtered)

    def combine_channels_to_image(self, filtered):
        """
        Combine filtered channels into a single image.

        Args:
            filtered: List of filtered images for each channel.

        Returns:
            Combined image.
        """
        # Convert each filtered channel to numpy array
        filtered_arrays = [np.array(channel) for channel in filtered]

        # Stack the filtered channels along the last axis to form the combined image
        combined_image = np.stack(filtered_arrays, axis=-1)

        return combined_image

    def update_histogram_and_hashes(self, frame, filtered):
        # Update histogram
        for i, ax in enumerate(self.histogram_canvas.figure.get_axes()):
            ax.clear()
            colors = ['red', 'green', 'blue']
            channel = filtered[i]  # Memilih saluran warna yang sesuai dengan indeks
            hist, bins = np.histogram(channel.ravel(), bins=32, range=(0, 255))
            ax.bar(bins[:-1], hist, color=colors[i], alpha=0.7, width=6)  # Menyesuaikan lebar batang histogram
            ax.set_title(f"Histogram of {colors[i]} Channel (Frame {self.frame_number})", fontsize=14, fontweight='bold', color='blue')
            ax.set_xlabel("Pixel Value", fontsize=12)
            ax.set_ylabel("Frequency", fontsize=12)
            ax.grid(True, linestyle='--', linewidth=0.5, color='gray', alpha=0.5)
            ax.tick_params(axis='both', which='major', labelsize=10)
            # Add frequency values above each bar
            for bar, frequency in zip(hist, bins[1:]):
                if bar > 0:
                    ax.annotate(f'{frequency:.0f}', xy=(bins[np.where(hist == bar)[0][0]] + (bins[1] - bins[0]) / 2, bar),
                                xytext=(0, 3), textcoords='offset points', ha='center', va='bottom', fontsize=8)
        self.histogram_canvas.draw()

        # Update hash values
        hash_algorithms = ['md5', 'sha1', 'sha256', 'sha224', 'sha384', 'sha512', 'blake2b', 'ripemd160']
        hash_values = {}
        for algorithm in hash_algorithms:
            hash_obj = hashlib.new(algorithm)
            for channel in filtered:
                hash_obj.update(channel.tobytes())  # Update hash values based on edge-detected image
            hash_value = hash_obj.hexdigest()
            hash_values[algorithm] = hash_value
```

```python
            self.hash_listbox.delete(0, tk.END)  # Clear existing hash values
            for algorithm, value in hash_values.items():
                self.hash_listbox.insert(tk.END, f"{algorithm}: {value}")

    def show_filterinng_result(self, filtered):
        # Combine channels into a single image
        combined_image = self.combine_channels_to_image(filtered)

        # Convert the combined image to a PIL Image
        pil_image = Image.fromarray(np.uint8(combined_image))

        # Convert PIL Image to Tkinter PhotoImage
        edge_photo = ImageTk.PhotoImage(image=pil_image)

        # Display the image in the canvas
        self.edge_canvas.create_image(0, 0, anchor="nw", image=edge_photo)
        self.edge_canvas.image = edge_photo

    def open_another_player(self):
        # Open another instance of the application
        root = tk.Toplevel(self.master)
        app = FrameFiltering(root)

def main():
    root = tk.Tk()
    app = FrameFiltering(root)
    root.mainloop()

if __name__ == "__main__":
    main()
```

RUNNING PROGRAM

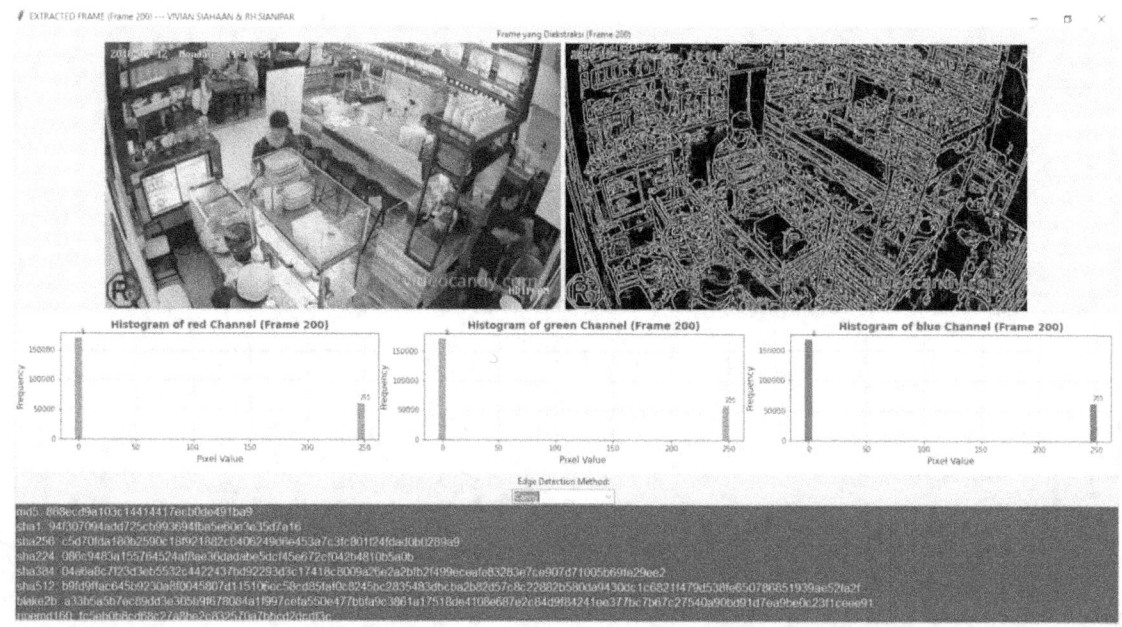

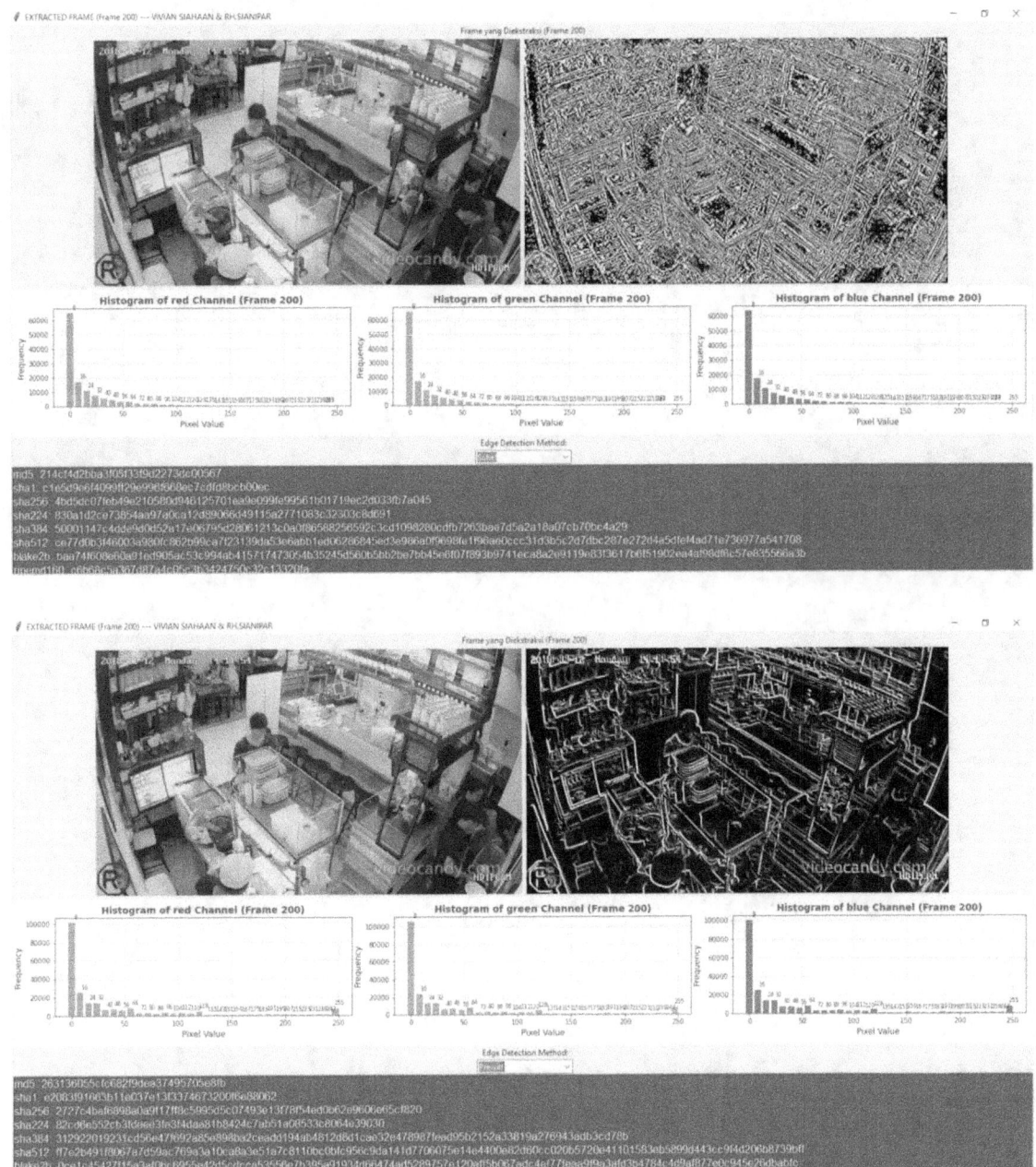

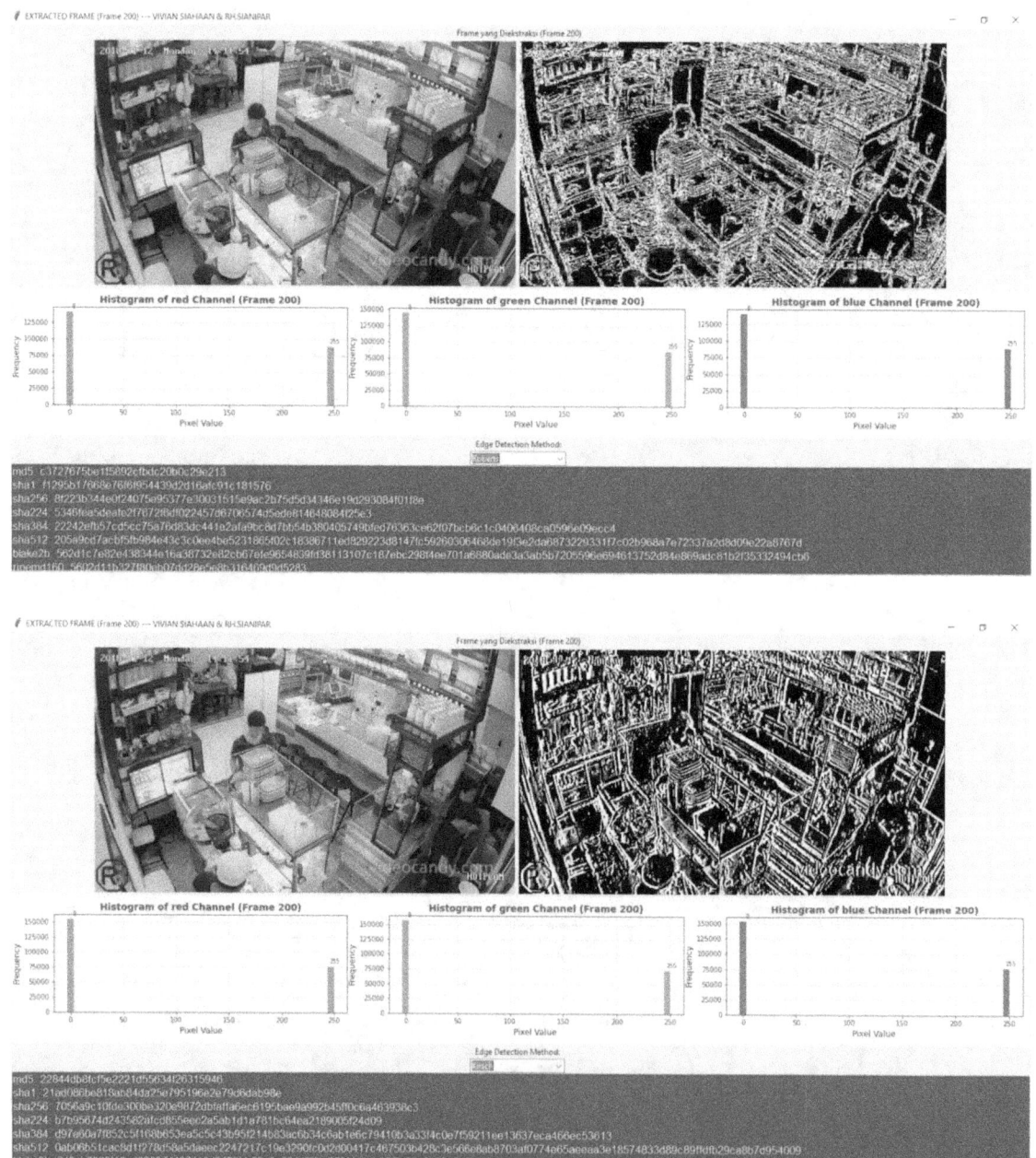

FRAME HASHING

DESCRIPTION

The project, represented by the hashing_each_frame.py script, is a graphical application designed to process video files, analyze their frames, and compute MD5 hashes for each frame. The main purpose of the project is to provide a tool that enables users to open video files, view individual frames, and generate and store hash values for these frames. This can be particularly useful for tasks such as video forensics, integrity verification, or content-based video retrieval.

Detailed Description

The project is built using Python with the following key libraries:
- Tkinter: For creating the graphical user interface (GUI).
- PIL (Pillow): For image handling and display.
- moviepy: For video processing.
- numpy: For numerical operations, particularly for handling frame data.
- hashlib: For computing MD5 hashes.

Key Features
GUI for Video Selection and Control:

- Users can open a video file through a file dialog.
- Basic video controls are provided, including play, pause, stop, and a seek slider.

Video Metadata Display:
- Metadata about the selected video (such as file name, duration, resolution, frame rate, codec, and bit rate) is extracted and displayed in a table format.

Frame Display and Hashing:
- As the video plays, each frame is displayed on a canvas.
- An MD5 hash is computed for each frame and displayed alongside the frame number.
- The frame hash is also saved to a text file for future reference.

Frame Histogram Display:
- The application calculates and displays histograms for the red, green, and blue channels of the current frame.
- Histograms provide a visual representation of the pixel intensity distribution, which can be useful for image analysis.

Detailed Walkthrough

Initialization:
The HashingEachFrame class initializes the GUI and sets up all the necessary widgets, including buttons, labels, sliders, and canvases.

Video Opening and Metadata Extraction:
The open_video method allows the user to select a video file. The selected video is loaded using moviepy, and metadata is extracted and displayed in a table.

Video Playback Controls:
- The play_video, pause_video, and stop_video methods control the video playback.
- The seek_video method updates the video frame based on the position set by the slider.

Frame Processing and Hashing:
- The update_video_frame method handles the frame-by-frame processing of the video during playback.
- For each frame, the method calculates its MD5 hash using the calculate_frame_hash method and updates the GUI to display the frame and its hash.
- The hash is saved to a text file for record-keeping.

Histogram Calculation and Display:
- The get_frame_histogram method calculates the histograms for the red, green, and blue channels of the current frame.
- The plot_histogram method displays these histograms on a separate canvas.

File I/O for Frame Hashes:
The save_frame_hash_to_file method saves the frame index and its corresponding hash to a text file named after the video file.

Conclusion

This project offers a comprehensive tool for video analysis, focusing on frame-by-frame hashing and visualization. It can be extended or modified for more specific use cases, such as more detailed video forensics, automated integrity checking of video files, or incorporating additional video processing features. The modular structure of the code allows for easy expansion and adaptation to various requirements in the field of video analysis.

SOURCE CODE

```python
#hashing_each_frame.py
import tkinter as tk
from tkinter import filedialog, ttk
from PIL import Image, ImageTk
import moviepy.editor as mp
import numpy as np
import os
import hashlib

class HashingEachFrame:
    def __init__(self, master):
        self.master = master
```

```python
        self.master.title("MD5 HASHING OF EVERY FRAME IN VIDEO")

        self.create_widgets()

    def create_widgets(self):
        self.open_button = tk.Button(self.master, text="Open Video", command=self.open_video)
        self.open_button.pack(pady=10)

        self.video_frame = tk.Label(self.master)
        self.video_frame.pack()

        self.metadata_table = ttk.Treeview(self.master, columns=('Property', 'Value'))
        self.metadata_table.heading('#0', text='Property')
        self.metadata_table.heading('#1', text='Value')
        self.metadata_table.pack(pady=10)

        # Frame for play, pause, and stop buttons
        self.button_frame = tk.Frame(self.master)
        self.button_frame.pack()

        self.play_button = tk.Button(self.button_frame, text="Play", command=self.play_video)
        self.play_button.pack(side=tk.LEFT, padx=5)

        self.pause_button = tk.Button(self.button_frame, text="Pause", command=self.pause_video)
        self.pause_button.pack(side=tk.LEFT, padx=5)

        self.stop_button = tk.Button(self.button_frame, text="Stop", command=self.stop_video)
        self.stop_button.pack(side=tk.LEFT, padx=5)

        self.seek_slider = tk.Scale(self.master, from_=0, to=100, orient=tk.HORIZONTAL, command=self.seek_video)
        self.seek_slider.pack()

        # Label widget for displaying frame hash
        self.frame_hash_label = tk.Label(self.master, text="Frame Hash:", font=("Helvetica", 30))  # Modified font size
        self.frame_hash_label.pack()

        self.video_clip = None
        self.playing = False
        self.video_frame_idx = 0
        self.video_filename = None  # Store video filename

        # Canvas for video frame
        self.canvas = tk.Canvas(self.master, width=600, height=300)
        self.canvas.pack(side=tk.LEFT)

        # Canvas for specific frame display
        self.frame_canvas = tk.Canvas(self.master, width=600, height=300)  # Adjusted size
        self.frame_canvas.pack(side=tk.RIGHT)

    def open_video(self):
        self.video_filename = filedialog.askopenfilename(filetypes=[("Video files", "*.mp4;*.avi;*.mpeg")])
        if self.video_filename:
            self.video_clip = mp.VideoFileClip(self.video_filename)
            self.update_metadata_table(self.video_filename)
            self.seek_slider.config(to=self.video_clip.duration)

    def play_video(self):
        if self.video_clip is not None and not self.playing:
            self.playing = True
            self.update_video_frame()
```

```python
    def update_video_frame(self):
        if self.playing:
            frame_np = self.video_clip.get_frame(self.video_frame_idx / self.video_clip.fps)
            frame_hash = self.calculate_frame_hash(frame_np)
            frame = Image.fromarray(frame_np)
            frame_tk = ImageTk.PhotoImage(frame)

            self.canvas.create_image(0, 0, anchor=tk.NW, image=frame_tk)
            self.canvas.image = frame_tk

            hist = self.get_frame_histogram(frame_np)
            if hist:
                self.plot_histogram(hist)

            # Update frame hash label with frame number
            self.frame_hash_label.config(text=f"Frame {self.video_frame_idx}: Frame Hash: {frame_hash}")

            # Save frame hash to a text file
            self.save_frame_hash_to_file(self.video_filename, self.video_frame_idx, frame_hash)

            self.video_frame_idx += 1
            if self.video_frame_idx < self.video_clip.duration * self.video_clip.fps:
                self.seek_slider.set(self.video_frame_idx / self.video_clip.fps)
                self.master.after(33, self.update_video_frame)
            else:
                self.stop_video()

    def save_frame_hash_to_file(self, video_filename, frame_idx, frame_hash):
        # Extract video filename without extension
        filename_without_extension = os.path.splitext(os.path.basename(video_filename))[0]
        txt_filename = f"{filename_without_extension}_frame_hash.txt"

        with open(txt_filename, "a") as file:
            file.write(f"{frame_idx}\t{frame_hash}\n")

    def pause_video(self):
        self.playing = False

    def stop_video(self):
        self.playing = False
        self.video_frame_idx = 0

    def seek_video(self, value):
        if self.video_clip is not None:
            pos_in_seconds = float(value)
            self.video_frame_idx = int(pos_in_seconds * self.video_clip.fps)
            if not self.playing:
                self.update_video_frame()
            else:
                frame_np = self.video_clip.get_frame(self.video_frame_idx / self.video_clip.fps)
                hist = self.get_frame_histogram(frame_np)
                if hist:
                    self.frame_canvas.delete('all')
                    self.plot_histogram(hist)
                    frame_number = int(self.video_frame_idx / self.video_clip.fps)
                    self.frame_canvas.create_text(300, 20, text=f"Histogram for Second {frame_number}", font=("Helvetica", 16), anchor=tk.CENTER)
                    self.frame_canvas.create_text(300, 280, text="Pixel Intensity", font=("Helvetica", 10), anchor=tk.CENTER)
```

```python
                self.frame_canvas.create_text(30, 150, text="Frequency", 
font=("Helvetica", 10), anchor=tk.CENTER)

    def update_metadata_table(self, file_path):
        metadata = self.get_video_metadata(file_path)
        for key, value in metadata.items():
            self.metadata_table.insert('', 'end', text=key, values=(value))

    def get_video_metadata(self, file_path):
        metadata = {}
        video = mp.VideoFileClip(file_path)
        metadata['File Name'] = os.path.basename(file_path)
        metadata['Duration (s)'] = video.duration
        metadata['Width (px)'] = video.size[0]
        metadata['Height (px)'] = video.size[1]
        metadata['FPS'] = video.fps

        if 'video' in video.reader.infos:
            metadata['Codec'] = video.reader.infos['video']['codec_name']
            metadata['Bit Rate (kbps)'] = video.reader.infos['video']['bit_rate'] // 1000
        else:
            metadata['Codec'] = "Unavailable"
            metadata['Bit Rate (kbps)'] = "Unavailable"

        return metadata

    def get_frame_histogram(self, frame):
        if len(frame.shape) == 3:
            hist_red, bins_red = np.histogram(frame[:,:,0].ravel(), bins=64, range=[0,64])
            hist_green, bins_green = np.histogram(frame[:,:,1].ravel(), bins=64, range=[0,64])
            hist_blue, bins_blue = np.histogram(frame[:,:,2].ravel(), bins=64, range=[0,64])
            return hist_red, hist_green, hist_blue
        else:
            return None

    def plot_histogram(self, hist):
        hist_red, hist_green, hist_blue = hist

        max_value = max(np.max(hist_red), np.max(hist_green), np.max(hist_blue))
        scale = 500 / max_value  # Adjusted scale

        bar_width = 8   # Lebar batang histogram
        max_height = 300  # Tinggi maksimum batang histogram
        for i in range(64):
            x0 = i * 10
            x1 = x0 + bar_width
            y0 = 500
            y1 = max(100, 500 - hist_red[i] * scale)  # Batasi tinggi maksimum batang histogram
            self.frame_canvas.create_rectangle(x0, y0, x1, y1, fill="red")

            y0 = y1
            y1 = max(100, 500 - hist_green[i] * scale)  # Batasi tinggi maksimum batang histogram
            self.frame_canvas.create_rectangle(x0, y0, x1, y1, fill="green")

            y0 = y1
            y1 = max(100, 500 - hist_blue[i] * scale)  # Batasi tinggi maksimum batang histogram
            self.frame_canvas.create_rectangle(x0, y0, x1, y1, fill="blue")

    def calculate_frame_hash(self, frame):
        return hashlib.md5(frame.tobytes()).hexdigest()
```

```python
def main():
    root = tk.Tk()
    app = HashingEachFrame(root)
    root.mainloop()

if __name__ == "__main__":
    main()
```

RUNNING PROGRAM

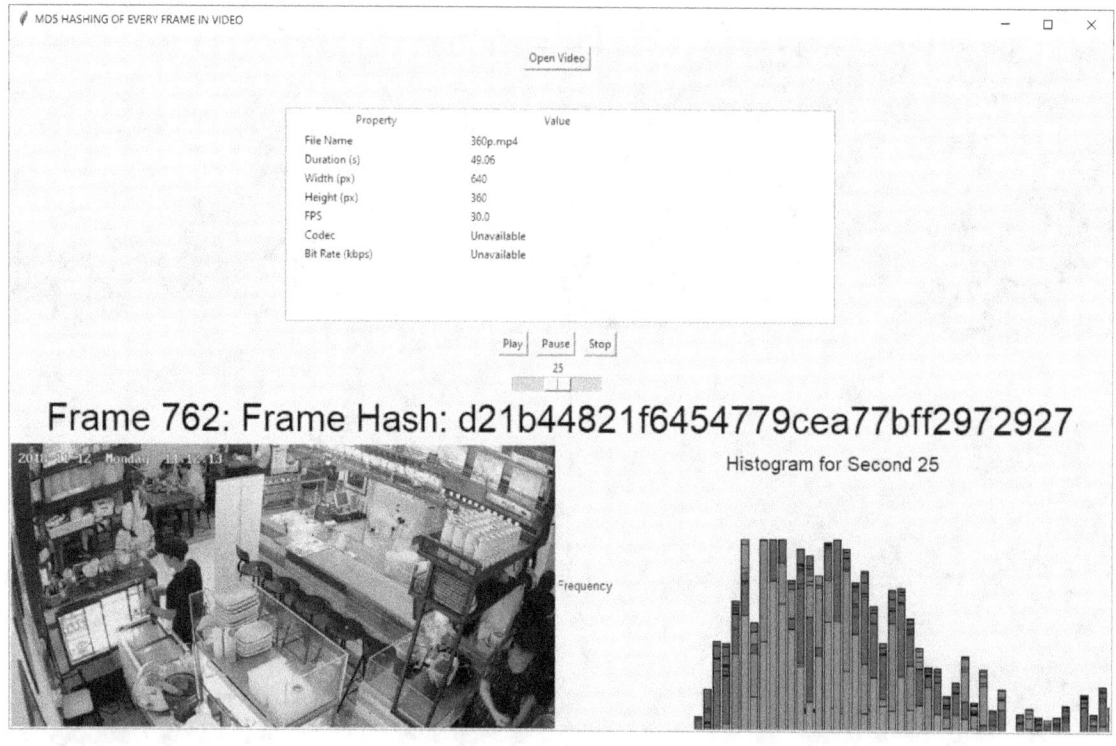

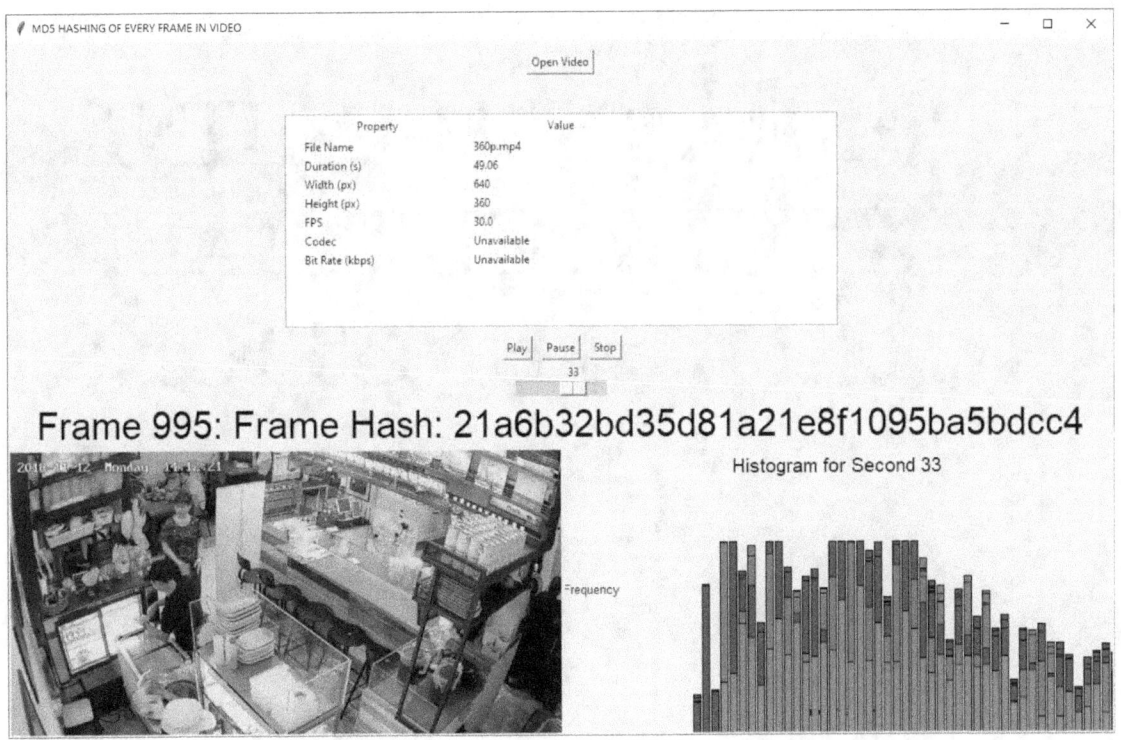

FRAME HASHING WITH EIGHT HASH FUNCTIONS

DESCRIPTION

The project, encapsulated in the eight_hash_functions_each_frame.py script, aims to provide a graphical tool for video analysis and frame extraction. It enables users to open video files, visualize frames, extract specific frames, and compute multiple hash values for these frames using eight different hash functions. The primary purpose is to offer a versatile platform for frame-level analysis and hash computation, which can be valuable for tasks such as video forensics, content authentication, and integrity verification.

Detailed Description

The project leverages Python and several libraries to achieve its functionality, including:
- Tkinter: For building the graphical user interface (GUI).
- PIL (Pillow): For image processing and display.
- imageio: For reading video files.
- matplotlib: For generating histograms and visualizations.
- hashlib: For computing hash values.

Key Features
Video Playback and Visualization:

- Users can open video files and visualize frames within a user-friendly interface.
- Playback controls allow for playing, pausing, and stopping the video.

Frame Extraction:
Users can extract specific frames from the video for detailed analysis.

Frame Zooming and Navigation:
- Zoom functionality enables users to adjust the scale of frame display.
- Navigation controls facilitate jumping to specific times or frames within the video.

Frame Analysis and Hashing:
- Upon frame extraction, the application computes histograms for each RGB channel of the frame.
- It calculates hash values for the extracted frame using eight different hash algorithms, including MD5, SHA-1, SHA-256, SHA-224, SHA-384, SHA-512, BLAKE2b, and RIPEMD-160.
- The computed hash values are displayed alongside the frame for reference and analysis.

Multiple Instances:
Users can open multiple instances of the application to analyze different videos simultaneously.

Detailed Walkthrough
Initialization:
- The FrameEightHashing class initializes the GUI and sets up all the necessary widgets, including canvas for video display, control buttons, entry fields, and comboboxes.

Video Opening and Playback:
- Users can open video files using the "Open Video" button. The selected video is loaded using imageio and displayed on the canvas.
- Playback controls allow users to play, pause, and stop the video.

Frame Extraction and Analysis:
- Users can extract frames by specifying the frame number. Extracted frames are displayed in a separate window along with their histograms and computed hash values using various algorithms.
- The application computes histograms for the RGB channels of the extracted frame and visualizes them using matplotlib.

Frame Zooming and Navigation:
Zoom controls enable users to adjust the scale of frame display for detailed analysis. Navigation controls allow users to jump to specific times or frames within the video.

Multiple Instances:
Users can open another instance of the application to analyze different videos simultaneously, providing flexibility and efficiency in video analysis tasks.

Conclusion
The project provides a comprehensive solution for video frame analysis, offering functionalities for visualization, extraction, and hash computation. Its modular design and integration of multiple hash algorithms make it a versatile tool for various applications, including video forensics, content verification, and integrity checking. With its user-friendly interface and rich feature set, the application facilitates efficient and detailed analysis of video content, catering to the needs of both casual users and professionals in the field.

SOURCE CODE

```python
#eight_hash_functions_each_frame.py
import tkinter as tk
from tkinter import ttk
from tkinter import filedialog
from PIL import Image, ImageTk
import imageio
import matplotlib.pyplot as plt
from matplotlib.backends.backend_tkagg import FigureCanvasTkAgg
import hashlib
import numpy as np


class FrameEightHashing:
    def __init__(self, master):
        self.master = master
```

```python
        self.master.title("FRAME HASHING AND HISTOGRAM---VIVIAN SIAHAAN & RH.SIANIPAR")
        
        self.video = None
        self.video_path = None
        self.paused = False
        self.zoom_scale = tk.IntVar(value=1)
        self.frame_index = 0
        self.start_x = None
        self.start_y = None
        self.current_x = 0
        self.current_y = 0
        self.photo = None  # Save object reference to PhotoImage globally
        
        self.create_widgets()

    def create_widgets(self):
        # Panel for video display
        video_panel = tk.Frame(self.master)
        video_panel.grid(row=0, column=0, padx=10, pady=10, sticky="nsew")
        
        # Canvas to display the video
        canvas_width = 800
        canvas_height = 600
        self.canvas = tk.Canvas(video_panel, width=canvas_width, height=canvas_height)
        self.canvas.pack(side="top", fill="both", expand=True)
        self.canvas.bind("<MouseWheel>", self.on_mousewheel)
        self.canvas.bind("<ButtonPress-1>", self.on_press)
        self.canvas.bind("<B1-Motion>", self.on_drag)
        
        # Scrollbar
        self.scrollbar = tk.Scrollbar(video_panel, orient="horizontal", command=self.on_scroll)
        self.scrollbar.pack(side="bottom", fill="x")
        
        self.canvas.configure(xscrollcommand=self.scrollbar.set)
        
        # Panel for control buttons
        control_panel = tk.Frame(self.master)
        control_panel.grid(row=1, column=0, padx=10, pady=(0, 10), sticky="ew")
        
        # Button to open a video file
        self.open_button = tk.Button(control_panel, text="Open Video", command=self.open_video)
        self.open_button.grid(row=0, column=0, padx=10, pady=5)
        
        # Combobox for selecting zoom scale
        self.zoom_combobox = ttk.Combobox(control_panel, textvariable=self.zoom_scale, values=list(range(1, 11)))
        self.zoom_combobox.grid(row=0, column=1, padx=10, pady=5)
        self.zoom_combobox.bind("<<ComboboxSelected>>", self.update_zoom)
        
        # Label and entry for specifying time
        self.time_label = tk.Label(control_panel, text="Jump to Time (s):")
        self.time_label.grid(row=0, column=2, padx=10, pady=5, sticky="e")
        self.time_entry = ttk.Entry(control_panel)
        self.time_entry.grid(row=0, column=3, padx=10, pady=5, sticky="w")
        self.time_entry.bind("<Return>", lambda event: self.jump_to_time())
        
        # Button to jump to specified time
        self.jump_button = tk.Button(control_panel, text="Jump to Time", command=self.jump_to_time)
        self.jump_button.grid(row=0, column=4, padx=10, pady=5)
        
        # Button to play/pause the video
        self.play_button = tk.Button(control_panel, text="Play/Pause", command=self.toggle_play_pause)
```

```python
        self.play_button.grid(row=0, column=5, padx=10, pady=5)

        # Button to stop the video
        self.stop_button = tk.Button(control_panel, text="Stop", command=self.stop_video)
        self.stop_button.grid(row=0, column=6, padx=10, pady=5)

        # Button to extract frame
        self.extract_button = tk.Button(control_panel, text="Extract Frame", command=self.extract_frame)
        self.extract_button.grid(row=1, column=0, padx=10, pady=5)

        # Label and entry for frame number
        self.frame_label = tk.Label(control_panel, text="Frame Number:")
        self.frame_label.grid(row=1, column=1, padx=10, pady=5, sticky="e")
        self.frame_entry = ttk.Entry(control_panel)
        self.frame_entry.grid(row=1, column=2, padx=10, pady=5, sticky="w")
        self.frame_entry.bind("<Return>", lambda event: self.extract_frame())

        # Button to open another instance of the application
        self.open_another_button = tk.Button(control_panel, text="Open Another Video Player", command=self.open_another_player)
        self.open_another_button.grid(row=2, column=0, columnspan=7, padx=10, pady=5)

    def open_video(self):
        self.video_path = filedialog.askopenfilename(filetypes=[("Video files", "*.mp4;*.avi;*.mkv")])
        if self.video_path:
            self.video = imageio.get_reader(self.video_path)
            self.play_video()

    def play_video(self):
        if self.video:
            self.paused = False
            self.show_frame()

    def stop_video(self):
        self.paused = True
        self.frame_index = 0
        self.current_x = 0
        self.current_y = 0  # Reset the current position
        self.show_frame()

    def toggle_play_pause(self):
        self.paused = not self.paused
        if not self.paused:
            self.play_video()

    def update_zoom(self, event=None):
        self.show_frame()

    def show_frame(self):
        if self.video:
            if not self.paused:
                self.frame_index += 1
                if self.frame_index >= len(self.video):
                    self.frame_index = 0  # Reset frame index if it exceeds the maximum index
            if 0 <= self.frame_index < len(self.video):  # Check if frame index is within range
                try:
                    frame = self.video.get_data(self.frame_index)
                    frame = Image.fromarray(frame)
                    frame = frame.resize((frame.width * self.zoom_scale.get(), frame.height * self.zoom_scale.get()))
                    photo = ImageTk.PhotoImage(frame)
```

```python
                self.photo = photo  # Save object reference to PhotoImage globally
                self.canvas.delete("video")  # Delete previous image
                self.canvas.create_image(self.current_x, self.current_y, anchor="nw", image=photo, tags="video")
                if not self.paused:
                    self.canvas.after(30, self.show_frame)
        except Exception as e:
            print("Error:", e)

    def on_mousewheel(self, event):
        direction = event.delta // 120
        current_value = int(self.zoom_scale.get())
        if direction == 1 and current_value < 10:
            current_value += 1
        elif direction == -1 and current_value > 1:
            current_value -= 1
        self.zoom_scale.set(current_value)
        self.update_zoom()

    def on_press(self, event):
        self.start_x = event.x
        self.start_y = event.y

    def on_drag(self, event):
        if self.start_x and self.start_y:
            x_offset = event.x - self.start_x
            y_offset = event.y - self.start_y
            self.current_x += x_offset  # Update current position
            self.current_y += y_offset  # Update current position
            self.canvas.move("video", x_offset, y_offset)
            self.start_x = event.x
            self.start_y = event.y

    def on_scroll(self, *args):
        scroll_pos = self.scrollbar.get()
        self.current_x = -scroll_pos * self.canvas.winfo_width()
        self.canvas.xview_moveto(scroll_pos)
        self.frame_index = int(scroll_pos * len(self.video))  # Update frame index
        self.show_frame()

    def jump_to_time(self):
        time_str = self.time_entry.get()
        try:
            time_seconds = float(time_str)
            if 0 <= time_seconds:
                self.frame_index = int(time_seconds * self.video.get_meta_data()['fps'])
                self.show_frame()
        except ValueError:
            pass

    def extract_frame(self):
        frame_number_str = self.frame_entry.get()
        try:
            frame_number = int(frame_number_str)
            if 0 <= frame_number < len(self.video):
                frame = self.video.get_data(frame_number)
                self.show_extracted_frame(frame, frame_number)
        except ValueError:
            pass

    def show_extracted_frame(self, frame, frame_number):
        extracted_frame_window = tk.Toplevel(self.master)
        extracted_frame_window.title(f"Frame yang Diekstraksi (Frame {frame_number}) --- RISMON HASIHOLAN SIANIPAR")
```

```python
        extracted_frame_label = tk.Label(extracted_frame_window, text=f"Frame yang Diekstraksi (Frame {frame_number})")
        extracted_frame_label.pack()

        height, width, _ = frame.shape  # Get dimensions of the frame
        extracted_photo = ImageTk.PhotoImage(image=Image.fromarray(frame))

        extracted_frame_canvas = tk.Canvas(extracted_frame_window, width=width, height=height)
        extracted_frame_canvas.pack()
        extracted_frame_canvas.create_image(0, 0, anchor="nw", image=extracted_photo)
        extracted_frame_canvas.image = extracted_photo

        # Plot histogram for each RGB channel
        fig, axs = plt.subplots(1, 3, figsize=(20, 3))
        colors = ['red', 'green', 'blue']
        for i, color in enumerate(['R', 'G', 'B']):
            hist, bins, _ = axs[i].hist(frame[:,:,i].ravel(), bins=64, range=(0, 255), color=colors[i], alpha=0.7)
            axs[i].set_title(f"Histogram of {color} Channel (Frame {frame_number})", fontsize=14, fontweight='bold', color='blue')
            axs[i].set_xlabel("Pixel Value", fontsize=12)
            axs[i].set_ylabel("Frequency", fontsize=12)
            axs[i].grid(True, linestyle='--', linewidth=0.5, color='gray', alpha=0.5)
            axs[i].tick_params(axis='both', which='major', labelsize=10)

            # Add frequency values above each bar
            for bar, frequency in zip(hist, bins[1:]):
                if bar > 0:
                    axs[i].annotate(f'{frequency:.0f}', xy=(bins[np.where(hist == bar)[0][0]] + (bins[1] - bins[0]) / 2, bar),
                                    xytext=(0, 3), textcoords='offset points', ha='center', va='bottom', fontsize=6)
        plt.tight_layout()

        # Calculate multiple hash values of the frame
        hash_algorithms = ['md5', 'sha1', 'sha256', 'sha224', 'sha384', 'sha512', 'blake2b', 'ripemd160']
        hash_values = {}
        for algorithm in hash_algorithms:
            hash_obj = hashlib.new(algorithm)
            hash_obj.update(frame.tobytes())
            hash_value = hash_obj.hexdigest()
            hash_values[algorithm] = hash_value

        # Display hash values
        hash_listbox = tk.Listbox(extracted_frame_window, height=8, width=40, font=("Arial", 13), bg="gray25", fg="white")
        hash_listbox.pack(fill=tk.BOTH, expand=True)

        # Add horizontal scrollbar if needed
        scrollbar = tk.Scrollbar(extracted_frame_window, orient=tk.HORIZONTAL, command=hash_listbox.xview)
        scrollbar.pack(side=tk.BOTTOM, fill=tk.X)
        hash_listbox.config(xscrollcommand=scrollbar.set)

        for algorithm, value in hash_values.items():
            hash_listbox.insert(tk.END, f"{algorithm}: {value}")

        hist_canvas = FigureCanvasTkAgg(fig, master=extracted_frame_window)
        hist_canvas.draw()
        hist_canvas.get_tk_widget().pack()
```

```python
    def open_another_player(self):
        # Open another instance of the application
        root = tk.Toplevel(self.master)
        app = FrameEightHashing(root)

def main():
    root = tk.Tk()
    app = FrameEightHashing(root)
    root.mainloop()

if __name__ == "__main__":
    main()
```

RUNNING PROGRAM

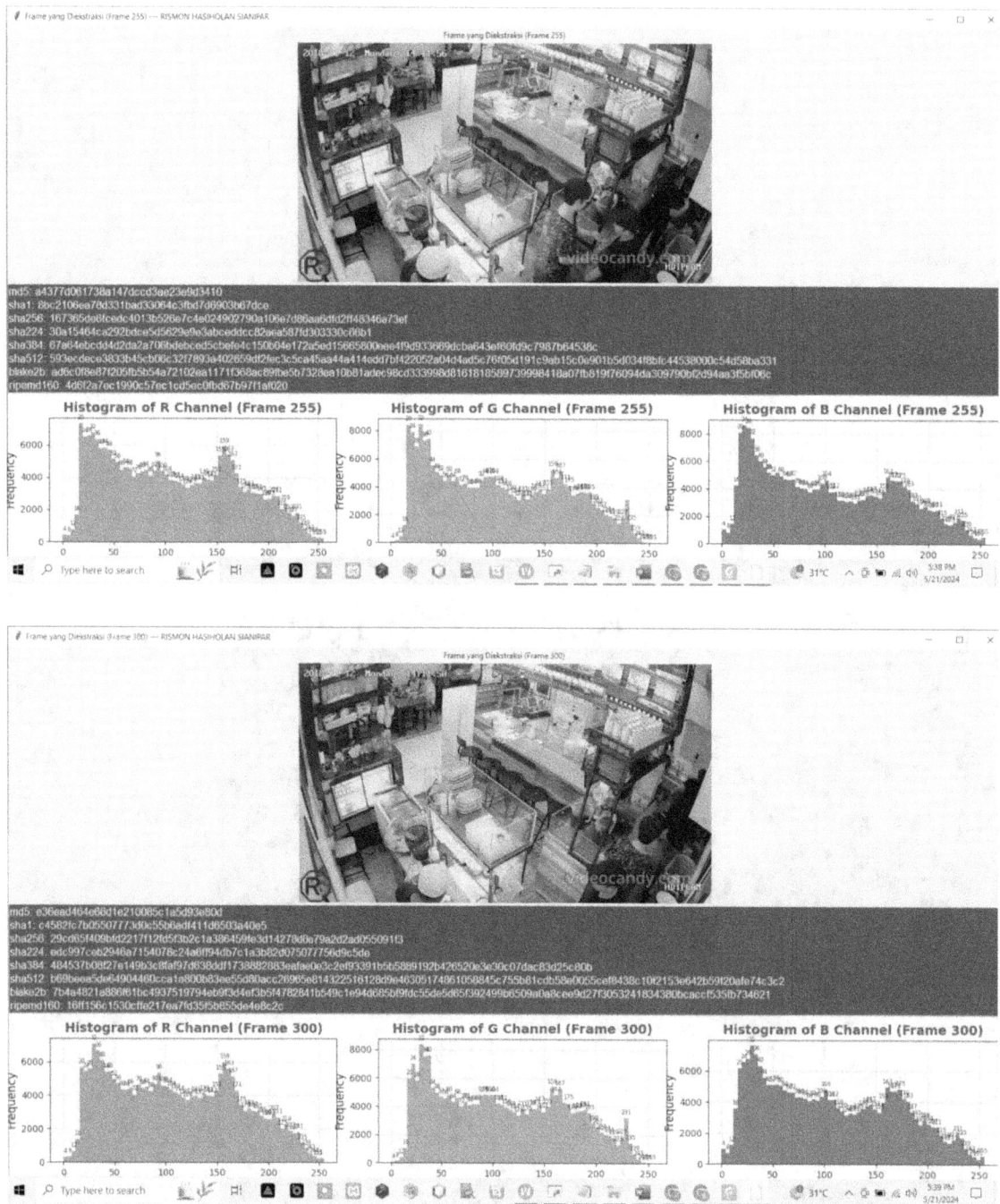

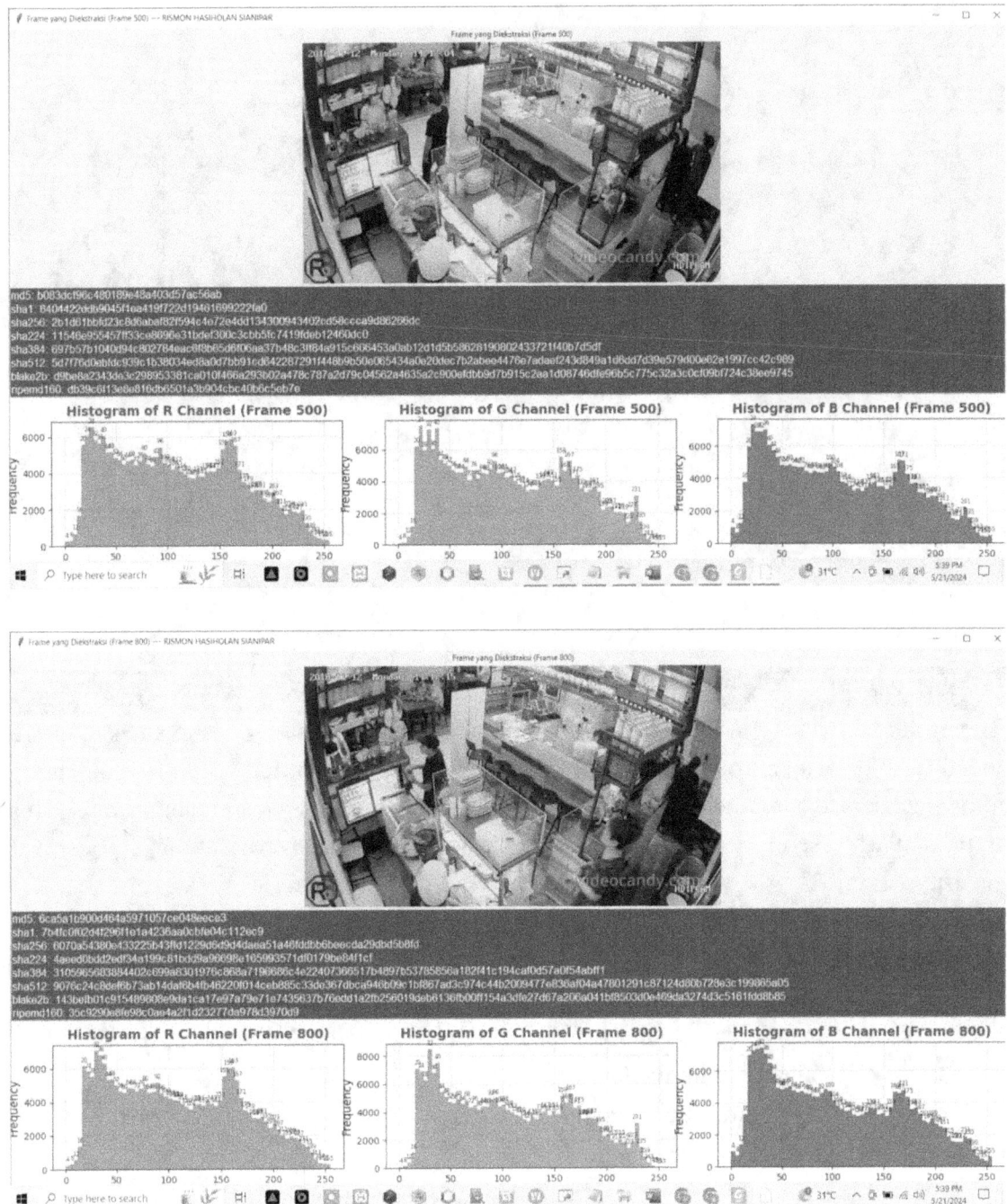

HASHING THE WHOLE VIDEO

DESCRIPTION

The project provides a graphical user interface (GUI) for computing hash values of entire video files. Its main purpose is to ensure the integrity and authenticity of video content by allowing users to compute and verify hash values using multiple hashing algorithms. This is particularly useful in fields such as digital forensics, data verification, and content security.

Functionalities

1. Video Playback and Display:
   - Open Video: Users can open video files (e.g., MP4, AVI) to view their content within the GUI.
   - Play: Start or resume the video playback.
   - Pause: Pause the video playback.
   - Stop: Stop the video playback and release the video resource.
2. Hash Calculation:
   - The application can compute hash values for the entire video using several hash algorithms, such as MD5, SHA-1, SHA-256, and others.
   - These hash values help in verifying that the video content has not been altered.

3. Displaying Hash Values:
   Computed hash values are displayed in a list within the GUI for easy viewing and reference.
4. Saving Hash Values:
   Users can save the computed hash values to a text file for future reference or verification purposes.
5. Multiple Instances:
   Users can open multiple instances of the application to compute hash values for different videos simultaneously.

Detailed Walkthrough
1. Initialization and GUI Setup:
   The application initializes the main window and sets up the GUI components, including labels for video display, a list for showing hash values, and various control buttons.
2. Video Opening and Display:
   - Users can select and open a video file using the "Open Video" button. The selected video is then displayed in the GUI.
   - The video frames are processed and converted into a format suitable for display.
3. Video Playback Controls:
   - Play: Users can play the video, and the frames are continuously displayed in the GUI.
   - Pause: Users can pause the video playback at any time.
   - Stop: Users can stop the video playback, which also resets the display.
4. Hash Calculation:
   - When the user clicks the "Calculate Hash" button, the application reads through the video frame by frame.
   - For each frame, the application updates hash objects corresponding to each selected hash algorithm.
   - Once all frames are processed, the final hash values for each algorithm are computed and displayed in the GUI.
5. Saving Hash Values:
   - Users can save the displayed hash values to a text file by clicking the "Save Hashes" button.

- The application prompts the user to select a file location and saves the hash values in the specified file.
6. Opening New Instances:
   The application allows users to open new instances of the GUI, enabling them to compute and compare hash values for different videos simultaneously.

Conclusion

The project provides a comprehensive tool for video hash computation, facilitating the verification of video integrity and authenticity. Its user-friendly interface and robust functionalities make it valuable for applications in digital forensics, content verification, and data security. By supporting multiple hash algorithms and offering easy playback controls, the tool ensures efficient and reliable hash value computation for video files.

SOURCE CODE

```python
#hash_functions_whole_video.py
import tkinter as tk
from tkinter import filedialog, messagebox
import cv2
import hashlib
import subprocess
from PIL import Image, ImageTk

class VideoHashGUI:
    def __init__(self, root):
        self.root = root
        self.root.title("Video Hash GUI---VIVIAN SIAHAAN & R.H. SIANIPAR")

        self.video_frame = tk.LabelFrame(self.root, text="Video")
        self.video_frame.pack(padx=10, pady=10)

        self.hash_frame = tk.LabelFrame(self.root, text="Hash Values")
        self.hash_frame.pack(padx=10, pady=10)

        self.video_label = tk.Label(self.video_frame)
        self.video_label.pack()

        self.hash_listbox = tk.Listbox(self.hash_frame, width=70, font=('Helvetica', 12))  #
Lebar diperbesar menjadi 70
        self.hash_listbox.pack()

        self.open_button = tk.Button(self.root, text="Open Video", command=self.open_video)
        self.open_button.pack(side=tk.LEFT, padx=5)

        self.play_button = tk.Button(self.root, text="Play", command=self.play_video)
        self.play_button.pack(side=tk.LEFT, padx=5)

        self.pause_button = tk.Button(self.root, text="Pause", command=self.pause_video)
        self.pause_button.pack(side=tk.LEFT, padx=5)
```

```python
        self.stop_button = tk.Button(self.root, text="Stop", command=self.stop_video)
        self.stop_button.pack(side=tk.LEFT, padx=5)

        self.calculate_button = tk.Button(self.root, text="Calculate Hash", command=self.calculate_hash)
        self.calculate_button.pack(side=tk.LEFT, padx=5)

        self.save_button = tk.Button(self.root, text="Save Hashes", command=self.save_hashes)
        self.save_button.pack(side=tk.LEFT, padx=5)

        self.open_new_instance_button = tk.Button(self.root, text="Open New Instance", command=self.open_new_instance)
        self.open_new_instance_button.pack(side=tk.LEFT, padx=5)

        self.video_capture = None
        self.playing = False

    def open_video(self):
        file_path = filedialog.askopenfilename(filetypes=[("Video files", "*.mp4;*.avi")])
        if file_path:
            self.video_capture = cv2.VideoCapture(file_path)
            self.display_video()

    def display_video(self):
        if self.video_capture:
            ret, frame = self.video_capture.read()
            if ret:
                frame = cv2.cvtColor(frame, cv2.COLOR_BGR2RGB)
                image = Image.fromarray(frame)
                imgtk = ImageTk.PhotoImage(image=image)
                self.video_label.imgtk = imgtk
                self.video_label.config(image=imgtk)
                if self.playing:
                    self.root.after(10, self.display_video)
            else:
                messagebox.showwarning("Warning", "End of video reached.")

    def play_video(self):
        if self.video_capture:
            self.playing = True
            self.display_video()

    def pause_video(self):
        self.playing = False

    def stop_video(self):
        self.playing = False
        if self.video_capture:
            self.video_capture.release()
            self.video_label.config(image='')

    def calculate_hash(self):
        if self.video_capture:
            hash_algorithms = ['md5', 'sha1', 'sha256', 'sha224', 'sha384', 'sha512', 'blake2b', 'ripemd160']
            self.hash_listbox.delete(0, tk.END)
            hash_values = {}
            while True:
                ret, frame = self.video_capture.read()
                if not ret:
                    break
                frame = cv2.cvtColor(frame, cv2.COLOR_BGR2RGB)
                for algorithm in hash_algorithms:
                    if algorithm not in hash_values:
```

```python
                    hash_values[algorithm] = hashlib.new(algorithm)
                    hash_values[algorithm].update(frame.tobytes())
            for algorithm, hash_obj in hash_values.items():
                hash_value = hash_obj.hexdigest()
                self.hash_listbox.insert(tk.END, f"{algorithm}--> {hash_value}")

    def save_hashes(self):
        if self.hash_listbox.size() > 0:
            file_path = filedialog.asksaveasfilename(defaultextension=".txt", filetypes=[("Text files", "*.txt")])
            if file_path:
                with open(file_path, "w") as file:
                    for index in range(self.hash_listbox.size()):
                        file.write(self.hash_listbox.get(index) + "\n")
                messagebox.showinfo("Success", "Hashes saved successfully.")

    def open_new_instance(self):
        subprocess.Popen(["python", __file__])

if __name__ == "__main__":
    root = tk.Tk()
    app = VideoHashGUI(root)
    root.mainloop()
```

RUNNING PROGRAM

MEAN FILTERING OF VIDEO

DESCRIPTION

The project's objective is to develop a graphical user interface (GUI) application that enables users to load and interact with video files. Users can play, pause, stop, navigate through video frames, jump to specific times, and apply a mean filter to the video frames to reduce noise. Additionally, the application supports zooming and can open multiple instances.

Functionalities

1. Open Video File: Allow users to select and load a video file.
2. Play/Pause Video: Control the playback of the video.
3. Stop Video: Stop the video and reset playback.
4. Navigate Frames: Move to the next or previous video frame.
5. Jump to Specific Time: Jump to a specific time within the video.
6. Zoom In/Out: Adjust the zoom level of the video frames.
7. Apply Mean Filter: Apply a mean filter to the video frames for noise reduction.
8. Open Another Instance: Launch a new instance of the application.

Detailed Explanation of Each Function

Open Video
- Purpose: To select and load a video file.
- Functionality: Opens a file dialog for users to choose a video file. Once a file is selected, it loads the video for playback.

Play Video
- Purpose: To start or resume video playback.
- Functionality: Sets the application to play mode and begins displaying video frames sequentially.

Play Filtered Video
- Purpose: To play the video with a mean filter applied.
- Functionality: Similar to regular play, but displays frames after applying a mean filter to reduce noise.

Stop Video
- Purpose: To stop video playback and reset the frame index and position.
- Functionality: Stops the video, resets the playback position, and clears the display.

Toggle Play/Pause
- Purpose: To switch between playing and pausing the video.
- Functionality: Changes the playback state from play to pause or vice versa.

Update Zoom
- Purpose: To change the zoom level of the video display.
- Functionality: Adjusts the scaling of the video frames based on the selected zoom level and refreshes the display.

Add Noise
- Purpose: To add random noise to the video frames for demonstration.
- Functionality: Adds Gaussian noise to the frames to simulate a noisy video.

Show Frame
- Purpose: To display the current frame of the video.
- Functionality: Retrieves the current frame, applies zoom and noise if necessary, and displays it on the canvas.

Show Mean Frame
- Purpose: To display the current frame with a mean filter applied.
- Functionality: Applies a mean filter to the frame to reduce noise and displays the filtered frame on a separate canvas.

Handle Mouse Wheel
- Purpose: To handle zooming using the mouse wheel.
- Functionality: Adjusts the zoom scale and updates the video display accordingly.

Handle Mouse Press and Drag
- Purpose: To handle dragging the video frames using the mouse.
- Functionality: Tracks mouse movements to allow users to drag and reposition the video frames within the canvas.

Handle Scroll
- Purpose: To handle horizontal scrolling of the video frames.
- Functionality: Moves the frames based on scrollbar input and updates the frame index accordingly.

Jump to Time
- Purpose: To jump to a specified time in the video.
- Functionality: Converts the specified time into a frame index and updates the video display to show the frame at that time.

Navigate Frames
- Purpose: To move to the previous or next frame in the video.
- Functionality: Changes the frame index to display the next or previous frame.

Open Another Player
- Purpose: To open a new instance of the video player application.
- Functionality: Launches a new window with another instance of the video player, allowing multiple videos to be opened and interacted with simultaneously.

SOURCE CODE

```python
#mean_filter_frame.py
import tkinter as tk
from tkinter import ttk
from tkinter import filedialog
from PIL import Image, ImageTk
import imageio
import cv2
import numpy as np

class MeanFilter:
    def __init__(self, master):
        self.master = master
        self.master.title("Filtering Frame Using Mean Filter")

        self.video = None
        self.video_path = None
        self.paused = False
        self.zoom_scale = tk.IntVar(value=1)
        self.frame_index = 0
        self.start_x1 = None
        self.start_y1 = None
        self.current_x1 = 0
        self.current_y1 = 0
        self.start_x2 = None
        self.start_y2 = None
        self.current_x2 = 0
        self.current_y2 = 0
        self.prev_frame = None

        self.create_widgets()

    def create_widgets(self):
        # Panel for video display
        video_panel = tk.Frame(self.master)
        video_panel.grid(row=0, column=0, padx=10, pady=10, sticky="nsew")

        # Canvas to display the original video
        canvas_width = 900
        canvas_height = 400
        self.canvas = tk.Canvas(video_panel, width=canvas_width, height=canvas_height)
        self.canvas.pack(side="left", fill="both", expand=True)
        self.canvas.bind("<MouseWheel>", self.on_mousewheel)
        self.canvas.bind("<ButtonPress-1>", self.on_press1)
        self.canvas.bind("<B1-Motion>", self.on_drag1)

        # Scrollbar for original video canvas
        self.scrollbar = tk.Scrollbar(video_panel, orient="horizontal", command=self.on_scroll)
        self.scrollbar.pack(side="bottom", fill="x")
        self.canvas.configure(xscrollcommand=self.scrollbar.set)
```

```python
        # Canvas to display the Canny edge video
        self.filter_canvas = tk.Canvas(video_panel, width=canvas_width, height=canvas_height)
        self.filter_canvas.pack(side="right", fill="both", expand=True)
        self.filter_canvas.bind("<MouseWheel>", self.on_mousewheel)
        self.filter_canvas.bind("<ButtonPress-1>", self.on_press2)
        self.filter_canvas.bind("<B1-Motion>", self.on_drag2)

        # Panel for control buttons
        control_panel = tk.Frame(self.master)
        control_panel.grid(row=1, column=0, padx=10, pady=(0, 10), sticky="ew")

        # Button to open a video file
        self.open_button = tk.Button(control_panel, text="Open Video", command=self.open_video)
        self.open_button.grid(row=0, column=0, padx=10, pady=5)

        # Combobox for selecting zoom scale
        self.zoom_combobox = ttk.Combobox(control_panel, textvariable=self.zoom_scale, values=list(range(1, 11)))
        self.zoom_combobox.grid(row=0, column=1, padx=10, pady=5)
        self.zoom_combobox.bind("<<ComboboxSelected>>", self.update_zoom)

        # Label and entry for specifying time
        self.time_label = tk.Label(control_panel, text="Jump to Time (s):")
        self.time_label.grid(row=0, column=2, padx=10, pady=5, sticky="e")
        self.time_entry = ttk.Entry(control_panel)
        self.time_entry.grid(row=0, column=3, padx=10, pady=5, sticky="w")
        self.time_entry.bind("<Return>", lambda event: self.jump_to_time())

        # Button to jump to specified time
        self.jump_button = tk.Button(control_panel, text="Jump to Time", command=self.jump_to_time)
        self.jump_button.grid(row=0, column=4, padx=10, pady=5)

        # Button to play/pause the video
        self.play_button = tk.Button(control_panel, text="Play/Pause", command=self.toggle_play_pause)
        self.play_button.grid(row=0, column=5, padx=10, pady=5)

        # Button to stop the video
        self.stop_button = tk.Button(control_panel, text="Stop", command=self.stop_video)
        self.stop_button.grid(row=0, column=6, padx=10, pady=5)

        # Button to navigate to the previous frame
        self.prev_frame_button = tk.Button(control_panel, text="Previous Frame", command=self.prev_frame)
        self.prev_frame_button.grid(row=0, column=7, padx=10, pady=5)

        # Button to navigate to the next frame
        self.next_frame_button = tk.Button(control_panel, text="Next Frame", command=self.next_frame)
        self.next_frame_button.grid(row=0, column=8, padx=10, pady=5)

        # Button to open another instance of the application
        self.open_another_button = tk.Button(control_panel, text="Open Another Video Player", command=self.open_another_player)
        self.open_another_button.grid(row=2, column=0, columnspan=9, padx=10, pady=5)

    def open_video(self):
        self.video_path = filedialog.askopenfilename(filetypes=[("Video files", "*.mp4;*.avi;*.mkv")])
        if self.video_path:
            self.video = imageio.get_reader(self.video_path)
            self.play_video()
            self.play_filtered_video()
```

```python
    def play_video(self):
        if self.video:
            self.paused = False
            self.show_frame()
            self.show_mean_frame()

    def play_filtered_video(self):
        if self.video:
            self.paused = False
            self.show_mean_frame()

    def stop_video(self):
        self.paused = True
        self.frame_index = 0
        self.current_x1 = 0
        self.current_y1 = 0   # Reset the current position
        self.current_x2 = 0
        self.current_y2 = 0   # Reset the current position
        self.show_frame()
        self.show_mean_frame()

    def toggle_play_pause(self):
        self.paused = not self.paused
        if not self.paused:
            self.play_video()
            self.play_filtered_video()

    def update_zoom(self, event=None):
        self.show_frame()
        self.show_mean_frame()
        self.canvas.scale("video", self.current_x1, self.current_y1, self.zoom_scale.get(), self.zoom_scale.get())
        self.filter_canvas.scale("mean_frame", self.current_x2, self.current_y2, self.zoom_scale.get(), self.zoom_scale.get())

    def add_noise(self, image):
        # Convert image to numpy array
        img_array = np.array(image)

        # Generate random noise
        noise = np.random.normal(0, 1, img_array.shape).astype(np.uint8)

        # Add noise to the image
        noisy_image = cv2.add(img_array, noise)

        # Ensure image values are within valid range
        noisy_image = np.clip(noisy_image, 0, 255)

        # Convert back to image format
        noisy_image = Image.fromarray(noisy_image)

        return noisy_image

    def show_frame(self):
        if self.video:
            if not self.paused:
                self.frame_index += 1
                if self.frame_index >= len(self.video):
                    self.frame_index = 0   # Reset frame index if it exceeds the maximum index
            if 0 <= self.frame_index < len(self.video):   # Check if frame index is within range
                try:
                    frame = self.video.get_data(self.frame_index)
```

```python
                        original_width, original_height = frame.shape[1], frame.shape[0]  # Save 
original dimensions

                        frame = Image.fromarray(frame)

                        # Resize frame according to zoom scale
                        frame = frame.resize((original_width * self.zoom_scale.get(), 
original_height * self.zoom_scale.get()))

                        # Add noise to the frame
                        self.noisy_frame = self.add_noise(frame)

                        photo = ImageTk.PhotoImage(self.noisy_frame)
                        self.photo = photo  # Save object reference to PhotoImage globally
                        self.canvas.delete("video")  # Delete previous image
                        self.canvas.create_image(self.current_x1, self.current_y1, anchor="nw", 
image=photo, tags="video")

                        if not self.paused:
                            self.canvas.after(30, self.show_frame)
                    except Exception as e:
                        print("Error: ", e)

    def show_mean_frame(self):
        if self.video:
            if not self.paused:
                self.frame_index += 1
                if self.frame_index >= len(self.video):
                    self.frame_index = 0  # Reset frame index if it exceeds the maximum index
            if 0 <= self.frame_index < len(self.video):  # Check if frame index is within 
range
                try:
                    # Apply mean filter to reduce noise
                    noisy_frame = cv2.cvtColor(np.array(self.noisy_frame), cv2.COLOR_RGB2BGR)
                    kernel_size = (7, 7)  # Define kernel size for mean filter
                    frame_smoothed = cv2.blur(noisy_frame, kernel_size)

                    # Convert frame back to RGB format
                    frame_rgb = cv2.cvtColor(frame_smoothed, cv2.COLOR_BGR2RGB)

                    # Convert to Image format
                    mean_frame = Image.fromarray(frame_rgb)

                    # Resize frame according to zoom scale using original dimensions
                    original_width, original_height = self.noisy_frame.width, 
self.noisy_frame.height
                    mean_frame = mean_frame.resize((int(original_width * 
self.zoom_scale.get()), 
                                                    int(original_height * 
self.zoom_scale.get())))

                    # Convert Image to PhotoImage
                    mean_photo = ImageTk.PhotoImage(mean_frame)
                    self.mean_photo = mean_photo

                    # Delete previous image
                    self.filter_canvas.delete("mean_frame")

                    # Create new image
                    self.filter_canvas.create_image(self.current_x2, self.current_y2, 
anchor="nw", image=mean_photo, tags="mean_frame")

                    if not self.paused:
                        self.master.after(30, self.show_mean_frame)
```

```python
            except Exception as e:
                print("Error: ", e)

    def on_mousewheel(self, event):
        direction = event.delta // 120
        current_value = int(self.zoom_scale.get())
        if direction == 1 and current_value < 10:
            current_value += 1
        elif direction == -1 and current_value > 1:
            current_value -= 1
        self.zoom_scale.set(current_value)
        self.update_zoom()

    def on_press1(self, event):
        self.start_x1 = event.x
        self.start_y1 = event.y

    def on_press2(self, event):
        self.start_x2 = event.x
        self.start_y2 = event.y

    def on_drag1(self, event):
        if self.start_x1 and self.start_y1:
            self.x_offset1 = event.x - self.start_x1
            self.y_offset1 = event.y - self.start_y1
            self.current_x1 += self.x_offset1  # Update current position
            self.current_y1 += self.y_offset1  # Update current position
            self.canvas.move("video", self.x_offset1, self.y_offset1) # Move original canvas

            self.start_x1 = event.x
            self.start_y1 = event.y

    def on_drag2(self, event):
        if self.start_x2 and self.start_y2:
            self.x_offset2 = event.x - self.start_x2
            self.y_offset2 = event.y - self.start_y2
            self.current_x2 += self.x_offset2  # Update current position
            self.current_y2 += self.y_offset2  # Update current position
            self.filter_canvas.move("mean_frame", self.x_offset2, self.y_offset2)  # Move filter canvas

            self.start_x2 = event.x
            self.start_y2 = event.y

    def on_scroll(self, *args):
        scroll_pos = self.scrollbar.get()
        self.current_x1 = -scroll_pos * self.canvas.winfo_width()  # Update current position for original canvas
        self.current_x2 = -scroll_pos * self.canvas.winfo_width()  # Update current position for filtered canvas
        self.canvas.xview_moveto(scroll_pos)
        self.filter_canvas.xview_moveto(scroll_pos)  # Move filter canvas along with original canvas
        self.frame_index = int(scroll_pos * len(self.video))  # Update frame index
        self.show_frame()
        self.show_mean_frame()  # Update filtered frame

    def jump_to_time(self):
        time_str = self.time_entry.get()
        try:
            time_seconds = float(time_str)
            if 0 <= time_seconds:
                self.frame_index = int(time_seconds * self.video.get_meta_data()['fps'])
                self.show_frame()
```

```python
                    self.show_mean_frame()  # Jump to specified time for Canny edge frame
        except ValueError:
            pass

    def prev_frame(self):
        if self.video and self.frame_index > 0:
            self.frame_index -= 1
            self.show_frame()
            self.show_mean_frame()

    def next_frame(self):
        if self.video and self.frame_index < len(self.video) - 1:
            self.frame_index += 1
            self.show_frame()
            self.show_mean_frame()

    def open_another_player(self):
        # Open another instance of the application
        root = tk.Toplevel(self.master)
        app = MeanFilter(root)

def main():
    root = tk.Tk()
    app = MeanFilter(root)
    root.mainloop()

if __name__ == "__main__":
    main()
```

RUNNING PROGRAM

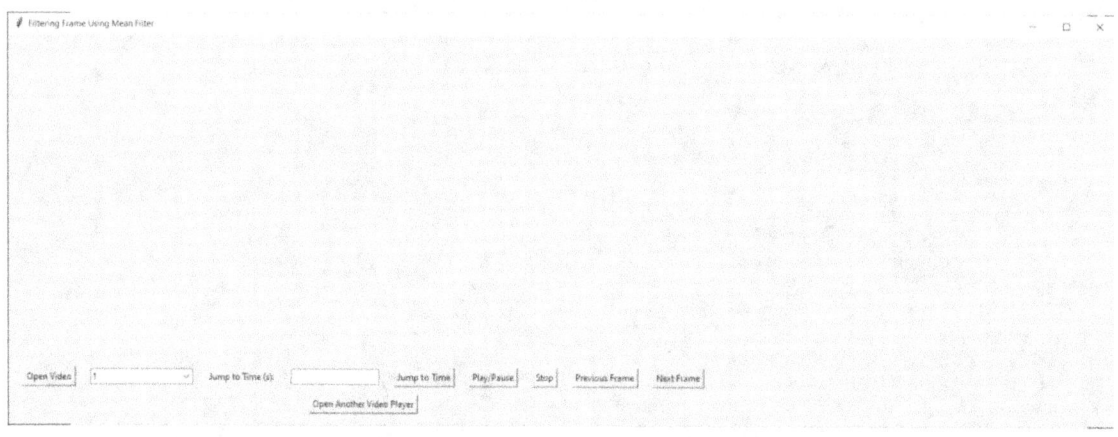

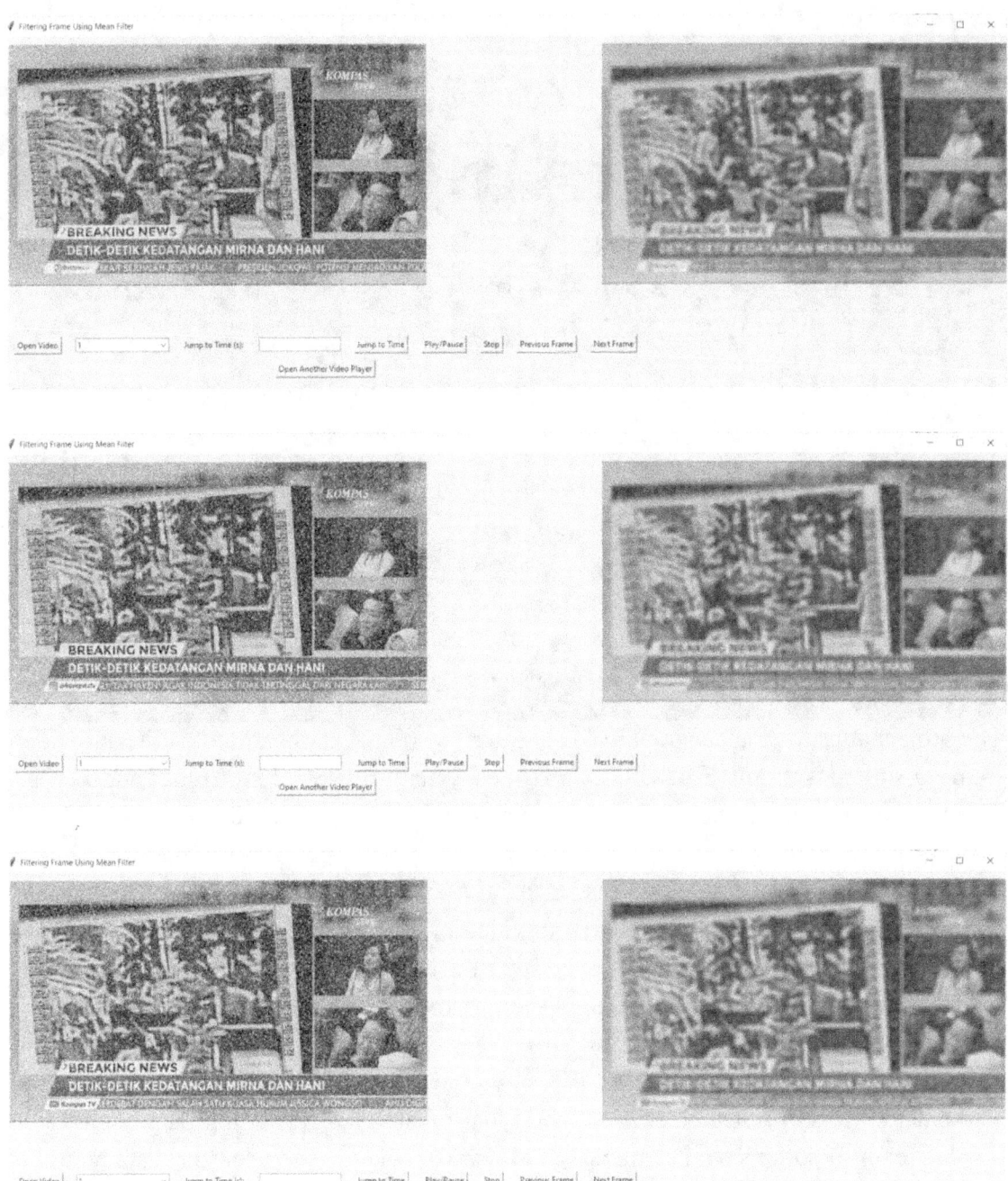

ANISOTROPIC DIFFUSING OF VIDEO

DESCRIPTION

The project aims to create a graphical user interface (GUI) application for filtering video frames using anisotropic diffusion. It provides a platform for users to load video files, apply the anisotropic diffusion filter, and interact with the filtered video frames.

The AnisotropicDiffusion class serves as the core component of the application, encapsulating all functionalities related to video processing and GUI interactions. Upon initialization, the GUI window is created with a title indicating the use of anisotropic diffusion for frame filtering. Attributes such as the video source, current frame index, zoom scale, and GUI elements are initialized.

The create_widgets() method sets up the layout of the GUI, including panels for video display, control buttons, and scrollbars. Two canvas widgets are used for displaying the original video frames and the filtered frames after anisotropic diffusion. Control buttons such as open video, play/pause, stop, jump to time, and navigation buttons are provided for user interaction.

Users can load video files using the open_video() method, which allows them to select a video file using a file dialog. Upon selection, the video is loaded for playback and filtering.

Playback controls such as play, pause, and stop are available for users to control video playback. Zooming functionality is implemented using the mouse wheel, and panning is enabled by dragging the mouse on the canvas.

Frame processing involves retrieving and displaying the current frame of the video, applying Gaussian noise to simulate real-world scenarios, and performing anisotropic diffusion on the noisy frame to reduce noise and enhance image quality. Both original and filtered frames are updated dynamically to reflect changes in playback, zoom, and frame navigation.

Event handlers are defined for mouse wheel scrolling, mouse press, drag actions, and scrollbar movements. Users can input a specific time to jump to within the video using the time entry field and the "Jump to Time" button. Navigation buttons allow users to move to the previous or next frame in the video sequence.

The application supports opening multiple instances of the video player using the "Open Another Video Player" button. The main() function initializes the root Tkinter window and creates an instance of the AnisotropicDiffusion class. The mainloop() function ensures that the GUI remains responsive by continuously listening for user inputs and updating the display accordingly.

Users are prompted to select video files with common formats such as MP4, AVI, and MKV using the file dialog. Error handling mechanisms are implemented to catch exceptions during video loading, frame processing, and display updates. Parameters such as sigma_s and sigma_r are adjustable to fine-tune the anisotropic diffusion filter's performance based on user requirements.

Original frame dimensions are preserved during resizing to maintain aspect ratio and ensure accurate display. Image data is converted between formats such as PIL Image, NumPy arrays, and OpenCV matrices to facilitate processing and display. Canvas widgets are interactive, allowing users to manipulate video frames through mouse gestures for a more intuitive user experience.

Frames are loaded dynamically from the video source, ensuring efficient memory usage and smooth playback even for large video files. The application leverages efficient rendering techniques to minimize latency and provide a responsive user interface. Frame updates occur in real-time, allowing users to observe changes instantly as they interact with the GUI controls.

Resources such as video objects, images, and GUI elements are managed efficiently to prevent memory leaks and optimize performance. The application provides feedback to users through console messages, informing them of errors or status updates during video processing. The codebase is modular and follows best practices to enhance maintainability and facilitate future enhancements or extensions. The design of the application prioritizes user experience, offering a rich set of features and intuitive controls for seamless interaction with video content.

SOURCE CODE

```python
#anisotopic_diffusion_frame.py
import tkinter as tk
from tkinter import ttk
from tkinter import filedialog
from PIL import Image, ImageTk
import imageio
import cv2
import numpy as np

class AnisotropicDiffusion:
    def __init__(self, master):
        self.master = master
        self.master.title("Filtering Frame Using Anisotropic Diffusion")

        self.video = None
        self.video_path = None
        self.paused = False
        self.zoom_scale = tk.IntVar(value=1)
        self.frame_index = 0
        self.start_x1 = None
        self.start_y1 = None
        self.current_x1 = 0
        self.current_y1 = 0
        self.start_x2 = None
        self.start_y2 = None
        self.current_x2 = 0
        self.current_y2 = 0
        self.prev_frame = None

        self.create_widgets()

    def create_widgets(self):
        # Panel for video display
        video_panel = tk.Frame(self.master)
        video_panel.grid(row=0, column=0, padx=10, pady=10, sticky="nsew")

        # Canvas to display the original video
        canvas_width = 900
        canvas_height = 400
```

```python
        self.canvas = tk.Canvas(video_panel, width=canvas_width, height=canvas_height)
        self.canvas.pack(side="left", fill="both", expand=True)
        self.canvas.bind("<MouseWheel>", self.on_mousewheel)
        self.canvas.bind("<ButtonPress-1>", self.on_press1)
        self.canvas.bind("<B1-Motion>", self.on_drag1)

        # Scrollbar for original video canvas
        self.scrollbar = tk.Scrollbar(video_panel, orient="horizontal", command=self.on_scroll)
        self.scrollbar.pack(side="bottom", fill="x")
        self.canvas.configure(xscrollcommand=self.scrollbar.set)

        # Canvas to display the Canny edge video
        self.filter_canvas = tk.Canvas(video_panel, width=canvas_width, height=canvas_height)
        self.filter_canvas.pack(side="right", fill="both", expand=True)
        self.filter_canvas.bind("<MouseWheel>", self.on_mousewheel)
        self.filter_canvas.bind("<ButtonPress-1>", self.on_press2)
        self.filter_canvas.bind("<B1-Motion>", self.on_drag2)

        # Panel for control buttons
        control_panel = tk.Frame(self.master)
        control_panel.grid(row=1, column=0, padx=10, pady=(0, 10), sticky="ew")

        # Button to open a video file
        self.open_button = tk.Button(control_panel, text="Open Video", command=self.open_video)
        self.open_button.grid(row=0, column=0, padx=10, pady=5)

        # Combobox for selecting zoom scale
        self.zoom_combobox = ttk.Combobox(control_panel, textvariable=self.zoom_scale, values=list(range(1, 11)))
        self.zoom_combobox.grid(row=0, column=1, padx=10, pady=5)
        self.zoom_combobox.bind("<<ComboboxSelected>>", self.update_zoom)

        # Label and entry for specifying time
        self.time_label = tk.Label(control_panel, text="Jump to Time (s):")
        self.time_label.grid(row=0, column=2, padx=10, pady=5, sticky="e")
        self.time_entry = ttk.Entry(control_panel)
        self.time_entry.grid(row=0, column=3, padx=10, pady=5, sticky="w")
        self.time_entry.bind("<Return>", lambda event: self.jump_to_time())

        # Button to jump to specified time
        self.jump_button = tk.Button(control_panel, text="Jump to Time", command=self.jump_to_time)
        self.jump_button.grid(row=0, column=4, padx=10, pady=5)

        # Button to play/pause the video
        self.play_button = tk.Button(control_panel, text="Play/Pause", command=self.toggle_play_pause)
        self.play_button.grid(row=0, column=5, padx=10, pady=5)

        # Button to stop the video
        self.stop_button = tk.Button(control_panel, text="Stop", command=self.stop_video)
        self.stop_button.grid(row=0, column=6, padx=10, pady=5)

        # Button to navigate to the previous frame
        self.prev_frame_button = tk.Button(control_panel, text="Previous Frame", command=self.prev_frame)
        self.prev_frame_button.grid(row=0, column=7, padx=10, pady=5)

        # Button to navigate to the next frame
        self.next_frame_button = tk.Button(control_panel, text="Next Frame", command=self.next_frame)
        self.next_frame_button.grid(row=0, column=8, padx=10, pady=5)

        # Button to open another instance of the application
```

```python
        self.open_another_button = tk.Button(control_panel, text="Open Another Video Player", command=self.open_another_player)
        self.open_another_button.grid(row=2, column=0, columnspan=9, padx=10, pady=5)

    def open_video(self):
        self.video_path = filedialog.askopenfilename(filetypes=[("Video files", "*.mp4;*.avi;*.mkv")])
        if self.video_path:
            self.video = imageio.get_reader(self.video_path)
            self.play_video()
            self.play_filtered_video()

    def play_video(self):
        if self.video:
            self.paused = False
            self.show_frame()
            self.show_anisotropic_frame()

    def play_filtered_video(self):
        if self.video:
            self.paused = False
            self.show_anisotropic_frame()

    def stop_video(self):
        self.paused = True
        self.frame_index = 0
        self.current_x1 = 0
        self.current_y1 = 0  # Reset the current position
        self.current_x2 = 0
        self.current_y2 = 0  # Reset the current position
        self.show_frame()
        self.show_anisotropic_frame()

    def toggle_play_pause(self):
        self.paused = not self.paused
        if not self.paused:
            self.play_video()
            self.play_filtered_video()

    def update_zoom(self, event=None):
        self.show_frame()
        self.show_anisotropic_frame()
        self.canvas.scale("video", self.current_x1, self.current_y1, self.zoom_scale.get(), self.zoom_scale.get())
        self.filter_canvas.scale("anisotropic_frame", self.current_x2, self.current_y2, self.zoom_scale.get(), self.zoom_scale.get())

    def add_noise(self, image):
        # Convert image to numpy array
        img_array = np.array(image)

        # Generate random noise
        noise = np.random.normal(0, 1, img_array.shape).astype(np.uint8)

        # Add noise to the image
        noisy_image = cv2.add(img_array, noise)

        # Ensure image values are within valid range
        noisy_image = np.clip(noisy_image, 0, 255)

        # Convert back to image format
        noisy_image = Image.fromarray(noisy_image)

        return noisy_image
```

```python
    def show_frame(self):
        if self.video:
            if not self.paused:
                self.frame_index += 1
                if self.frame_index >= len(self.video):
                    self.frame_index = 0  # Reset frame index if it exceeds the maximum index
            if 0 <= self.frame_index < len(self.video):  # Check if frame index is within range
                try:
                    frame = self.video.get_data(self.frame_index)
                    original_width, original_height = frame.shape[1], frame.shape[0]  # Save original dimensions

                    frame = Image.fromarray(frame)

                    # Resize frame according to zoom scale
                    frame = frame.resize((original_width * self.zoom_scale.get(), original_height * self.zoom_scale.get()))

                    # Add noise to the frame
                    self.noisy_frame = self.add_noise(frame)

                    photo = ImageTk.PhotoImage(self.noisy_frame)
                    self.photo = photo  # Save object reference to PhotoImage globally
                    self.canvas.delete("video")  # Delete previous image
                    self.canvas.create_image(self.current_x1, self.current_y1, anchor="nw", image=photo, tags="video")

                    if not self.paused:
                        self.canvas.after(30, self.show_frame)
                except Exception as e:
                    print("Error: ", e)

    def apply_anisotropic_diffusion(self, frame):
        # Apply anisotropic diffusion
        anisotropic_frame = cv2.edgePreservingFilter(frame, flags=1, sigma_s=150, sigma_r=0.75)
        # Adjust parameters sigma_s and sigma_r as needed
        return anisotropic_frame

    def show_anisotropic_frame(self):
        if self.video:
            if not self.paused:
                self.frame_index += 1
                if self.frame_index >= len(self.video):
                    self.frame_index = 0  # Reset frame index if it exceeds the maximum index
            if 0 <= self.frame_index < len(self.video):  # Check if frame index is within range
                try:
                    # Convert noisy frame to BGR format
                    noisy_frame = cv2.cvtColor(np.array(self.noisy_frame), cv2.COLOR_RGB2BGR)

                    # Apply anisotropic diffusion
                    frame_denoised = self.apply_anisotropic_diffusion(noisy_frame)

                    # Convert frame back to RGB format
                    frame_rgb = cv2.cvtColor(frame_denoised, cv2.COLOR_BGR2RGB)

                    # Convert to Image format
                    anisotropic_frame = Image.fromarray(frame_rgb)

                    # Resize frame according to zoom scale using original dimensions
```

```python
                            original_width, original_height = self.noisy_frame.width, 
self.noisy_frame.height
                            anisotropic_frame = anisotropic_frame.resize((int(original_width * 
self.zoom_scale.get()),
                                                       int(original_height * 
self.zoom_scale.get())))

                            # Convert Image to PhotoImage
                            denoised_photo = ImageTk.PhotoImage(anisotropic_frame)
                            self.denoised_photo = denoised_photo

                            # Delete previous image
                            self.filter_canvas.delete("anisotropic_frame")

                            # Create new image
                            self.filter_canvas.create_image(self.current_x2, self.current_y2, 
anchor="nw", image=denoised_photo, tags="anisotropic_frame")

                        if not self.paused:
                            self.master.after(30, self.show_anisotropic_frame)
                except Exception as e:
                    print("Error: ", e)

    def on_mousewheel(self, event):
        direction = event.delta // 120
        current_value = int(self.zoom_scale.get())
        if direction == 1 and current_value < 10:
            current_value += 1
        elif direction == -1 and current_value > 1:
            current_value -= 1
        self.zoom_scale.set(current_value)
        self.update_zoom()

    def on_press1(self, event):
        self.start_x1 = event.x
        self.start_y1 = event.y

    def on_press2(self, event):
        self.start_x2 = event.x
        self.start_y2 = event.y

    def on_drag1(self, event):
        if self.start_x1 and self.start_y1:
            self.x_offset1 = event.x - self.start_x1
            self.y_offset1 = event.y - self.start_y1
            self.current_x1 += self.x_offset1  # Update current position
            self.current_y1 += self.y_offset1  # Update current position
            self.canvas.move("video", self.x_offset1, self.y_offset1) # Move original canvas

            self.start_x1 = event.x
            self.start_y1 = event.y

    def on_drag2(self, event):
        if self.start_x2 and self.start_y2:
            self.x_offset2 = event.x - self.start_x2
            self.y_offset2 = event.y - self.start_y2
            self.current_x2 += self.x_offset2  # Update current position
            self.current_y2 += self.y_offset2  # Update current position
            self.filter_canvas.move("anisotropic_frame", self.x_offset2, self.y_offset2)  # 
Move filter canvas

            self.start_x2 = event.x
            self.start_y2 = event.y
```

```python
    def on_scroll(self, *args):
        scroll_pos = self.scrollbar.get()
        self.current_x1 = -scroll_pos * self.canvas.winfo_width()  # Update current position for original canvas
        self.current_x2 = -scroll_pos * self.canvas.winfo_width()  # Update current position for filtered canvas
        self.canvas.xview_moveto(scroll_pos)
        self.filter_canvas.xview_moveto(scroll_pos)  # Move filter canvas along with original canvas
        self.frame_index = int(scroll_pos * len(self.video))  # Update frame index
        self.show_frame()
        self.show_anisotropic_frame()  # Update filtered frame

    def jump_to_time(self):
        time_str = self.time_entry.get()
        try:
            time_seconds = float(time_str)
            if 0 <= time_seconds:
                self.frame_index = int(time_seconds * self.video.get_meta_data()['fps'])
                self.show_frame()
                self.show_anisotropic_frame()  # Jump to specified time for Canny edge frame
        except ValueError:
            pass

    def prev_frame(self):
        if self.video and self.frame_index > 0:
            self.frame_index -= 1
            self.show_frame()
            self.show_anisotropic_frame()

    def next_frame(self):
        if self.video and self.frame_index < len(self.video) - 1:
            self.frame_index += 1
            self.show_frame()
            self.show_anisotropic_frame()

    def open_another_player(self):
        # Open another instance of the application
        root = tk.Toplevel(self.master)
        app = AnisotropicDiffusion(root)

def main():
    root = tk.Tk()
    app = AnisotropicDiffusion(root)
    root.mainloop()

if __name__ == "__main__":
    main()
```

RUNNING PROGRAM

BILATERAL FILTERING OF VIDEO

DESCRIPTION

The project involves the development of a graphical user interface (GUI) application for filtering video frames using the bilateral filter technique. It provides users with the capability to load video files, apply the bilateral filter, and interact with the filtered video frames.

The BilateralFilter class serves as the central component of the application, responsible for managing video processing and GUI interactions. Upon initialization, the GUI window is created with a title indicating the use of the bilateral filter for frame filtering. Various attributes such as the video source, current frame index, zoom scale, and GUI elements are initialized within this class.

The create_widgets() method configures the layout of the GUI, including panels for displaying the original video frames and the filtered frames, as well as control buttons for user interaction. Canvas widgets are used for displaying video frames, while buttons allow users to open video files, control playback, adjust zoom level, and navigate through frames.

Users can load video files by clicking the "Open Video" button, which opens a file dialog for selecting video files in common formats such as MP4, AVI, or MKV. Once a video file is selected, it is loaded for playback and filtering using the bilateral filter.

Playback controls such as play, pause, stop, previous frame, and next frame are provided to enable users to control video playback. The GUI also includes features such as zooming using the mouse wheel and panning by dragging the mouse on the canvas.

Frame processing involves retrieving the current frame of the video, adding Gaussian noise to simulate real-world conditions, and applying the bilateral filter to reduce noise and enhance image quality. Both the original and filtered frames are dynamically updated to reflect changes in playback, zoom, and frame navigation.

Event handlers are defined for mouse wheel scrolling, mouse press, drag actions, and scrollbar movements to facilitate user interaction with the GUI. Users can input a specific time to jump to within the video using the time entry field and the "Jump to Time" button.

The application supports opening multiple instances of the video player using the "Open Another Video Player" button. This feature allows users to simultaneously view and compare different video files using separate instances of the application.

The main() function initializes the root Tkinter window and creates an instance of the BilateralFilter class, ensuring that the GUI remains responsive by continuously listening for user inputs and updating the display accordingly.

Error handling mechanisms are implemented to catch exceptions during video loading, frame processing, and display updates. Parameters such as the filter size and sigma values are adjustable to fine-tune the bilateral filter's performance based on user preferences and the characteristics of the input video.

The application preserves the original dimensions of the video frames during resizing to maintain aspect ratio and ensure accurate display. Image data is converted between formats such as PIL Image, NumPy arrays, and OpenCV matrices to facilitate processing and display.

Efficient rendering techniques are employed to minimize latency and provide a responsive user interface, ensuring smooth playback even for large video files. Resources such as video objects, images, and GUI elements are managed efficiently to optimize performance and prevent memory leaks.

Console messages are used to provide feedback to users, informing them of errors or status updates during video processing. The codebase follows modular design principles and best practices to enhance maintainability and facilitate future enhancements or extensions of the application.

Overall, the design of the application prioritizes user experience, offering a rich set of features and intuitive controls for seamless interaction with video content.

SOURCE CODE

```python
#bilateral_filter_frame.py
import tkinter as tk
from tkinter import ttk
from tkinter import filedialog
from PIL import Image, ImageTk
import imageio
import cv2
import numpy as np

class BilateralFilter:
    def __init__(self, master):
        self.master = master
        self.master.title("Filtering Frame Using Bilateral Filter")

        self.video = None
        self.video_path = None
        self.paused = False
        self.zoom_scale = tk.IntVar(value=1)
        self.frame_index = 0
        self.start_x1 = None
        self.start_y1 = None
        self.current_x1 = 0
        self.current_y1 = 0
        self.start_x2 = None
        self.start_y2 = None
        self.current_x2 = 0
        self.current_y2 = 0
        self.prev_frame = None

        self.create_widgets()

    def create_widgets(self):
        # Panel for video display
        video_panel = tk.Frame(self.master)
        video_panel.grid(row=0, column=0, padx=10, pady=10, sticky="nsew")

        # Canvas to display the original video
        canvas_width = 900
        canvas_height = 400
```

```python
        self.canvas = tk.Canvas(video_panel, width=canvas_width, height=canvas_height)
        self.canvas.pack(side="left", fill="both", expand=True)
        self.canvas.bind("<MouseWheel>", self.on_mousewheel)
        self.canvas.bind("<ButtonPress-1>", self.on_press1)
        self.canvas.bind("<B1-Motion>", self.on_drag1)

        # Scrollbar for original video canvas
        self.scrollbar = tk.Scrollbar(video_panel, orient="horizontal", command=self.on_scroll)
        self.scrollbar.pack(side="bottom", fill="x")
        self.canvas.configure(xscrollcommand=self.scrollbar.set)

        # Canvas to display the Canny edge video
        self.filter_canvas = tk.Canvas(video_panel, width=canvas_width, height=canvas_height)
        self.filter_canvas.pack(side="right", fill="both", expand=True)
        self.filter_canvas.bind("<MouseWheel>", self.on_mousewheel)
        self.filter_canvas.bind("<ButtonPress-1>", self.on_press2)
        self.filter_canvas.bind("<B1-Motion>", self.on_drag2)

        # Panel for control buttons
        control_panel = tk.Frame(self.master)
        control_panel.grid(row=1, column=0, padx=10, pady=(0, 10), sticky="ew")

        # Button to open a video file
        self.open_button = tk.Button(control_panel, text="Open Video", command=self.open_video)
        self.open_button.grid(row=0, column=0, padx=10, pady=5)

        # Combobox for selecting zoom scale
        self.zoom_combobox = ttk.Combobox(control_panel, textvariable=self.zoom_scale, values=list(range(1, 11)))
        self.zoom_combobox.grid(row=0, column=1, padx=10, pady=5)
        self.zoom_combobox.bind("<<ComboboxSelected>>", self.update_zoom)

        # Label and entry for specifying time
        self.time_label = tk.Label(control_panel, text="Jump to Time (s):")
        self.time_label.grid(row=0, column=2, padx=10, pady=5, sticky="e")
        self.time_entry = ttk.Entry(control_panel)
        self.time_entry.grid(row=0, column=3, padx=10, pady=5, sticky="w")
        self.time_entry.bind("<Return>", lambda event: self.jump_to_time())

        # Button to jump to specified time
        self.jump_button = tk.Button(control_panel, text="Jump to Time", command=self.jump_to_time)
        self.jump_button.grid(row=0, column=4, padx=10, pady=5)

        # Button to play/pause the video
        self.play_button = tk.Button(control_panel, text="Play/Pause", command=self.toggle_play_pause)
        self.play_button.grid(row=0, column=5, padx=10, pady=5)

        # Button to stop the video
        self.stop_button = tk.Button(control_panel, text="Stop", command=self.stop_video)
        self.stop_button.grid(row=0, column=6, padx=10, pady=5)

        # Button to navigate to the previous frame
        self.prev_frame_button = tk.Button(control_panel, text="Previous Frame", command=self.prev_frame)
        self.prev_frame_button.grid(row=0, column=7, padx=10, pady=5)

        # Button to navigate to the next frame
        self.next_frame_button = tk.Button(control_panel, text="Next Frame", command=self.next_frame)
        self.next_frame_button.grid(row=0, column=8, padx=10, pady=5)

        # Button to open another instance of the application
```

```python
        self.open_another_button = tk.Button(control_panel, text="Open Another Video Player", 
command=self.open_another_player)
        self.open_another_button.grid(row=2, column=0, columnspan=9, padx=10, pady=5)

    def open_video(self):
        self.video_path = filedialog.askopenfilename(filetypes=[("Video files", 
"*.mp4;*.avi;*.mkv")])
        if self.video_path:
            self.video = imageio.get_reader(self.video_path)
            self.play_video()
            self.play_filtered_video()

    def play_video(self):
        if self.video:
            self.paused = False
            self.show_frame()
            self.show_bilateral_frame()

    def play_filtered_video(self):
        if self.video:
            self.paused = False
            self.show_bilateral_frame()

    def stop_video(self):
        self.paused = True
        self.frame_index = 0
        self.current_x1 = 0
        self.current_y1 = 0  # Reset the current position
        self.current_x2 = 0
        self.current_y2 = 0  # Reset the current position
        self.show_frame()
        self.show_bilateral_frame()

    def toggle_play_pause(self):
        self.paused = not self.paused
        if not self.paused:
            self.play_video()
            self.play_filtered_video()

    def update_zoom(self, event=None):
        self.show_frame()
        self.show_bilateral_frame()
        self.canvas.scale("video", self.current_x1, self.current_y1, self.zoom_scale.get(), 
self.zoom_scale.get())
        self.filter_canvas.scale("bilateral_frame", self.current_x2, self.current_y2, 
self.zoom_scale.get(), self.zoom_scale.get())

    def add_noise(self, image):
        # Convert image to numpy array
        img_array = np.array(image)

        # Generate random noise
        noise = np.random.normal(0, 1, img_array.shape).astype(np.uint8)

        # Add noise to the image
        noisy_image = cv2.add(img_array, noise)

        # Ensure image values are within valid range
        noisy_image = np.clip(noisy_image, 0, 255)

        # Convert back to image format
        noisy_image = Image.fromarray(noisy_image)

        return noisy_image
```

```python
    def show_frame(self):
        if self.video:
            if not self.paused:
                self.frame_index += 1
                if self.frame_index >= len(self.video):
                    self.frame_index = 0  # Reset frame index if it exceeds the maximum index
            if 0 <= self.frame_index < len(self.video):  # Check if frame index is within range
                try:
                    frame = self.video.get_data(self.frame_index)
                    original_width, original_height = frame.shape[1], frame.shape[0]  # Save original dimensions

                    frame = Image.fromarray(frame)

                    # Resize frame according to zoom scale
                    frame = frame.resize((original_width * self.zoom_scale.get(), original_height * self.zoom_scale.get()))

                    # Add noise to the frame
                    self.noisy_frame = self.add_noise(frame)

                    photo = ImageTk.PhotoImage(self.noisy_frame)
                    self.photo = photo  # Save object reference to PhotoImage globally
                    self.canvas.delete("video")  # Delete previous image
                    self.canvas.create_image(self.current_x1, self.current_y1, anchor="nw", image=photo, tags="video")

                    if not self.paused:
                        self.canvas.after(30, self.show_frame)
                except Exception as e:
                    print("Error: ", e)

    def apply_bilateral_filter(self, frame):
        # Apply bilateral filter to reduce noise
        bilateral_filtered_frame = cv2.bilateralFilter(frame, 13, 125, 125)  # Adjust parameters as needed
        return bilateral_filtered_frame

    def show_bilateral_frame(self):
        if self.video:
            if not self.paused:
                self.frame_index += 1
                if self.frame_index >= len(self.video):
                    self.frame_index = 0  # Reset frame index if it exceeds the maximum index
            if 0 <= self.frame_index < len(self.video):  # Check if frame index is within range
                try:
                    # Convert noisy frame to BGR format
                    noisy_frame = cv2.cvtColor(np.array(self.noisy_frame), cv2.COLOR_RGB2BGR)

                    # Apply bilateral filter
                    frame_smoothed = self.apply_bilateral_filter(noisy_frame)

                    # Convert frame back to RGB format
                    frame_rgb = cv2.cvtColor(frame_smoothed, cv2.COLOR_BGR2RGB)

                    # Convert to Image format
                    bilateral_frame = Image.fromarray(frame_rgb)

                    # Resize frame according to zoom scale using original dimensions
                    original_width, original_height = self.noisy_frame.width, self.noisy_frame.height
```

```
                            bilateral_frame = bilateral_frame.resize((int(original_width *
self.zoom_scale.get()),
                                                        int(original_height *
self.zoom_scale.get())))

                        # Convert Image to PhotoImage
                        median_photo = ImageTk.PhotoImage(bilateral_frame)
                        self.median_photo = median_photo

                        # Delete previous image
                        self.filter_canvas.delete("bilateral_frame")

                        # Create new image
                        self.filter_canvas.create_image(self.current_x2, self.current_y2,
anchor="nw", image=median_photo, tags="bilateral_frame")

                        if not self.paused:
                            self.master.after(30, self.show_bilateral_frame)
                    except Exception as e:
                        print("Error: ", e)

    def on_mousewheel(self, event):
        direction = event.delta // 120
        current_value = int(self.zoom_scale.get())
        if direction == 1 and current_value < 10:
            current_value += 1
        elif direction == -1 and current_value > 1:
            current_value -= 1
        self.zoom_scale.set(current_value)
        self.update_zoom()

    def on_press1(self, event):
        self.start_x1 = event.x
        self.start_y1 = event.y

    def on_press2(self, event):
        self.start_x2 = event.x
        self.start_y2 = event.y

    def on_drag1(self, event):
        if self.start_x1 and self.start_y1:
            self.x_offset1 = event.x - self.start_x1
            self.y_offset1 = event.y - self.start_y1
            self.current_x1 += self.x_offset1  # Update current position
            self.current_y1 += self.y_offset1  # Update current position
            self.canvas.move("video", self.x_offset1, self.y_offset1) # Move original canvas

            self.start_x1 = event.x
            self.start_y1 = event.y

    def on_drag2(self, event):
        if self.start_x2 and self.start_y2:
            self.x_offset2 = event.x - self.start_x2
            self.y_offset2 = event.y - self.start_y2
            self.current_x2 += self.x_offset2  # Update current position
            self.current_y2 += self.y_offset2  # Update current position
            self.filter_canvas.move("bilateral_frame", self.x_offset2, self.y_offset2) # Move
filter canvas

            self.start_x2 = event.x
            self.start_y2 = event.y

    def on_scroll(self, *args):
        scroll_pos = self.scrollbar.get()
```

```python
        self.current_x1 = -scroll_pos * self.canvas.winfo_width()  # Update current position for original canvas
        self.current_x2 = -scroll_pos * self.canvas.winfo_width()  # Update current position for filtered canvas
        self.canvas.xview_moveto(scroll_pos)
        self.filter_canvas.xview_moveto(scroll_pos)  # Move filter canvas along with original canvas
        self.frame_index = int(scroll_pos * len(self.video))  # Update frame index
        self.show_frame()
        self.show_bilateral_frame()  # Update filtered frame

    def jump_to_time(self):
        time_str = self.time_entry.get()
        try:
            time_seconds = float(time_str)
            if 0 <= time_seconds:
                self.frame_index = int(time_seconds * self.video.get_meta_data()['fps'])
                self.show_frame()
                self.show_bilateral_frame()  # Jump to specified time for Canny edge frame
        except ValueError:
            pass

    def prev_frame(self):
        if self.video and self.frame_index > 0:
            self.frame_index -= 1
            self.show_frame()
            self.show_bilateral_frame()

    def next_frame(self):
        if self.video and self.frame_index < len(self.video) - 1:
            self.frame_index += 1
            self.show_frame()
            self.show_bilateral_frame()

    def open_another_player(self):
        # Open another instance of the application
        root = tk.Toplevel(self.master)
        app = BilateralFilter(root)

def main():
    root = tk.Tk()
    app = BilateralFilter(root)
    root.mainloop()

if __name__ == "__main__":
    main()
```

RUNNING PROGRAM

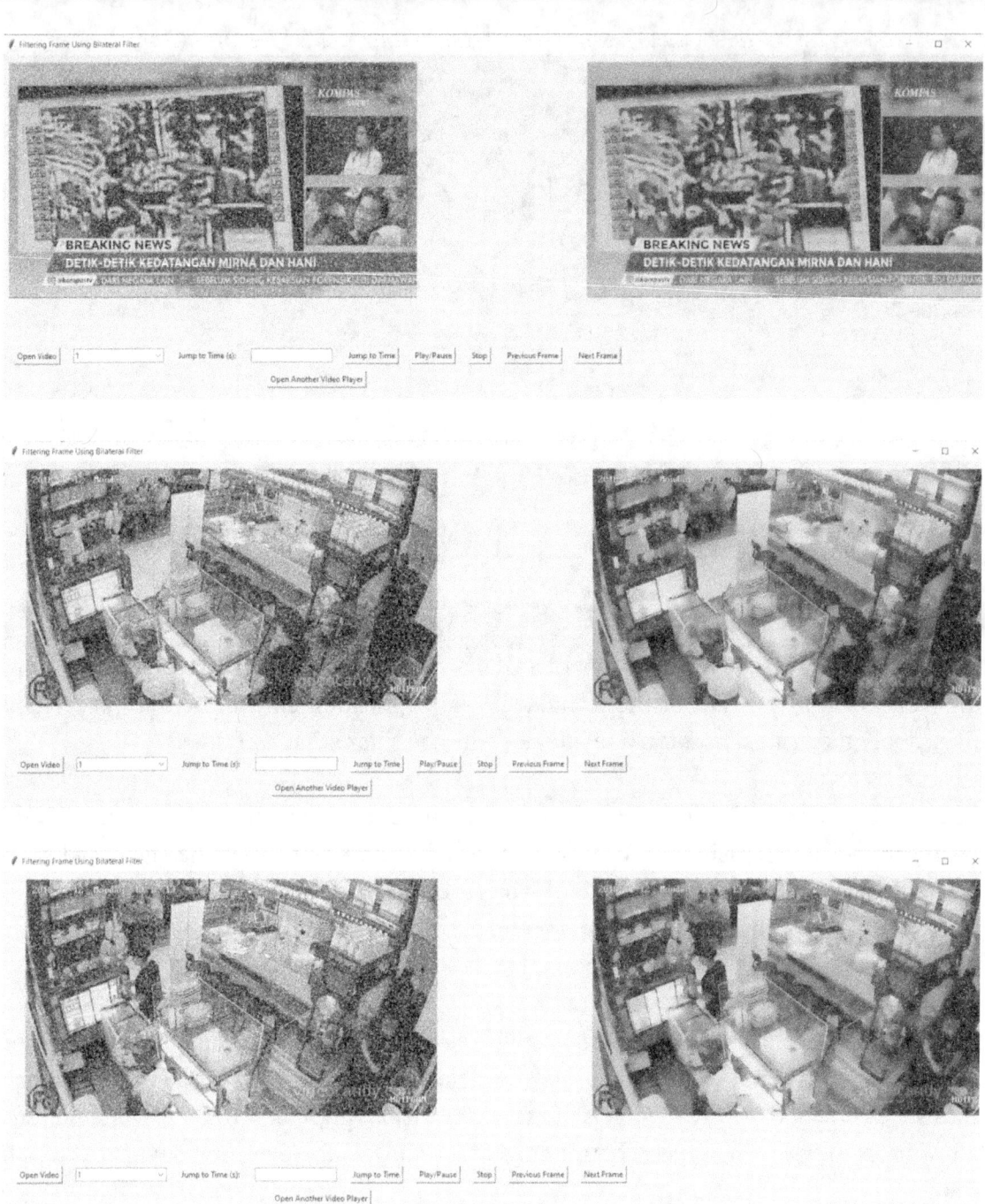

NON-LOCAL MEANS DENOISING OF VIDEO

DESCRIPTION

The project involves the development of a GUI application for filtering video frames using the Non-Local Means Denoising technique. The application allows users to load video files, apply the denoising filter, and interact with the filtered video frames.

The NonLocalMeansDenoising class serves as the core component of the application, managing video processing and GUI interactions. Upon initialization, the GUI window is created with a title indicating the use of Non-Local Means Denoising for frame filtering. Various attributes such as the video source, current frame index, zoom scale, and GUI elements are initialized within this class.

The create_widgets() method configures the layout of the GUI, including panels for displaying the original video frames and the denoised frames, as well as control buttons for user interaction. Canvas widgets are used for displaying video frames, while buttons allow users to open video files, control playback, adjust zoom level, and navigate through frames.

Users can load video files by clicking the "Open Video" button, which opens a file dialog for selecting video files in common formats such as MP4, AVI, or MKV. Once a video file is selected, it is loaded for playback and denoising using the Non-Local Means Denoising filter.

Playback controls such as play, pause, stop, previous frame, and next frame are provided to enable users to control video playback. The GUI also includes features such as zooming using the mouse wheel and panning by dragging the mouse on the canvas.

Frame processing involves retrieving the current frame of the video, adding Gaussian noise to simulate real-world conditions, and applying the Non-Local Means Denoising filter to reduce noise and enhance image quality. Both the original and denoised frames are dynamically updated to reflect changes in playback, zoom, and frame navigation.

Event handlers are defined for mouse wheel scrolling, mouse press, drag actions, and scrollbar movements to facilitate user interaction with the GUI. Users can input a specific time to jump to within the video using the time entry field and the "Jump to Time" button.

The application supports opening multiple instances of the video player using the "Open Another Video Player" button. This feature allows users to simultaneously view and compare different video files using separate instances of the application.

The main() function initializes the root Tkinter window and creates an instance of the NonLocalMeansDenoising class, ensuring that the GUI remains responsive by continuously listening for user inputs and updating the display accordingly.

Error handling mechanisms are implemented to catch exceptions during video loading, frame processing, and display updates. Parameters such as the filter strength, template size, and search window size are adjustable to fine-tune the Non-Local Means Denoising filter's performance based on user preferences and the characteristics of the input video.

The application preserves the original dimensions of the video frames during resizing to maintain aspect ratio and ensure accurate display. Image data is converted between formats such as PIL Image, NumPy arrays, and OpenCV matrices to facilitate processing and display.

Efficient rendering techniques are employed to minimize latency and provide a responsive user interface, ensuring smooth playback even for large video files. Resources such as video objects, images, and GUI elements are managed efficiently to optimize performance and prevent memory leaks.

Console messages are used to provide feedback to users, informing them of errors or status updates during video processing. The codebase follows modular design principles and best practices to enhance maintainability and facilitate future enhancements or extensions of the application.

Overall, the design of the application prioritizes user experience, offering a rich set of features and intuitive controls for seamless interaction with video content.

SOURCE CODE

```python
#non_local_denoising_frame.py
import tkinter as tk
from tkinter import ttk
from tkinter import filedialog
from PIL import Image, ImageTk
import imageio
import cv2
import numpy as np

class NonLocalMeansDenoising:
    def __init__(self, master):
        self.master = master
        self.master.title("Filtering Frame Using Non-Local Means Denoising")

        self.video = None
        self.video_path = None
        self.paused = False
        self.zoom_scale = tk.IntVar(value=1)
        self.frame_index = 0
        self.start_x1 = None
        self.start_y1 = None
        self.current_x1 = 0
        self.current_y1 = 0
        self.start_x2 = None
        self.start_y2 = None
        self.current_x2 = 0
        self.current_y2 = 0
        self.prev_frame = None

        self.create_widgets()

    def create_widgets(self):
        # Panel for video display
        video_panel = tk.Frame(self.master)
        video_panel.grid(row=0, column=0, padx=10, pady=10, sticky="nsew")

        # Canvas to display the original video
        canvas_width = 900
        canvas_height = 400
```

```python
        self.canvas = tk.Canvas(video_panel, width=canvas_width, height=canvas_height)
        self.canvas.pack(side="left", fill="both", expand=True)
        self.canvas.bind("<MouseWheel>", self.on_mousewheel)
        self.canvas.bind("<ButtonPress-1>", self.on_press1)
        self.canvas.bind("<B1-Motion>", self.on_drag1)

        # Scrollbar for original video canvas
        self.scrollbar = tk.Scrollbar(video_panel, orient="horizontal", command=self.on_scroll)
        self.scrollbar.pack(side="bottom", fill="x")
        self.canvas.configure(xscrollcommand=self.scrollbar.set)

        # Canvas to display the Canny edge video
        self.filter_canvas = tk.Canvas(video_panel, width=canvas_width, height=canvas_height)
        self.filter_canvas.pack(side="right", fill="both", expand=True)
        self.filter_canvas.bind("<MouseWheel>", self.on_mousewheel)
        self.filter_canvas.bind("<ButtonPress-1>", self.on_press2)
        self.filter_canvas.bind("<B1-Motion>", self.on_drag2)

        # Panel for control buttons
        control_panel = tk.Frame(self.master)
        control_panel.grid(row=1, column=0, padx=10, pady=(0, 10), sticky="ew")

        # Button to open a video file
        self.open_button = tk.Button(control_panel, text="Open Video", command=self.open_video)
        self.open_button.grid(row=0, column=0, padx=10, pady=5)

        # Combobox for selecting zoom scale
        self.zoom_combobox = ttk.Combobox(control_panel, textvariable=self.zoom_scale, values=list(range(1, 11)))
        self.zoom_combobox.grid(row=0, column=1, padx=10, pady=5)
        self.zoom_combobox.bind("<<ComboboxSelected>>", self.update_zoom)

        # Label and entry for specifying time
        self.time_label = tk.Label(control_panel, text="Jump to Time (s):")
        self.time_label.grid(row=0, column=2, padx=10, pady=5, sticky="e")
        self.time_entry = ttk.Entry(control_panel)
        self.time_entry.grid(row=0, column=3, padx=10, pady=5, sticky="w")
        self.time_entry.bind("<Return>", lambda event: self.jump_to_time())

        # Button to jump to specified time
        self.jump_button = tk.Button(control_panel, text="Jump to Time", command=self.jump_to_time)
        self.jump_button.grid(row=0, column=4, padx=10, pady=5)

        # Button to play/pause the video
        self.play_button = tk.Button(control_panel, text="Play/Pause", command=self.toggle_play_pause)
        self.play_button.grid(row=0, column=5, padx=10, pady=5)

        # Button to stop the video
        self.stop_button = tk.Button(control_panel, text="Stop", command=self.stop_video)
        self.stop_button.grid(row=0, column=6, padx=10, pady=5)

        # Button to navigate to the previous frame
        self.prev_frame_button = tk.Button(control_panel, text="Previous Frame", command=self.prev_frame)
        self.prev_frame_button.grid(row=0, column=7, padx=10, pady=5)

        # Button to navigate to the next frame
        self.next_frame_button = tk.Button(control_panel, text="Next Frame", command=self.next_frame)
        self.next_frame_button.grid(row=0, column=8, padx=10, pady=5)

        # Button to open another instance of the application
```

```python
        self.open_another_button = tk.Button(control_panel, text="Open Another Video Player", 
command=self.open_another_player)
        self.open_another_button.grid(row=2, column=0, columnspan=9, padx=10, pady=5)

    def open_video(self):
        self.video_path = filedialog.askopenfilename(filetypes=[("Video files", 
"*.mp4;*.avi;*.mkv")])
        if self.video_path:
            self.video = imageio.get_reader(self.video_path)
            self.play_video()
            self.play_filtered_video()

    def play_video(self):
        if self.video:
            self.paused = False
            self.show_frame()
            self.show_non_local_frame()

    def play_filtered_video(self):
        if self.video:
            self.paused = False
            self.show_non_local_frame()

    def stop_video(self):
        self.paused = True
        self.frame_index = 0
        self.current_x1 = 0
        self.current_y1 = 0  # Reset the current position
        self.current_x2 = 0
        self.current_y2 = 0  # Reset the current position
        self.show_frame()
        self.show_non_local_frame()

    def toggle_play_pause(self):
        self.paused = not self.paused
        if not self.paused:
            self.play_video()
            self.play_filtered_video()

    def update_zoom(self, event=None):
        self.show_frame()
        self.show_non_local_frame()
        self.canvas.scale("video", self.current_x1, self.current_y1, self.zoom_scale.get(), 
self.zoom_scale.get())
        self.filter_canvas.scale("denoised_frame", self.current_x2, self.current_y2, 
self.zoom_scale.get(), self.zoom_scale.get())

    def add_noise(self, image):
        # Convert image to numpy array
        img_array = np.array(image)

        # Generate random noise
        noise = np.random.normal(0, 1, img_array.shape).astype(np.uint8)

        # Add noise to the image
        noisy_image = cv2.add(img_array, noise)

        # Ensure image values are within valid range
        noisy_image = np.clip(noisy_image, 0, 255)

        # Convert back to image format
        noisy_image = Image.fromarray(noisy_image)

        return noisy_image
```

```python
    def show_frame(self):
        if self.video:
            if not self.paused:
                self.frame_index += 1
                if self.frame_index >= len(self.video):
                    self.frame_index = 0  # Reset frame index if it exceeds the maximum index
            if 0 <= self.frame_index < len(self.video):  # Check if frame index is within range
                try:
                    frame = self.video.get_data(self.frame_index)
                    original_width, original_height = frame.shape[1], frame.shape[0]  # Save original dimensions

                    frame = Image.fromarray(frame)

                    # Resize frame according to zoom scale
                    frame = frame.resize((original_width * self.zoom_scale.get(), original_height * self.zoom_scale.get()))

                    # Add noise to the frame
                    self.noisy_frame = self.add_noise(frame)

                    photo = ImageTk.PhotoImage(self.noisy_frame)
                    self.photo = photo  # Save object reference to PhotoImage globally
                    self.canvas.delete("video")  # Delete previous image
                    self.canvas.create_image(self.current_x1, self.current_y1, anchor="nw", image=photo, tags="video")

                    if not self.paused:
                        self.canvas.after(30, self.show_frame)
                except Exception as e:
                    print("Error: ", e)

    def apply_non_local_denoising(self, frame):
        # Apply non-local means denoising
        denoised_frame = cv2.fastNlMeansDenoisingColored(frame, None, 15, 10, 7, 21)  # Adjust parameters as needed
        return denoised_frame

    def show_non_local_frame(self):
        if self.video:
            if not self.paused:
                self.frame_index += 1
                if self.frame_index >= len(self.video):
                    self.frame_index = 0  # Reset frame index if it exceeds the maximum index
            if 0 <= self.frame_index < len(self.video):  # Check if frame index is within range
                try:
                    # Convert noisy frame to BGR format
                    noisy_frame = cv2.cvtColor(np.array(self.noisy_frame), cv2.COLOR_RGB2BGR)

                    # Apply non-local means denoising
                    frame_denoised = self.apply_non_local_denoising(noisy_frame)

                    # Convert frame back to RGB format
                    frame_rgb = cv2.cvtColor(frame_denoised, cv2.COLOR_BGR2RGB)

                    # Convert to Image format
                    denoised_frame = Image.fromarray(frame_rgb)

                    # Resize frame according to zoom scale using original dimensions
                    original_width, original_height = self.noisy_frame.width, self.noisy_frame.height
```

```python
                        denoised_frame = denoised_frame.resize((int(original_width * 
self.zoom_scale.get()), 
                                                                int(original_height * 
self.zoom_scale.get())))
                        
                        # Convert Image to PhotoImage
                        denoised_photo = ImageTk.PhotoImage(denoised_frame)
                        self.denoised_photo = denoised_photo
                        
                        # Delete previous image
                        self.filter_canvas.delete("denoised_frame")
                        
                        # Create new image
                        self.filter_canvas.create_image(self.current_x2, self.current_y2, 
anchor="nw", image=denoised_photo, tags="denoised_frame")
                        
                        if not self.paused:
                            self.master.after(30, self.show_non_local_frame)
                except Exception as e:
                    print("Error: ", e)

    def on_mousewheel(self, event):
        direction = event.delta // 120
        current_value = int(self.zoom_scale.get())
        if direction == 1 and current_value < 10:
            current_value += 1
        elif direction == -1 and current_value > 1:
            current_value -= 1
        self.zoom_scale.set(current_value)
        self.update_zoom()

    def on_press1(self, event):
        self.start_x1 = event.x
        self.start_y1 = event.y

    def on_press2(self, event):
        self.start_x2 = event.x
        self.start_y2 = event.y

    def on_drag1(self, event):
        if self.start_x1 and self.start_y1:
            self.x_offset1 = event.x - self.start_x1
            self.y_offset1 = event.y - self.start_y1
            self.current_x1 += self.x_offset1  # Update current position
            self.current_y1 += self.y_offset1  # Update current position
            self.canvas.move("video", self.x_offset1, self.y_offset1) # Move original canvas

            self.start_x1 = event.x
            self.start_y1 = event.y

    def on_drag2(self, event):
        if self.start_x2 and self.start_y2:
            self.x_offset2 = event.x - self.start_x2
            self.y_offset2 = event.y - self.start_y2
            self.current_x2 += self.x_offset2  # Update current position
            self.current_y2 += self.y_offset2  # Update current position
            self.filter_canvas.move("denoised_frame", self.x_offset2, self.y_offset2)  # Move 
filter canvas

            self.start_x2 = event.x
            self.start_y2 = event.y

    def on_scroll(self, *args):
        scroll_pos = self.scrollbar.get()
```

```python
            self.current_x1 = -scroll_pos * self.canvas.winfo_width()  # Update current position for original canvas
            self.current_x2 = -scroll_pos * self.canvas.winfo_width()  # Update current position for filtered canvas
            self.canvas.xview_moveto(scroll_pos)
            self.filter_canvas.xview_moveto(scroll_pos)  # Move filter canvas along with original canvas
            self.frame_index = int(scroll_pos * len(self.video))  # Update frame index
            self.show_frame()
            self.show_non_local_frame()  # Update filtered frame

    def jump_to_time(self):
        time_str = self.time_entry.get()
        try:
            time_seconds = float(time_str)
            if 0 <= time_seconds:
                self.frame_index = int(time_seconds * self.video.get_meta_data()['fps'])
                self.show_frame()
                self.show_non_local_frame()  # Jump to specified time for Canny edge frame
        except ValueError:
            pass

    def prev_frame(self):
        if self.video and self.frame_index > 0:
            self.frame_index -= 1
            self.show_frame()
            self.show_non_local_frame()

    def next_frame(self):
        if self.video and self.frame_index < len(self.video) - 1:
            self.frame_index += 1
            self.show_frame()
            self.show_non_local_frame()

    def open_another_player(self):
        # Open another instance of the application
        root = tk.Toplevel(self.master)
        app = NonLocalMeansDenoising(root)

def main():
    root = tk.Tk()
    app = NonLocalMeansDenoising(root)
    root.mainloop()

if __name__ == "__main__":
    main()
```

RUNNING PROGRAM

DETECTING CANNY EDGES OF VIDEO

DESCRIPTION

The project is a GUI application designed for performing Canny edge detection on video frames. Developed by Vivian Siahaan and Rh. Sianipar, the application provides users with tools to load video files, visualize the original video frames, and display the corresponding Canny edge detection results.

Upon launching the application, a window titled "CANNY EDGE DETECTOR" is displayed, indicating its purpose. The GUI consists of panels for displaying both the original video frames and the Canny edge-detected frames, along with control buttons for user interaction.

The VideoCanny class serves as the main component of the application, managing video processing and GUI interactions. It initializes attributes such as the video source, current frame index, zoom scale, and GUI elements within its constructor.

The GUI layout is organized using frames and canvases, allowing for flexible arrangement of visual elements. The original video frames and the Canny edge-detected frames are displayed side by side within the video panel using separate canvas widgets.

Control buttons are provided to open video files, adjust zoom level, jump to specific times within the video, toggle play/pause, stop playback, navigate to previous and next frames, and open additional instances of the application for simultaneous use.

Video files can be opened using the "Open Video" button, which prompts the user to select a compatible video file (e.g., MP4, AVI, MKV). Once a video file is loaded, both the original and Canny edge-detected frames are displayed in their respective canvas widgets.

Playback controls allow users to play, pause, and stop video playback, as well as navigate through frames using the previous and next frame buttons. The application dynamically updates the displayed frames based on user interactions and video playback status.

Zoom functionality is provided to enable users to adjust the scale of the displayed frames using the mouse wheel. Additionally, panning is supported by allowing users to drag the frames within the canvas widgets.

The Canny edge detection algorithm is applied to each video frame to detect edges, which are then visualized in real-time within the Canny edge canvas. The algorithm enhances edges in the frame while suppressing noise and non-edge details.

Error handling mechanisms are implemented to catch exceptions during video loading, frame processing, and display updates, ensuring robustness and stability of the application.

The application supports opening multiple instances of the video player to facilitate comparison of different video files or simultaneous analysis of multiple videos.

Efficient rendering techniques are employed to minimize latency and provide a responsive user interface, ensuring smooth playback and real-time edge detection even for large video files.

Overall, the application prioritizes usability and functionality, offering a user-friendly interface for performing Canny edge detection on video content.

SOURCE CODE

```python
#canny_edge_detection_frame.py
import tkinter as tk
from tkinter import ttk
from tkinter import filedialog
from PIL import Image, ImageTk
import imageio
import cv2
import numpy as np

class VideoCanny:
    def __init__(self, master):
        self.master = master
        self.master.title("CANNY EDGE DETECTOR---VIVIAN SIAHAAN & RH.SIANIPAR")

        self.video = None
        self.video_path = None
        self.paused = False
        self.zoom_scale = tk.IntVar(value=1)
        self.frame_index = 0
        self.start_x = None
        self.start_y = None
        self.current_x = 0
        self.current_y = 0

        self.create_widgets()

    def create_widgets(self):
        # Panel for video display
        video_panel = tk.Frame(self.master)
        video_panel.grid(row=0, column=0, padx=10, pady=10, sticky="nsew")

        # Canvas to display the original video
        canvas_width = 700
        canvas_height = 450
        self.canvas = tk.Canvas(video_panel, width=canvas_width, height=canvas_height)
        self.canvas.pack(side="left", fill="both", expand=True)
        self.canvas.bind("<MouseWheel>", self.on_mousewheel)
        self.canvas.bind("<ButtonPress-1>", self.on_press)
        self.canvas.bind("<B1-Motion>", self.on_drag)

        # Scrollbar for original video canvas
        self.scrollbar = tk.Scrollbar(video_panel, orient="horizontal", command=self.on_scroll)
        self.scrollbar.pack(side="bottom", fill="x")
        self.canvas.configure(xscrollcommand=self.scrollbar.set)

        # Canvas to display the Canny edge video
        self.edge_canvas = tk.Canvas(video_panel, width=canvas_width, height=canvas_height)
        self.edge_canvas.pack(side="right", fill="both", expand=True)
        self.edge_canvas.bind("<MouseWheel>", self.on_mousewheel)
        self.edge_canvas.bind("<ButtonPress-1>", self.on_press)
        self.edge_canvas.bind("<B1-Motion>", self.on_drag)

        # Panel for control buttons
        control_panel = tk.Frame(self.master)
        control_panel.grid(row=1, column=0, padx=10, pady=(0, 10), sticky="ew")

        # Button to open a video file
        self.open_button = tk.Button(control_panel, text="Open Video", command=self.open_video)
        self.open_button.grid(row=0, column=0, padx=10, pady=5)
```

```python
        # Combobox for selecting zoom scale
        self.zoom_combobox = ttk.Combobox(control_panel, textvariable=self.zoom_scale, values=list(range(1, 11)))
        self.zoom_combobox.grid(row=0, column=1, padx=10, pady=5)
        self.zoom_combobox.bind("<<ComboboxSelected>>", self.update_zoom)

        # Label and entry for specifying time
        self.time_label = tk.Label(control_panel, text="Jump to Time (s):")
        self.time_label.grid(row=0, column=2, padx=10, pady=5, sticky="e")
        self.time_entry = ttk.Entry(control_panel)
        self.time_entry.grid(row=0, column=3, padx=10, pady=5, sticky="w")
        self.time_entry.bind("<Return>", lambda event: self.jump_to_time())

        # Button to jump to specified time
        self.jump_button = tk.Button(control_panel, text="Jump to Time", command=self.jump_to_time)
        self.jump_button.grid(row=0, column=4, padx=10, pady=5)

        # Button to play/pause the video
        self.play_button = tk.Button(control_panel, text="Play/Pause", command=self.toggle_play_pause)
        self.play_button.grid(row=0, column=5, padx=10, pady=5)

        # Button to stop the video
        self.stop_button = tk.Button(control_panel, text="Stop", command=self.stop_video)
        self.stop_button.grid(row=0, column=6, padx=10, pady=5)

        # Button to navigate to the previous frame
        self.prev_frame_button = tk.Button(control_panel, text="Previous Frame", command=self.prev_frame)
        self.prev_frame_button.grid(row=0, column=7, padx=10, pady=5)

        # Button to navigate to the next frame
        self.next_frame_button = tk.Button(control_panel, text="Next Frame", command=self.next_frame)
        self.next_frame_button.grid(row=0, column=8, padx=10, pady=5)

        # Button to open another instance of the application
        self.open_another_button = tk.Button(control_panel, text="Open Another Video Player", command=self.open_another_player)
        self.open_another_button.grid(row=2, column=0, columnspan=9, padx=10, pady=5)

    def open_video(self):
        self.video_path = filedialog.askopenfilename(filetypes=[("Video files", "*.mp4;*.avi;*.mkv")])
        if self.video_path:
            self.video = imageio.get_reader(self.video_path)
            self.play_video()
            self.play_edged_video()

    def play_video(self):
        if self.video:
            self.paused = False
            self.show_frame()
            self.show_canny_frame()

    def stop_video(self):
        self.paused = True
        self.frame_index = 0
        self.current_x = 0
        self.current_y = 0  # Reset the current position
        self.show_frame()
        self.show_canny_frame()
```

```python
    def toggle_play_pause(self):
        self.paused = not self.paused
        if not self.paused:
            self.play_video()
            self.play_edged_video()

    def play_edged_video(self):
        if self.video:
            self.paused = False
            self.show_canny_frame()

    def update_zoom(self, event=None):
        self.show_frame()
        self.show_canny_frame()

    def show_frame(self):
        if self.video:
            if not self.paused:
                self.frame_index += 1
                if self.frame_index >= len(self.video):
                    self.frame_index = 0  # Reset frame index if it exceeds the maximum index
            if 0 <= self.frame_index < len(self.video):  # Check if frame index is within range
                try:
                    frame = self.video.get_data(self.frame_index)
                    frame = Image.fromarray(frame)
                    frame = frame.resize((frame.width * self.zoom_scale.get(), frame.height * self.zoom_scale.get()))
                    photo = ImageTk.PhotoImage(frame)
                    self.photo = photo  # Save object reference to PhotoImage globally
                    self.canvas.delete("video")  # Delete previous image
                    self.canvas.create_image(self.current_x, self.current_y, anchor="nw", image=photo, tags="video")
                    if not self.paused:
                        self.canvas.after(30, self.show_frame)
                except Exception as e:
                    print("Error: ", e)

    def show_canny_frame(self):
        if self.video:
            if not self.paused:
                self.frame_index += 1
                if self.frame_index >= len(self.video):
                    self.frame_index = 0  # Reset frame index if it exceeds the maximum index
            if 0 <= self.frame_index < len(self.video):  # Check if frame index is within range
                try:
                    frame = self.video.get_data(self.frame_index)
                    frame = cv2.cvtColor(frame, cv2.COLOR_RGB2BGR)  # Convert to BGR format for OpenCV
                    edge_frame = cv2.Canny(frame, 50, 200)

                    # Perform dilation to make edges thicker
                    kernel = np.ones((2,2), np.uint8)
                    edge_frame = cv2.dilate(edge_frame, kernel, iterations=1)

                    edge_frame = cv2.resize(edge_frame, None, fx=self.zoom_scale.get(), fy=self.zoom_scale.get())
                    edge_frame = cv2.cvtColor(edge_frame, cv2.COLOR_GRAY2RGB)  # Convert back to RGB
                    edge_photo = ImageTk.PhotoImage(image=Image.fromarray(edge_frame))
                    self.edge_photo = edge_photo
                    self.edge_canvas.delete("edges")  # Delete previous edge detection result
```

```python
                        self.edge_canvas.create_image(0, 0, anchor="nw", image=edge_photo, tags="edges")
                        if not self.paused:
                            self.master.after(30, self.show_canny_frame)
                except Exception as e:
                    print("Error: ", e)

    def on_mousewheel(self, event):
        direction = event.delta // 120
        current_value = int(self.zoom_scale.get())
        if direction == 1 and current_value < 10:
            current_value += 1
        elif direction == -1 and current_value > 1:
            current_value -= 1
        self.zoom_scale.set(current_value)
        self.update_zoom()

    def on_press(self, event):
        self.start_x = event.x
        self.start_y = event.y

    def on_drag(self, event):
        if self.start_x and self.start_y:
            self.x_offset = event.x - self.start_x
            self.y_offset = event.y - self.start_y
            self.current_x += self.x_offset  # Update current position
            self.current_y += self.y_offset  # Update current position
            self.canvas.move("video", self.x_offset, self.y_offset)
            self.edge_canvas.move("edges", self.x_offset, self.y_offset)  # Move Canny edge canvas along with original canvas

            # Calculate the corresponding movement for the Canny edge canvas
            edge_x_offset = int(self.x_offset * (self.edge_canvas.winfo_width() / self.canvas.winfo_width()))
            edge_y_offset = int(self.y_offset * (self.edge_canvas.winfo_height() / self.canvas.winfo_height()))
            self.edge_canvas.move("edges", edge_x_offset, edge_y_offset)

            self.start_x = event.x
            self.start_y = event.y

    def on_scroll(self, *args):
        scroll_pos = self.scrollbar.get()
        self.current_x = -scroll_pos * self.canvas.winfo_width()
        self.canvas.xview_moveto(scroll_pos)
        self.edge_canvas.xview_moveto(scroll_pos)  # Move Canny edge canvas along with original canvas
        self.frame_index = int(scroll_pos * len(self.video))  # Update frame index
        self.show_frame()
        self.show_canny_frame()  # Update Canny edge frame

    def jump_to_time(self):
        time_str = self.time_entry.get()
        try:
            time_seconds = float(time_str)
            if 0 <= time_seconds:
                self.frame_index = int(time_seconds * self.video.get_meta_data()['fps'])
                self.show_frame()
                self.show_canny_frame()  # Jump to specified time for Canny edge frame
        except ValueError:
            pass

    def prev_frame(self):
        if self.frame_index > 0:
```

```python
            self.frame_index -= 1
            self.show_frame()
            self.show_canny_frame()

    def next_frame(self):
        if self.frame_index < len(self.video) - 1:
            self.frame_index += 1
            self.show_frame()
            self.show_canny_frame()

    def open_another_player(self):
        # Open another instance of the application
        root = tk.Toplevel(self.master)
        app = VideoCanny(root)

def main():
    root = tk.Tk()
    app = VideoCanny(root)
    root.mainloop()

if __name__ == "__main__":
    main()
```

RUNNING PROGRAM

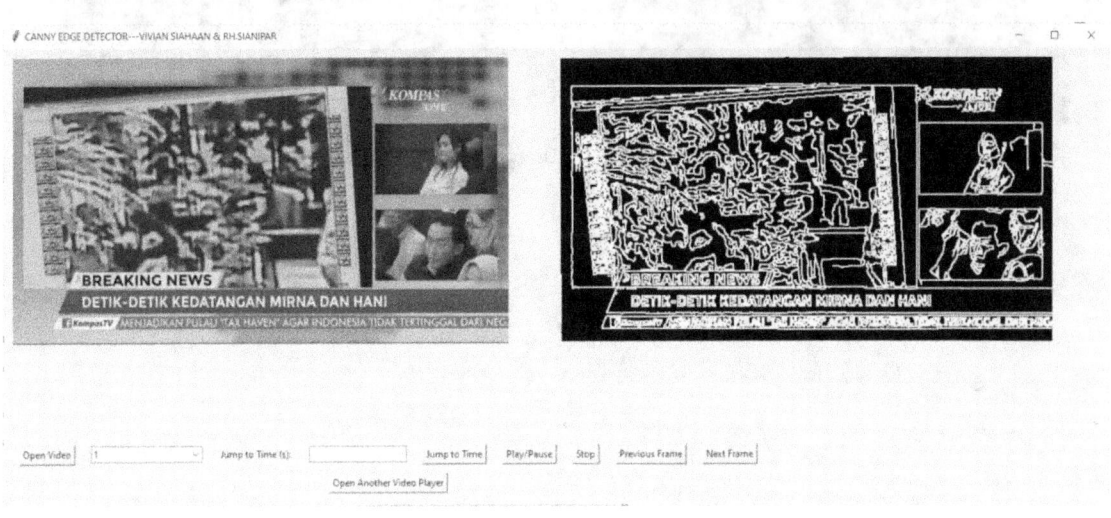

DETECTING KIRSCH EDGES OF VIDEO

DESCRIPTION

The "KIRSCH EDGE DETECTOR" project is a graphical user interface (GUI) application built using Tkinter and OpenCV libraries. It is designed for real-time edge detection in video streams using the Kirsch edge detection algorithm.

The application's main class, VideoKirsch, initializes the GUI components upon instantiation. It includes features such as video loading, frame display, zoom control, playback control, and edge detection using the Kirsch algorithm.

The GUI layout consists of panels for displaying the original video frames and the Kirsch edge-detected frames side by side. Control buttons are provided for user interaction, allowing video loading, zoom adjustment, time jumping, playback control, and navigation through frames.

Video files can be loaded using the "Open Video" button, which prompts the user to select a compatible video file (e.g., MP4, AVI, MKV). Once a video file is loaded, both the original and Kirsch edge-detected frames are displayed in their respective canvas widgets.

Playback controls enable users to play, pause, and stop video playback, as well as navigate through frames using the previous and next frame buttons. The application dynamically updates the displayed frames based on user interactions and video playback status.

Zoom functionality allows users to adjust the scale of the displayed frames using the mouse wheel. Panning is supported by allowing users to drag the frames within the canvas widgets.

The Kirsch edge detection algorithm is applied to each video frame to detect edges, which are then visualized in real-time within the Kirsch edge canvas. The algorithm enhances edges in the frame while suppressing noise and non-edge details.

Error handling mechanisms are implemented to catch exceptions during video loading, frame processing, and display updates, ensuring robustness and stability of the application.

The application also supports opening multiple instances of the video player to facilitate comparison of different video files or simultaneous analysis of multiple videos.

Efficient rendering techniques are employed to minimize latency and provide a responsive user interface, ensuring smooth playback and real-time edge detection even for large video files.

Overall, the "KIRSCH EDGE DETECTOR" application offers a user-friendly interface for performing real-time edge detection using the Kirsch algorithm, making it a valuable tool for image processing and computer vision tasks.

SOURCE CODE

```python
#kirsch__edge_detection_frame.py
import tkinter as tk
from tkinter import ttk
from tkinter import filedialog
from PIL import Image, ImageTk
import imageio
import cv2
import numpy as np

class VideoKirsch:
    def __init__(self, master):
        self.master = master
        self.master.title("KIRSCH EDGE DETECTOR---VIVIAN SIAHAAN & RH.SIANIPAR")
```

```python
        self.video = None
        self.video_path = None
        self.paused = False
        self.zoom_scale = tk.IntVar(value=1)
        self.frame_index = 0
        self.start_x = None
        self.start_y = None
        self.current_x = 0
        self.current_y = 0

        self.create_widgets()

    def create_widgets(self):
        # Panel for video display
        video_panel = tk.Frame(self.master)
        video_panel.grid(row=0, column=0, padx=10, pady=10, sticky="nsew")

        # Canvas to display the original video
        canvas_width = 900
        canvas_height = 500
        self.canvas = tk.Canvas(video_panel, width=canvas_width, height=canvas_height)
        self.canvas.pack(side="left", fill="both", expand=True)
        self.canvas.bind("<MouseWheel>", self.on_mousewheel)
        self.canvas.bind("<ButtonPress-1>", self.on_press)
        self.canvas.bind("<B1-Motion>", self.on_drag)

        # Scrollbar for original video canvas
        self.scrollbar = tk.Scrollbar(video_panel, orient="horizontal", command=self.on_scroll)
        self.scrollbar.pack(side="bottom", fill="x")
        self.canvas.configure(xscrollcommand=self.scrollbar.set)

        # Canvas to display the Canny edge video
        self.edge_canvas = tk.Canvas(video_panel, width=canvas_width, height=canvas_height)
        self.edge_canvas.pack(side="right", fill="both", expand=True)
        self.edge_canvas.bind("<MouseWheel>", self.on_mousewheel)
        self.edge_canvas.bind("<ButtonPress-1>", self.on_press)
        self.edge_canvas.bind("<B1-Motion>", self.on_drag)

        # Panel for control buttons
        control_panel = tk.Frame(self.master)
        control_panel.grid(row=1, column=0, padx=10, pady=(0, 10), sticky="ew")

        # Button to open a video file
        self.open_button = tk.Button(control_panel, text="Open Video", command=self.open_video)
        self.open_button.grid(row=0, column=0, padx=10, pady=5)

        # Combobox for selecting zoom scale
        self.zoom_combobox = ttk.Combobox(control_panel, textvariable=self.zoom_scale, values=list(range(1, 11)))
        self.zoom_combobox.grid(row=0, column=1, padx=10, pady=5)
        self.zoom_combobox.bind("<<ComboboxSelected>>", self.update_zoom)

        # Label and entry for specifying time
        self.time_label = tk.Label(control_panel, text="Jump to Time (s):")
        self.time_label.grid(row=0, column=2, padx=10, pady=5, sticky="e")
        self.time_entry = ttk.Entry(control_panel)
        self.time_entry.grid(row=0, column=3, padx=10, pady=5, sticky="w")
        self.time_entry.bind("<Return>", lambda event: self.jump_to_time())

        # Button to jump to specified time
        self.jump_button = tk.Button(control_panel, text="Jump to Time", command=self.jump_to_time)
        self.jump_button.grid(row=0, column=4, padx=10, pady=5)
```

```python
        # Button to play/pause the video
        self.play_button = tk.Button(control_panel, text="Play/Pause", command=self.toggle_play_pause)
        self.play_button.grid(row=0, column=5, padx=10, pady=5)

        # Button to stop the video
        self.stop_button = tk.Button(control_panel, text="Stop", command=self.stop_video)
        self.stop_button.grid(row=0, column=6, padx=10, pady=5)

        # Button to navigate to the previous frame
        self.prev_frame_button = tk.Button(control_panel, text="Previous Frame", command=self.prev_frame)
        self.prev_frame_button.grid(row=0, column=7, padx=10, pady=5)

        # Button to navigate to the next frame
        self.next_frame_button = tk.Button(control_panel, text="Next Frame", command=self.next_frame)
        self.next_frame_button.grid(row=0, column=8, padx=10, pady=5)

        # Button to open another instance of the application
        self.open_another_button = tk.Button(control_panel, text="Open Another Video Player", command=self.open_another_player)
        self.open_another_button.grid(row=2, column=0, columnspan=9, padx=10, pady=5)

    def open_video(self):
        self.video_path = filedialog.askopenfilename(filetypes=[("Video files", "*.mp4;*.avi;*.mkv")])
        if self.video_path:
            self.video = imageio.get_reader(self.video_path)
            self.play_video()
            self.play_edged_video()

    def play_video(self):
        if self.video:
            self.paused = False
            self.show_frame()
            self.show_kirsch_frame()

    def stop_video(self):
        self.paused = True
        self.frame_index = 0
        self.current_x = 0
        self.current_y = 0  # Reset the current position
        self.show_frame()
        self.show_kirsch_frame()

    def toggle_play_pause(self):
        self.paused = not self.paused
        if not self.paused:
            self.play_video()
            self.play_edged_video()

    def update_zoom(self, event=None):
        self.show_frame()
        self.show_kirsch_frame()

    def show_frame(self):
        if self.video:
            if not self.paused:
                self.frame_index += 1
                if self.frame_index >= len(self.video):
                    self.frame_index = 0  # Reset frame index if it exceeds the maximum index
```

```python
            if 0 <= self.frame_index < len(self.video):  # Check if frame index is within range
                try:
                    frame = self.video.get_data(self.frame_index)
                    frame = Image.fromarray(frame)
                    frame = frame.resize((frame.width * self.zoom_scale.get(), frame.height * self.zoom_scale.get()))
                    photo = ImageTk.PhotoImage(frame)
                    self.photo = photo  # Save object reference to PhotoImage globally
                    self.canvas.delete("video")  # Delete previous image
                    self.canvas.create_image(self.current_x, self.current_y, anchor="nw", image=photo, tags="video")
                    if not self.paused:
                        self.canvas.after(30, self.show_frame)
                except Exception as e:
                    print("Error: ", e)

    def play_edged_video(self):
        if self.video:
            self.paused = False
            self.show_kirsch_frame()

    def show_kirsch_frame(self):
        if self.video:
            if not self.paused:
                self.frame_index += 1
                if self.frame_index >= len(self.video):
                    self.frame_index = 0  # Reset frame index if it exceeds the maximum index
            if 0 <= self.frame_index < len(self.video):  # Check if frame index is within range
                try:
                    frame = self.video.get_data(self.frame_index)
                    frame = cv2.cvtColor(frame, cv2.COLOR_RGB2BGR)  # Convert to BGR format for OpenCV

                    # Apply Gaussian filter to reduce noise
                    frame_smoothed = cv2.GaussianBlur(frame, (5, 5), 0)

                    # Apply Kirsch edge detection
                    edge_frame = self.apply_kirsch(frame_smoothed)

                    # Apply thresholding to convert to black and white
                    edge_frame[edge_frame > 240] = 255
                    edge_frame[edge_frame <= 240] = 0

                    edge_frame = cv2.resize(edge_frame, None, fx=self.zoom_scale.get(), fy=self.zoom_scale.get())
                    edge_frame = cv2.cvtColor(edge_frame, cv2.COLOR_BGR2RGB)  # Convert back to RGB
                    edge_photo = ImageTk.PhotoImage(image=Image.fromarray(edge_frame))
                    self.edge_photo = edge_photo
                    self.edge_canvas.delete("edges")  # Delete previous edge detection result
                    self.edge_canvas.create_image(0, 0, anchor="nw", image=edge_photo, tags="edges")
                    if not self.paused:
                        self.master.after(30, self.show_kirsch_frame)
                except Exception as e:
                    print("Error: ", e)

    def apply_kirsch(self, frame):
        kernels = [
            np.array([[-3, -3, 5], [-3, 0, 5], [-3, -3, 5]]),
            np.array([[-3, 5, 5], [-3, 0, 5], [-3, -3, -3]]),
            np.array([[5, 5, 5], [-3, 0, -3], [-3, -3, -3]]),
```

```python
            np.array([[5, 5, -3], [5, 0, -3], [-3, -3, -3]]),
            np.array([[5, -3, -3], [5, 0, -3], [5, -3, -3]]),
            np.array([[-3, -3, -3], [5, 0, -3], [5, 5, -3]]),
            np.array([[-3, -3, -3], [-3, 0, -3], [5, 5, 5]]),
            np.array([[-3, -3, -3], [-3, 0, 5], [-3, 5, 5]])
        ]
        sobel_frames = [cv2.filter2D(frame, -1, kernel) for kernel in kernels]
        magnitude = np.max(np.stack(sobel_frames, axis=-1), axis=-1)
        return np.uint8(magnitude)

    def on_mousewheel(self, event):
        direction = event.delta // 120
        current_value = int(self.zoom_scale.get())
        if direction == 1 and current_value < 10:
            current_value += 1
        elif direction == -1 and current_value > 1:
            current_value -= 1
        self.zoom_scale.set(current_value)
        self.update_zoom()

    def on_press(self, event):
        self.start_x = event.x
        self.start_y = event.y

    def on_drag(self, event):
        if self.start_x and self.start_y:
            self.x_offset = event.x - self.start_x
            self.y_offset = event.y - self.start_y
            self.current_x += self.x_offset  # Update current position
            self.current_y += self.y_offset  # Update current position
            self.canvas.move("video", self.x_offset, self.y_offset)
            self.edge_canvas.move("edges", self.x_offset, self.y_offset)  # Move Canny edge canvas along with original canvas

            # Calculate the corresponding movement for the Canny edge canvas
            edge_x_offset = int(self.x_offset * (self.edge_canvas.winfo_width() / self.canvas.winfo_width()))
            edge_y_offset = int(self.y_offset * (self.edge_canvas.winfo_height() / self.canvas.winfo_height()))
            self.edge_canvas.move("edges", edge_x_offset, edge_y_offset)

            self.start_x = event.x
            self.start_y = event.y

    def on_scroll(self, *args):
        scroll_pos = self.scrollbar.get()
        self.current_x = -scroll_pos * self.canvas.winfo_width()
        self.canvas.xview_moveto(scroll_pos)
        self.edge_canvas.xview_moveto(scroll_pos)  # Move Canny edge canvas along with original canvas
        self.frame_index = int(scroll_pos * len(self.video))  # Update frame index
        self.show_frame()
        self.show_kirsch_frame()  # Update Canny edge frame

    def jump_to_time(self):
        time_str = self.time_entry.get()
        try:
            time_seconds = float(time_str)
            if 0 <= time_seconds:
                self.frame_index = int(time_seconds * self.video.get_meta_data()['fps'])
                self.show_frame()
                self.show_kirsch_frame()  # Jump to specified time for Canny edge frame
        except ValueError:
```

```python
        pass

    def prev_frame(self):
        if self.frame_index > 0:
            self.frame_index -= 1
            self.show_frame()
            self.show_kirsch_frame()

    def next_frame(self):
        if self.frame_index < len(self.video) - 1:
            self.frame_index += 1
            self.show_frame()
            self.show_kirsch_frame()

    def open_another_player(self):
        # Open another instance of the application
        root = tk.Toplevel(self.master)
        app = VideoKirsch(root)

def main():
    root = tk.Tk()
    app = VideoKirsch(root)
    root.mainloop()

if __name__ == "__main__":
    main()
```

RUNNING PROGRAM

LUCAS-KANADE OPTICAL FLOW

DESCRIPTION

The "Lucas-Kanade Optical Flow" project is a Python application that provides a graphical user interface (GUI) for computing and visualizing optical flow in video streams using the Lucas-Kanade method. The project utilizes several libraries, including tkinter, PIL (Python Imaging Library), imageio, OpenCV (cv2), and numpy, to create the GUI, process video frames, and calculate optical flow.

Upon execution, the application creates a main window with various components, including panels for displaying the original video frames and the optical flow result, control buttons for interacting with the video, and widgets for adjusting parameters such as zoom scale and time.

The VideoOpticalFlow class serves as the core component of the application, encapsulating functionalities such as video loading, playback control, optical flow computation, canvas interactions, and error handling.

The GUI layout consists of two main panels: the video display panel and the control panel. The video display panel contains two canvas widgets for displaying the original video frames and the optical flow result side by side. Users can interact with these canvases by clicking and dragging to pan the displayed frames within the widgets.

The control panel houses various buttons and widgets for controlling the video playback, adjusting zoom scale, specifying time for jumping to a particular frame, and opening another instance of the application. Users can open video files using the "Open Video" button, which prompts them to select a file via a file dialog.

The application supports smooth video playback, allowing users to play, pause, stop, and navigate through the video frames using the corresponding control buttons. Optical flow is computed and visualized in real-time as the video plays, providing users with insights into motion patterns within the video stream.

Optical flow computation is performed using the Lucas-Kanade method (cv2.calcOpticalFlowFarneback), which estimates motion vectors between consecutive frames. These motion vectors are visualized as line segments and markers on the optical flow canvas, allowing users to observe the direction and magnitude of motion.

Users can adjust the zoom scale to magnify or shrink the displayed frames for better visualization. Additionally, they can jump to a specific time in the video by entering the time in seconds and pressing the "Jump to Time" button.

The application includes error handling mechanisms to catch and display any exceptions that may occur during video loading, frame processing, or optical flow computation, ensuring a robust user experience.

Furthermore, users can open multiple instances of the application using the "Open Another Video Player" button, enabling them to analyze multiple videos simultaneously.

Overall, the "Lucas-Kanade Optical Flow" project offers a user-friendly interface for analyzing motion patterns in video streams, making it a valuable tool for various applications in computer vision and video analysis.

SOURCE CODE

```python
#gui_optical_flow_lucas_kanade.py
import tkinter as tk
from tkinter import ttk
from tkinter import filedialog
from PIL import Image, ImageTk
import imageio
import cv2
import numpy as np

class VideoOpticalFlow:
    def __init__(self, master):
        self.master = master
        self.master.title("Lucas-Kanade Optical Flow")

        self.video = None
        self.video_path = None
        self.paused = False
        self.zoom_scale = tk.IntVar(value=1)
        self.frame_index = 0
        self.start_x1 = None
        self.start_y1 = None
        self.current_x1 = 0
        self.current_y1 = 0
        self.start_x2 = None
        self.start_y2 = None
        self.current_x2 = 0
        self.current_y2 = 0

        self.prev_frame_gray = None  # Initialize prev_frame_gray variable

        self.create_widgets()

    def create_widgets(self):
        # Panel for video display
        video_panel = tk.Frame(self.master)
        video_panel.grid(row=0, column=0, padx=10, pady=10, sticky="nsew")

        # Canvas to display the original video
        canvas_width = 700
        canvas_height = 500
        self.canvas = tk.Canvas(video_panel, width=canvas_width, height=canvas_height)
        self.canvas.pack(side="left", fill="both", expand=True)
        self.canvas.bind("<MouseWheel>", self.on_mousewheel)
        self.canvas.bind("<ButtonPress-1>", self.on_press1)
        self.canvas.bind("<B1-Motion>", self.on_drag1)

        # Canvas to display the optical flow result
        self.flow_canvas = tk.Canvas(video_panel, width=canvas_width, height=canvas_height)
        self.flow_canvas.pack(side="right", fill="both", expand=True)
        self.flow_canvas.bind("<MouseWheel>", self.on_mousewheel)
        self.flow_canvas.bind("<ButtonPress-1>", self.on_press2)
        self.flow_canvas.bind("<B1-Motion>", self.on_drag2)

        # Panel for control buttons
        control_panel = tk.Frame(self.master)
        control_panel.grid(row=1, column=0, padx=10, pady=(0, 10), sticky="ew")

        # Button to open a video file
        self.open_button = tk.Button(control_panel, text="Open Video", command=self.open_video)
        self.open_button.grid(row=0, column=0, padx=10, pady=5)
```

```python
        # Combobox for selecting zoom scale
        self.zoom_combobox = ttk.Combobox(control_panel, textvariable=self.zoom_scale, values=list(range(1, 11)))
        self.zoom_combobox.grid(row=0, column=1, padx=10, pady=5)
        self.zoom_combobox.bind("<<ComboboxSelected>>", self.update_zoom)

        # Label and entry for specifying time
        self.time_label = tk.Label(control_panel, text="Jump to Time (s):")
        self.time_label.grid(row=0, column=2, padx=10, pady=5, sticky="e")
        self.time_entry = ttk.Entry(control_panel)
        self.time_entry.grid(row=0, column=3, padx=10, pady=5, sticky="w")
        self.time_entry.bind("<Return>", lambda event: self.jump_to_time())

        # Button to jump to specified time
        self.jump_button = tk.Button(control_panel, text="Jump to Time", command=self.jump_to_time)
        self.jump_button.grid(row=0, column=4, padx=10, pady=5)

        # Button to play/pause the video
        self.play_button = tk.Button(control_panel, text="Play/Pause", command=self.toggle_play_pause)
        self.play_button.grid(row=0, column=5, padx=10, pady=5)

        # Button to stop the video
        self.stop_button = tk.Button(control_panel, text="Stop", command=self.stop_video)
        self.stop_button.grid(row=0, column=6, padx=10, pady=5)

        # Button to navigate to the previous frame
        self.prev_frame_button = tk.Button(control_panel, text="Previous Frame", command=self.prev_frame)
        self.prev_frame_button.grid(row=0, column=7, padx=10, pady=5)

        # Button to navigate to the next frame
        self.next_frame_button = tk.Button(control_panel, text="Next Frame", command=self.next_frame)
        self.next_frame_button.grid(row=0, column=8, padx=10, pady=5)

        # Button to open another instance of the application
        self.open_another_button = tk.Button(control_panel, text="Open Another Video Player", command=self.open_another_player)
        self.open_another_button.grid(row=2, column=0, columnspan=9, padx=10, pady=5)

    def open_video(self):
        self.video_path = filedialog.askopenfilename(filetypes=[("Video files", "*.mp4;*.avi;*.mkv")])
        if self.video_path:
            self.video = imageio.get_reader(self.video_path)
            self.play_video()

    def play_video(self):
        if self.video:
            self.paused = False
            self.show_frame()
            self.show_optical_flow()

    def stop_video(self):
        self.paused = True
        self.frame_index = 0
        self.current_x1 = 0
        self.current_y1 = 0  # Reset the current position
        self.show_frame()
        self.show_optical_flow()
```

```python
    def toggle_play_pause(self):
        self.paused = not self.paused
        if not self.paused:
            self.play_video()

    def update_zoom(self, event=None):
        self.show_frame()
        self.show_optical_flow()

    def show_frame(self):
        if self.video:
            if not self.paused:
                if 0 <= self.frame_index < len(self.video):  # Check if frame index is within range
                    try:
                        frame = self.video.get_data(self.frame_index)
                        frame_gray = cv2.cvtColor(frame, cv2.COLOR_RGB2GRAY)  # Convert to grayscale

                        # Initialize prev_frame_gray on first frame
                        if self.prev_frame_gray is None:
                            self.prev_frame_gray = frame_gray.copy()

                        # Display current frame
                        frame = Image.fromarray(frame)
                        frame = frame.resize((frame.width * self.zoom_scale.get(), frame.height * self.zoom_scale.get()))
                        photo = ImageTk.PhotoImage(frame)
                        self.photo = photo  # Save object reference to PhotoImage globally
                        self.canvas.delete("video")  # Delete previous image
                        self.canvas.create_image(self.current_x1, self.current_y1, anchor="nw", image=photo, tags="video")

                        # Update prev_frame_gray
                        self.prev_frame_gray = frame_gray.copy()

                        if not self.paused:
                            self.frame_index += 1
                            self.canvas.after(30, self.show_frame)
                    except Exception as e:
                        print("Error: ", e)

    def show_optical_flow(self):
        if self.video:
            if not self.paused:
                if 0 <= self.frame_index < len(self.video):  # Check if frame index is within range
                    try:
                        frame = self.video.get_data(self.frame_index)
                        frame_gray = cv2.cvtColor(frame, cv2.COLOR_RGB2GRAY)  # Convert to grayscale

                        # Calculate optical flow
                        optical_flow = cv2.calcOpticalFlowFarneback(self.prev_frame_gray, frame_gray, None, 0.5, 3, 15, 3, 5, 1.2, 0)

                        # Create an empty mask image for visualization
                        mask = np.zeros_like(frame)

                        # Compute flow visualization
                        step = 6  # Adjust this value to change the density of the flow visualization
                        for y in range(0, int(frame.shape[0] * self.zoom_scale.get()), step):
```

```python
                            for x in range(0, int(frame.shape[1] * self.zoom_scale.get()), step):
                                dx, dy = optical_flow[int(y / self.zoom_scale.get()), int(x / self.zoom_scale.get())]
                                # Scale the optical flow vectors based on the zoom scale
                                dx *= 15  # Adjust this scaling factor as needed
                                dy *= 15  # Adjust this scaling factor as needed
                                cv2.line(mask, (x, y), (int(x + dx), int(y + dy)), (255, 255, 255), 1)
                                cv2.circle(mask, (int(x + dx), int(y + dy)), 1, (0, 255, 0), -1)

                        # Resize mask for display
                        mask = cv2.resize(mask, (int(frame.shape[1] * self.zoom_scale.get()), int(frame.shape[0] * self.zoom_scale.get())))

                        # Convert mask to PIL format and display on canvas
                        mask = Image.fromarray(mask)
                        mask = ImageTk.PhotoImage(mask)
                        self.mask = mask
                        self.flow_canvas.delete("mask")  # Delete previous optical flow
                        self.flow_canvas.create_image(self.current_x2, self.current_y2, anchor="nw", image=mask, tags="mask")

                        if not self.paused:
                            self.frame_index += 1
                            self.master.after(30, self.show_optical_flow)

                        # Update previous frame
                        self.prev_frame_gray = frame_gray.copy()

                except Exception as e:
                    print("Error in show_optical_flow:", e)  # Print error message

    def on_mousewheel(self, event):
        direction = event.delta // 120
        current_value = int(self.zoom_scale.get())
        if direction == 1 and current_value < 10:
            current_value += 1
        elif direction == -1 and current_value > 1:
            current_value -= 1
        self.zoom_scale.set(current_value)
        self.update_zoom()

    def on_press1(self, self, event):
        self.start_x1 = event.x
        self.start_y1 = event.y

    def on_drag1(self, event):
        if self.start_x1 and self.start_y1:
            self.x_offset1 = event.x - self.start_x1
            self.y_offset1 = event.y - self.start_y1
            self.current_x1 += self.x_offset1  # Update current position
            self.current_y1 += self.y_offset1  # Update current position
            self.canvas.move("video", self.x_offset1, self.y_offset1)
            self.start_x1 = event.x
            self.start_y1 = event.y

    def on_press2(self, event):
        self.start_x2 = event.x
        self.start_y2 = event.y

    def on_drag2(self, event):
        if self.start_x2 and self.start_y2:
```

```python
            self.x_offset2 = event.x - self.start_x2
            self.y_offset2 = event.y - self.start_y2
            self.current_x2 += self.x_offset2  # Update current position
            self.current_y2 += self.y_offset2  # Update current position
            self.flow_canvas.move("mask", self.x_offset2, self.y_offset2)  # Move optical flow
canvas along with original canvas
            self.start_x2 = event.x
            self.start_y2 = event.y

    def jump_to_time(self):
        time_str = self.time_entry.get()
        try:
            time_seconds = float(time_str)
            if 0 <= time_seconds:
                self.frame_index = int(time_seconds * self.video.get_meta_data()['fps'])
                self.show_frame()
                self.show_optical_flow()  # Jump to specified time for optical flow
        except ValueError:
            pass

    def prev_frame(self):
        if self.frame_index > 0:
            self.frame_index -= 1
            self.show_frame()
            self.show_optical_flow()

    def next_frame(self):
        if self.video and self.frame_index < len(self.video) - 1:
            self.frame_index += 1
            self.show_frame()
            self.show_optical_flow()

    def open_another_player(self):
        # Open another instance of the application
        root = tk.Toplevel(self.master)
        app = VideoOpticalFlow(root)

def main():
    root = tk.Tk()
    app = VideoOpticalFlow(root)
    root.mainloop()

if __name__ == "__main__":
    main()
```

RUNNING PROGRAM

KALMAN FILTER OPTICAL FLOW

DESCRIPTION

The "Optical Flow Analysis with Kalman Filter" project is a Python application designed to analyze optical flow in video streams using the Kalman filter method. It utilizes various libraries such as tkinter, PIL (Python Imaging Library), imageio, OpenCV (cv2), and numpy to create a graphical user interface (GUI), process video frames, and implement the Kalman filter algorithm.

Upon execution, the application creates a main window with components including panels for displaying the original video frames and the optical flow result, as well as control buttons for interacting with the video and adjusting parameters.

The VideoKalmanOpticalFlow class serves as the core component, encapsulating functionalities such as video loading, playback control, optical flow computation, canvas interactions, and Kalman filter implementation.

The GUI layout consists of two main panels: the video display panel and the control panel. The video display panel contains two canvas widgets for displaying the original video frames and the optical flow result side by side. Users can interact with these canvases by clicking and dragging to pan the displayed frames within the widgets.

The control panel houses various buttons and widgets for controlling the video playback, adjusting zoom scale, specifying step size, specifying displacement parameters, and opening another instance of the application.

Users can open video files using the "Open Video" button, which prompts them to select a file via a file dialog. Once a video is loaded, users can play, pause, stop, and navigate through the video frames using the corresponding control buttons.

Optical flow is computed and visualized in real-time as the video plays, providing users with insights into motion patterns within the video stream. The Kalman filter is applied to improve the accuracy of the optical flow estimation by incorporating temporal dynamics and reducing noise.

The Kalman filter parameters, including the measurement matrix, transition matrix, and process noise covariance, are initialized during object instantiation. These parameters define the behavior of the Kalman filter in predicting the state of the system and updating the state estimate based on measurements.

During optical flow computation, the Kalman filter is used to predict the next state of the motion vectors based on the current state and update the state estimate using the measured optical flow vectors.

Users can adjust the zoom scale to magnify or shrink the displayed frames for better visualization. Additionally, they can specify the step size and displacement parameters to control the density and scale of the optical flow visualization.

The application includes error handling mechanisms to catch and display any exceptions that may occur during video loading, frame processing, optical flow computation, or Kalman filter implementation, ensuring a robust user experience.

Furthermore, users can open multiple instances of the application using the "Open Another Video Player" button, enabling them to analyze multiple videos simultaneously.

Overall, the "Optical Flow Analysis with Kalman Filter" project offers a user-friendly interface for analyzing motion patterns in video streams with improved accuracy using the

Kalman filter algorithm, making it a valuable tool for various applications in computer vision and video analysis.

SOURCE CODE

```python
#gui_optical_flow_kalman_filter.py
import tkinter as tk
from tkinter import ttk
from tkinter import filedialog
from PIL import Image, ImageTk
import imageio
import cv2
import numpy as np

class VideoKalmanOpticalFlow:
    def __init__(self, master):
        self.master = master
        self.master.title("Optical Flow Analysis with Kalman Filter")

        self.video = None
        self.video_path = None
        self.paused = False
        self.zoom_scale = tk.IntVar(value=1)
        self.frame_index = 0
        self.start_x1 = None
        self.start_y1 = None
        self.current_x1 = 0
        self.current_y1 = 0
        self.start_x2 = None
        self.start_y2 = None
        self.current_x2 = 0
        self.current_y2 = 0

        self.prev_frame_gray = None  # Initialize prev_frame_gray variable
        self.kalman = cv2.KalmanFilter(4, 2)
        self.kalman.measurementMatrix = np.array([[1, 0, 0, 0],
                                                   [0, 1, 0, 0]], np.float32)
        self.kalman.transitionMatrix = np.array([[1, 0, 1, 0],
                                                  [0, 1, 0, 1],
                                                  [0, 0, 1, 0],
                                                  [0, 0, 0, 1]], np.float32)
        self.kalman.processNoiseCov = np.array([[1, 0, 0, 0],
                                                 [0, 1, 0, 0],
                                                 [0, 0, 1, 0],
                                                 [0, 0, 0, 1]], np.float32) * 0.03

        self.create_widgets()

    def create_widgets(self):
        # Panel for video display
        video_panel = tk.Frame(self.master)
        video_panel.grid(row=0, column=0, padx=10, pady=10, sticky="nsew")

        # Canvas to display the original video
        canvas_width = 800
        canvas_height = 500
        self.canvas = tk.Canvas(video_panel, width=canvas_width, height=canvas_height)
        self.canvas.pack(side="left", fill="both", expand=True)
```

```python
        self.canvas.bind("<MouseWheel>", self.on_mousewheel)
        self.canvas.bind("<ButtonPress-1>", self.on_press1)
        self.canvas.bind("<B1-Motion>", self.on_drag1)

        # Canvas to display the optical flow result
        self.flow_canvas = tk.Canvas(video_panel, width=canvas_width, height=canvas_height)
        self.flow_canvas.pack(side="right", fill="both", expand=True)
        self.flow_canvas.bind("<MouseWheel>", self.on_mousewheel)
        self.flow_canvas.bind("<ButtonPress-1>", self.on_press2)
        self.flow_canvas.bind("<B1-Motion>", self.on_drag2)

        # Panel for control buttons
        control_panel = tk.Frame(self.master)
        control_panel.grid(row=1, column=0, padx=10, pady=(0, 10), sticky="ew")

        # Button to open a video file
        self.open_button = tk.Button(control_panel, text="Open Video", command=self.open_video)
        self.open_button.grid(row=0, column=0, padx=10, pady=5)

        # Combobox for selecting zoom scale
        self.zoom_combobox = ttk.Combobox(control_panel, textvariable=self.zoom_scale, values=list(range(1, 11)))
        self.zoom_combobox.grid(row=0, column=1, padx=10, pady=5)
        self.zoom_combobox.bind("<<ComboboxSelected>>", self.update_zoom)

        # Label and entry for specifying step
        self.step_label = tk.Label(control_panel, text="Step:")
        self.step_label.grid(row=0, column=2, padx=10, pady=5, sticky="e")
        self.step_default = tk.StringVar(value="6")
        self.step_entry = ttk.Entry(control_panel, textvariable=self.step_default)
        self.step_entry.grid(row=0, column=3, padx=10, pady=5, sticky="w")
        self.step_entry.bind("<Return>", lambda event: self.toggle_play_pause())

        # Label and entry for specifying dx (same as dy)
        self.dx_label = tk.Label(control_panel, text="dx (same as dy):")
        self.dx_label.grid(row=0, column=4, padx=10, pady=5, sticky="e")
        self.dx_default = tk.StringVar(value="15")
        self.dx_entry = ttk.Entry(control_panel, textvariable=self.dx_default)
        self.dx_entry.grid(row=0, column=5, padx=10, pady=5, sticky="w")
        self.dx_entry.bind("<Return>", lambda event: self.toggle_play_pause())

        # Button to jump to specified time
        self.jump_button = tk.Button(control_panel, text="Jump to Time", command=self.jump_to_time)
        self.jump_button.grid(row=0, column=6, padx=10, pady=5)

        # Button to play/pause the video
        self.play_button = tk.Button(control_panel, text="Play/Pause", command=self.toggle_play_pause)
        self.play_button.grid(row=0, column=7, padx=10, pady=5)

        # Button to stop the video
        self.stop_button = tk.Button(control_panel, text="Stop", command=self.stop_video)
        self.stop_button.grid(row=0, column=8, padx=10, pady=5)

        # Button to navigate to the previous frame
        self.prev_frame_button = tk.Button(control_panel, text="Previous Frame", command=self.prev_frame)
        self.prev_frame_button.grid(row=0, column=9, padx=10, pady=5)

        # Button to navigate to the next frame
        self.next_frame_button = tk.Button(control_panel, text="Next Frame", command=self.next_frame)
        self.next_frame_button.grid(row=0, column=10, padx=10, pady=5)
```

```python
        # Button to open another instance of the application
        self.open_another_button = tk.Button(control_panel, text="Open Another Video Player", command=self.open_another_player)
        self.open_another_button.grid(row=2, column=0, columnspan=11, padx=10, pady=5)

    def open_video(self):
        self.video_path = filedialog.askopenfilename(filetypes=[("Video files", "*.mp4;*.avi;*.mkv")])
        if self.video_path:
            self.video = imageio.get_reader(self.video_path)
            self.play_video()

    def play_video(self):
        if self.video:
            self.paused = False
            self.show_frame()
            self.show_optical_flow()

    def stop_video(self):
        self.paused = True
        self.frame_index = 0
        self.current_x1 = 0
        self.current_y1 = 0  # Reset the current position
        self.show_frame()
        self.show_optical_flow()

    def toggle_play_pause(self):
        self.paused = not self.paused
        if not self.paused:
            self.play_video()

    def update_zoom(self, event=None):
        self.show_frame()
        self.show_optical_flow()

    def show_frame(self):
        if self.video:
            if not self.paused:
                if 0 <= self.frame_index < len(self.video):  # Check if frame index is within range
                    try:
                        frame = self.video.get_data(self.frame_index)
                        frame_gray = cv2.cvtColor(frame, cv2.COLOR_RGB2GRAY)  # Convert to grayscale

                        # Initialize prev_frame_gray on first frame
                        if self.prev_frame_gray is None:
                            self.prev_frame_gray = frame_gray.copy()

                        # Display current frame
                        frame = Image.fromarray(frame)
                        frame = frame.resize((frame.width * self.zoom_scale.get(), frame.height * self.zoom_scale.get()))
                        photo = ImageTk.PhotoImage(frame)
                        self.photo = photo  # Save object reference to PhotoImage globally
                        self.canvas.delete("video")  # Delete previous image
                        self.canvas.create_image(self.current_x1, self.current_y1, anchor="nw", image=photo, tags="video")

                        # Update prev_frame_gray
                        self.prev_frame_gray = frame_gray.copy()

                        self.frame_index += 1  # Move to the next frame
```

```python
                    except Exception as e:
                        print("Error: ", e)

    def show_optical_flow(self):
        if self.video:
            if not self.paused:
                if 0 <= self.frame_index < len(self.video):  # Check if frame index is within range
                    try:
                        frame = self.video.get_data(self.frame_index)
                        frame_gray = cv2.cvtColor(frame, cv2.COLOR_RGB2GRAY)  # Convert to grayscale

                        # Calculate optical flow
                        optical_flow = cv2.calcOpticalFlowFarneback(self.prev_frame_gray, frame_gray, None, 0.5, 3, 15, 3, 5, 1.2, 0)

                        # Create an empty mask image for visualization
                        mask = np.zeros_like(frame)

                        # Compute flow visualization
                        step = int(self.step_entry.get())
                        for y in range(0, frame.shape[0], step):
                            for x in range(0, frame.shape[1], step):
                                dx, dy = optical_flow[y, x]
                                # Scale the optical flow vectors based on the zoom scale
                                dx *= int(self.dx_entry.get())
                                dy *= int(self.dx_entry.get())
                                pt1 = (x, y)
                                pt2 = (int(x + dx), int(y + dy))
                                cv2.line(mask, pt1, pt2, (255, 255, 255), 1)
                                cv2.circle(mask, pt2, 1, (0, 255, 0), -1)

                        # Resize mask for display
                        mask = cv2.resize(mask, (frame.shape[1] * self.zoom_scale.get(), frame.shape[0] * self.zoom_scale.get()))

                        # Convert mask to PIL format and display on canvas
                        mask = Image.fromarray(mask)
                        mask = ImageTk.PhotoImage(mask)
                        self.mask = mask
                        self.flow_canvas.delete("mask")  # Delete previous optical flow
                        self.flow_canvas.create_image(self.current_x2, self.current_y2, anchor="nw", image=mask, tags="mask")

                        self.frame_index += 1  # Move to the next frame

                        # Update previous frame
                        self.prev_frame_gray = frame_gray.copy()

                    except Exception as e:
                        print("Error in show_optical_flow:", e)  # Print error message

    def on_mousewheel(self, event):
        direction = event.delta // 120
        current_value = int(self.zoom_scale.get())
        if direction == 1 and current_value < 10:
            current_value += 1
        elif direction == -1 and current_value > 1:
            current_value -= 1
        self.zoom_scale.set(current_value)
        self.update_zoom()
```

```python
def on_press1(self, event):
    self.start_x1 = event.x
    self.start_y1 = event.y

def on_drag1(self, event):
    if self.start_x1 and self.start_y1:
        self.x_offset1 = event.x - self.start_x1
        self.y_offset1 = event.y - self.start_y1
        self.current_x1 += self.x_offset1  # Update current position
        self.current_y1 += self.y_offset1  # Update current position
        self.canvas.move("video", self.x_offset1, self.y_offset1)
        self.start_x1 = event.x
        self.start_y1 = event.y

def on_press2(self, event):
    self.start_x2 = event.x
    self.start_y2 = event.y

def on_drag2(self, event):
    if self.start_x2 and self.start_y2:
        self.x_offset2 = event.x - self.start_x2
        self.y_offset2 = event.y - self.start_y2
        self.current_x2 += self.x_offset2  # Update current position
        self.current_y2 += self.y_offset2  # Update current position
        self.flow_canvas.move("mask", self.x_offset2, self.y_offset2)  # Move optical flow canvas along with original canvas
        self.start_x2 = event.x
        self.start_y2 = event.y

def jump_to_time(self):
    time_str = self.time_entry.get()
    try:
        time_seconds = float(time_str)
        if 0 <= time_seconds:
            self.frame_index = int(time_seconds * self.video.get_meta_data()['fps'])
            self.show_frame()
            self.show_optical_flow()  # Jump to specified time for optical flow
    except ValueError:
        pass

def prev_frame(self):
    if self.frame_index > 0:
        self.frame_index -= 3
        #self.paused = True   # Pause the video when navigating to the previous frame
        self.show_frame()
        self.show_optical_flow()
        print(self.frame_index)

def next_frame(self):
    if self.video and self.frame_index < len(self.video) - 1:
        self.frame_index -= 1
        #self.frame_index += 1
        #self.paused = True   # Pause the video when navigating to the next frame
        self.show_frame()
        self.show_optical_flow()
        print(self.frame_index)


def open_another_player(self):
    # Open another instance of the application
    root = tk.Toplevel(self.master)
    app = VideoKalmanOpticalFlow(root)
```

```
def main():
    root = tk.Tk()
    app = VideoKalmanOpticalFlow(root)
    root.mainloop()

if __name__ == "__main__":
    main()
```

RUNNING PROGRAM

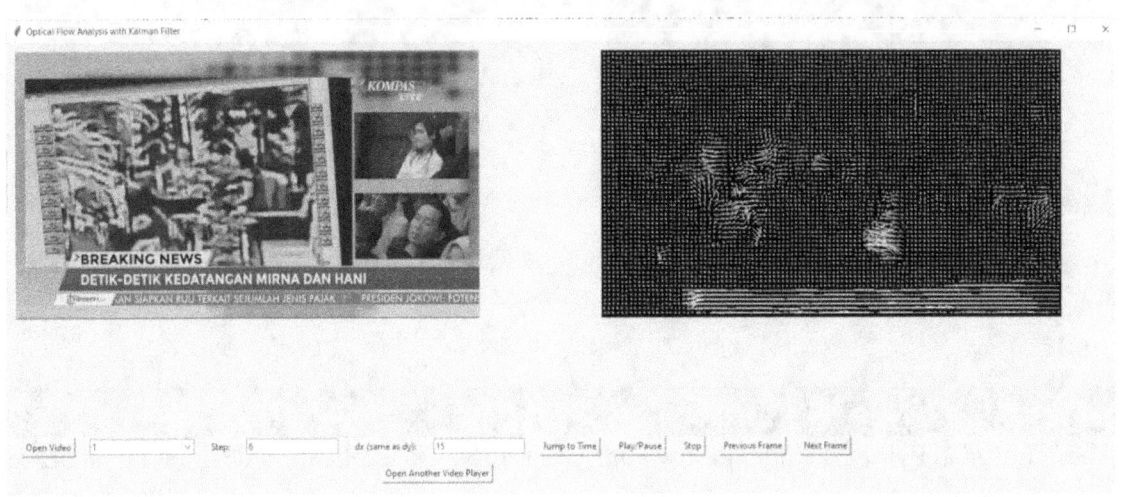

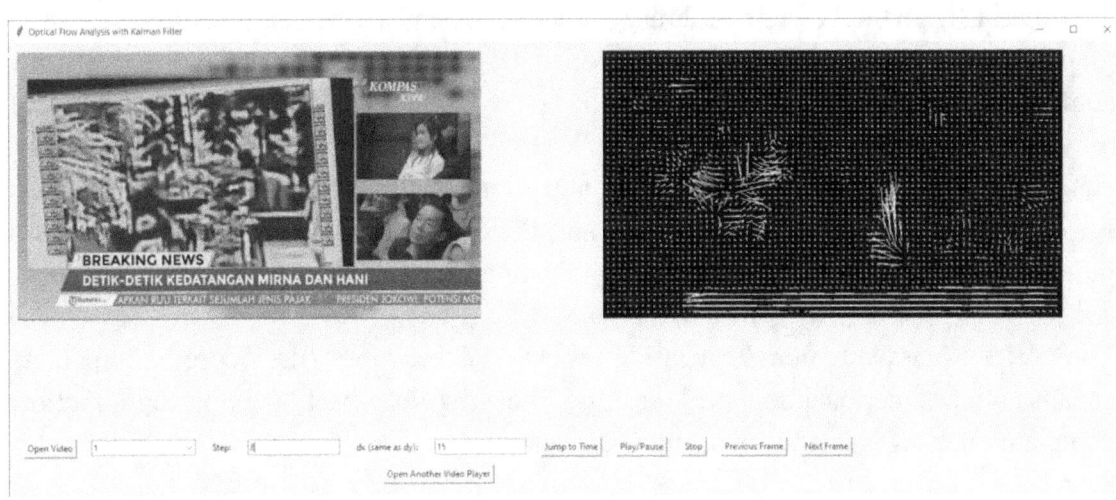

GAUSSIAN PYRAMID OPTICAL FLOW

DESCRIPTION

The "Gaussian Pyramid Optical Flow" project is a Python application designed to analyze optical flow in video streams using the Gaussian pyramid method. It utilizes libraries such as tkinter, PIL (Python Imaging Library), imageio, OpenCV (cv2), and numpy to create a graphical user interface (GUI), process video frames, and implement the optical flow computation.

Upon execution, the application creates a main window with components including panels for displaying the original video frames and the optical flow result, as well as control buttons for interacting with the video and adjusting parameters.

The VideoGaussianPyramidOpticalFlow class serves as the core component, encapsulating functionalities such as video loading, playback control, optical flow computation, canvas interactions, and GUI creation.

The GUI layout consists of two main panels: the video display panel and the control panel. The video display panel contains two canvas widgets for displaying the original video frames and the optical flow result side by side. Users can interact with these canvases by clicking and dragging to pan the displayed frames within the widgets.

The control panel houses various buttons and widgets for controlling the video playback, adjusting zoom scale, specifying step size, specifying displacement parameters, and opening another instance of the application.

Users can open video files using the "Open Video" button, which prompts them to select a file via a file dialog. Once a video is loaded, users can play, pause, stop, and navigate through the video frames using the corresponding control buttons.

Optical flow is computed and visualized in real-time as the video plays, providing users with insights into motion patterns within the video stream. The Gaussian pyramid method is used to compute optical flow, which involves building multi-scale representations of the image and estimating motion between these representations.

Users can adjust the zoom scale to magnify or shrink the displayed frames for better visualization. Additionally, they can specify the step size and displacement parameters to control the density and scale of the optical flow visualization.

The application includes error handling mechanisms to catch and display any exceptions that may occur during video loading, frame processing, or optical flow computation, ensuring a robust user experience.

Furthermore, users can open multiple instances of the application using the "Open Another Video Player" button, enabling them to analyze multiple videos simultaneously.

Overall, the "Gaussian Pyramid Optical Flow" project offers a user-friendly interface for analyzing motion patterns in video streams using the Gaussian pyramid method, making it a valuable tool for various applications in computer vision and video analysis.

SOURCE CODE

```
#gui_optical_flow_gaussian_pyramid.py
import tkinter as tk
from tkinter import ttk
from tkinter import filedialog
from PIL import Image, ImageTk
import imageio
import cv2
import numpy as np
```

```python
class VideoGaussianPyramidOpticalFlow:
    def __init__(self, master):
        self.master = master
        self.master.title("Gaussian Pyramid Optical Flow")

        self.video = None
        self.video_path = None
        self.paused = False
        self.zoom_scale = tk.IntVar(value=1)
        self.frame_index = 0
        self.start_x1 = None
        self.start_y1 = None
        self.current_x1 = 0
        self.current_y1 = 0
        self.start_x2 = None
        self.start_y2 = None
        self.current_x2 = 0
        self.current_y2 = 0

        self.prev_frame_gray = None  # Initialize prev_frame_gray variable

        self.create_widgets()

    def create_widgets(self):
        # Panel for video display
        video_panel = tk.Frame(self.master)
        video_panel.grid(row=0, column=0, padx=10, pady=10, sticky="nsew")

        # Canvas to display the original video
        canvas_width = 800
        canvas_height = 500
        self.canvas = tk.Canvas(video_panel, width=canvas_width, height=canvas_height)
        self.canvas.pack(side="left", fill="both", expand=True)
        self.canvas.bind("<MouseWheel>", self.on_mousewheel)
        self.canvas.bind("<ButtonPress-1>", self.on_press1)
        self.canvas.bind("<B1-Motion>", self.on_drag1)

        # Canvas to display the optical flow result
        self.flow_canvas = tk.Canvas(video_panel, width=canvas_width, height=canvas_height)
        self.flow_canvas.pack(side="right", fill="both", expand=True)
        self.flow_canvas.bind("<MouseWheel>", self.on_mousewheel)
        self.flow_canvas.bind("<ButtonPress-1>", self.on_press2)
        self.flow_canvas.bind("<B1-Motion>", self.on_drag2)

        # Panel for control buttons
        control_panel = tk.Frame(self.master)
        control_panel.grid(row=1, column=0, padx=10, pady=(0, 10), sticky="ew")

        # Button to open a video file
        self.open_button = tk.Button(control_panel, text="Open Video", command=self.open_video)
        self.open_button.grid(row=0, column=0, padx=10, pady=5)

        # Combobox for selecting zoom scale
        self.zoom_combobox = ttk.Combobox(control_panel, textvariable=self.zoom_scale, values=list(range(1, 11)))
        self.zoom_combobox.grid(row=0, column=1, padx=10, pady=5)
        self.zoom_combobox.bind("<<ComboboxSelected>>", self.update_zoom)

        # Label and entry for specifying step
        self.step_label = tk.Label(control_panel, text="Step:")
        self.step_label.grid(row=0, column=2, padx=10, pady=5, sticky="e")
        self.step_default = tk.StringVar(value="6")
        self.step_entry = ttk.Entry(control_panel, textvariable=self.step_default)
```

```python
        self.step_entry.grid(row=0, column=3, padx=10, pady=5, sticky="w")
        self.step_entry.bind("<Return>", lambda event: self.toggle_play_pause())

        # Label and entry for specifying dx (same as dy)
        self.dx_label = tk.Label(control_panel, text="dx (same as dy):")
        self.dx_label.grid(row=0, column=4, padx=10, pady=5, sticky="e")
        self.dx_default = tk.StringVar(value="15")
        self.dx_entry = ttk.Entry(control_panel, textvariable=self.dx_default)
        self.dx_entry.grid(row=0, column=5, padx=10, pady=5, sticky="w")
        self.dx_entry.bind("<Return>", lambda event: self.toggle_play_pause())

        # Button to jump to specified time
        self.jump_button = tk.Button(control_panel, text="Jump to Time", command=self.jump_to_time)
        self.jump_button.grid(row=0, column=6, padx=10, pady=5)

        # Button to play/pause the video
        self.play_button = tk.Button(control_panel, text="Play/Pause", command=self.toggle_play_pause)
        self.play_button.grid(row=0, column=7, padx=10, pady=5)

        # Button to stop the video
        self.stop_button = tk.Button(control_panel, text="Stop", command=self.stop_video)
        self.stop_button.grid(row=0, column=8, padx=10, pady=5)

        # Button to navigate to the previous frame
        self.prev_frame_button = tk.Button(control_panel, text="Previous Frame", command=self.prev_frame)
        self.prev_frame_button.grid(row=0, column=9, padx=10, pady=5)

        # Button to navigate to the next frame
        self.next_frame_button = tk.Button(control_panel, text="Next Frame", command=self.next_frame)
        self.next_frame_button.grid(row=0, column=10, padx=10, pady=5)

        # Button to open another instance of the application
        self.open_another_button = tk.Button(control_panel, text="Open Another Video Player", command=self.open_another_player)
        self.open_another_button.grid(row=2, column=0, columnspan=11, padx=10, pady=5)

    def open_video(self):
        self.video_path = filedialog.askopenfilename(filetypes=[("Video files", "*.mp4;*.avi;*.mkv")])
        if self.video_path:
            self.video = imageio.get_reader(self.video_path)
            self.play_video()

    def play_video(self):
        if self.video:
            self.paused = False
            self.show_frame()
            self.show_optical_flow()

    def stop_video(self):
        self.paused = True
        self.frame_index = 0
        self.current_x1 = 0
        self.current_y1 = 0  # Reset the current position
        self.show_frame()
        self.show_optical_flow()

    def toggle_play_pause(self):
        self.paused = not self.paused
```

```python
            if not self.paused:
                self.play_video()

    def update_zoom(self, event=None):
        self.show_frame()
        self.show_optical_flow()

    def show_frame(self):
        if self.video:
            if not self.paused:
                if 0 <= self.frame_index < len(self.video):  # Check if frame index is within range
                    try:
                        frame = self.video.get_data(self.frame_index)
                        frame_gray = cv2.cvtColor(frame, cv2.COLOR_RGB2GRAY)  # Convert to grayscale

                        # Initialize prev_frame_gray on first frame
                        if self.prev_frame_gray is None:
                            self.prev_frame_gray = frame_gray.copy()

                        # Display current frame
                        frame = Image.fromarray(frame)
                        frame = frame.resize((frame.width * self.zoom_scale.get(), frame.height * self.zoom_scale.get()))
                        photo = ImageTk.PhotoImage(frame)
                        self.photo = photo  # Save object reference to PhotoImage globally
                        self.canvas.delete("video")  # Delete previous image
                        self.canvas.create_image(self.current_x1, self.current_y1, anchor="nw", image=photo, tags="video")

                        # Update prev_frame_gray
                        self.prev_frame_gray = frame_gray.copy()

                        self.frame_index += 1  # Move to the next frame

                        #self.canvas.after(30, self.show_frame)
                    except Exception as e:
                        print("Error: ", e)

    def show_optical_flow(self):
        if self.video:
            if not self.paused:
                if 0 <= self.frame_index < len(self.video):  # Check if frame index is within range
                    try:
                        frame = self.video.get_data(self.frame_index)
                        frame_gray = cv2.cvtColor(frame, cv2.COLOR_RGB2GRAY)  # Convert to grayscale

                        # Calculate optical flow
                        optical_flow = cv2.calcOpticalFlowFarneback(self.prev_frame_gray, frame_gray, None, 0.5, 3, 15, 3, 5, 1.2, 0)

                        # Create an empty mask image for visualization
                        mask = np.zeros_like(frame)

                        # Compute flow visualization
                        step = int(self.step_entry.get())
                        for y in range(0, frame.shape[0], step):
                            for x in range(0, frame.shape[1], step):
                                dx, dy = optical_flow[y, x]
                                # Scale the optical flow vectors based on the zoom scale
                                dx *= int(self.dx_entry.get())
```

```python
                        dy *= int(self.dx_entry.get())
                        pt1 = (x, y)
                        pt2 = (int(x + dx), int(y + dy))
                        cv2.line(mask, pt1, pt2, (255, 255, 255), 1)
                        cv2.circle(mask, pt2, 1, (0, 255, 0), -1)

                    # Resize mask for display
                    mask = cv2.resize(mask, (frame.shape[1] * self.zoom_scale.get(), frame.shape[0] * self.zoom_scale.get()))

                    # Convert mask to PIL format and display on canvas
                    mask = Image.fromarray(mask)
                    mask = ImageTk.PhotoImage(mask)
                    self.mask = mask
                    self.flow_canvas.delete("mask")  # Delete previous optical flow
                    self.flow_canvas.create_image(self.current_x2, self.current_y2, anchor="nw", image=mask, tags="mask")

                    self.frame_index += 1  # Move to the next frame

                    # Update previous frame
                    self.prev_frame_gray = frame_gray.copy()

            except Exception as e:
                print("Error in show_optical_flow:", e)  # Print error message

    def on_mousewheel(self, event):
        direction = event.delta // 120
        current_value = int(self.zoom_scale.get())
        if direction == 1 and current_value < 10:
            current_value += 1
        elif direction == -1 and current_value > 1:
            current_value -= 1
        self.zoom_scale.set(current_value)
        self.update_zoom()

    def on_press1(self, event):
        self.start_x1 = event.x
        self.start_y1 = event.y

    def on_drag1(self, event):
        if self.start_x1 and self.start_y1:
            self.x_offset1 = event.x - self.start_x1
            self.y_offset1 = event.y - self.start_y1
            self.current_x1 += self.x_offset1  # Update current position
            self.current_y1 += self.y_offset1  # Update current position
            self.canvas.move("video", self.x_offset1, self.y_offset1)
            self.start_x1 = event.x
            self.start_y1 = event.y

    def on_press2(self, event):
        self.start_x2 = event.x
        self.start_y2 = event.y

    def on_drag2(self, event):
        if self.start_x2 and self.start_y2:
            self.x_offset2 = event.x - self.start_x2
            self.y_offset2 = event.y - self.start_y2
            self.current_x2 += self.x_offset2  # Update current position
            self.current_y2 += self.y_offset2  # Update current position
            self.flow_canvas.move("mask", self.x_offset2, self.y_offset2)  # Move optical flow canvas along with original canvas
            self.start_x2 = event.x
            self.start_y2 = event.y
```

```python
    def jump_to_time(self):
        time_str = self.time_entry.get()
        try:
            time_seconds = float(time_str)
            if 0 <= time_seconds:
                self.frame_index = int(time_seconds * self.video.get_meta_data()['fps'])
                self.show_frame()
                self.show_optical_flow()  # Jump to specified time for optical flow
        except ValueError:
            pass

    def prev_frame(self):
        if self.frame_index > 0:
            self.frame_index -= 3
            #self.paused = True  # Pause the video when navigating to the previous frame
            self.show_frame()
            self.show_optical_flow()
            print(self.frame_index)

    def next_frame(self):
        if self.video and self.frame_index < len(self.video) - 1:
            self.frame_index -= 1
            #self.frame_index += 1
            #self.paused = True  # Pause the video when navigating to the next frame
            self.show_frame()
            self.show_optical_flow()
            print(self.frame_index)


    def open_another_player(self):
        # Open another instance of the application
        root = tk.Toplevel(self.master)
        app = VideoGaussianPyramidOpticalFlow(root)

def main():
    root = tk.Tk()
    app = VideoGaussianPyramidOpticalFlow(root)
    root.mainloop()

if __name__ == "__main__":
    main()
```

RUNNING PROGRAM

OBJECT TRACKING WITH LUCAS-KANADE

DESCRIPTION

The "Object Tracking with Lucas Kanade" project is a Python application developed to track objects in video streams using the Lucas-Kanade optical flow algorithm. It leverages libraries such as tkinter, PIL (Python Imaging Library), imageio, OpenCV (cv2), and numpy to create a graphical user interface (GUI), process video frames, and implement object tracking functionalities.

Upon execution, the application launches a main window with components including a panel for video display, a list box for displaying center coordinates of tracked objects, and a control panel containing various buttons for interacting with the video and managing tracking operations.

The ObjectTrackingLucasKanade class serves as the central component, encapsulating functionalities such as video loading, playback control, object tracking using Lucas-Kanade algorithm, GUI creation, and event handling.

The GUI layout comprises a video display panel featuring a canvas widget for displaying the original video frames and a list box for presenting the center coordinates of tracked objects. Users can interact with the video canvas by clicking and dragging to define bounding boxes around objects of interest for tracking.

The control panel contains buttons for opening video files, adjusting zoom scale, playing/pausing the video, stopping the video, navigating through frames, and clearing the list box. These buttons enable users to control the playback and tracking process efficiently.

Users can open video files by clicking the "Open Video" button, which prompts them to select a file via a file dialog. Once a video is loaded, users can play, pause, stop, and navigate through the video frames using the corresponding control buttons.

Object tracking is performed using the Lucas-Kanade optical flow algorithm, which estimates the motion of objects in consecutive frames. The application tracks objects based on user-defined bounding boxes, updating the coordinates of the bounding boxes using the calculated optical flow.

The list box displays the center coordinates of tracked objects, providing users with real-time feedback on the positions of objects throughout the video stream.

The application includes functionalities for adjusting the zoom scale to magnify or shrink the displayed frames for better visualization, as well as for clearing the list box to reset the tracked object data.

Error handling mechanisms are incorporated to catch and display any exceptions that may occur during video loading, frame processing, or object tracking, ensuring a smooth user experience.

Overall, the "Object Tracking with Lucas Kanade" project offers a user-friendly interface for tracking objects in video streams using the Lucas-Kanade optical flow algorithm, making it a valuable tool for various applications in computer vision and video analysis.

SOURCE CODE

```python
#object_tracking_lucas_kanade_new.py
import tkinter as tk
from tkinter import ttk
from tkinter import filedialog
from PIL import Image, ImageTk
import imageio
import cv2
import numpy as np

class ObjectTrackingLucasKanade:
    def __init__(self, master):
        self.master = master
        self.master.title("Object Tracking with Lucas Kanade")
        self.file_name = ""
        self.set_window_title()  # Set window title initially

        self.frame_number_label = tk.Label(master, text="Frame: 0")
        self.frame_number_label.pack()

        self.video = None
        self.video_path = None
        self.paused = False
        self.zoom_scale = tk.IntVar(value=1)
        self.frame_index = 0
        self.bbox = None
        self.tracking_started = False  # Initialize tracking_started to False
        self.prev_frame_gray = None

        self.bbox_rect = None  # Initialize bbox_rect attribute to None
        self.frame_processing = False  # Initialize frame_processing attribute to False

        self.create_widgets()

    def create_widgets(self):
        # Panel for video display
        video_panel = tk.Frame(self.master)
        video_panel.pack(padx=10, pady=10)

        # Canvas to display the original video
        canvas_width = 800
        canvas_height = 500
        self.canvas = tk.Canvas(video_panel, width=canvas_width, height=canvas_height)
        self.canvas.pack(side="left", fill="both", expand=True)
        self.canvas.bind("<MouseWheel>", self.on_mousewheel)
        self.canvas.bind("<ButtonPress-1>", self.on_press)
        self.canvas.bind("<B1-Motion>", self.on_drag)

        # List box to display center coordinates
        self.center_listbox = tk.Listbox(video_panel, width=30, height=20, font=("Helvetica", 14))
        self.center_listbox.pack(side="right", fill="y")
        # Scrollbar for the listbox
        scrollbar = tk.Scrollbar(video_panel, orient="vertical")
        scrollbar.pack(side="left", fill="y")
        scrollbar.config(command=self.center_listbox.yview)

        # Attach scrollbar to listbox
        self.center_listbox.config(yscrollcommand=scrollbar.set)

        # Panel for control buttons
```

```python
        control_panel = tk.Frame(self.master)
        control_panel.pack(padx=10, pady=(0, 10), fill="x")

        # Button to open a video file
        self.open_button = tk.Button(control_panel, text="Open Video", command=self.open_video)
        self.open_button.grid(row=0, column=0, padx=10, pady=5)

        # Combobox for selecting zoom scale
        self.zoom_combobox = ttk.Combobox(control_panel, textvariable=self.zoom_scale, values=list(range(1, 11)))
        self.zoom_combobox.grid(row=0, column=1, padx=10, pady=5)
        self.zoom_combobox.bind("<<ComboboxSelected>>", self.update_zoom)

        # Button to play/pause the video
        self.play_button = tk.Button(control_panel, text="Play/Pause", command=self.toggle_play_pause)
        self.play_button.grid(row=0, column=2, padx=10, pady=5)

        # Button to stop the video
        self.stop_button = tk.Button(control_panel, text="Stop", command=self.stop_video)
        self.stop_button.grid(row=0, column=3, padx=10, pady=5)

        # Button to navigate to the previous frame
        self.prev_frame_button = tk.Button(control_panel, text="Previous Frame", command=self.prev_frame)
        self.prev_frame_button.grid(row=0, column=4, padx=10, pady=5)

        # Button to navigate to the next frame
        self.next_frame_button = tk.Button(control_panel, text="Next Frame", command=self.next_frame)
        self.next_frame_button.grid(row=0, column=5, padx=10, pady=5)

        # Button to clear the listbox
        self.clear_button = tk.Button(control_panel, text="Clear Listbox", command=self.clear_listbox)
        self.clear_button.grid(row=0, column=6, padx=10, pady=5)

    def open_video(self):
        self.video_path = filedialog.askopenfilename(filetypes=[("Video files", "*.mp4;*.avi;*.mkv")])
        if self.video_path:
            self.video = imageio.get_reader(self.video_path)
            self.file_name = self.video_path.split('/')[-1]
            self.set_window_title()
            self.play_video()

    def play_video(self):
        if self.video:
            self.paused = False
            self.tracking_started = True
            self.show_frame()

    def stop_video(self):
        self.paused = True
        self.frame_index = 0
        self.bbox = None
        self.show_frame()

    def toggle_play_pause(self):
        self.paused = not self.paused
        if not self.paused:
            if self.bbox is not None:
                self.tracking_started = True
            self.play_video()
```

```python
    def update_zoom(self, event=None):
        self.show_frame()

    def track_object(self, frame, bbox):
        if bbox:
            x1, y1, x2, y2 = map(int, bbox)
            roi = frame[y1:y2, x1:x2]
            if roi.size > 0:
                # Convert the ROI to grayscale
                roi_gray = cv2.cvtColor(roi, cv2.COLOR_BGR2GRAY)
                # Initialize the previous frame if not already initialized or if its dimensions don't match the current frame
                if self.prev_frame_gray is None or self.prev_frame_gray.shape != roi_gray.shape:
                    self.prev_frame_gray = roi_gray.copy()

                # Calculate optical flow using Lucas-Kanade algorithm
                optical_flow = cv2.calcOpticalFlowFarneback(self.prev_frame_gray, roi_gray, None, 0.5, 3, 15, 3, 5, 1.2, 0)

                # Calculate the mean optical flow within the bounding box
                max_flow = np.max(optical_flow, axis=(0, 1))

                # Update the bounding box coordinates based on the mean optical flow
                x1 += int(max_flow[0])
                y1 += int(max_flow[1])
                x2 += int(max_flow[0])
                y2 += int(max_flow[1])

                # Update the previous frame
                self.prev_frame_gray = roi_gray.copy()

                # Calculate the center of the bounding box
                center_x = (x1 + x2) // 2
                center_y = (y1 + y2) // 2

                # Add the center coordinates to the list box
                self.center_listbox.insert(tk.END, f"(center_x = {center_x}, center_y = {center_y})")

                return x1, y1, x2, y2
        return None

    def update_bbox_rectangle(self, bbox):
        if bbox is not None:
            x1, y1, x2, y2 = map(int, bbox)
            if self.bbox_rect is not None:
                self.canvas.coords(self.bbox_rect, x1, y1, x2, y2)
                self.canvas.tag_raise(self.bbox_rect)  # Raise the bounding box to the front
            else:
                self.bbox_rect = self.canvas.create_rectangle(x1, y1, x2-50, y2-50, outline='#fc3d3d', width=8, tags="bbox")

    def show_frame(self):
        if self.video:
            if not self.paused:
                if 0 <= self.frame_index < len(self.video):
                    if not self.frame_processing:  # Check if the frame is already being processed
                        try:
                            self.frame_processing = True  # Set frame_processing flag to True to indicate frame processing
```

```python
                            frame = self.video.get_data(self.frame_index)
                            frame = cv2.cvtColor(frame, cv2.COLOR_RGB2BGR)

                            if self.bbox is not None:
                                if not self.tracking_started:
                                    self.tracking_started = True

                                self.bbox = self.track_object(frame, self.bbox)
                                if self.bbox:
                                    frame = cv2.cvtColor(frame, cv2.COLOR_BGR2RGB)
                                    frame = Image.fromarray(frame)
                                    frame = frame.resize((frame.width * self.zoom_scale.get(), frame.height * self.zoom_scale.get()))
                                    photo = ImageTk.PhotoImage(frame)
                                    self.photo = photo
                                    self.canvas.delete("video")
                                    self.canvas.create_image(0, 0, anchor="nw", image=photo, tags="video")
                                    self.update_bbox_rectangle(self.bbox)

                            else:
                                frame = cv2.cvtColor(frame, cv2.COLOR_BGR2RGB)
                                frame = Image.fromarray(frame)
                                frame = frame.resize((frame.width * self.zoom_scale.get(), frame.height * self.zoom_scale.get()))
                                photo = ImageTk.PhotoImage(frame)
                                self.photo = photo
                                self.canvas.delete("video")
                                self.canvas.create_image(0, 0, anchor="nw", image=photo, tags="video")

                            self.frame_number_label.config(text=f"Frame: {self.frame_index} / {self.video.count_frames()}", font=("Helvetica", 18))

                            self.frame_index += 1

                    except Exception as e:
                        print("Error: ", e)
                    finally:
                        self.frame_processing = False  # Reset frame_processing flag to False after processing the frame

    def on_mousewheel(self, event):
        direction = event.delta // 120
        current_value = int(self.zoom_scale.get())
        if direction == 1 and current_value < 10:
            current_value += 1
        elif direction == -1 and current_value > 1:
            current_value -= 1
        self.zoom_scale.set(current_value)
        self.update_zoom()

    def on_press(self, self, event):
        self.start_x = self.canvas.canvasx(event.x)
        self.start_y = self.canvas.canvasy(event.y)
        self.bbox = None

    def on_drag(self, event):
        cur_x = self.canvas.canvasx(event.x)
        cur_y = self.canvas.canvasy(event.y)
        if self.bbox_rect:
            self.canvas.delete(self.bbox_rect)
        self.bbox = (self.start_x, self.start_y, cur_x, cur_y)
```

```python
        self.bbox_rect = self.canvas.create_rectangle(*self.bbox, outline='#fc3d3d', width=6)

    def prev_frame(self):
        if self.frame_index > 0:
            self.frame_index -= 1
            self.show_frame()

    def next_frame(self):
        if self.video and self.frame_index < len(self.video) - 1:
            self.show_frame()

    def clear_listbox(self):
        self.center_listbox.delete(0, tk.END)

    def set_window_title(self):
        if self.file_name:
            self.master.title(f"Object Tracking with Lucas Kanade- {self.file_name}")
            self.master.title_font = ("Helvetica", 16, "bold")
        else:
            self.master.title("Object Tracking with Lucas Kanade")

def main():
    root = tk.Tk()
    app = ObjectTrackingLucasKanade(root)
    root.mainloop()

if __name__ == "__main__":
    main()
```

RUNNING PROGRAM

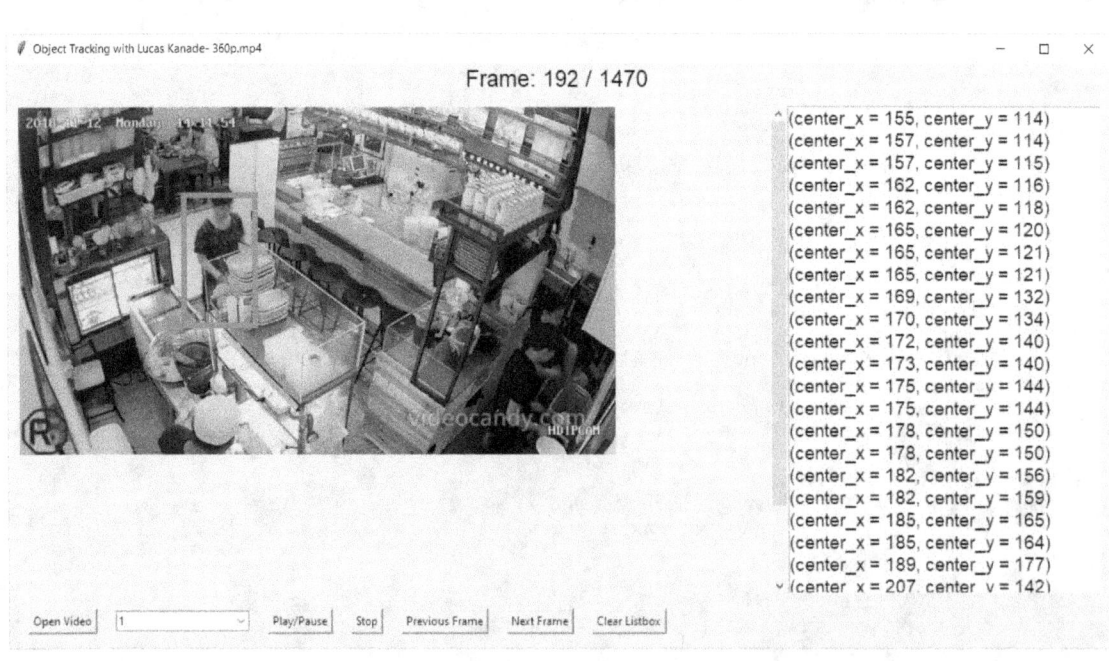

CROPPED FRAME FILTERING

DESCRIPTION

The rgb_cropped_filtered_frame.py project is a Python application built using the Tkinter library for creating a graphical user interface (GUI) to analyze RGB histograms of frames extracted from videos. Let's break down its functionality:

The application consists of a class called Filter_CroppedFrame, which represents the main window of the GUI. This class initializes various GUI elements such as buttons, comboboxes, and canvas for displaying videos.

Upon opening the application, users can select a video file (supported formats include mp4, avi, mkv, wmv) using the "Open Video" button.

Once a video is opened, users can play/pause, stop, and navigate through frames using the control buttons provided.

The GUI allows users to zoom in/out on the displayed video frames using a combobox to select the desired zoom scale.

Users can also draw a bounding box (bbox) on the video frame by clicking and dragging the mouse. The application then analyzes the RGB histogram of the selected region.

Various filters can be applied to the cropped frame, including Gaussian, Mean, Median, Bilateral Filtering, Non-local Means Denoising, Anisotropic Diffusion, Total Variation Denoising, Wiener Filter, Adaptive Thresholding, Haar Wavelet Transform, and Daubechies Wavelet Transform.

After applying a filter, the application displays the filtered image along with its RGB histograms in a popup window.

The RGB histograms are displayed both as line plots and bar graphs, showing the frequency distribution of pixel values for each color channel (Red, Green, Blue).

The matplotlib library is used for plotting histograms, and the resulting plots are converted to images for display in the Tkinter GUI.

Additionally, the application provides functionality to open multiple instances of the GUI simultaneously using the "Open New Instance" button.

The main() function initializes the Tkinter root window and creates an instance of the Filter_CroppedFrame class, starting the GUI application.

Overall, the rgb_cropped_filtered_frame.py project provides a user-friendly interface for analyzing RGB histograms of video frames with the flexibility to apply various filters for image enhancement and denoising.

SOURCE CODE

```python
#rgb_cropped_filtered_frame.py
import tkinter as tk
from tkinter import ttk
from tkinter import filedialog
from PIL import Image, ImageTk
import imageio
import pywt
import cv2
import numpy as np
import matplotlib.pyplot as plt
import os
```

```python
class Filter_CroppedFrame:
    def __init__(self, master):
        self.master = master
        self.master.title("Analyzing RGB Histogram of Frame")
        self.file_name = ""
        self.set_window_title()  # Set window title initially

        self.frame_number_label = tk.Label(master, text="Frame: 0")
        self.frame_number_label.pack()

        self.video = None
        self.video_path = None
        self.paused = False
        self.zoom_scale = tk.IntVar(value=1)
        self.frame_index = 0
        self.bbox = None
        self.bbox_rect = None  # Initialize bbox_rect attribute to None

        # Available filters
        self.filters = ["None", "Gaussian", "Mean", "Median", "Bilateral Filtering",
                        "Non-local Means Denoising", "Anisotropic Diffusion",
                        "Total Variation Denoising", "Wiener Filter",
                        "Adaptive Thresholding", "Haar Wavelet Transform",
                        "Daubechies Wavelet Transform"]

        self.create_widgets()

    def create_widgets(self):
        # Panel for video display
        video_panel = tk.Frame(self.master)
        video_panel.pack(padx=10, pady=10)

        # Canvas to display the original video
        canvas_width = 800
        canvas_height = 500
        self.canvas = tk.Canvas(video_panel, width=canvas_width, height=canvas_height)
        self.canvas.pack(side="left", fill="both", expand=True)
        self.canvas.bind("<MouseWheel>", self.on_mousewheel)
        self.canvas.bind("<ButtonPress-1>", self.on_press)
        self.canvas.bind("<B1-Motion>", self.on_drag)
        self.canvas.bind("<ButtonRelease-1>", self.on_release)  # Bind ButtonRelease event

        # Panel for control buttons
        control_panel = tk.Frame(self.master)
        control_panel.pack(padx=10, pady=(0, 10), fill="x")

        # Button to open a video file
        self.open_button = tk.Button(control_panel, text="Open Video", command=self.open_video)
        self.open_button.grid(row=0, column=0, padx=10, pady=5)

        # Combobox for selecting zoom scale
        self.zoom_combobox = ttk.Combobox(control_panel, textvariable=self.zoom_scale, values=list(range(1, 11)))
        self.zoom_combobox.grid(row=0, column=1, padx=10, pady=5)
        self.zoom_combobox.bind("<<ComboboxSelected>>", self.update_zoom)

        # Button to play/pause the video
        self.play_button = tk.Button(control_panel, text="Play/Pause", command=self.toggle_play_pause)
        self.play_button.grid(row=0, column=2, padx=10, pady=5)

        # Button to stop the video
        self.stop_button = tk.Button(control_panel, text="Stop", command=self.stop_video)
```

```python
        self.stop_button.grid(row=0, column=3, padx=10, pady=5)

        # Button to navigate to the previous frame
        self.prev_frame_button = tk.Button(control_panel, text="Previous Frame", command=self.prev_frame)
        self.prev_frame_button.grid(row=0, column=4, padx=10, pady=5)

        # Button to navigate to the next frame
        self.next_frame_button = tk.Button(control_panel, text="Next Frame", command=self.next_frame)
        self.next_frame_button.grid(row=0, column=5, padx=10, pady=5)

        # Button to open new instance
        self.open_new_instance_button = tk.Button(control_panel, text="Open New Instance", command=self.open_new_instance)
        self.open_new_instance_button.grid(row=0, column=6, padx=10, pady=5)

        # Combobox for selecting filters
        self.filter_combobox = ttk.Combobox(control_panel, values=self.filters)
        self.filter_combobox.grid(row=0, column=7, padx=10, pady=5)
        self.filter_combobox.current(0)  # Set default value

    def open_video(self):
        self.video_path = filedialog.askopenfilename(filetypes=[("Video files", "*.mp4;*.avi;*.mkv;*.wmv")])
        if self.video_path:
            self.video = imageio.get_reader(self.video_path)
            self.file_name = self.video_path.split('/')[-1]
            self.set_window_title()
            self.play_video()  # Auto-play the video when opened
            self.show_frame()  # Show the first frame when the video is opened

    def play_video(self):
        if self.video:
            self.paused = False
            self.show_frame()

    def toggle_play_pause(self):
        if self.video:
            self.paused = not self.paused
            self.play_video()  # Play/pause the video based on the current state

    def stop_video(self):
        self.paused = True
        self.frame_index = 0
        self.bbox = None
        self.show_frame()

    def update_zoom(self, event=None):
        self.show_frame()

    def show_frame(self):
        if self.video:
            if not self.paused:
                if 0 <= self.frame_index < len(self.video):
                    frame = self.video.get_data(self.frame_index)
                    frame = cv2.cvtColor(frame, cv2.COLOR_RGB2BGR)

                    if self.bbox is not None:
                        if self.bbox:
                            frame = cv2.cvtColor(frame, cv2.COLOR_BGR2RGB)
                            frame = Image.fromarray(frame)
                            frame = frame.resize((frame.width * self.zoom_scale.get(), frame.height * self.zoom_scale.get()))
```

```python
                            photo = ImageTk.PhotoImage(frame)
                            self.photo = photo
                            self.canvas.delete("video")
                            self.canvas.create_image(0, 0, anchor="nw", image=photo, tags="video")
                    else:
                        frame = cv2.cvtColor(frame, cv2.COLOR_BGR2RGB)
                        frame = Image.fromarray(frame)
                        frame = frame.resize((frame.width * self.zoom_scale.get(), frame.height * self.zoom_scale.get()))
                        photo = ImageTk.PhotoImage(frame)
                        self.photo = photo
                        self.canvas.delete("video")
                        self.canvas.create_image(0, 0, anchor="nw", image=photo, tags="video")

                    self.frame_number_label.config(text=f"Frame: {self.frame_index} / {self.video.count_frames()}", font=("Helvetica", 18))

                    self.frame_index += 1

    def on_mousewheel(self, event):
        direction = event.delta // 120
        current_value = int(self.zoom_scale.get())
        if direction == 1 and current_value < 10:
            current_value += 1
        elif direction == -1 and current_value > 1:
            current_value -= 1
        self.zoom_scale.set(current_value)
        self.update_zoom()

    def on_press(self, event):
        self.start_x = self.canvas.canvasx(event.x)
        self.start_y = self.canvas.canvasy(event.y)
        self.bbox = None

    def on_drag(self, event):
        cur_x = self.canvas.canvasx(event.x)
        cur_y = self.canvas.canvasy(event.y)
        if self.bbox_rect:
            self.canvas.delete(self.bbox_rect)
        self.bbox = (self.start_x, self.start_y, cur_x, cur_y)
        self.bbox_rect = self.canvas.create_rectangle(*self.bbox, outline='#fc3d3d', width=5)

    def on_release(self, event):
        self.analyze_histogram()  # Call analyze_histogram() method when the mouse button is released

    def prev_frame(self):
        if self.frame_index > 0:
            self.frame_index -= 2
            self.show_frame()

    def next_frame(self):
        if self.video and self.frame_index < len(self.video) - 1:
            self.show_frame()

    def set_window_title(self):
        if self.file_name:
            self.master.title(f"Analyzing RGB Histogram of Frame - {self.file_name}")
            self.master.title_font = ("Helvetica", 16, "bold")
        else:
            self.master.title("Analyzing RGB Histogram of Frame")
```

```python
def analyze_histogram(self):
    if self.bbox is not None:
        x1, y1, x2, y2 = map(int, self.bbox)
        if x1 != x2 and y1 != y2:
            frame = self.video.get_data(self.frame_index)
            cropped_frame = frame[y1:y2, x1:x2]
            cropped_frame = cv2.cvtColor(cropped_frame, cv2.COLOR_BGR2RGB)

            # Get selected filter from combobox
            selected_filter = self.filter_combobox.get()
            # Apply selected filter
            filtered_frame = self.apply_filter(selected_filter, cropped_frame)

            self.create_popup_window(filtered_frame)
            self.display_cropped_image(filtered_frame)
            self.display_histograms(filtered_frame)

def create_popup_window(self, cropped_frame):
    self.popup_window = tk.Toplevel(self.master)
    self.popup_window.title("Cropped Image and Its Histogram")
    self.popup_window.geometry("1500x700")


def display_cropped_image(self, cropped_frame):
    cropped_frame_frame = tk.Frame(self.popup_window)
    cropped_frame_frame.pack(side="left")

    cropped_frame_rgb = cv2.cvtColor(cropped_frame, cv2.COLOR_BGR2RGB)
    cropped_img = Image.fromarray(cropped_frame_rgb)
    cropped_img = cropped_img.resize((600, 600))

    cropped_photo = ImageTk.PhotoImage(cropped_img)
    cropped_canvas = tk.Canvas(cropped_frame_frame, width=600, height=600)
    cropped_canvas.pack(side="left", anchor="nw")
    cropped_canvas.create_image(0, 0, anchor="nw", image=cropped_photo)
    cropped_canvas.image = cropped_photo

def display_histograms(self, cropped_frame):
    histograms_frame = tk.Frame(self.popup_window)
    histograms_frame.pack(side="right", padx=20)

    self.display_line_histogram(cropped_frame, histograms_frame)
    self.display_bar_histogram(cropped_frame, histograms_frame)

def display_line_histogram(self, cropped_frame, histograms_frame):
    line_histogram_frame = tk.Frame(histograms_frame)
    line_histogram_frame.pack(side="top", pady=10)

    plt.figure(figsize=(12, 4))
    color = ('r', 'g', 'b')
    for i, col in enumerate(color):
        histr = cv2.calcHist([cropped_frame], [i], None, [256], [0, 256])
        plt.plot(histr, color=col, label=f'Channel {col.upper()}', linewidth=2)
        plt.xlim([0, 256])
    plt.title('Line Histogram')
    plt.xlabel('Pixel Value')
    plt.ylabel('Frequency')
    plt.tight_layout()
    plt.grid(True)
    plt.legend()

    line_histogram_img = self.plot_to_image(plt)
    self.display_histogram_image(line_histogram_frame, line_histogram_img)
```

```python
    def display_bar_histogram(self, cropped_frame, histograms_frame):
        bar_histogram_frame = tk.Frame(histograms_frame)
        bar_histogram_frame.pack(side="bottom", pady=10)

        plt.figure(figsize=(12, 4))
        color = ('r', 'g', 'b')
        for i, col in enumerate(color):
            hist_range = (0, 256)
            hist_counts, _ = np.histogram(cropped_frame[:, :, i], bins=64, range=hist_range)
            plt.bar(np.arange(64), hist_counts, color=col, alpha=0.7, label=f'Channel {col.upper()}')
            for index, value in enumerate(hist_counts):
                plt.text(index, value + 10, str(int(value)), ha='center', va='bottom', fontsize=9)

        plt.title('Bar Histogram')
        plt.xlabel('Pixel Value')
        plt.ylabel('Frequency')
        plt.xticks(np.linspace(0, 63, num=5), np.linspace(0, 255, num=5, dtype=int))  # Adjust x-axis ticks
        plt.tight_layout()
        plt.grid(True)
        plt.legend()

        bar_histogram_img = self.plot_to_image(plt)
        self.display_histogram_image(bar_histogram_frame, bar_histogram_img)

    def display_histogram_image(self, parent_frame, img):
        histogram_photo = ImageTk.PhotoImage(image=img)
        histogram_canvas = tk.Canvas(parent_frame, width=900, height=300)
        histogram_canvas.pack(side="bottom", anchor="se")
        histogram_canvas.create_image(0, 0, anchor="nw", image=histogram_photo)
        histogram_canvas.image = histogram_photo

    def plot_histogram_bar_to_image(self, image):
        # Calculate histogram for each channel
        histograms = []
        for i in range(3):
            hist_range = (0, 256)
            hist_counts, _ = np.histogram(image[:, :, i], bins=64, range=hist_range)  # Adjust bins to 64
            histograms.append(hist_counts)

        # Extracting only 64 bins from the histogram
        num_bins = 64  # Adjusted to 64 bins

        # Generating colors for each channel
        colors = ['red', 'green', 'blue']

        plt.figure()
        for i, histogram in enumerate(histograms):
            # Normalize the histogram counts for better visualization
            hist_counts = histogram / np.sum(histogram)
            # Setting the color for each channel
            plt.bar(np.arange(num_bins), hist_counts[:num_bins], color=colors[i], alpha=0.7, label=f'Channel {["Red", "Green", "Blue"][i]}')

        plt.xlabel('Pixel Value')
        plt.ylabel('Normalized Frequency')
        plt.title('RGB Channel Histograms')
        plt.grid(True)
        plt.tight_layout()
        plt.legend()
```

```python
        # Convert the histogram bar graph to an image
        histogram_bar_img = self.plot_to_image(plt)
        histogram_bar_photo = ImageTk.PhotoImage(image=histogram_bar_img)

        return histogram_bar_photo

    def plot_to_image(self, plt):
        plt.savefig('temp_plot.png')
        img = Image.open('temp_plot.png')
        return img

    def apply_filter(self, filter_name, frame):
        if filter_name == "None":
            return frame
        elif filter_name == "Gaussian":
            return cv2.GaussianBlur(frame, (5, 5), 0)
        elif filter_name == "Mean":
            return cv2.blur(frame, (5, 5))
        elif filter_name == "Median":
            return cv2.medianBlur(frame, 5)
        elif filter_name == "Bilateral Filtering":
            return cv2.bilateralFilter(frame, 9, 75, 75)
        elif filter_name == "Non-local Means Denoising":
            return cv2.fastNlMeansDenoisingColored(frame, None, 10, 10, 7, 21)
        elif filter_name == "Anisotropic Diffusion":
            return self.anisotropic_diffusion(frame)
        elif filter_name == "Total Variation Denoising":
            return self.total_variation_denoising(frame)
        elif filter_name == "Wiener Filter":
            return self.wiener_filter(frame)
        elif filter_name == "Adaptive Thresholding":
            return self.adaptive_threshold_each_channel(frame)
        elif filter_name == "Haar Wavelet Transform":
            return self.haar_wavelet_transform(frame)
        elif filter_name == "Daubechies Wavelet Transform":
            return self.daubechies_wavelet_transform(frame)
        else:
            return frame  # Default: return original frame if filter not found

    def wiener_filter(self, frame, kernel_size=(5, 5), noise_var=0.01):
        # Check if frame is None
        if frame is None:
            print("Error: Input frame is None.")
            return None

        # Check if frame is a valid numpy array
        if not isinstance(frame, np.ndarray):
            print("Error: Input frame is not a numpy array.")
            return None

        # Check if frame is an empty array
        if frame.size == 0:
            print("Error: Input frame is empty.")
            return None

        # Check if frame is in BGR color space
        if frame.shape[-1] != 3:
            print("Error: Input frame is not in BGR color space.")
            return None

        # Apply Wiener filter
        filtered_frame = cv2.medianBlur(frame, kernel_size[0])  # Use kernel_size[0] as the kernel size
        filtered_frame = cv2.fastNlMeansDenoising(filtered_frame, h=noise_var)
```

```python
        return filtered_frame

    def adaptive_threshold_each_channel(self, frame):
        # Split the frame into individual channels
        b, g, r = cv2.split(frame)

        # Apply adaptive thresholding to each channel separately
        b_thresh = cv2.adaptiveThreshold(b, 255, cv2.ADAPTIVE_THRESH_GAUSSIAN_C, cv2.THRESH_BINARY, 11, 2)
        g_thresh = cv2.adaptiveThreshold(g, 255, cv2.ADAPTIVE_THRESH_GAUSSIAN_C, cv2.THRESH_BINARY, 11, 2)
        r_thresh = cv2.adaptiveThreshold(r, 255, cv2.ADAPTIVE_THRESH_GAUSSIAN_C, cv2.THRESH_BINARY, 11, 2)

        # Merge the thresholded channels back together
        return cv2.merge([b_thresh, g_thresh, r_thresh])

    def haar_wavelet_transform(self, frame):
        # Split the frame into its individual color channels
        b, g, r = cv2.split(frame)

        # Perform the wavelet transform on each channel separately
        b_coeffs = pywt.dwt2(b, 'haar')
        g_coeffs = pywt.dwt2(g, 'haar')
        r_coeffs = pywt.dwt2(r, 'haar')

        # Reconstruct the channels from the coefficients
        b_reconstructed = pywt.idwt2(b_coeffs, 'haar')
        g_reconstructed = pywt.idwt2(g_coeffs, 'haar')
        r_reconstructed = pywt.idwt2(r_coeffs, 'haar')

        # Clip the values to ensure they are within the valid range
        b_reconstructed = np.clip(b_reconstructed, 0, 255).astype(np.uint8)
        g_reconstructed = np.clip(g_reconstructed, 0, 255).astype(np.uint8)
        r_reconstructed = np.clip(r_reconstructed, 0, 255).astype(np.uint8)

        # Merge the channels back together
        return cv2.merge([b_reconstructed, g_reconstructed, r_reconstructed])

    def daubechies_wavelet_transform(self, frame):
        # Split the frame into its individual color channels
        b, g, r = cv2.split(frame)

        # Choose the wavelet function (Daubechies 5)
        wavelet = 'db5'

        # Perform the wavelet transform on each channel separately
        b_coeffs = pywt.dwt2(b, wavelet)
        g_coeffs = pywt.dwt2(g, wavelet)
        r_coeffs = pywt.dwt2(r, wavelet)

        # Reconstruct the channels from the coefficients
        b_reconstructed = pywt.idwt2(b_coeffs, wavelet)
        g_reconstructed = pywt.idwt2(g_coeffs, wavelet)
        r_reconstructed = pywt.idwt2(r_coeffs, wavelet)

        # Clip the values to ensure they are within the valid range
        b_reconstructed = np.clip(b_reconstructed, 0, 255).astype(np.uint8)
        g_reconstructed = np.clip(g_reconstructed, 0, 255).astype(np.uint8)
        r_reconstructed = np.clip(r_reconstructed, 0, 255).astype(np.uint8)

        # Merge the channels back together
        return cv2.merge([b_reconstructed, g_reconstructed, r_reconstructed])
```

```python
    def anisotropic_diffusion(self, img):
        return cv2.fastNlMeansDenoisingColored(img, None, 10, 10, 7, 21)

    def apply_total_variation_denoising_channel(self, channel, weight, iterations):
        # Initialize the result with the original channel
        result = channel.copy().astype(np.float64)  # Convert to float64

        # Perform total variation denoising
        for _ in range(iterations):
            # Compute the gradient of the channel
            dx = cv2.Sobel(result, cv2.CV_64F, 1, 0, ksize=3)
            dy = cv2.Sobel(result, cv2.CV_64F, 0, 1, ksize=3)

            # Update the channel using the gradient and the weight
            result -= weight * np.sqrt(dx**2 + dy**2)

        # Clip the values to ensure they are within the valid range
        result = np.clip(result, 0, 255).astype(np.uint8)

        return result

    def total_variation_denoising(self, img, weight=0.01, iterations=20):
        # Split the image into its individual color channels
        b, g, r = cv2.split(img)

        # Apply total variation denoising to each channel separately
        b_denoised = self.apply_total_variation_denoising_channel(b, weight, iterations)
        g_denoised = self.apply_total_variation_denoising_channel(g, weight, iterations)
        r_denoised = self.apply_total_variation_denoising_channel(r, weight, iterations)

        # Merge the denoised channels back together
        return cv2.merge([b_denoised, g_denoised, r_denoised])

    def open_new_instance(self):
        # Open another instance of the application
        root = tk.Toplevel(self.master)
        app = Filter_CroppedFrame(root)

def main():
    root = tk.Tk()
    app = Filter_CroppedFrame(root)
    root.mainloop()

if __name__ == "__main__":
    main()
```

RUNNING PROGRAM

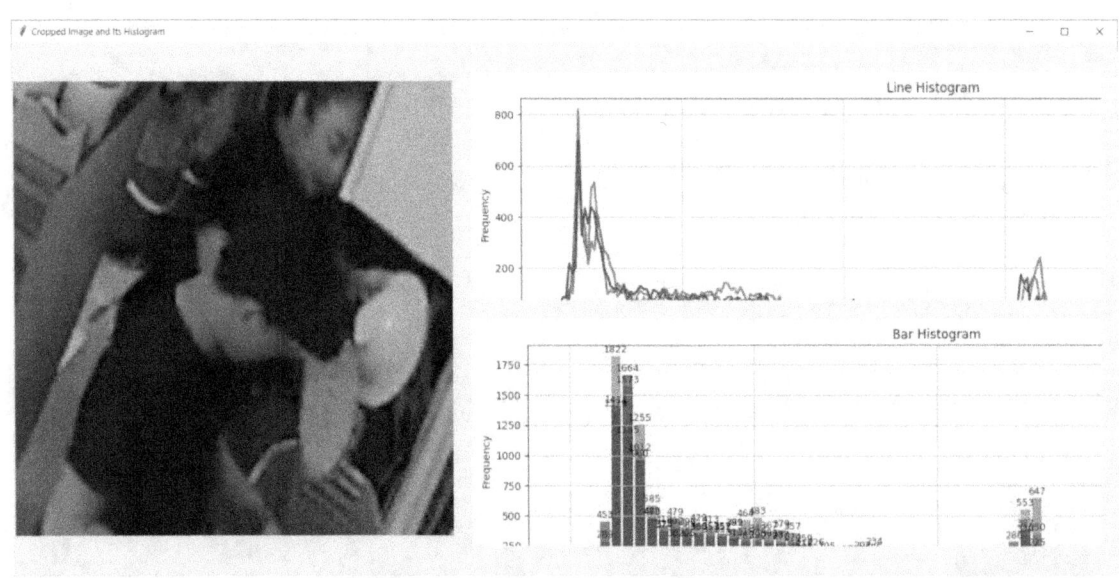

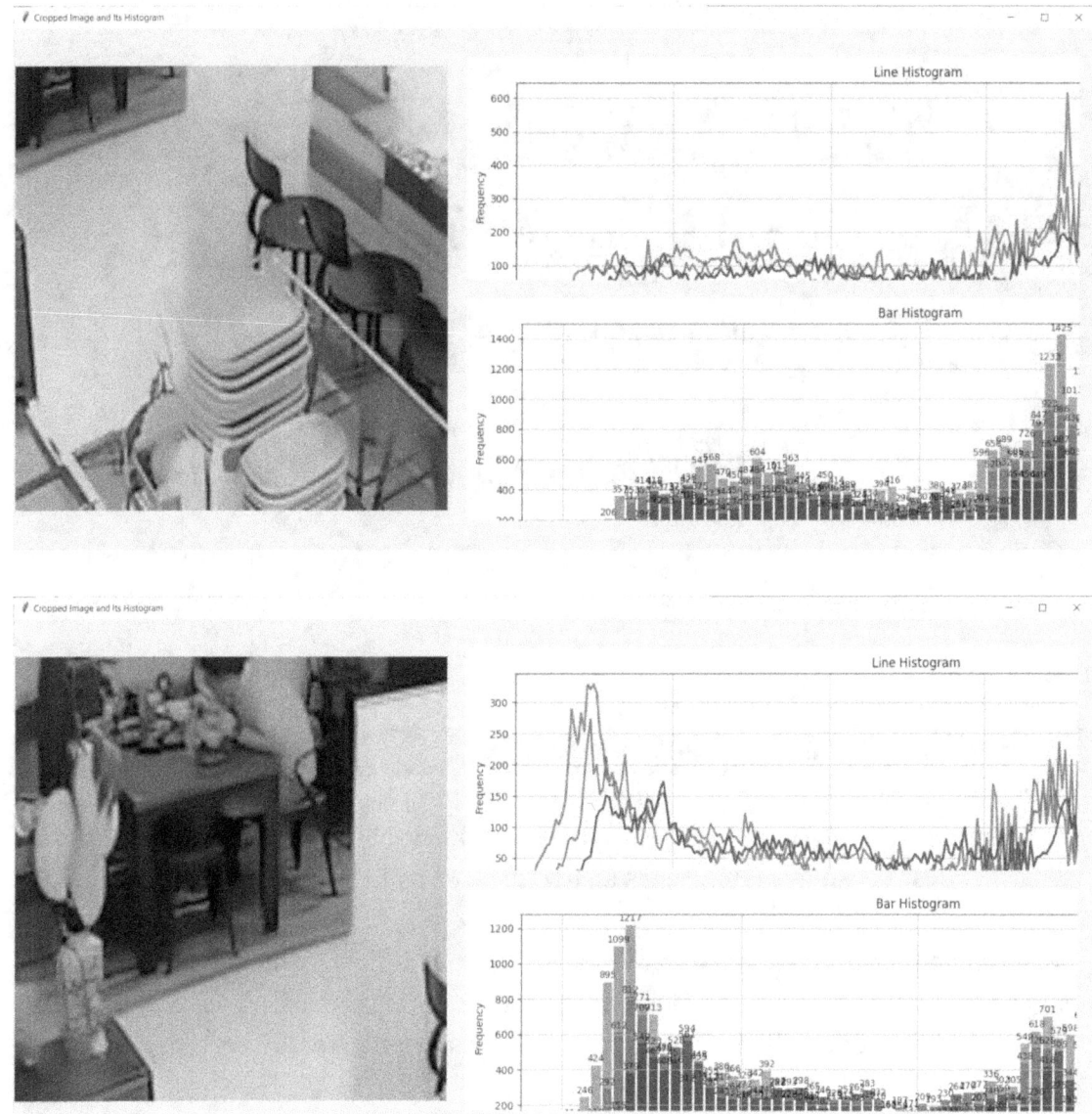

MOTION ANALYSIS WITH BLOCK-BASED GRADIENT DESCENT SEARCH (BGDS)

DESCRIPTION

The Python script gui_motion_analysis_bgds.py is a project designed to create a graphical user interface (GUI) for motion analysis using the Block-based Gradient Descent Search (BGDS) optical flow algorithm. Here's an overview of its functionality:

The script initializes a class called VideoBGDSOpticalFlow, which acts as the main application window for the GUI. Upon initialization, various attributes such as file name, video variables, zoom scale, frame index, and canvas coordinates are set.

The create_widgets method sets up the GUI layout, including frames for video display, control buttons, and parameter input fields. Control buttons such as open, play/pause, stop, jump to time, previous frame, next frame, and open another player are created and linked to corresponding methods for functionality.

Parameter input fields are provided for specifying step, dx (same as dy), block size, iteration limit, learning rate, and convergence threshold.

Methods like open_video, play_video, and toggle_play_pause facilitate video file selection, playback, and control toggling. The update_zoom method adjusts the zoom level of displayed video frames.

For each frame, the show_frame method displays it on the canvas and updates the frame number label. The block_based_gradient_descent_search method implements the BGDS algorithm to calculate optical flow motion vectors between consecutive frames.

The show_optical_flow method visualizes the calculated optical flow vectors on the canvas using line segments and circles. Event handlers are defined for mouse wheel scrolling and canvas dragging for both the original video display and optical flow visualization.

Navigation methods like jump_to_time, prev_frame, and next_frame allow users to navigate through video frames. The set_window_title method updates the window title with the current video file name.

The open_another_player method opens another instance of the application in a new window. Finally, the main function creates an instance of the VideoBGDSOpticalFlow class and starts the Tkinter event loop.

Overall, the GUI provides an intuitive interface for motion analysis tasks, allowing users to interact with video playback controls and optical flow analysis tools efficiently.

SOURCE CODE

```python
#gui_motion_analysis_bgds.py
import tkinter as tk
from tkinter import ttk
from tkinter import filedialog
from PIL import Image, ImageTk
import imageio
import cv2
import numpy as np
import math

class VideoBGDSOpticalFlow:
    def __init__(self, master):
        self.master = master
        self.master.title("Motion Analysis with Block-based Gradient Descent Search (BGDS)")
        self.file_name = ""
        self.set_window_title()  # Set window title initially
```

```python
        # Frame number label
        self.frame_number_label = tk.Label(master, text="Frame: 0")
        self.frame_number_label.pack()

        self.video = None
        self.video_path = None
        self.paused = False
        self.zoom_scale = tk.IntVar(value=1)
        self.frame_index = 0
        self.start_x1 = None
        self.start_y1 = None
        self.current_x1 = 0
        self.current_y1 = 0
        self.start_x2 = None
        self.start_y2 = None
        self.current_x2 = 0
        self.current_y2 = 0

        self.prev_frame_gray = None  # Initialize prev_frame_gray variable
        self.create_widgets()

    def create_widgets(self):
        # Panel for video display
        video_panel = tk.Frame(self.master)
        video_panel.pack(padx=10, pady=10)

        # Canvas to display the original video
        canvas_width = 800
        canvas_height = 500
        self.canvas = tk.Canvas(video_panel, width=canvas_width, height=canvas_height)
        self.canvas.pack(side="left", fill="both", expand=True)
        self.canvas.bind("<MouseWheel>", self.on_mousewheel)
        self.canvas.bind("<ButtonPress-1>", self.on_press1)
        self.canvas.bind("<B1-Motion>", self.on_drag1)

        # Canvas to display the optical flow result
        self.flow_canvas = tk.Canvas(video_panel, width=canvas_width, height=canvas_height)
        self.flow_canvas.pack(side="right", fill="both", expand=True)
        self.flow_canvas.bind("<MouseWheel>", self.on_mousewheel)
        self.flow_canvas.bind("<ButtonPress-1>", self.on_press2)
        self.flow_canvas.bind("<B1-Motion>", self.on_drag2)

        # Panel for control buttons
        control_panel = tk.Frame(self.master)
        control_panel.pack(padx=10, pady=(0, 10), fill="x")

        # Button to open a video file
        self.open_button = tk.Button(control_panel, text="Open Video", command=self.open_video)
        self.open_button.grid(row=0, column=0, padx=10, pady=5)

        # Combobox for selecting zoom scale
        self.zoom_combobox = ttk.Combobox(control_panel, textvariable=self.zoom_scale, values=list(range(1, 11)))
        self.zoom_combobox.grid(row=0, column=1, padx=10, pady=5)
        self.zoom_combobox.bind("<<ComboboxSelected>>", self.update_zoom)

        # Label and entry for specifying step
        self.step_label = tk.Label(control_panel, text="Step:")
        self.step_label.grid(row=0, column=2, padx=10, pady=5, sticky="e")
        self.step_default = tk.StringVar(value="20")
        self.step_entry = ttk.Entry(control_panel, textvariable=self.step_default)
        self.step_entry.grid(row=0, column=3, padx=10, pady=5, sticky="w")
        self.step_entry.bind("<Return>", lambda event: self.toggle_play_pause())
```

```python
        # Label and entry for specifying dx (same as dy)
        self.dx_label = tk.Label(control_panel, text="dx (same as dy):")
        self.dx_label.grid(row=0, column=4, padx=10, pady=5, sticky="e")
        self.dx_default = tk.StringVar(value="10")
        self.dx_entry = ttk.Entry(control_panel, textvariable=self.dx_default)
        self.dx_entry.grid(row=0, column=5, padx=10, pady=5, sticky="w")
        self.dx_entry.bind("<Return>", lambda event: self.toggle_play_pause())

        # Label and entry for specifying block size
        self.block_size_label = tk.Label(control_panel, text="Block Size:")
        self.block_size_label.grid(row=0, column=6, padx=10, pady=5, sticky="e")
        self.block_size_default = tk.StringVar(value="16")
        self.block_size_entry = ttk.Entry(control_panel, textvariable=self.block_size_default)
        self.block_size_entry.grid(row=0, column=7, padx=10, pady=5, sticky="w")
        self.block_size_entry.bind("<Return>", lambda event: self.toggle_play_pause())

        # Button to jump to specified time
        self.jump_button = tk.Button(control_panel, text="Jump to Time", command=self.jump_to_time)
        self.jump_button.grid(row=0, column=10, padx=10, pady=5)

        # Button to play/pause the video
        self.play_button = tk.Button(control_panel, text="Play/Pause", command=self.toggle_play_pause)
        self.play_button.grid(row=0, column=11, padx=10, pady=5)

        # Button to stop the video
        self.stop_button = tk.Button(control_panel, text="Stop", command=self.stop_video)
        self.stop_button.grid(row=0, column=12, padx=10, pady=5)

        # Button to navigate to the previous frame
        self.prev_frame_button = tk.Button(control_panel, text="Previous Frame", command=self.prev_frame)
        self.prev_frame_button.grid(row=2, column=1, padx=10, pady=5)

        # Button to navigate to the next frame
        self.next_frame_button = tk.Button(control_panel, text="Next Frame", command=self.next_frame)
        self.next_frame_button.grid(row=2, column=2, padx=10, pady=5)

        # Button to open another instance of the application
        self.open_another_button = tk.Button(control_panel, text="Open Another Video Player", command=self.open_another_player)
        self.open_another_button.grid(row=2, column=9, columnspan=15, padx=10, pady=5)

        # Add labels and textboxes for parameters in the create_widgets method
        self.iteration_limit_label = tk.Label(control_panel, text="Iteration Limit:")
        self.iteration_limit_label.grid(row=2, column=3, padx=10, pady=5, sticky="e")
        self.iteration_limit_default = tk.StringVar(value="50")  # Default value
        self.iteration_limit_entry = ttk.Entry(control_panel, textvariable=self.iteration_limit_default)
        self.iteration_limit_entry.grid(row=2, column=4, padx=10, pady=5, sticky="w")

        self.learning_rate_label = tk.Label(control_panel, text="Learning Rate:")
        self.learning_rate_label.grid(row=2, column=5, padx=10, pady=5, sticky="e")
        self.learning_rate_default = tk.StringVar(value="0.01")  # Default value
        self.learning_rate_entry = ttk.Entry(control_panel, textvariable=self.learning_rate_default)
        self.learning_rate_entry.grid(row=2, column=6, padx=10, pady=5, sticky="w")

        self.convergence_threshold_label = tk.Label(control_panel, text="Convergence Threshold:")
        self.convergence_threshold_label.grid(row=2, column=7, padx=10, pady=5, sticky="e")
        self.convergence_threshold_default = tk.StringVar(value="0.01")  # Default value
```

```python
        self.convergence_threshold_entry = ttk.Entry(control_panel, 
textvariable=self.convergence_threshold_default)
        self.convergence_threshold_entry.grid(row=2, column=8, padx=10, pady=5, sticky="w")

    def open_video(self):
        self.video_path = filedialog.askopenfilename(filetypes=[("Video files", 
"*.mp4;*.avi;*.mkv")])
        if self.video_path:
            self.video = imageio.get_reader(self.video_path)
            self.file_name = self.video_path.split('/')[-1]  # Extract file name
            self.set_window_title()  # Update window title with file name
            self.play_video()

    def play_video(self):
        if self.video:
            self.paused = False
            self.show_frame()
            self.show_optical_flow()

    def stop_video(self):
        self.paused = True
        self.frame_index = 0
        self.current_x1 = 0
        self.current_y1 = 0  # Reset the current position
        self.show_frame()
        self.show_optical_flow()

    def toggle_play_pause(self):
        self.paused = not self.paused
        if not self.paused:
            self.play_video()

    def update_zoom(self, event=None):
        self.show_frame()
        self.show_optical_flow()

    def show_frame(self):
        if self.video:
            if not self.paused:
                if 0 <= self.frame_index < len(self.video):  # Check if frame index is within 
range
                    try:
                        frame = self.video.get_data(self.frame_index)
                        frame_gray = cv2.cvtColor(frame, cv2.COLOR_RGB2GRAY)  # Convert to 
grayscale

                        # Initialize prev_frame_gray on first frame
                        if self.prev_frame_gray is None:
                            self.prev_frame_gray = frame_gray.copy()

                        # Display current frame
                        frame = Image.fromarray(frame)
                        frame = frame.resize((frame.width * self.zoom_scale.get(), frame.height 
* self.zoom_scale.get()))
                        photo = ImageTk.PhotoImage(frame)
                        self.photo = photo  # Save object reference to PhotoImage globally
                        self.canvas.delete("video")  # Delete previous image
                        self.canvas.create_image(self.current_x1, self.current_y1, anchor="nw", 
image=photo, tags="video")

                        # Update prev_frame_gray
                        self.prev_frame_gray = frame_gray.copy()

                        # Update frame number label
```

```python
                        self.frame_number_label.config(text=f"Frame: {self.frame_index} / {self.video.count_frames()}", font=("Helvetica", 18))
                        
                        self.frame_index += 1  # Move to the next frame
                    
                    except Exception as e:
                        print("Error: ", e)
    
    def block_based_gradient_descent_search(self, prev_frame_gray, frame_gray):
        iteration_limit = int(self.iteration_limit_entry.get())  # Get iteration limit from entry
        learning_rate = float(self.learning_rate_entry.get())  # Get learning rate from entry
        convergence_threshold = float(self.convergence_threshold_entry.get())  # Get convergence threshold from entry
        step = int(self.step_entry.get())  # Get iteration limit from entry
        
        # BGDS implementation
        block_size = int(self.block_size_entry.get())  # Get block size from entry
        rows, cols = frame_gray.shape[0] // step, frame_gray.shape[1] // step
        motion_vectors = np.zeros((rows, cols, 2))
        
        # Iterate through image blocks
        for i in range(rows):
            for j in range(cols):
                y = i * step  # Calculate starting y-coordinate of the block
                x = j * step  # Calculate starting x-coordinate of the block
                # Initial motion vector guess
                motion_vector = [0, 0]
                prev_block = prev_frame_gray[y:y + block_size, x:x + block_size]
                
                # Check if the current block is too close to the edges to compute the gradient
                if y + block_size >= frame_gray.shape[0] or x + block_size >= frame_gray.shape[1]:
                    continue
                
                # Gradient descent iterations
                for _ in range(iteration_limit):
                    # Compute error between current block and previous block
                    current_block = frame_gray[y:y + block_size, x:x + block_size]
                    error = np.sum((prev_block - current_block) ** 2)
                    
                    # Compute gradient if the block size is large enough
                    if current_block.shape[0] > 1 and current_block.shape[1] > 1:
                        gradient = np.gradient(current_block)
                        # Update motion vector using gradient descent
                        motion_vector[0] -= learning_rate * gradient[0].mean()
                        motion_vector[1] -= learning_rate * gradient[1].mean()
                    
                    # Check convergence
                    if error < convergence_threshold:
                        break
                
                # Store motion vector
                motion_vectors[i, j] = motion_vector
        
        return motion_vectors
    
    def show_optical_flow(self):
        if self.video:
            if not self.paused:
                if 0 <= self.frame_index < len(self.video):  # Check if frame index is within range
                    try:
                        frame = self.video.get_data(self.frame_index)
```

```python
                    frame_gray = cv2.cvtColor(frame, cv2.COLOR_RGB2GRAY)  # Convert to grayscale

                    # Calculate optical flow using Block-based Gradient Descent Search (BGDS)
                    motion_vectors = self.block_based_gradient_descent_search(self.prev_frame_gray, frame_gray)

                    # Create an empty mask image for visualization
                    mask = np.zeros_like(frame)

                    # Compute flow visualization
                    step = int(self.step_entry.get())
                    for i in range(0, frame.shape[0], step):
                        for j in range(0, frame.shape[1], step):
                            # Ensure the motion vectors index does not exceed the bounds
                            if i // step < motion_vectors.shape[0] and j // step < motion_vectors.shape[1]:
                                dx, dy = motion_vectors[i // step, j // step]  # Unpack motion vectors tuple

                                # Scale the optical flow vectors based on the zoom scale
                                dx *= int(self.dx_entry.get())
                                dy *= int(self.dx_entry.get())
                                # Convert coordinates to integers
                                x1, y1 = int(j), int(i)
                                x2, y2 = int(j + dx), int(i + dy)
                                # Draw the line and circle
                                cv2.line(mask, (x1, y1), (x2, y2), (255, 255, 255), 1)
                                cv2.circle(mask, (x2, y2), 1, (0, 255, 0), -1)

                    # Convert mask to PIL format and display on canvas
                    mask = Image.fromarray(mask)
                    mask = ImageTk.PhotoImage(mask)
                    self.mask = mask
                    self.flow_canvas.delete("mask")  # Delete previous optical flow
                    self.flow_canvas.create_image(self.current_x2, self.current_y2, anchor="nw", image=mask, tags="mask")

                    # Update previous frame
                    self.prev_frame_gray = frame_gray.copy()

        except Exception as e:
            print("Error in show_optical_flow:", e)  # Print error message

    def on_mousewheel(self, event):
        direction = event.delta // 120
        current_value = int(self.zoom_scale.get())
        if direction == 1 and current_value < 10:
            current_value += 1
        elif direction == -1 and current_value > 1:
            current_value -= 1
        self.zoom_scale.set(current_value)
        self.update_zoom()

    def on_press1(self, self, event):
        self.start_x1 = event.x
        self.start_y1 = event.y

    def on_drag1(self, event):
        if self.start_x1 and self.start_y1:
            self.x_offset1 = event.x - self.start_x1
            self.y_offset1 = event.y - self.start_y1
            self.current_x1 += self.x_offset1  # Update current position
            self.current_y1 += self.y_offset1  # Update current position
```

```python
            self.canvas.move("video", self.x_offset1, self.y_offset1)
            self.start_x1 = event.x
            self.start_y1 = event.y

    def on_press2(self, event):
        self.start_x2 = event.x
        self.start_y2 = event.y

    def on_drag2(self, event):
        if self.start_x2 and self.start_y2:
            self.x_offset2 = event.x - self.start_x2
            self.y_offset2 = event.y - self.start_y2
            self.current_x2 += self.x_offset2  # Update current position
            self.current_y2 += self.y_offset2  # Update current position
            self.flow_canvas.move("mask", self.x_offset2, self.y_offset2)  # Move optical flow canvas along with original canvas
            self.start_x2 = event.x
            self.start_y2 = event.y

    def jump_to_time(self):
        time_str = self.time_entry.get()
        try:
            time_seconds = float(time_str)
            if 0 <= time_seconds:
                self.frame_index = int(time_seconds * self.video.get_meta_data()['fps'])
                self.show_frame()
                self.show_optical_flow()  # Jump to specified time for optical flow
        except ValueError:
            pass

    def prev_frame(self):
        if self.frame_index > 0:
            self.frame_index -= 1
            self.show_frame()
            self.show_optical_flow()
            print(self.frame_index)

    def next_frame(self):
        if self.video and self.frame_index < len(self.video) - 1:
            self.show_frame()
            self.show_optical_flow()
            print(self.frame_index)

    def set_window_title(self):
        if self.file_name:
            self.master.title(f"Block-based Gradient Descent Search (BGDS) Optical Flow - {self.file_name}")
            self.master.title_font = ("Helvetica", 16, "bold")
        else:
            self.master.title("Block-based Gradient Descent Search (BGDS) Optical Flow")

    def open_another_player(self):
        # Open another instance of the application
        root = tk.Toplevel(self.master)
        app = VideoBGDSOpticalFlow(root)

def main():
    root = tk.Tk()
    app = VideoBGDSOpticalFlow(root)
    root.mainloop()

if __name__ == "__main__":
    main()
```

RUNNING PROGRAM

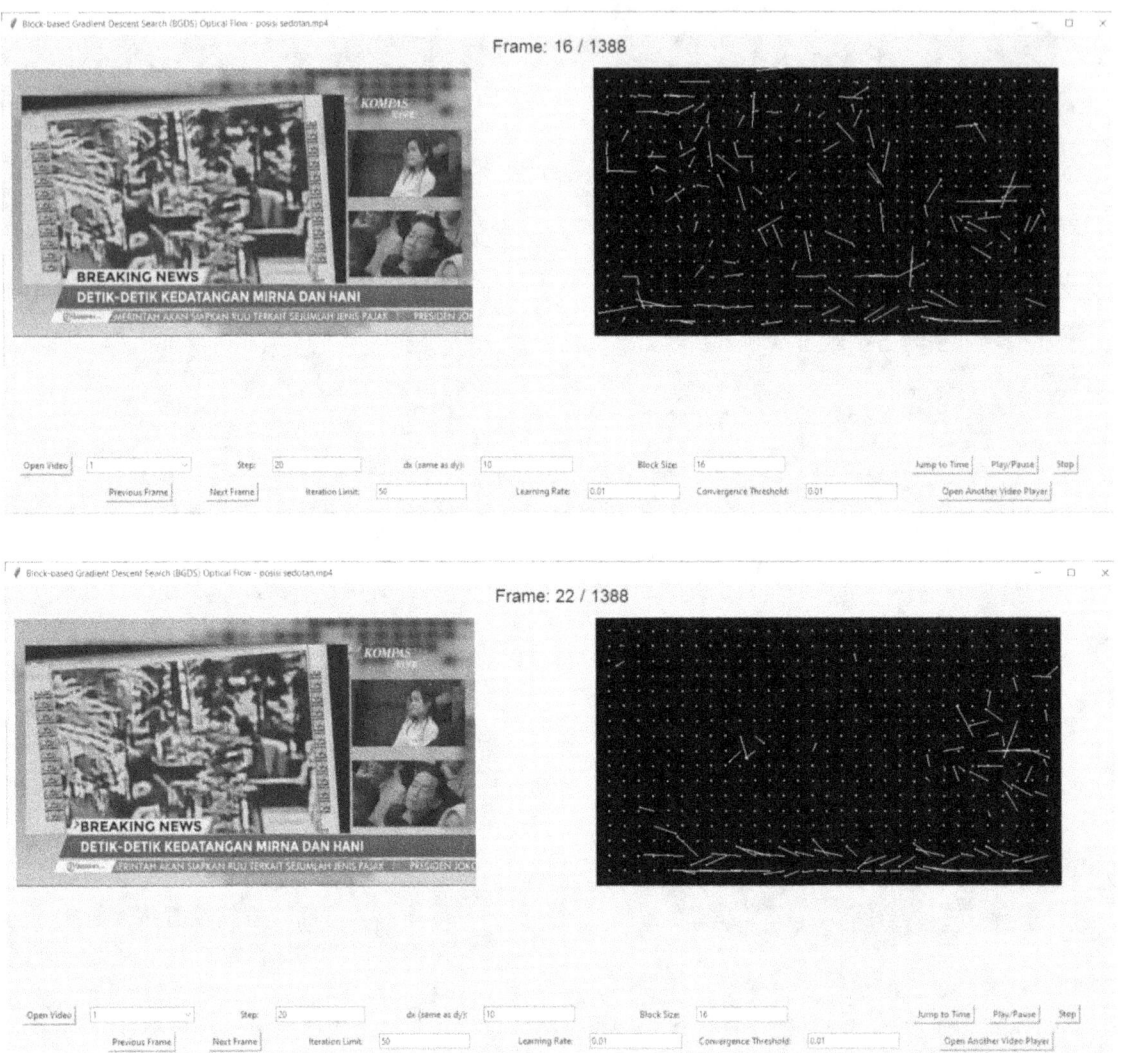

MOTION ANALYSIS WITH DIAMOND SEARCH ALGORITHM (DSA)

DESCRIPTION

The gui_motion_analysis_fsbm_dsa.py script is a Python project aimed at providing a graphical user interface (GUI) for optical flow analysis using the Diamond Search Algorithm (DSA). Here's a breakdown of its functionality:

The script begins by importing necessary libraries, including Tkinter for GUI development, Pillow for image processing, imageio for reading video files, OpenCV for computer vision tasks, NumPy for numerical operations, and math for mathematical calculations.

A class named VideoFSBM_DSAOpticalFlow is defined, representing the main application window for the GUI. The constructor initializes various attributes such as the window title, file name, video variables, zoom scale, frame index, and canvas coordinates.

The create_widgets method sets up the GUI layout, including frames for video display, control buttons, and parameter input fields. The layout includes separate canvas widgets for displaying the original video and optical flow result.

Control buttons for opening a video file, selecting zoom scale, specifying algorithm parameters, jumping to a specific time, playing/pausing the video, stopping the video, navigating between frames, and opening another instance of the application are created and placed within the control panel frame.

Methods such as open_video, play_video, stop_video, and toggle_play_pause handle video file selection, playback, pausing, and stopping functionalities, respectively. These methods interact with the video player and update the displayed frames accordingly.

The update_zoom method adjusts the zoom level of displayed video frames based on user input. It interacts with the canvas widgets to update the zoomed-in/out frames.

The show_frame method displays video frames on the canvas, updates the frame number label, and implements grayscale conversion for processing.

The full_search_block_matching_dsa method implements the full search block matching algorithm with DSA to calculate optical flow motion vectors between consecutive frames.

The show_optical_flow method visualizes the calculated optical flow vectors on the canvas using line segments and circles. It computes and displays flow visualization based on motion vectors obtained from the DSA algorithm.

Event handlers are defined for mouse wheel scrolling and canvas dragging to facilitate user interaction with the displayed video frames and optical flow visualization.

Additional methods such as jump_to_time, prev_frame, next_frame, and set_window_title handle functionalities like jumping to a specific time, navigating between frames, and updating the window title.

Finally, the open_another_player method allows users to open another instance of the application in a new window, providing flexibility in analyzing multiple videos simultaneously.

The main function initializes the Tkinter root window and creates an instance of the VideoFSBM_DSAOpticalFlow class, starting the GUI application loop.

Overall, the GUI offers an intuitive interface for optical flow analysis tasks, allowing users to interact with video playback controls and visualize motion vectors efficiently.

SOURCE CODE

```python
#gui_motion_analysis_fsbm_dsa.py
import tkinter as tk
from tkinter import ttk
from tkinter import filedialog
from PIL import Image, ImageTk
import imageio
import cv2
import numpy as np
import math

class VideoFSBM_DSAOpticalFlow:
    def __init__(self, master):
        self.master = master
        self.master.title("Optical Flow Analysis with Diamond Search Algorithm (DSA)")
        self.file_name = ""
        self.set_window_title()  # Set window title initially

        # Frame number label
        self.frame_number_label = tk.Label(master, text="Frame: 0")
        self.frame_number_label.pack()

        self.video = None
        self.video_path = None
        self.paused = False
        self.zoom_scale = tk.IntVar(value=1)
        self.frame_index = 0
        self.start_x1 = None
        self.start_y1 = None
        self.current_x1 = 0
        self.current_y1 = 0
        self.start_x2 = None
        self.start_y2 = None
        self.current_x2 = 0
        self.current_y2 = 0

        self.prev_frame_gray = None  # Initialize prev_frame_gray variable
        self.create_widgets()

    def create_widgets(self):
        # Panel for video display
        video_panel = tk.Frame(self.master)
        video_panel.pack(padx=10, pady=10)

        # Canvas to display the original video
        canvas_width = 800
        canvas_height = 500
        self.canvas = tk.Canvas(video_panel, width=canvas_width, height=canvas_height)
        self.canvas.pack(side="left", fill="both", expand=True)
        self.canvas.bind("<MouseWheel>", self.on_mousewheel)
        self.canvas.bind("<ButtonPress-1>", self.on_press1)
        self.canvas.bind("<B1-Motion>", self.on_drag1)

        # Canvas to display the optical flow result
```

```python
        self.flow_canvas = tk.Canvas(video_panel, width=canvas_width, height=canvas_height)
        self.flow_canvas.pack(side="right", fill="both", expand=True)
        self.flow_canvas.bind("<MouseWheel>", self.on_mousewheel)
        self.flow_canvas.bind("<ButtonPress-1>", self.on_press2)
        self.flow_canvas.bind("<B1-Motion>", self.on_drag2)

        # Panel for control buttons
        control_panel = tk.Frame(self.master)
        control_panel.pack(padx=10, pady=(0, 10), fill="x")

        # Button to open a video file
        self.open_button = tk.Button(control_panel, text="Open Video", command=self.open_video)
        self.open_button.grid(row=0, column=0, padx=10, pady=5)

        # Combobox for selecting zoom scale
        self.zoom_combobox = ttk.Combobox(control_panel, textvariable=self.zoom_scale,
values=list(range(1, 11)))
        self.zoom_combobox.grid(row=0, column=1, padx=10, pady=5)
        self.zoom_combobox.bind("<<ComboboxSelected>>", self.update_zoom)

        # Label and entry for specifying step
        self.step_label = tk.Label(control_panel, text="Step:")
        self.step_label.grid(row=0, column=2, padx=10, pady=5, sticky="e")
        self.step_default = tk.StringVar(value="20")
        self.step_entry = ttk.Entry(control_panel, textvariable=self.step_default)
        self.step_entry.grid(row=0, column=3, padx=10, pady=5, sticky="w")
        self.step_entry.bind("<Return>", lambda event: self.toggle_play_pause())

        # Label and entry for specifying dx (same as dy)
        self.dx_label = tk.Label(control_panel, text="dx (same as dy):")
        self.dx_label.grid(row=0, column=4, padx=10, pady=5, sticky="e")
        self.dx_default = tk.StringVar(value="10")
        self.dx_entry = ttk.Entry(control_panel, textvariable=self.dx_default)
        self.dx_entry.grid(row=0, column=5, padx=10, pady=5, sticky="w")
        self.dx_entry.bind("<Return>", lambda event: self.toggle_play_pause())

        # Label and entry for specifying block size
        self.block_size_label = tk.Label(control_panel, text="Block Size:")
        self.block_size_label.grid(row=0, column=6, padx=10, pady=5, sticky="e")
        self.block_size_default = tk.StringVar(value="16")
        self.block_size_entry = ttk.Entry(control_panel, textvariable=self.block_size_default)
        self.block_size_entry.grid(row=0, column=7, padx=10, pady=5, sticky="w")
        self.block_size_entry.bind("<Return>", lambda event: self.toggle_play_pause())

        # Label and entry for specifying search range
        self.search_range_label = tk.Label(control_panel, text="Search Range:")
        self.search_range_label.grid(row=0, column=8, padx=10, pady=5, sticky="e")
        self.search_range_default = tk.StringVar(value="16")
        self.search_range_entry = ttk.Entry(control_panel,
textvariable=self.search_range_default)
        self.search_range_entry.grid(row=0, column=9, padx=10, pady=5, sticky="w")
        self.search_range_entry.bind("<Return>", lambda event: self.toggle_play_pause())

        # Button to jump to specified time
        self.jump_button = tk.Button(control_panel, text="Jump to Time",
command=self.jump_to_time)
        self.jump_button.grid(row=0, column=10, padx=10, pady=5)

        # Button to play/pause the video
        self.play_button = tk.Button(control_panel, text="Play/Pause",
command=self.toggle_play_pause)
        self.play_button.grid(row=0, column=11, padx=10, pady=5)

        # Button to stop the video
```

```python
        self.stop_button = tk.Button(control_panel, text="Stop", command=self.stop_video)
        self.stop_button.grid(row=0, column=12, padx=10, pady=5)

        # Button to navigate to the previous frame
        self.prev_frame_button = tk.Button(control_panel, text="Previous Frame", command=self.prev_frame)
        self.prev_frame_button.grid(row=2, column=1, padx=10, pady=5)

        # Button to navigate to the next frame
        self.next_frame_button = tk.Button(control_panel, text="Next Frame", command=self.next_frame)
        self.next_frame_button.grid(row=2, column=2, padx=10, pady=5)

        # Button to open another instance of the application
        self.open_another_button = tk.Button(control_panel, text="Open Another Video Player", command=self.open_another_player)
        self.open_another_button.grid(row=2, column=0, columnspan=15, padx=10, pady=5)

    def open_video(self):
        self.video_path = filedialog.askopenfilename(filetypes=[("Video files", "*.mp4;*.avi;*.mkv")])
        if self.video_path:
            self.video = imageio.get_reader(self.video_path)
            self.file_name = self.video_path.split('/')[-1]  # Extract file name
            self.set_window_title()  # Update window title with file name
            self.play_video()

    def play_video(self):
        if self.video:
            self.paused = False
            self.show_frame()
            self.show_optical_flow()

    def stop_video(self):
        self.paused = True
        self.frame_index = 0
        self.current_x1 = 0
        self.current_y1 = 0  # Reset the current position
        self.show_frame()
        self.show_optical_flow()

    def toggle_play_pause(self):
        self.paused = not self.paused
        if not self.paused:
            self.play_video()

    def update_zoom(self, event=None):
        self.show_frame()
        self.show_optical_flow()

    def show_frame(self):
        if self.video:
            if not self.paused:
                if 0 <= self.frame_index < len(self.video):  # Check if frame index is within range
                    try:
                        frame = self.video.get_data(self.frame_index)
                        frame_gray = cv2.cvtColor(frame, cv2.COLOR_RGB2GRAY)  # Convert to grayscale

                        # Initialize prev_frame_gray on first frame
                        if self.prev_frame_gray is None:
                            self.prev_frame_gray = frame_gray.copy()
```

```python
                        # Display current frame
                        frame = Image.fromarray(frame)
                        frame = frame.resize((frame.width * self.zoom_scale.get(), frame.height * self.zoom_scale.get()))
                        photo = ImageTk.PhotoImage(frame)
                        self.photo = photo  # Save object reference to PhotoImage globally
                        self.canvas.delete("video")  # Delete previous image
                        self.canvas.create_image(self.current_x1, self.current_y1, anchor="nw", image=photo, tags="video")

                        # Update prev_frame_gray
                        self.prev_frame_gray = frame_gray.copy()

                        # Update frame number label
                        self.frame_number_label.config(text=f"Frame: {self.frame_index} / {self.video.count_frames()}", font=("Helvetica", 18))

                        self.frame_index += 1  # Move to the next frame

                except Exception as e:
                    print("Error: ", e)

    def full_search_block_matching_dsa(self, prev_frame_gray, frame_gray):
        # FSBM implementation
        block_size = int(self.block_size_entry.get())  # Get block size from entry
        search_range = int(self.search_range_entry.get())  # Get search range from entry
        motion_vectors = np.zeros((frame_gray.shape[0] // block_size, frame_gray.shape[1] // block_size, 3))

        for y in range(0, frame_gray.shape[0] - block_size, block_size):
            for x in range(0, frame_gray.shape[1] - block_size, block_size):
                min_ssd = float('inf')
                best_dx = 0
                best_dy = 0

                # Diamond Search Algorithm
                step_size = search_range
                while step_size >= 1:
                    dx_values = [0, -step_size, 0, step_size, 0]
                    dy_values = [-step_size, 0, step_size, 0, -step_size]

                    for dx, dy in zip(dx_values, dy_values):
                        if 0 <= y + dy < frame_gray.shape[0] - block_size and 0 <= x + dx < frame_gray.shape[1] - block_size:
                            template = prev_frame_gray[y:y+block_size, x:x+block_size]
                            search_area = frame_gray[y+dy:y+dy+block_size, x+dx:x+dx+block_size]
                            ssd = np.sum((template - search_area) ** 2)
                            if ssd < min_ssd:
                                min_ssd = ssd
                                best_dx = dx
                                best_dy = dy

                    step_size //= 2

                # Calculate angle
                angle = math.atan2(best_dy, best_dx)
                # Calculate magnitude
                magnitude = math.sqrt(best_dx**2 + best_dy**2)

                motion_vectors[y // block_size, x // block_size] = [best_dx, best_dy, angle]

        return motion_vectors
```

```python
    def show_optical_flow(self):
        if self.video:
            if not self.paused:
                if 0 <= self.frame_index < len(self.video):  # Check if frame index is within range
                    try:
                        frame = self.video.get_data(self.frame_index)
                        frame_gray = cv2.cvtColor(frame, cv2.COLOR_RGB2GRAY)  # Convert to grayscale

                        # Calculate optical flow using Diamond Search Algorithm (DSA)
                        motion_vectors = self.full_search_block_matching_dsa(self.prev_frame_gray, frame_gray)

                        # Create an empty mask image for visualization
                        mask = np.zeros_like(frame)

                        # Compute flow visualization
                        step = int(self.step_entry.get())
                        for y in range(0, frame.shape[0], step):
                            for x in range(0, frame.shape[1], step):
                                # Ensure the motion vectors index does not exceed the bounds
                                if y // step < motion_vectors.shape[0] and x // step < motion_vectors.shape[1]:
                                    dx, dy, angle = motion_vectors[y // step, x // step]
                                    # Scale the optical flow vectors based on the zoom scale
                                    dx *= int(self.dx_entry.get())
                                    dy *= int(self.dx_entry.get())
                                    # Convert coordinates to integers
                                    x1, y1 = int(x), int(y)
                                    x2, y2 = int(x + dx), int(y + dy)
                                    # Draw the line and circle
                                    cv2.line(mask, (x1, y1), (x2, y2), (255, 255, 255), 1)
                                    cv2.circle(mask, (x2, y2), 1, (0, 255, 0), -1)

                        # Convert mask to PIL format and display on canvas
                        mask = Image.fromarray(mask)
                        mask = ImageTk.PhotoImage(mask)
                        self.mask = mask
                        self.flow_canvas.delete("mask")  # Delete previous optical flow
                        self.flow_canvas.create_image(self.current_x2, self.current_y2, anchor="nw", image=mask, tags="mask")

                        # Update previous frame
                        self.prev_frame_gray = frame_gray.copy()

                    except Exception as e:
                        print("Error in show_optical_flow:", e)  # Print error message

    def on_mousewheel(self, event):
        direction = event.delta // 120
        current_value = int(self.zoom_scale.get())
        if direction == 1 and current_value < 10:
            current_value += 1
        elif direction == -1 and current_value > 1:
            current_value -= 1
        self.zoom_scale.set(current_value)
        self.update_zoom()

    def on_press1(self, event):
        self.start_x1 = event.x
        self.start_y1 = event.y

    def on_drag1(self, event):
```

```python
            if self.start_x1 and self.start_y1:
                self.x_offset1 = event.x - self.start_x1
                self.y_offset1 = event.y - self.start_y1
                self.current_x1 += self.x_offset1  # Update current position
                self.current_y1 += self.y_offset1  # Update current position
                self.canvas.move("video", self.x_offset1, self.y_offset1)
                self.start_x1 = event.x
                self.start_y1 = event.y

    def on_press2(self, event):
        self.start_x2 = event.x
        self.start_y2 = event.y

    def on_drag2(self, event):
            if self.start_x2 and self.start_y2:
                self.x_offset2 = event.x - self.start_x2
                self.y_offset2 = event.y - self.start_y2
                self.current_x2 += self.x_offset2  # Update current position
                self.current_y2 += self.y_offset2  # Update current position
                self.flow_canvas.move("mask", self.x_offset2, self.y_offset2)  # Move optical flow canvas along with original canvas
                self.start_x2 = event.x
                self.start_y2 = event.y

    def jump_to_time(self):
        time_str = self.time_entry.get()
        try:
            time_seconds = float(time_str)
            if 0 <= time_seconds:
                self.frame_index = int(time_seconds * self.video.get_meta_data()['fps'])
                self.show_frame()
                self.show_optical_flow()  # Jump to specified time for optical flow
        except ValueError:
            pass

    def prev_frame(self):
        if self.frame_index > 0:
            self.frame_index -= 1
            self.show_frame()
            self.show_optical_flow()
            print(self.frame_index)

    def next_frame(self):
        if self.video and self.frame_index < len(self.video) - 1:
            self.show_frame()
            self.show_optical_flow()
            print(self.frame_index)

    def set_window_title(self):
        if self.file_name:
            self.master.title(f"Diamond Search Algorithm (DSA) Optical Flow - {self.file_name}")
            self.master.title_font = ("Helvetica", 16, "bold")
        else:
            self.master.title("Diamond Search Algorithm (DSA) Optical Flow")

    def open_another_player(self):
        # Open another instance of the application
        root = tk.Toplevel(self.master)
        app = VideoFSBM_DSAOpticalFlow(root)

def main():
    root = tk.Tk()
    app = VideoFSBM_DSAOpticalFlow(root)
```

```
    root.mainloop()

if __name__ == "__main__":
    main()
```

RUNNING PROGRAM

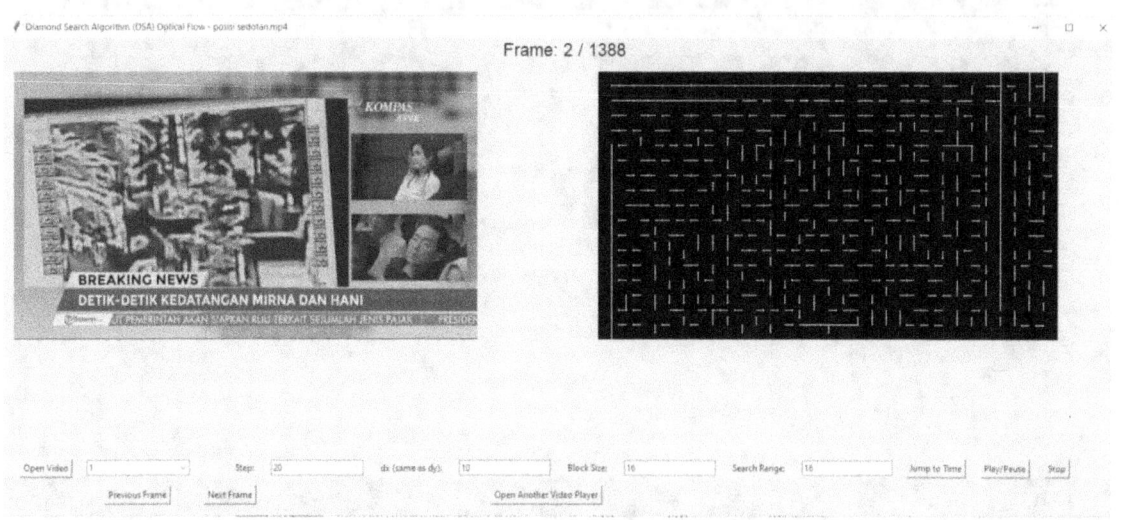

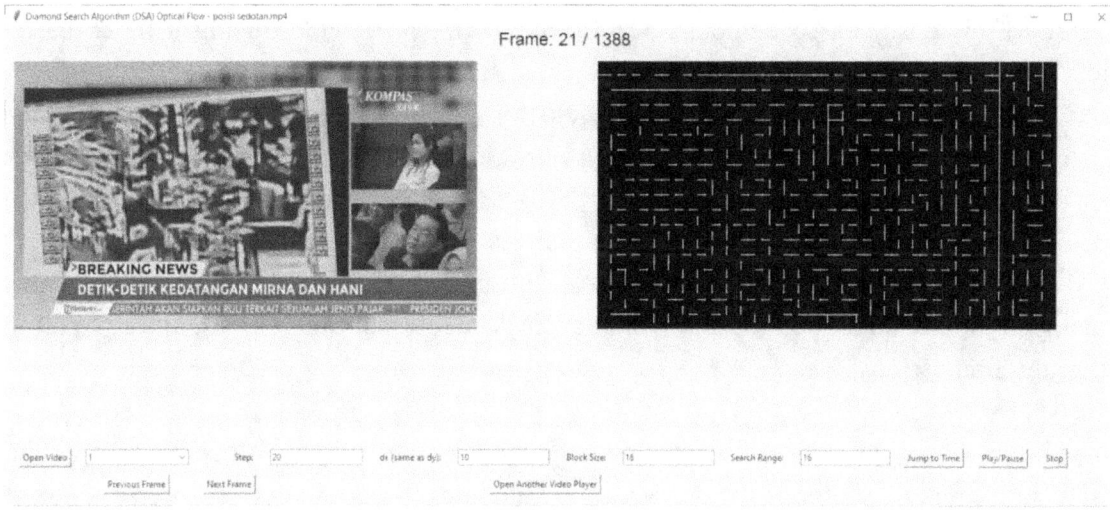

OBJECT TRACKING WITH BLOCK-BASED GRADIENT DESCENT SEARCH (BGDS)

DESCRIPTION

This Python project, titled "Object Tracking with Block-based Gradient Descent Search (BGDS)", is designed to demonstrate object tracking in a video using a block-based gradient descent search algorithm. The project utilizes various libraries such as tkinter for the GUI, PIL for image processing, imageio for reading video files, and OpenCV for computer vision tasks.

The main class ObjectTracking_BGDS initializes the GUI application window and sets up the interface for video display, control buttons, and parameter inputs. It includes methods for opening video files, playing/pausing videos, stopping videos, and navigating through frames.

The block_based_gradient_descent_search method implements the block-based gradient descent search algorithm, which iteratively updates motion vectors to track object movements between frames. This algorithm involves computing gradients and minimizing error between blocks in consecutive frames.

The track_object method utilizes the BGDS algorithm to track the object within the bounding box specified by the user. It calculates motion vectors and updates the bounding box coordinates based on the mean motion vector.

The show_frame method is responsible for displaying video frames on the canvas. It handles frame processing, including object tracking, resizing frames based on zoom scale, and updating the frame number label.

The GUI elements include buttons for opening video files, controlling playback, navigating frames, and clearing the listbox displaying center coordinates. Parameter inputs are provided for adjusting block size, search range, iteration limit, learning rate, convergence threshold, and step size.

The application allows users to interactively select a bounding box around the object of interest using mouse clicks and drags. The selected bounding box is used as the initial region for object tracking.

Overall, this project provides a user-friendly interface for object tracking in videos using the block-based gradient descent search algorithm, demonstrating the application of computer vision techniques for motion analysis.

SOURCE CODE

```python
#object_tracking_bgds.py
import tkinter as tk
from tkinter import ttk
from tkinter import filedialog
from PIL import Image, ImageTk
import imageio
import cv2
import numpy as np
import math

class ObjectTracking_BGDS:
    def __init__(self, master):
        self.master = master
        self.master.title("Object Tracking with Block-based Gradient Descent Search (BGDS)")
        self.file_name = ""
        self.set_window_title()  # Set window title initially

        self.frame_number_label = tk.Label(master, text="Frame: 0")
        self.frame_number_label.pack()

        self.video = None
        self.video_path = None
```

```python
        self.paused = False
        self.zoom_scale = tk.IntVar(value=1)
        self.frame_index = 0
        self.bbox = None
        self.tracking_started = False  # Initialize tracking_started to False
        self.prev_frame_gray = None

        self.bbox_rect = None  # Initialize bbox_rect attribute to None
        self.frame_processing = False  # Initialize frame_processing attribute to False

        self.create_widgets()

    def create_widgets(self):
        # Panel for video display
        video_panel = tk.Frame(self.master)
        video_panel.pack(padx=10, pady=10)

        # Canvas to display the original video
        canvas_width = 800
        canvas_height = 500
        self.canvas = tk.Canvas(video_panel, width=canvas_width, height=canvas_height)
        self.canvas.pack(side="left", fill="both", expand=True)
        self.canvas.bind("<MouseWheel>", self.on_mousewheel)
        self.canvas.bind("<ButtonPress-1>", self.on_press)
        self.canvas.bind("<B1-Motion>", self.on_drag)

        # List box to display center coordinates
        self.center_listbox = tk.Listbox(video_panel, width=30, height=20, font=("Helvetica", 14))
        self.center_listbox.pack(side="right", fill="y")
        # Scrollbar for the listbox
        scrollbar = tk.Scrollbar(video_panel, orient="vertical")
        scrollbar.pack(side="left", fill="y")
        scrollbar.config(command=self.center_listbox.yview)

        # Attach scrollbar to listbox
        self.center_listbox.config(yscrollcommand=scrollbar.set)

        # Panel for control buttons
        control_panel = tk.Frame(self.master)
        control_panel.pack(padx=10, pady=(0, 10), fill="x")

        # Button to open a video file
        self.open_button = tk.Button(control_panel, text="Open Video", command=self.open_video)
        self.open_button.grid(row=0, column=0, padx=10, pady=5)

        # Combobox for selecting zoom scale
        self.zoom_combobox = ttk.Combobox(control_panel, textvariable=self.zoom_scale, values=list(range(1, 11)))
        self.zoom_combobox.grid(row=0, column=1, padx=10, pady=5)
        self.zoom_combobox.bind("<<ComboboxSelected>>", self.update_zoom)

        # Button to play/pause the video
        self.play_button = tk.Button(control_panel, text="Play/Pause", command=self.toggle_play_pause)
        self.play_button.grid(row=0, column=2, padx=10, pady=5)

        # Button to stop the video
        self.stop_button = tk.Button(control_panel, text="Stop", command=self.stop_video)
        self.stop_button.grid(row=0, column=3, padx=10, pady=5)

        # Button to navigate to the previous frame
        self.prev_frame_button = tk.Button(control_panel, text="Previous Frame", command=self.prev_frame)
```

```python
        self.prev_frame_button.grid(row=0, column=4, padx=10, pady=5)

        # Button to navigate to the next frame
        self.next_frame_button = tk.Button(control_panel, text="Next Frame", command=self.next_frame)
        self.next_frame_button.grid(row=0, column=5, padx=10, pady=5)

        # Button to clear the listbox
        self.clear_button = tk.Button(control_panel, text="Clear Listbox", command=self.clear_listbox)
        self.clear_button.grid(row=0, column=6, padx=10, pady=5)

        # Label and entry for specifying block size
        self.block_size_label = tk.Label(control_panel, text="Block Size:")
        self.block_size_label.grid(row=0, column=7, padx=10, pady=5, sticky="e")
        self.block_size_default = tk.StringVar(value="16")
        self.block_size_entry = ttk.Entry(control_panel, textvariable=self.block_size_default)
        self.block_size_entry.grid(row=0, column=8, padx=10, pady=5, sticky="w")
        self.block_size_entry.bind("<Return>", lambda event: self.toggle_play_pause())

        # Label and entry for specifying search range
        self.search_range_label = tk.Label(control_panel, text="Search Range:")
        self.search_range_label.grid(row=1, column=0, padx=10, pady=5, sticky="e")
        self.search_range_default = tk.StringVar(value="16")
        self.search_range_entry = ttk.Entry(control_panel, textvariable=self.search_range_default)
        self.search_range_entry.grid(row=1, column=1, padx=10, pady=5, sticky="w")
        self.search_range_entry.bind("<Return>", lambda event: self.toggle_play_pause())

        # Add labels and textboxes for parameters in the create_widgets method
        self.iteration_limit_label = tk.Label(control_panel, text="Iteration Limit:")
        self.iteration_limit_label.grid(row=1, column=2, padx=10, pady=5, sticky="e")
        self.iteration_limit_default = tk.StringVar(value="50")  # Default value
        self.iteration_limit_entry = ttk.Entry(control_panel, textvariable=self.iteration_limit_default)
        self.iteration_limit_entry.grid(row=1, column=3, padx=10, pady=5, sticky="w")

        self.learning_rate_label = tk.Label(control_panel, text="Learning Rate:")
        self.learning_rate_label.grid(row=1, column=4, padx=10, pady=5, sticky="e")
        self.learning_rate_default = tk.StringVar(value="0.01")  # Default value
        self.learning_rate_entry = ttk.Entry(control_panel, textvariable=self.learning_rate_default)
        self.learning_rate_entry.grid(row=1, column=5, padx=10, pady=5, sticky="w")

        self.convergence_threshold_label = tk.Label(control_panel, text="Convergence Threshold:")
        self.convergence_threshold_label.grid(row=1, column=6, padx=10, pady=5, sticky="e")
        self.convergence_threshold_default = tk.StringVar(value="0.01")  # Default value
        self.convergence_threshold_entry = ttk.Entry(control_panel, textvariable=self.convergence_threshold_default)
        self.convergence_threshold_entry.grid(row=1, column=7, padx=10, pady=5, sticky="w")

        # Label and entry for specifying step
        self.step_label = tk.Label(control_panel, text="Step:")
        self.step_label.grid(row=1, column=8, padx=10, pady=5, sticky="e")
        self.step_default = tk.StringVar(value="20")
        self.step_entry = ttk.Entry(control_panel, textvariable=self.step_default)
        self.step_entry.grid(row=1, column=9, padx=10, pady=5, sticky="w")
        self.step_entry.bind("<Return>", lambda event: self.toggle_play_pause())

    def open_video(self):
        self.video_path = filedialog.askopenfilename(filetypes=[("Video files", "*.mp4;*.avi;*.mkv;*.wmv")])
        if self.video_path:
```

```python
        self.video = imageio.get_reader(self.video_path)
        self.file_name = self.video_path.split('/')[-1]
        self.set_window_title()
        self.play_video()

def play_video(self):
    if self.video:
        self.paused = False
        self.tracking_started = True
        self.show_frame()

def stop_video(self):
    self.paused = True
    self.frame_index = 0
    self.bbox = None
    self.show_frame()

def toggle_play_pause(self):
    self.paused = not self.paused
    if not self.paused:
        if self.bbox is not None:
            self.tracking_started = True
        self.play_video()

def update_zoom(self, event=None):
    self.show_frame()

def block_based_gradient_descent_search(self, prev_frame_gray, frame_gray):
    iteration_limit = int(self.iteration_limit_entry.get())  # Get iteration limit from entry
    learning_rate = float(self.learning_rate_entry.get())  # Get learning rate from entry
    convergence_threshold = float(self.convergence_threshold_entry.get())  # Get convergence threshold from entry
    step = int(self.step_entry.get())  # Get iteration limit from entry

    # BGDS implementation
    block_size = int(self.block_size_entry.get())  # Get block size from entry
    rows, cols = frame_gray.shape[0] // step, frame_gray.shape[1] // step
    motion_vectors = np.zeros((rows, cols, 2))

    # Iterate through image blocks
    for i in range(rows):
        for j in range(cols):
            y = i * step  # Calculate starting y-coordinate of the block
            x = j * step  # Calculate starting x-coordinate of the block
            # Initial motion vector guess
            motion_vector = [0, 0]
            prev_block = prev_frame_gray[y:y + block_size, x:x + block_size]

            # Check if the current block is too close to the edges to compute the gradient
            if y + block_size >= frame_gray.shape[0] or x + block_size >= frame_gray.shape[1]:
                continue

            # Gradient descent iterations
            for _ in range(iteration_limit):
                # Compute error between current block and previous block
                current_block = frame_gray[y:y + block_size, x:x + block_size]
                error = np.sum((prev_block - current_block) ** 2)

                # Compute gradient if the block size is large enough
                if current_block.shape[0] > 1 and current_block.shape[1] > 1:
                    gradient = np.gradient(current_block)
                    # Update motion vector using gradient descent
```

```python
                        motion_vector[0] -= learning_rate * gradient[0].mean()
                        motion_vector[1] -= learning_rate * gradient[1].mean()

                    # Check convergence
                    if error < convergence_threshold:
                        break

                # Store motion vector
                motion_vectors[i, j] = motion_vector

        return motion_vectors

    def track_object(self, frame, bbox):
        if bbox:
            x1, y1, x2, y2 = map(int, bbox)
            roi = frame[y1:y2, x1:x2]
            if roi.size > 0:
                # Convert the ROI to grayscale
                roi_gray = cv2.cvtColor(roi, cv2.COLOR_BGR2GRAY)
                # Initialize the previous frame if not already initialized or if its dimensions don't match the current frame
                if self.prev_frame_gray is None or self.prev_frame_gray.shape != roi_gray.shape:
                    self.prev_frame_gray = roi_gray.copy()

                # Calculate motion vectors using Block-based Gradient Descent Search (BGDS)
                motion_vectors = self.block_based_gradient_descent_search(self.prev_frame_gray, roi_gray)

                # Calculate the mean motion vector within the bounding box
                mean_motion_vector = np.mean(motion_vectors, axis=(0, 1))

                # Update the bounding box coordinates based on the mean motion vector
                x1 += int(mean_motion_vector[0])
                y1 += int(mean_motion_vector[1])
                x2 += int(mean_motion_vector[0])
                y2 += int(mean_motion_vector[1])

                # Update the previous frame
                self.prev_frame_gray = roi_gray.copy()

                # Calculate the center of the bounding box
                center_x = (x1 + x2) // 2
                center_y = (y1 + y2) // 2

                # Add the center coordinates to the list box
                self.center_listbox.insert(tk.END, f"(center_x = {center_x}, center_y = {center_y})")

                return x1, y1, x2, y2
        return None

    def update_bbox_rectangle(self, bbox):
        if bbox is not None:
            x1, y1, x2, y2 = map(int, bbox)
            if self.bbox_rect is not None:
                self.canvas.coords(self.bbox_rect, x1, y1, x2, y2)
                self.canvas.tag_raise(self.bbox_rect)  # Raise the bounding box to the front
            else:
                self.bbox_rect = self.canvas.create_rectangle(x1, y1, x2-50, y2-50, outline='#fc3d3d', width=8, tags="bbox")

    def show_frame(self):
```

```python
        if self.video:
            if not self.paused:
                if 0 <= self.frame_index < len(self.video):
                    if not self.frame_processing:  # Check if the frame is already being processed
                        try:
                            self.frame_processing = True  # Set frame_processing flag to True to indicate frame processing

                            frame = self.video.get_data(self.frame_index)
                            frame = cv2.cvtColor(frame, cv2.COLOR_RGB2BGR)

                            if self.bbox is not None:
                                if not self.tracking_started:
                                    self.tracking_started = True

                                self.bbox = self.track_object(frame, self.bbox)
                                if self.bbox:
                                    frame = cv2.cvtColor(frame, cv2.COLOR_BGR2RGB)
                                    frame = Image.fromarray(frame)
                                    frame = frame.resize((frame.width * self.zoom_scale.get(), frame.height * self.zoom_scale.get()))
                                    photo = ImageTk.PhotoImage(frame)
                                    self.photo = photo
                                    self.canvas.delete("video")
                                    self.canvas.create_image(0, 0, anchor="nw", image=photo, tags="video")

                                    self.update_bbox_rectangle(self.bbox)

                            else:
                                frame = cv2.cvtColor(frame, cv2.COLOR_BGR2RGB)
                                frame = Image.fromarray(frame)
                                frame = frame.resize((frame.width * self.zoom_scale.get(), frame.height * self.zoom_scale.get()))
                                photo = ImageTk.PhotoImage(frame)
                                self.photo = photo
                                self.canvas.delete("video")
                                self.canvas.create_image(0, 0, anchor="nw", image=photo, tags="video")

                            self.frame_number_label.config(text=f"Frame: {self.frame_index} / {self.video.count_frames()}", font=("Helvetica", 18))

                            self.frame_index += 1

                        except Exception as e:
                            print("Error: ", e)
                        finally:
                            self.frame_processing = False  # Reset frame_processing flag to False after processing the frame

    def on_mousewheel(self, event):
        direction = event.delta // 120
        current_value = int(self.zoom_scale.get())
        if direction == 1 and current_value < 10:
            current_value += 1
        elif direction == -1 and current_value > 1:
            current_value -= 1
        self.zoom_scale.set(current_value)
        self.update_zoom()

    def on_press(self, event):
        self.start_x = self.canvas.canvasx(event.x)
        self.start_y = self.canvas.canvasy(event.y)
```

```python
        self.bbox = None

    def on_drag(self, event):
        cur_x = self.canvas.canvasx(event.x)
        cur_y = self.canvas.canvasy(event.y)
        if self.bbox_rect:
            self.canvas.delete(self.bbox_rect)
        self.bbox = (self.start_x, self.start_y, cur_x, cur_y)
        self.bbox_rect = self.canvas.create_rectangle(*self.bbox, outline='#fc3d3d', width=6)

    def prev_frame(self):
        if self.frame_index > 0:
            self.frame_index -= 1
            self.show_frame()

    def next_frame(self):
        if self.video and self.frame_index < len(self.video) - 1:
            self.show_frame()

    def clear_listbox(self):
        self.center_listbox.delete(0, tk.END)

    def set_window_title(self):
        if self.file_name:
            self.master.title(f"Object Tracking with Block-based Gradient Descent Search (BGDS)- {self.file_name}")
            self.master.title_font = ("Helvetica", 16, "bold")
        else:
            self.master.title("Object Tracking with Block-based Gradient Descent Search (BGDS)")

def main():
    root = tk.Tk()
    app = ObjectTracking_BGDS(root)
    root.mainloop()

if __name__ == "__main__":
    main()
```

RUNNING PROGRAM

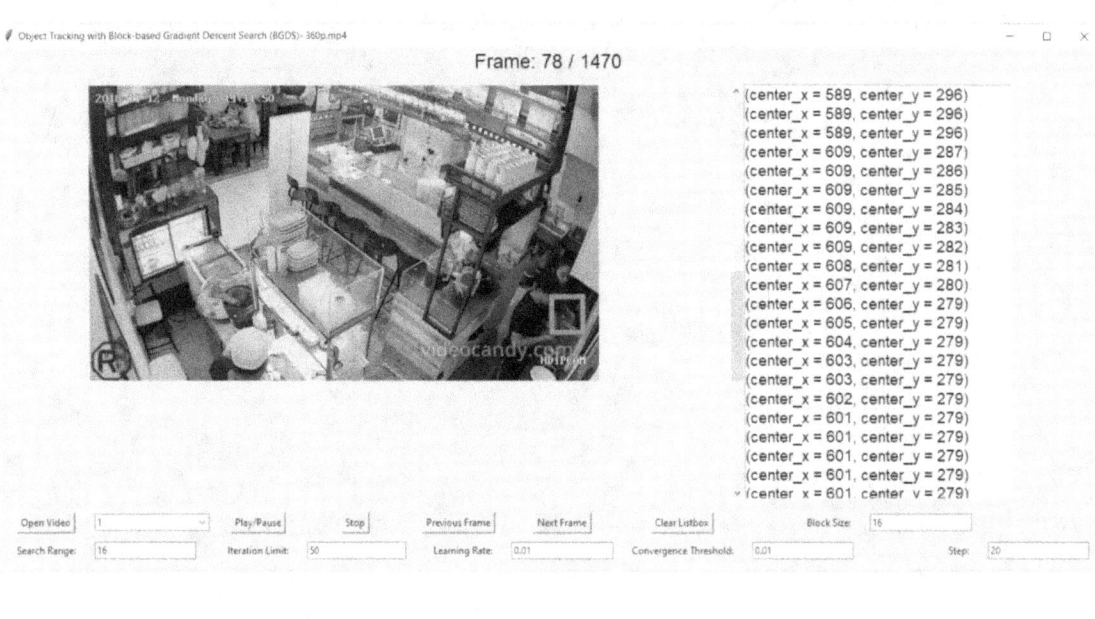

OBJECT TRACKING WITH AGAST (ADAPTIVE AND GENERIC ACCELERATED SEGMENT TEST)

DESCRIPTION

The "Object Tracking with AGAST (Adaptive and Generic Accelerated Segment Test)" project is a Python application designed for tracking objects within videos using the AGAST algorithm. It leverages libraries like tkinter for the GUI, PIL for image processing, imageio for video reading, and OpenCV for computer vision tasks.

The main class, ObjectTracking_AGAST, initializes the application window and sets up the interface for video display, control buttons, and parameter inputs. It includes methods for opening video files, playing/pausing videos, stopping videos, and navigating through frames.

The GUI elements consist of buttons for opening video files, controlling playback, navigating frames, and clearing the listbox displaying center coordinates. Additionally, there's a combobox for selecting zoom scale and a canvas for displaying the video frames.

The heart of the project lies in the agast_vectors method, which implements the AGAST algorithm for detecting keypoints and computing motion vectors between consecutive frames. It utilizes OpenCV's AGAST feature detector to detect keypoints and match them between frames using a brute-force matcher.

The track_object method utilizes the AGAST algorithm to track the object within the bounding box specified by the user. It calculates motion vectors and updates the bounding box coordinates based on the mean motion vector.

The show_frame method is responsible for displaying video frames on the canvas. It handles frame processing, including object tracking, resizing frames based on zoom scale, and updating the frame number label.

Users can interactively select a bounding box around the object of interest using mouse clicks and drags. The selected bounding box serves as the initial region for object tracking.

Overall, this project provides a user-friendly interface for object tracking in videos using the AGAST algorithm, showcasing the practical application of computer vision techniques for motion analysis and object tracking tasks.

SOURCE CODE

```python
# object_tracking_agast.py
import tkinter as tk
from tkinter import ttk
from tkinter import filedialog
from PIL import Image, ImageTk
import imageio
import cv2
import numpy as np

class ObjectTracking_AGAST:
    def __init__(self, master):
        self.master = master
        self.master.title("Object Tracking with AGAST (Adaptive and Generic Accelerated Segment Test)")
        self.file_name = ""
        self.set_window_title()  # Set window title initially
        
        self.frame_number_label = tk.Label(master, text="Frame: 0")
        self.frame_number_label.pack()
        
        self.video = None
        self.video_path = None
```

```python
        self.paused = False
        self.zoom_scale = tk.IntVar(value=1)
        self.frame_index = 0
        self.bbox = None
        self.tracking_started = False  # Initialize tracking_started to False
        self.prev_frame_gray = None

        self.bbox_rect = None  # Initialize bbox_rect attribute to None
        self.frame_processing = False  # Initialize frame_processing attribute to False

        self.create_widgets()

    def create_widgets(self):
        # Panel for video display
        video_panel = tk.Frame(self.master)
        video_panel.pack(padx=10, pady=10)

        # Canvas to display the original video
        canvas_width = 800
        canvas_height = 500
        self.canvas = tk.Canvas(video_panel, width=canvas_width, height=canvas_height)
        self.canvas.pack(side="left", fill="both", expand=True)
        self.canvas.bind("<MouseWheel>", self.on_mousewheel)
        self.canvas.bind("<ButtonPress-1>", self.on_press)
        self.canvas.bind("<B1-Motion>", self.on_drag)

        # List box to display center coordinates
        self.center_listbox = tk.Listbox(video_panel, width=30, height=20, font=("Helvetica", 14))
        self.center_listbox.pack(side="right", fill="y")
        # Scrollbar for the listbox
        scrollbar = tk.Scrollbar(video_panel, orient="vertical")
        scrollbar.pack(side="left", fill="y")
        scrollbar.config(command=self.center_listbox.yview)

        # Attach scrollbar to listbox
        self.center_listbox.config(yscrollcommand=scrollbar.set)

        # Panel for control buttons
        control_panel = tk.Frame(self.master)
        control_panel.pack(padx=10, pady=(0, 10), fill="x")

        # Button to open a video file
        self.open_button = tk.Button(control_panel, text="Open Video", command=self.open_video)
        self.open_button.grid(row=0, column=0, padx=10, pady=5)

        # Combobox for selecting zoom scale
        self.zoom_combobox = ttk.Combobox(control_panel, textvariable=self.zoom_scale, values=list(range(1, 11)))
        self.zoom_combobox.grid(row=0, column=1, padx=10, pady=5)
        self.zoom_combobox.bind("<<ComboboxSelected>>", self.update_zoom)

        # Button to play/pause the video
        self.play_button = tk.Button(control_panel, text="Play/Pause", command=self.toggle_play_pause)
        self.play_button.grid(row=0, column=2, padx=10, pady=5)

        # Button to stop the video
        self.stop_button = tk.Button(control_panel, text="Stop", command=self.stop_video)
        self.stop_button.grid(row=0, column=3, padx=10, pady=5)

        # Button to navigate to the previous frame
        self.prev_frame_button = tk.Button(control_panel, text="Previous Frame", command=self.prev_frame)
```

```python
        self.prev_frame_button.grid(row=0, column=4, padx=10, pady=5)

        # Button to navigate to the next frame
        self.next_frame_button = tk.Button(control_panel, text="Next Frame", command=self.next_frame)
        self.next_frame_button.grid(row=0, column=5, padx=10, pady=5)

        # Button to clear the listbox
        self.clear_button = tk.Button(control_panel, text="Clear Listbox", command=self.clear_listbox)
        self.clear_button.grid(row=0, column=6, padx=10, pady=5)

    def open_video(self):
        self.video_path = filedialog.askopenfilename(filetypes=[("Video files", "*.mp4;*.avi;*.mkv;*.wmv")])
        if self.video_path:
            self.video = imageio.get_reader(self.video_path)
            self.file_name = self.video_path.split('/')[-1]
            self.set_window_title()
            self.play_video()

    def play_video(self):
        if self.video:
            self.paused = False
            self.tracking_started = True
            self.show_frame()

    def stop_video(self):
        self.paused = True
        self.frame_index = 0
        self.bbox = None
        self.show_frame()

    def toggle_play_pause(self):
        self.paused = not self.paused
        if not self.paused:
            if self.bbox is not None:
                self.tracking_started = True
            self.play_video()

    def update_zoom(self, event=None):
        self.show_frame()

    def agast_vectors(self, prev_frame_gray, frame_gray):
        # Create AGAST detector with custom parameters
        agast = cv2.AgastFeatureDetector_create(threshold=30, nonmaxSuppression=True)

        # Detect keypoints and compute descriptors for the previous frame
        keypoints_prev = agast.detect(prev_frame_gray)
        keypoints_prev_np = np.array([kp.pt for kp in keypoints_prev], dtype=np.float32)

        # Detect keypoints and compute descriptors for the current frame
        keypoints_frame = agast.detect(frame_gray)
        keypoints_frame_np = np.array([kp.pt for kp in keypoints_frame], dtype=np.float32)

        # Match keypoints between previous and current frames
        bf = cv2.BFMatcher()
        matches = bf.knnMatch(keypoints_prev_np, keypoints_frame_np, k=2)

        # Apply ratio test
        good_matches = []
        for m, n in matches:
            if m.distance < 0.75 * n.distance:
                good_matches.append(m)
```

```python
            # Estimate motion vectors from good matches
            motion_vectors = np.zeros((len(good_matches), 2))
            for i, match in enumerate(good_matches):
                # Get the keypoints for the matched points
                prev_point = keypoints_prev_np[match.queryIdx]
                frame_point = keypoints_frame_np[match.trainIdx]

                # Calculate the motion vector
                dx = frame_point[0] - prev_point[0]
                dy = frame_point[1] - prev_point[1]

                # Store the motion vector
                motion_vectors[i] = [dx, dy]

            return motion_vectors

    def track_object(self, frame, bbox):
        if bbox:
            x1, y1, x2, y2 = map(int, bbox)
            roi = frame[y1:y2, x1:x2]
            if roi.size > 0:
                # Convert the ROI to grayscale
                roi_gray = cv2.cvtColor(roi, cv2.COLOR_BGR2GRAY)
                # Initialize the previous frame if not already initialized or if its dimensions don't match the current frame
                if self.prev_frame_gray is None or self.prev_frame_gray.shape != roi_gray.shape:
                    self.prev_frame_gray = roi_gray.copy()

                # Calculate motion vectors using AGAST Algorithm
                motion_vectors = self.agast_vectors(self.prev_frame_gray, roi_gray)

                # Calculate the mean motion vector within the bounding box
                mean_motion_vector = np.mean(motion_vectors, axis=0)

                # Update the bounding box coordinates based on the mean motion vector
                x1 += int(mean_motion_vector[0])
                y1 += int(mean_motion_vector[1])
                x2 += int(mean_motion_vector[0])
                y2 += int(mean_motion_vector[1])

                # Update the previous frame
                self.prev_frame_gray = roi_gray.copy()

                # Calculate the center of the bounding box
                center_x = (x1 + x2) // 2
                center_y = (y1 + y2) // 2

                # Add the center coordinates to the list box
                self.center_listbox.insert(tk.END, f"(center_x = {center_x}, center_y = {center_y})")

                return x1, y1, x2, y2
        return None

    def update_bbox_rectangle(self, bbox):
        if bbox is not None:
            x1, y1, x2, y2 = map(int, bbox)
            if self.bbox_rect is not None:
                self.canvas.coords(self.bbox_rect, x1, y1, x2, y2)
                self.canvas.tag_raise(self.bbox_rect)  # Raise the bounding box to the front
            else:
```

```python
                    self.bbox_rect = self.canvas.create_rectangle(x1, y1, x2-50, y2-50, outline='lightgreen', width=8, tags="bbox")

    def show_frame(self):
        if self.video:
            if not self.paused:
                if 0 <= self.frame_index < len(self.video):
                    if not self.frame_processing:  # Check if the frame is already being processed
                        try:
                            self.frame_processing = True  # Set frame_processing flag to True to indicate frame processing

                            frame = self.video.get_data(self.frame_index)
                            frame = cv2.cvtColor(frame, cv2.COLOR_RGB2BGR)

                            if self.bbox is not None:
                                if not self.tracking_started:
                                    self.tracking_started = True

                                self.bbox = self.track_object(frame, self.bbox)
                                if self.bbox:
                                    frame = cv2.cvtColor(frame, cv2.COLOR_BGR2RGB)
                                    frame = Image.fromarray(frame)
                                    frame = frame.resize((frame.width * self.zoom_scale.get(), frame.height * self.zoom_scale.get()))
                                    photo = ImageTk.PhotoImage(frame)
                                    self.photo = photo
                                    self.canvas.delete("video")
                                    self.canvas.create_image(0, 0, anchor="nw", image=photo, tags="video")

                                    self.update_bbox_rectangle(self.bbox)

                            else:
                                frame = cv2.cvtColor(frame, cv2.COLOR_BGR2RGB)
                                frame = Image.fromarray(frame)
                                frame = frame.resize((frame.width * self.zoom_scale.get(), frame.height * self.zoom_scale.get()))
                                photo = ImageTk.PhotoImage(frame)
                                self.photo = photo
                                self.canvas.delete("video")
                                self.canvas.create_image(0, 0, anchor="nw", image=photo, tags="video")

                            self.frame_number_label.config(text=f"Frame: {self.frame_index} / {self.video.count_frames()}", font=("Helvetica", 18))

                            self.frame_index += 1

                        except Exception as e:
                            print("Error: ", e)
                        finally:
                            self.frame_processing = False  # Reset frame_processing flag to False after processing the frame

    def on_mousewheel(self, event):
        direction = event.delta // 120
        current_value = int(self.zoom_scale.get())
        if direction == 1 and current_value < 10:
            current_value += 1
        elif direction == -1 and current_value > 1:
            current_value -= 1
        self.zoom_scale.set(current_value)
        self.update_zoom()
```

```python
    def on_press(self, event):
        self.start_x = self.canvas.canvasx(event.x)
        self.start_y = self.canvas.canvasy(event.y)
        self.bbox = None

    def on_drag(self, event):
        cur_x = self.canvas.canvasx(event.x)
        cur_y = self.canvas.canvasy(event.y)
        if self.bbox_rect:
            self.canvas.delete(self.bbox_rect)
        self.bbox = (self.start_x, self.start_y, cur_x, cur_y)
        self.bbox_rect = self.canvas.create_rectangle(*self.bbox, outline='lightgreen', width=6)

    def prev_frame(self):
        if self.frame_index > 0:
            self.frame_index -= 1
            self.show_frame()

    def next_frame(self):
        if self.video and self.frame_index < len(self.video) - 1:
            self.show_frame()

    def clear_listbox(self):
        self.center_listbox.delete(0, tk.END)

    def set_window_title(self):
        if self.file_name:
            self.master.title(f"Object Tracking with AGAST (Adaptive and Generic Accelerated Segment Test) - {self.file_name}")
            self.master.title_font = ("Helvetica", 16, "bold")
        else:
            self.master.title("Object Tracking with AGAST (Adaptive and Generic Accelerated Segment Test)")

def main():
    root = tk.Tk()
    app = ObjectTracking_AGAST(root)
    root.mainloop()

if __name__ == "__main__":
    main()
```

RUNNING PROGRAM

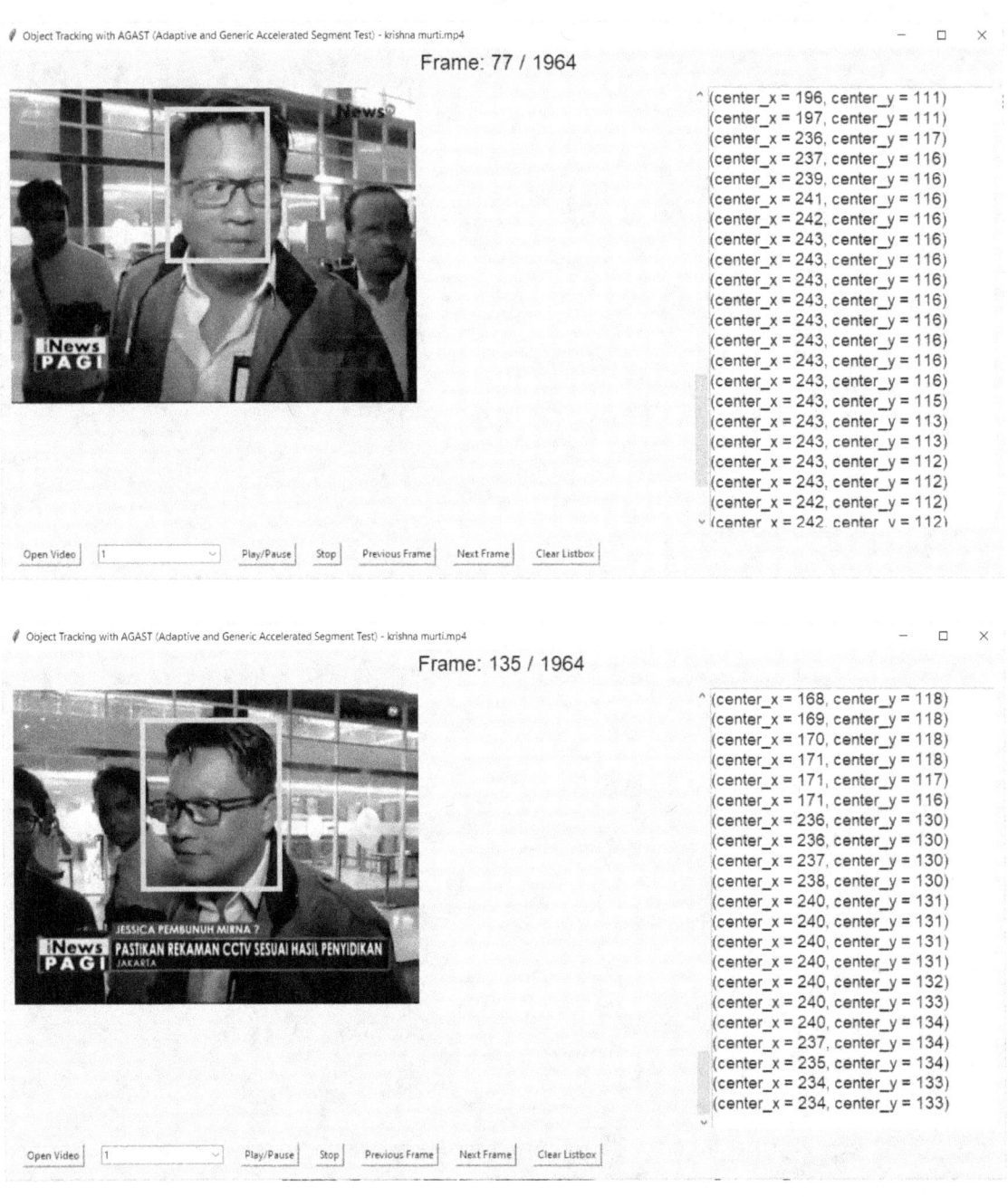

OBJECT TRACKING WITH AKAZE (ACCELERATED-KAZE)

DESCRIPTION

The "Object Tracking with AKAZE (Accelerated-KAZE)" project is a Python application designed to facilitate real-time object tracking within videos. It utilizes the AKAZE (Accelerated-KAZE) algorithm, known for its speed and effectiveness in feature detection and matching, enabling precise and reliable tracking of objects as they move within a video.

Upon launching the application, users are greeted with a graphical user interface (GUI) created using the tkinter library. This GUI provides a user-friendly environment, comprising various components tailored to support video playback, object tracking, and visualization of tracking outcomes.

At the heart of the GUI lies the Video Display Panel, housing a canvas where original video frames are showcased in real-time. Here, users can observe video playback and monitor the movement of objects within the video stream.

The Control Buttons Panel is another essential feature, offering users a range of controls for managing video playback. These controls include options to open video files, play or pause the video, stop the video, navigate to previous and next frames, and clear the listbox displaying center coordinates.

To enhance user experience, a Zoom Scale Combobox is provided, enabling users to adjust the zoom level of the video display. This feature empowers users to zoom in or out, allowing them to focus on specific details within the video.

Additionally, the Center Coordinates Listbox is incorporated to display the coordinates of the center of the bounding box around the tracked object. This information offers insights into the movement patterns of the tracked object over time, aiding in comprehensive analysis.

The core functionality of the application is encapsulated within the ObjectTracking_AKAZE class, housing methods for video playback, object tracking using the AKAZE algorithm, and GUI event handling.

Key functionalities of the application include opening video files, controlling video playback, performing object tracking with AKAZE, and displaying frames along with tracking results.

Through interactive features like selecting the initial bounding box around the object of interest by clicking and dragging on the canvas, users can actively participate in the object tracking process.

Overall, the "Object Tracking with AKAZE" project provides a robust platform for real-time object tracking in videos, offering users an intuitive interface and harnessing advanced computer vision techniques for accurate and efficient tracking of objects.

SOURCE CODE

```python
# object_tracking_akaze.py
import tkinter as tk
from tkinter import ttk
from tkinter import filedialog
from PIL import Image, ImageTk
import imageio
import cv2
import numpy as np

class ObjectTracking_AKAZE:
    def __init__(self, master):
        self.master = master
        self.master.title("Object Tracking with AKAZE (Accelerated-KAZE)")
        self.file_name = ""
        self.set_window_title()  # Set window title initially

        self.frame_number_label = tk.Label(master, text="Frame: 0")
        self.frame_number_label.pack()

        self.video = None
        self.video_path = None
        self.paused = False
        self.zoom_scale = tk.IntVar(value=1)
        self.frame_index = 0
        self.bbox = None
        self.tracking_started = False  # Initialize tracking_started to False
        self.prev_frame_gray = None

        self.bbox_rect = None  # Initialize bbox_rect attribute to None
        self.frame_processing = False  # Initialize frame_processing attribute to False

        self.create_widgets()

    def create_widgets(self):
        # Panel for video display
        video_panel = tk.Frame(self.master)
        video_panel.pack(padx=10, pady=10)

        # Canvas to display the original video
        canvas_width = 800
        canvas_height = 500
        self.canvas = tk.Canvas(video_panel, width=canvas_width, height=canvas_height)
        self.canvas.pack(side="left", fill="both", expand=True)
        self.canvas.bind("<MouseWheel>", self.on_mousewheel)
        self.canvas.bind("<ButtonPress-1>", self.on_press)
        self.canvas.bind("<B1-Motion>", self.on_drag)

        # List box to display center coordinates
        self.center_listbox = tk.Listbox(video_panel, width=30, height=20, font=("Helvetica", 14))
        self.center_listbox.pack(side="right", fill="y")
        # Scrollbar for the listbox
        scrollbar = tk.Scrollbar(video_panel, orient="vertical")
        scrollbar.pack(side="left", fill="y")
        scrollbar.config(command=self.center_listbox.yview)

        # Attach scrollbar to listbox
        self.center_listbox.config(yscrollcommand=scrollbar.set)

        # Panel for control buttons
```

```python
        control_panel = tk.Frame(self.master)
        control_panel.pack(padx=10, pady=(0, 10), fill="x")

        # Button to open a video file
        self.open_button = tk.Button(control_panel, text="Open Video", command=self.open_video)
        self.open_button.grid(row=0, column=0, padx=10, pady=5)

        # Combobox for selecting zoom scale
        self.zoom_combobox = ttk.Combobox(control_panel, textvariable=self.zoom_scale, values=list(range(1, 11)))
        self.zoom_combobox.grid(row=0, column=1, padx=10, pady=5)
        self.zoom_combobox.bind("<<ComboboxSelected>>", self.update_zoom)

        # Button to play/pause the video
        self.play_button = tk.Button(control_panel, text="Play/Pause", command=self.toggle_play_pause)
        self.play_button.grid(row=0, column=2, padx=10, pady=5)

        # Button to stop the video
        self.stop_button = tk.Button(control_panel, text="Stop", command=self.stop_video)
        self.stop_button.grid(row=0, column=3, padx=10, pady=5)

        # Button to navigate to the previous frame
        self.prev_frame_button = tk.Button(control_panel, text="Previous Frame", command=self.prev_frame)
        self.prev_frame_button.grid(row=0, column=4, padx=10, pady=5)

        # Button to navigate to the next frame
        self.next_frame_button = tk.Button(control_panel, text="Next Frame", command=self.next_frame)
        self.next_frame_button.grid(row=0, column=5, padx=10, pady=5)

        # Button to clear the listbox
        self.clear_button = tk.Button(control_panel, text="Clear Listbox", command=self.clear_listbox)
        self.clear_button.grid(row=0, column=6, padx=10, pady=5)

    def open_video(self):
        self.video_path = filedialog.askopenfilename(filetypes=[("Video files", "*.mp4;*.avi;*.mkv;*.wmv")])
        if self.video_path:
            self.video = imageio.get_reader(self.video_path)
            self.file_name = self.video_path.split('/')[-1]
            self.set_window_title()
            self.play_video()

    def play_video(self):
        if self.video:
            self.paused = False
            self.tracking_started = True
            self.show_frame()

    def stop_video(self):
        self.paused = True
        self.frame_index = 0
        self.bbox = None
        self.show_frame()

    def toggle_play_pause(self):
        self.paused = not self.paused
        if not self.paused:
            if self.bbox is not None:
                self.tracking_started = True
            self.play_video()
```

```python
    def update_zoom(self, event=None):
        self.show_frame()

    def akaze_vectors(self, prev_frame_gray, frame_gray):
        # Create AKAZE object with custom parameters
        akaze = cv2.AKAZE_create(descriptor_type=cv2.AKAZE_DESCRIPTOR_MLDB,
                                 descriptor_size=0,
                                 descriptor_channels=3,
                                 threshold=0.001,
                                 nOctaves=4,
                                 nOctaveLayers=4,
                                 diffusivity=cv2.KAZE_DIFF_PM_G2)

        # Detect and compute keypoints and descriptors for the previous frame
        keypoints_prev, descriptors_prev = akaze.detectAndCompute(prev_frame_gray, None)

        # Detect and compute keypoints and descriptors for the current frame
        keypoints_frame, descriptors_frame = akaze.detectAndCompute(frame_gray, None)

        # Create BFMatcher object
        bf = cv2.BFMatcher()

        # Match descriptors
        matches = bf.knnMatch(descriptors_prev, descriptors_frame, k=2)

        # Apply ratio test
        good_matches = []
        for m, n in matches:
            if m.distance < 0.75 * n.distance:
                good_matches.append(m)

        # Estimate motion vectors from good matches
        motion_vectors = np.zeros((len(good_matches), 2))
        for i, match in enumerate(good_matches):
            # Get the keypoints for the matched points
            prev_point = keypoints_prev[match.queryIdx].pt
            frame_point = keypoints_frame[match.trainIdx].pt

            # Calculate the motion vector
            dx = frame_point[0] - prev_point[0]
            dy = frame_point[1] - prev_point[1]

            # Store the motion vector
            motion_vectors[i] = [dx, dy]

        return motion_vectors

    def track_object(self, frame, bbox):
        if bbox:
            x1, y1, x2, y2 = map(int, bbox)
            roi = frame[y1:y2, x1:x2]
            if roi.size > 0:
                # Convert the ROI to grayscale
                roi_gray = cv2.cvtColor(roi, cv2.COLOR_BGR2GRAY)
                # Initialize the previous frame if not already initialized or if its dimensions don't match the current frame
                if self.prev_frame_gray is None or self.prev_frame_gray.shape != roi_gray.shape:
                    self.prev_frame_gray = roi_gray.copy()

                # Calculate motion vectors using AKAZE Algorithm
                motion_vectors = self.akaze_vectors(self.prev_frame_gray, roi_gray)
```

```python
            # Calculate the mean motion vector within the bounding box
            mean_motion_vector = np.mean(motion_vectors, axis=0)

            # Update the bounding box coordinates based on the mean motion vector
            x1 += int(mean_motion_vector[0])
            y1 += int(mean_motion_vector[1])
            x2 += int(mean_motion_vector[0])
            y2 += int(mean_motion_vector[1])

            # Update the previous frame
            self.prev_frame_gray = roi_gray.copy()

            # Calculate the center of the bounding box
            center_x = (x1 + x2) // 2
            center_y = (y1 + y2) // 2

            # Add the center coordinates to the list box
            self.center_listbox.insert(tk.END, f"(center_x = {center_x}, center_y = {center_y})")

            return x1, y1, x2, y2
        return None

    def update_bbox_rectangle(self, bbox):
        if bbox is not None:
            x1, y1, x2, y2 = map(int, bbox)
            if self.bbox_rect is not None:
                self.canvas.coords(self.bbox_rect, x1, y1, x2, y2)
                self.canvas.tag_raise(self.bbox_rect)  # Raise the bounding box to the front
            else:
                self.bbox_rect = self.canvas.create_rectangle(x1, y1, x2-50, y2-50, outline='lightgreen', width=8, tags="bbox")

    def show_frame(self):
        if self.video:
            if not self.paused:
                if 0 <= self.frame_index < len(self.video):
                    if not self.frame_processing:  # Check if the frame is already being processed
                        try:
                            self.frame_processing = True  # Set frame_processing flag to True to indicate frame processing

                            frame = self.video.get_data(self.frame_index)
                            frame = cv2.cvtColor(frame, cv2.COLOR_RGB2BGR)

                            if self.bbox is not None:
                                if not self.tracking_started:
                                    self.tracking_started = True

                                self.bbox = self.track_object(frame, self.bbox)
                                if self.bbox:
                                    frame = cv2.cvtColor(frame, cv2.COLOR_BGR2RGB)
                                    frame = Image.fromarray(frame)
                                    frame = frame.resize((frame.width * self.zoom_scale.get(), frame.height * self.zoom_scale.get()))
                                    photo = ImageTk.PhotoImage(frame)
                                    self.photo = photo
                                    self.canvas.delete("video")
                                    self.canvas.create_image(0, 0, anchor="nw", image=photo, tags="video")

                                    self.update_bbox_rectangle(self.bbox)
                                else:
```

```python
                                frame = cv2.cvtColor(frame, cv2.COLOR_BGR2RGB)
                                frame = Image.fromarray(frame)
                                frame = frame.resize((frame.width * self.zoom_scale.get(), frame.height * self.zoom_scale.get()))
                                photo = ImageTk.PhotoImage(frame)
                                self.photo = photo
                                self.canvas.delete("video")
                                self.canvas.create_image(0, 0, anchor="nw", image=photo, tags="video")

                                self.frame_number_label.config(text=f"Frame: {self.frame_index} / {self.video.count_frames()}", font=("Helvetica", 18))

                                self.frame_index += 1

                        except Exception as e:
                            print("Error: ", e)
                        finally:
                            self.frame_processing = False  # Reset frame_processing flag to False after processing the frame

    def on_mousewheel(self, event):
        direction = event.delta // 120
        current_value = int(self.zoom_scale.get())
        if direction == 1 and current_value < 10:
            current_value += 1
        elif direction == -1 and current_value > 1:
            current_value -= 1
        self.zoom_scale.set(current_value)
        self.update_zoom()

    def on_press(self, event):
        self.start_x = self.canvas.canvasx(event.x)
        self.start_y = self.canvas.canvasy(event.y)
        self.bbox = None

    def on_drag(self, event):
        cur_x = self.canvas.canvasx(event.x)
        cur_y = self.canvas.canvasy(event.y)
        if self.bbox_rect:
            self.canvas.delete(self.bbox_rect)
        self.bbox = (self.start_x, self.start_y, cur_x, cur_y)
        self.bbox_rect = self.canvas.create_rectangle(*self.bbox, outline='lightgreen', width=6)

    def prev_frame(self):
        if self.frame_index > 0:
            self.frame_index -= 1
            self.show_frame()

    def next_frame(self):
        if self.video and self.frame_index < len(self.video) - 1:
            self.show_frame()

    def clear_listbox(self):
        self.center_listbox.delete(0, tk.END)

    def set_window_title(self):
        if self.file_name:
            self.master.title(f"Object Tracking with AKAZE (Accelerated-KAZE) - {self.file_name}")
            self.master.title_font = ("Helvetica", 16, "bold")
        else:
            self.master.title("Object Tracking with AKAZE (Accelerated-KAZE)")
```

```
def main():
    root = tk.Tk()
    app = ObjectTracking_AKAZE(root)
    root.mainloop()

if __name__ == "__main__":
    main()
```

RUNNING PROGRAM

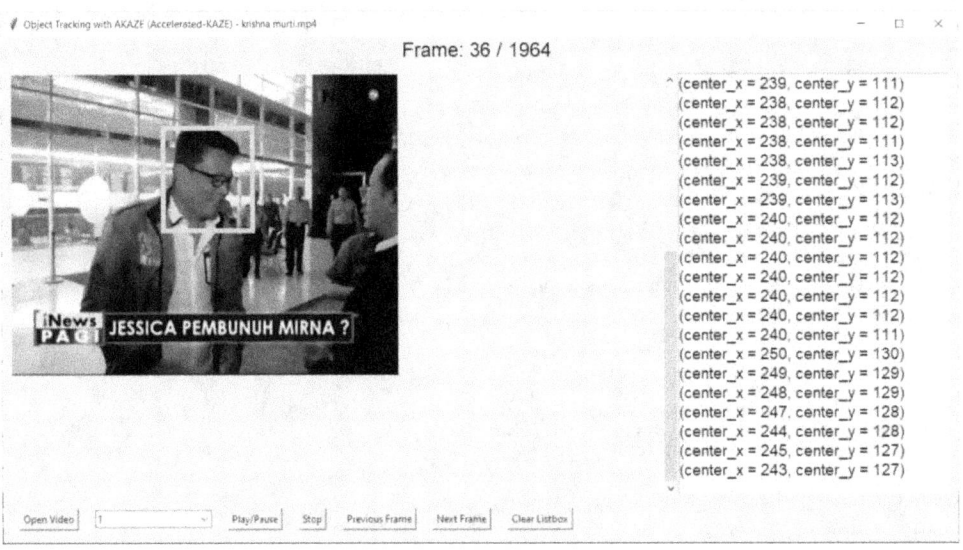

OBJECT TRACKING WITH BRISK (BINARY ROBUST INVARIANT SCALABLE KEYPOINTS)

DESCRIPTION

The "Object Tracking with BRISK" project is a Python application designed for real-time object tracking within videos using the BRISK (Binary Robust Invariant Scalable Keypoints) algorithm. This project features a graphical user interface (GUI) built with the tkinter library, offering users an intuitive and interactive environment for video playback and object tracking.

When the application starts, it presents users with a window titled "Object Tracking with BRISK (Binary Robust Invariant Scalable Keypoints)." The window contains several elements, including a label displaying the current frame number, a video display panel, a control panel with various buttons, and a list box showing the center coordinates of the tracked object.

The main interface element is the Video Display Panel, which features a canvas for displaying video frames. Users can view the video playback and interact with the canvas to select the region of interest (ROI) for tracking. The canvas supports mouse wheel events for zooming and mouse button events for drawing the bounding box around the object to be tracked.

Adjacent to the canvas is the Center Coordinates Listbox, which displays the coordinates of the object's center as it moves. This information helps users understand the object's trajectory over time. The list box is scrollable, making it easy to review the coordinates of previous frames.

The Control Buttons Panel houses several buttons that allow users to manage video playback and tracking. The "Open Video" button lets users select a video file from their system. The "Play/Pause" button toggles the video playback, and the "Stop" button stops the video and resets the frame index. Users can navigate through the video frames using the "Previous Frame" and "Next Frame" buttons. The "Clear Listbox" button empties the list box displaying the center coordinates.

The Zoom Scale Combobox allows users to adjust the zoom level of the video display. This feature enables users to focus on specific details within the video, providing better control over the tracking process. The zoom level can be adjusted from 1 to 10, offering a range of magnification options.

The core functionality of the application lies in the ObjectTracking_BRISK class. This class contains methods for handling video playback, managing user interactions, and performing object tracking using the BRISK algorithm. The BRISK algorithm is known for its speed and robustness in detecting and matching keypoints, making it suitable for real-time tracking applications.

The open_video method allows users to select and open a video file. Once a video is opened, the play_video method starts the playback and initializes the tracking process. The show_frame method is responsible for displaying the current frame on the canvas and updating the bounding box if tracking is active.

The track_object method performs the actual tracking by calculating motion vectors between consecutive frames using the BRISK algorithm. These motion vectors are used to update the coordinates of the bounding box, ensuring that the object is accurately tracked as it moves. The method also calculates the center of the bounding box and adds the coordinates to the list box.

The update_bbox_rectangle method updates the position of the bounding box on the canvas, ensuring it remains visible and accurately represents the tracked object's location. The bounding box is drawn as a rectangle with a red outline, making it easy to distinguish from the video content.

User interactions with the canvas are handled by the on_press and on_drag methods. These methods allow users to define the initial bounding box by clicking and dragging on the canvas. The bounding box coordinates are then used by the track_object method for tracking the selected object.

The play_video method manages the playback state, ensuring that frames are displayed in sequence. It also checks if tracking is active and updates the bounding box and list box accordingly. The toggle_play_pause method toggles the playback state, allowing users to pause and resume the video as needed.

The stop_video method stops the video playback and resets the tracking state. It clears the bounding box and resets the frame index to the beginning of the video. This method is useful for users who want to restart the tracking process or load a different video.

The prev_frame and next_frame methods allow users to navigate through the video frames. These methods are useful for reviewing specific frames or adjusting the bounding box if tracking needs to be corrected manually.

The clear_listbox method clears the list box displaying the center coordinates, providing a clean slate for new tracking sessions. This is particularly useful when users want to track a different object or start tracking from a different point in the video.

The update_zoom method adjusts the zoom level of the video display based on user input from the combobox or mouse wheel events. This feature enhances the user's ability to focus on specific areas of the video, improving the tracking accuracy.

The set_window_title method updates the window title to include the name of the currently opened video file. This provides a clear indication of the video being tracked, making it easier for users to manage multiple tracking sessions.

In summary, the "Object Tracking with BRISK" project provides a comprehensive and user-friendly platform for real-time object tracking in videos. It combines a robust tracking algorithm with an intuitive GUI, enabling users to interactively select and track objects within video streams. With features like zoom adjustment, frame navigation, and a list box for tracking coordinates, the application offers a versatile tool for analyzing object movements in video content. The project demonstrates the effective integration of computer vision techniques and user interface design, making advanced tracking capabilities accessible to a wide range of users.

SOURCE CODE

```python
# object_tracking_brisk.py
import tkinter as tk
from tkinter import ttk
from tkinter import filedialog
from PIL import Image, ImageTk
import imageio
import cv2
import numpy as np

class ObjectTracking_BRISK:
    def __init__(self, master):
        self.master = master
        self.master.title("Object Tracking with BRISK (Binary Robust Invariant Scalable Keypoints)")
        self.file_name = ""
        self.set_window_title()  # Set window title initially

        self.frame_number_label = tk.Label(master, text="Frame: 0")
        self.frame_number_label.pack()

        self.video = None
        self.video_path = None
        self.paused = False
        self.zoom_scale = tk.IntVar(value=1)
        self.frame_index = 0
        self.bbox = None
        self.tracking_started = False  # Initialize tracking_started to False
        self.prev_frame_gray = None

        self.bbox_rect = None  # Initialize bbox_rect attribute to None
        self.frame_processing = False  # Initialize frame_processing attribute to False

        self.create_widgets()

    def create_widgets(self):
        # Panel for video display
        video_panel = tk.Frame(self.master)
        video_panel.pack(padx=10, pady=10)

        # Canvas to display the original video
        canvas_width = 800
        canvas_height = 500
        self.canvas = tk.Canvas(video_panel, width=canvas_width, height=canvas_height)
        self.canvas.pack(side="left", fill="both", expand=True)
        self.canvas.bind("<MouseWheel>", self.on_mousewheel)
        self.canvas.bind("<ButtonPress-1>", self.on_press)
```

```python
        self.canvas.bind("<B1-Motion>", self.on_drag)

        # List box to display center coordinates
        self.center_listbox = tk.Listbox(video_panel, width=30, height=20, font=("Helvetica", 14))
        self.center_listbox.pack(side="right", fill="y")
        # Scrollbar for the listbox
        scrollbar = tk.Scrollbar(video_panel, orient="vertical")
        scrollbar.pack(side="left", fill="y")
        scrollbar.config(command=self.center_listbox.yview)

        # Attach scrollbar to listbox
        self.center_listbox.config(yscrollcommand=scrollbar.set)

        # Panel for control buttons
        control_panel = tk.Frame(self.master)
        control_panel.pack(padx=10, pady=(0, 10), fill="x")

        # Button to open a video file
        self.open_button = tk.Button(control_panel, text="Open Video", command=self.open_video)
        self.open_button.grid(row=0, column=0, padx=10, pady=5)

        # Combobox for selecting zoom scale
        self.zoom_combobox = ttk.Combobox(control_panel, textvariable=self.zoom_scale, values=list(range(1, 11)))
        self.zoom_combobox.grid(row=0, column=1, padx=10, pady=5)
        self.zoom_combobox.bind("<<ComboboxSelected>>", self.update_zoom)

        # Button to play/pause the video
        self.play_button = tk.Button(control_panel, text="Play/Pause", command=self.toggle_play_pause)
        self.play_button.grid(row=0, column=2, padx=10, pady=5)

        # Button to stop the video
        self.stop_button = tk.Button(control_panel, text="Stop", command=self.stop_video)
        self.stop_button.grid(row=0, column=3, padx=10, pady=5)

        # Button to navigate to the previous frame
        self.prev_frame_button = tk.Button(control_panel, text="Previous Frame", command=self.prev_frame)
        self.prev_frame_button.grid(row=0, column=4, padx=10, pady=5)

        # Button to navigate to the next frame
        self.next_frame_button = tk.Button(control_panel, text="Next Frame", command=self.next_frame)
        self.next_frame_button.grid(row=0, column=5, padx=10, pady=5)

        # Button to clear the listbox
        self.clear_button = tk.Button(control_panel, text="Clear Listbox", command=self.clear_listbox)
        self.clear_button.grid(row=0, column=6, padx=10, pady=5)

    def open_video(self):
        self.video_path = filedialog.askopenfilename(filetypes=[("Video files", "*.mp4;*.avi;*.mkv;*.wmv")])
        if self.video_path:
            self.video = imageio.get_reader(self.video_path)
            self.file_name = self.video_path.split('/')[-1]
            self.set_window_title()
            self.play_video()

    def play_video(self):
        if self.video:
            self.paused = False
```

```python
            self.tracking_started = True
            self.show_frame()

    def stop_video(self):
        self.paused = True
        self.frame_index = 0
        self.bbox = None
        self.show_frame()

    def toggle_play_pause(self):
        self.paused = not self.paused
        if not self.paused:
            if self.bbox is not None:
                self.tracking_started = True
            self.play_video()

    def update_zoom(self, event=None):
        self.show_frame()

    def brisk_vectors(self, prev_frame_gray, frame_gray):
        # Create BRISK object with custom parameters
        brisk = cv2.BRISK_create(thresh=30, octaves=3, patternScale=1.0)

        # Detect and compute keypoints and descriptors for the previous frame
        keypoints_prev, descriptors_prev = brisk.detectAndCompute(prev_frame_gray, None)

        # Detect and compute keypoints and descriptors for the current frame
        keypoints_frame, descriptors_frame = brisk.detectAndCompute(frame_gray, None)

        # Create BFMatcher object
        bf = cv2.BFMatcher()

        # Match descriptors
        matches = bf.knnMatch(descriptors_prev, descriptors_frame, k=2)

        # Apply ratio test
        good_matches = []
        for m, n in matches:
            if m.distance < 0.75 * n.distance:
                good_matches.append(m)

        # Estimate motion vectors from good matches
        motion_vectors = np.zeros((len(good_matches), 2))
        for i, match in enumerate(good_matches):
            # Get the keypoints for the matched points
            prev_point = keypoints_prev[match.queryIdx].pt
            frame_point = keypoints_frame[match.trainIdx].pt

            # Calculate the motion vector
            dx = frame_point[0] - prev_point[0]
            dy = frame_point[1] - prev_point[1]

            # Store the motion vector
            motion_vectors[i] = [dx, dy]

        return motion_vectors

    def track_object(self, frame, bbox):
        if bbox:
            x1, y1, x2, y2 = map(int, bbox)
            roi = frame[y1:y2, x1:x2]
            if roi.size > 0:
                # Convert the ROI to grayscale
                roi_gray = cv2.cvtColor(roi, cv2.COLOR_BGR2GRAY)
```

```python
            # Initialize the previous frame if not already initialized or if its dimensions don't match the current frame
            if self.prev_frame_gray is None or self.prev_frame_gray.shape != roi_gray.shape:
                self.prev_frame_gray = roi_gray.copy()

            # Calculate motion vectors using BRISK Algorithm
            motion_vectors = self.brisk_vectors(self.prev_frame_gray, roi_gray)

            # Calculate the mean motion vector within the bounding box
            mean_motion_vector = np.mean(motion_vectors, axis=0)

            # Update the bounding box coordinates based on the mean motion vector
            x1 += int(mean_motion_vector[0])
            y1 += int(mean_motion_vector[1])
            x2 += int(mean_motion_vector[0])
            y2 += int(mean_motion_vector[1])

            # Update the previous frame
            self.prev_frame_gray = roi_gray.copy()

            # Calculate the center of the bounding box
            center_x = (x1 + x2) // 2
            center_y = (y1 + y2) // 2

            # Add the center coordinates to the list box
            self.center_listbox.insert(tk.END, f"(center_x = {center_x}, center_y = {center_y})")

            return x1, y1, x2, y2
        return None

    def update_bbox_rectangle(self, bbox):
        if bbox is not None:
            x1, y1, x2, y2 = map(int, bbox)
            if self.bbox_rect is not None:
                self.canvas.coords(self.bbox_rect, x1, y1, x2, y2)
                self.canvas.tag_raise(self.bbox_rect)  # Raise the bounding box to the front
            else:
                self.bbox_rect = self.canvas.create_rectangle(x1, y1, x2-50, y2-50, outline='#fc3d3d', width=8, tags="bbox")

    def show_frame(self):
        if self.video:
            if not self.paused:
                if 0 <= self.frame_index < len(self.video):
                    if not self.frame_processing:  # Check if the frame is already being processed
                        try:
                            self.frame_processing = True  # Set frame_processing flag to True to indicate frame processing

                            frame = self.video.get_data(self.frame_index)
                            frame = cv2.cvtColor(frame, cv2.COLOR_RGB2BGR)

                            if self.bbox is not None:
                                if not self.tracking_started:
                                    self.tracking_started = True

                                self.bbox = self.track_object(frame, self.bbox)
                                if self.bbox:
                                    frame = cv2.cvtColor(frame, cv2.COLOR_BGR2RGB)
                                    frame = Image.fromarray(frame)
```

```
                                        frame = frame.resize((frame.width * self.zoom_scale.get(),
frame.height * self.zoom_scale.get()))
                                        photo = ImageTk.PhotoImage(frame)
                                        self.photo = photo
                                        self.canvas.delete("video")
                                        self.canvas.create_image(0, 0, anchor="nw", image=photo,
tags="video")
                                        self.update_bbox_rectangle(self.bbox)

                            else:
                                frame = cv2.cvtColor(frame, cv2.COLOR_BGR2RGB)
                                frame = Image.fromarray(frame)
                                frame = frame.resize((frame.width * self.zoom_scale.get(),
frame.height * self.zoom_scale.get()))
                                photo = ImageTk.PhotoImage(frame)
                                self.photo = photo
                                self.canvas.delete("video")
                                self.canvas.create_image(0, 0, anchor="nw", image=photo,
tags="video")

                            self.frame_number_label.config(text=f"Frame: {self.frame_index} /
{self.video.count_frames()}", font=("Helvetica", 18))

                            self.frame_index += 1

                except Exception as e:
                    print("Error: ", e)
                finally:
                    self.frame_processing = False  # Reset frame_processing flag to
False after processing the frame

    def on_mousewheel(self, event):
        direction = event.delta // 120
        current_value = int(self.zoom_scale.get())
        if direction == 1 and current_value < 10:
            current_value += 1
        elif direction == -1 and current_value > 1:
            current_value -= 1
        self.zoom_scale.set(current_value)
        self.update_zoom()

    def on_press(self, event):
        self.start_x = self.canvas.canvasx(event.x)
        self.start_y = self.canvas.canvasy(event.y)
        self.bbox = None

    def on_drag(self, event):
        cur_x = self.canvas.canvasx(event.x)
        cur_y = self.canvas.canvasy(event.y)
        if self.bbox_rect:
            self.canvas.delete(self.bbox_rect)
        self.bbox = (self.start_x, self.start_y, cur_x, cur_y)
        self.bbox_rect = self.canvas.create_rectangle(*self.bbox, outline='#fc3d3d', width=6)

    def prev_frame(self):
        if self.frame_index > 0:
            self.frame_index -= 1
            self.show_frame()

    def next_frame(self):
        if self.video and self.frame_index < len(self.video) - 1:
            self.show_frame()

    def clear_listbox(self):
```

```python
            self.center_listbox.delete(0, tk.END)

    def set_window_title(self):
        if self.file_name:
            self.master.title(f"Object Tracking with BRISK (Binary Robust Invariant Scalable Keypoints) - {self.file_name}")
            self.master.title_font = ("Helvetica", 16, "bold")
        else:
            self.master.title("Object Tracking with BRISK (Binary Robust Invariant Scalable Keypoints)")

def main():
    root = tk.Tk()
    app = ObjectTracking_BRISK(root)
    root.mainloop()

if __name__ == "__main__":
    main()
```

RUNNING PROGRAM

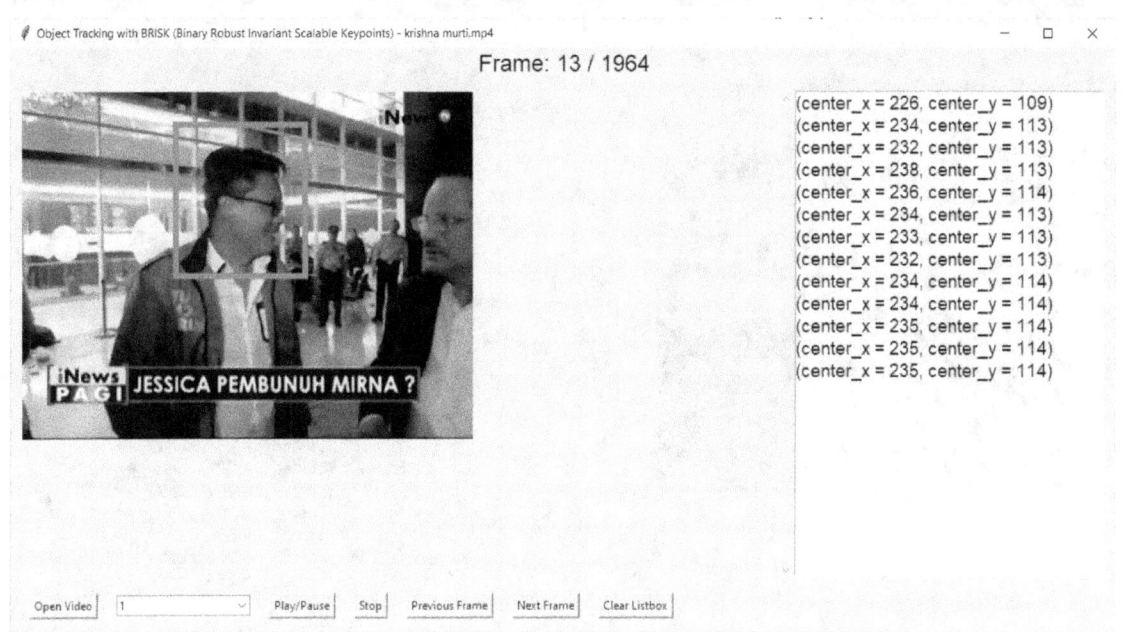

OBJECT TRACKING WITH GLOH (GRADIENT LOCATION-ORIENTATION HISTOGRAM)

DESCRIPTION

The object_tracking_gloh.py project is a Python application that utilizes the Tkinter library for the graphical user interface (GUI) and OpenCV for computer vision tasks. This project is designed to perform object tracking in video files using the Gradient Location-Orientation Histogram (GLOH) method. The application features a robust user interface that allows users to load videos, navigate through frames, and visualize tracking results.

Upon launching the application, the main window is initialized with a title indicating that the program is for "Object Tracking with GLOH (Gradient Location-Orientation Histogram)." The interface includes a label displaying the current frame number, a video canvas for displaying frames, and a list box to show the coordinates of tracked object centers. The window title dynamically updates based on the loaded video file.

The main functionalities are encapsulated within the ObjectTracking_GLOH class. This class handles various tasks such as video loading, playback controls, and object tracking.

The constructor of this class sets up initial values for several instance variables, including the video path, frame index, and bounding box coordinates. It also initializes the tracking state and sets up the GUI components.

The create_widgets method is responsible for creating and organizing the GUI components. It sets up a video panel with a canvas to display video frames and binds mouse events for zooming and drawing bounding boxes. The method also creates a control panel with buttons for opening videos, controlling playback, and navigating frames. Additionally, it includes a combobox for zoom scaling and a list box with a scrollbar to display tracked coordinates.

The open_video method allows users to select a video file from their filesystem. Upon selecting a file, the video is loaded using the imageio library, and the filename is extracted and displayed in the window title. The method then initiates video playback by calling play_video.

The play_video method starts the video playback by setting the paused state to false and begins showing frames by calling show_frame. This method ensures continuous frame display unless paused. If tracking has started, it updates the bounding box coordinates and displays the tracked object on each frame.

The stop_video method stops the video playback, resets the frame index to zero, and clears the bounding box. This method is useful for restarting the video or halting the tracking process.

The toggle_play_pause method toggles between playing and pausing the video. When the video is resumed, it ensures that tracking continues if a bounding box is present. This method provides a simple way to control video playback without losing the current frame position.

The update_zoom method updates the zoom level of the displayed video frame based on user input. It ensures that the zoom scale changes are immediately reflected in the video display, enhancing the user's ability to inspect details within the frame.

The gloh_vectors method implements the GLOH algorithm for detecting keypoints and computing descriptors. It uses the SIFT (Scale-Invariant Feature Transform) implementation in OpenCV to detect keypoints and match them between frames. The method applies a ratio test to filter good matches and computes motion vectors based on the matched keypoints.

The track_object method handles the core tracking functionality. It extracts the region of interest (ROI) based on the bounding box, converts it to grayscale, and calculates motion vectors using the gloh_vectors method. The method then updates the bounding box coordinates based on the mean motion vector, ensuring the tracked object is accurately followed across frames. The center coordinates of the bounding box are added to the list box for user reference.

The update_bbox_rectangle method visually updates the bounding box on the video canvas. It ensures that the bounding box is correctly drawn and positioned according to the updated coordinates, providing a clear visual indication of the tracked object.

The show_frame method is responsible for displaying the current frame of the video. It checks if the video is paused and if the frame index is within the valid range. This method processes each frame, updates the bounding box if tracking is enabled, and displays the frame on the canvas. It also updates the frame number label to reflect the current frame index.

The on_mousewheel method handles zooming in and out of the video frame based on mouse wheel input. It adjusts the zoom scale variable and updates the frame display accordingly, providing an intuitive way for users to zoom.

The on_press and on_drag methods enable users to draw a bounding box on the video frame using mouse events. These methods capture the starting point and dynamically update the bounding box as the user drags the mouse, allowing for easy initialization of the tracking region.

The prev_frame and next_frame methods allow users to navigate through the video frames manually. These methods adjust the frame index and call show_frame to display the previous or next frame, respectively. This functionality is useful for precise frame-by-frame analysis.

The clear_listbox method clears the list box that displays the coordinates of the tracked object centers. This method is helpful for resetting the tracking data and starting a new tracking session without residual data.

The set_window_title method updates the window title based on the loaded video file name. It ensures that the title reflects the current state of the application, providing context to the user.

The main function initializes the Tkinter root window and creates an instance of the ObjectTracking_GLOH class. It starts the Tkinter main loop, which keeps the application running and responsive to user interactions.

Overall, the object_tracking_gloh.py project provides a comprehensive tool for object tracking in videos using the GLOH method. It combines advanced computer vision techniques with an intuitive graphical interface, making it accessible for users to load videos, define tracking regions, and visualize tracking results in real-time. The project demonstrates the effective integration of Tkinter for GUI development and OpenCV for computer vision tasks, showcasing the potential for creating powerful and user-friendly applications in Python.

SOURCE CODE

```python
# object_tracking_gloh.py
import tkinter as tk
from tkinter import ttk
from tkinter import filedialog
from PIL import Image, ImageTk
import imageio
import cv2
import numpy as np

class ObjectTracking_GLOH:
    def __init__(self, master):
        self.master = master
        self.master.title("Object Tracking with GLOH (Gradient Location-Orientation Histogram)")
        self.file_name = ""
        self.set_window_title()  # Set window title initially

        self.frame_number_label = tk.Label(master, text="Frame: 0")
        self.frame_number_label.pack()

        self.video = None
        self.video_path = None
        self.paused = False
        self.zoom_scale = tk.IntVar(value=1)
        self.frame_index = 0
        self.bbox = None
        self.tracking_started = False  # Initialize tracking_started to False
        self.prev_frame_gray = None
```

```python
        self.bbox_rect = None  # Initialize bbox_rect attribute to None
        self.frame_processing = False  # Initialize frame_processing attribute to False

        self.create_widgets()

    def create_widgets(self):
        # Panel for video display
        video_panel = tk.Frame(self.master)
        video_panel.pack(padx=10, pady=10)

        # Canvas to display the original video
        canvas_width = 800
        canvas_height = 500
        self.canvas = tk.Canvas(video_panel, width=canvas_width, height=canvas_height)
        self.canvas.pack(side="left", fill="both", expand=True)
        self.canvas.bind("<MouseWheel>", self.on_mousewheel)
        self.canvas.bind("<ButtonPress-1>", self.on_press)
        self.canvas.bind("<B1-Motion>", self.on_drag)

        # List box to display center coordinates
        self.center_listbox = tk.Listbox(video_panel, width=30, height=20, font=("Helvetica", 14))
        self.center_listbox.pack(side="right", fill="y")
        # Scrollbar for the listbox
        scrollbar = tk.Scrollbar(video_panel, orient="vertical")
        scrollbar.pack(side="left", fill="y")
        scrollbar.config(command=self.center_listbox.yview)

        # Attach scrollbar to listbox
        self.center_listbox.config(yscrollcommand=scrollbar.set)

        # Panel for control buttons
        control_panel = tk.Frame(self.master)
        control_panel.pack(padx=10, pady=(0, 10), fill="x")

        # Button to open a video file
        self.open_button = tk.Button(control_panel, text="Open Video", command=self.open_video)
        self.open_button.grid(row=0, column=0, padx=10, pady=5)

        # Combobox for selecting zoom scale
        self.zoom_combobox = ttk.Combobox(control_panel, textvariable=self.zoom_scale, values=list(range(1, 11)))
        self.zoom_combobox.grid(row=0, column=1, padx=10, pady=5)
        self.zoom_combobox.bind("<<ComboboxSelected>>", self.update_zoom)

        # Button to play/pause the video
        self.play_button = tk.Button(control_panel, text="Play/Pause", command=self.toggle_play_pause)
        self.play_button.grid(row=0, column=2, padx=10, pady=5)

        # Button to stop the video
        self.stop_button = tk.Button(control_panel, text="Stop", command=self.stop_video)
        self.stop_button.grid(row=0, column=3, padx=10, pady=5)

        # Button to navigate to the previous frame
        self.prev_frame_button = tk.Button(control_panel, text="Previous Frame", command=self.prev_frame)
        self.prev_frame_button.grid(row=0, column=4, padx=10, pady=5)

        # Button to navigate to the next frame
        self.next_frame_button = tk.Button(control_panel, text="Next Frame", command=self.next_frame)
        self.next_frame_button.grid(row=0, column=5, padx=10, pady=5)
```

```python
        # Button to clear the listbox
        self.clear_button = tk.Button(control_panel, text="Clear Listbox", command=self.clear_listbox)
        self.clear_button.grid(row=0, column=6, padx=10, pady=5)

    def open_video(self):
        self.video_path = filedialog.askopenfilename(filetypes=[("Video files", "*.mp4;*.avi;*.mkv;*.wmv")])
        if self.video_path:
            self.video = imageio.get_reader(self.video_path)
            self.file_name = self.video_path.split('/')[-1]
            self.set_window_title()
            self.play_video()

    def play_video(self):
        if self.video:
            self.paused = False
            self.tracking_started = True
            self.show_frame()

    def stop_video(self):
        self.paused = True
        self.frame_index = 0
        self.bbox = None
        self.show_frame()

    def toggle_play_pause(self):
        self.paused = not self.paused
        if not self.paused:
            if self.bbox is not None:
                self.tracking_started = True
            self.play_video()

    def update_zoom(self, event=None):
        self.show_frame()

    def gloh_vectors(self, prev_frame_gray, frame_gray):
        # Create SIFT object
        sift = cv2.SIFT_create()

        # Detect keypoints and compute descriptors for the previous frame
        keypoints_prev, descriptors_prev = sift.detectAndCompute(prev_frame_gray, None)

        # Detect keypoints and compute descriptors for the current frame
        keypoints_frame, descriptors_frame = sift.detectAndCompute(frame_gray, None)

        # Create BFMatcher object
        bf = cv2.BFMatcher()

        # Match descriptors
        matches = bf.knnMatch(descriptors_prev, descriptors_frame, k=2)

        # Apply ratio test
        good_matches = []
        for m, n in matches:
            if m.distance < 0.75 * n.distance:
                good_matches.append(m)

        # Estimate motion vectors from good matches
        motion_vectors = np.zeros((len(good_matches), 2))
        for i, match in enumerate(good_matches):
            # Get the keypoints for the matched points
            prev_point = keypoints_prev[match.queryIdx].pt
            frame_point = keypoints_frame[match.trainIdx].pt
```

```python
            # Calculate the motion vector
            dx = frame_point[0] - prev_point[0]
            dy = frame_point[1] - prev_point[1]

            # Store the motion vector
            motion_vectors[i] = [dx, dy]

        return motion_vectors

    def track_object(self, frame, bbox):
        if bbox:
            x1, y1, x2, y2 = map(int, bbox)
            roi = frame[y1:y2, x1:x2]
            if roi.size > 0:
                # Convert the ROI to grayscale
                roi_gray = cv2.cvtColor(roi, cv2.COLOR_BGR2GRAY)
                # Initialize the previous frame if not already initialized or if its dimensions don't match the current frame
                if self.prev_frame_gray is None or self.prev_frame_gray.shape != roi_gray.shape:
                    self.prev_frame_gray = roi_gray.copy()

                # Calculate motion vectors using GLOH Algorithm
                motion_vectors = self.gloh_vectors(self.prev_frame_gray, roi_gray)

                # Calculate the mean motion vector within the bounding box
                mean_motion_vector = np.mean(motion_vectors, axis=0)

                # Update the bounding box coordinates based on the mean motion vector
                x1 += int(mean_motion_vector[0])
                y1 += int(mean_motion_vector[1])
                x2 += int(mean_motion_vector[0])
                y2 += int(mean_motion_vector[1])

                # Update the previous frame
                self.prev_frame_gray = roi_gray.copy()

                # Calculate the center of the bounding box
                center_x = (x1 + x2) // 2
                center_y = (y1 + y2) // 2

                # Add the center coordinates to the list box
                self.center_listbox.insert(tk.END, f"(center_x = {center_x}, center_y = {center_y})")

                return x1, y1, x2, y2
        return None

    def update_bbox_rectangle(self, bbox):
        if bbox is not None:
            x1, y1, x2, y2 = map(int, bbox)
            if self.bbox_rect is not None:
                self.canvas.coords(self.bbox_rect, x1, y1, x2, y2)
                self.canvas.tag_raise(self.bbox_rect)  # Raise the bounding box to the front
            else:
                self.bbox_rect = self.canvas.create_rectangle(x1, y1, x2-50, y2-50, outline='lightgreen', width=8, tags="bbox")

    def show_frame(self):
        if self.video:
            if not self.paused:
                if 0 <= self.frame_index < len(self.video):
```

```python
                        if not self.frame_processing:  # Check if the frame is already being processed
                            try:
                                self.frame_processing = True  # Set frame_processing flag to True to indicate frame processing

                                frame = self.video.get_data(self.frame_index)
                                frame = cv2.cvtColor(frame, cv2.COLOR_RGB2BGR)

                                if self.bbox is not None:
                                    if not self.tracking_started:
                                        self.tracking_started = True

                                    self.bbox = self.track_object(frame, self.bbox)
                                    if self.bbox:
                                        frame = cv2.cvtColor(frame, cv2.COLOR_BGR2RGB)
                                        frame = Image.fromarray(frame)
                                        frame = frame.resize((frame.width * self.zoom_scale.get(), frame.height * self.zoom_scale.get()))
                                        photo = ImageTk.PhotoImage(frame)
                                        self.photo = photo
                                        self.canvas.delete("video")
                                        self.canvas.create_image(0, 0, anchor="nw", image=photo, tags="video")

                                        self.update_bbox_rectangle(self.bbox)

                                else:
                                    frame = cv2.cvtColor(frame, cv2.COLOR_BGR2RGB)
                                    frame = Image.fromarray(frame)
                                    frame = frame.resize((frame.width * self.zoom_scale.get(), frame.height * self.zoom_scale.get()))
                                    photo = ImageTk.PhotoImage(frame)
                                    self.photo = photo
                                    self.canvas.delete("video")
                                    self.canvas.create_image(0, 0, anchor="nw", image=photo, tags="video")

                                self.frame_number_label.config(text=f"Frame: {self.frame_index} / {self.video.count_frames()}", font=("Helvetica", 18))

                                self.frame_index += 1

                            except Exception as e:
                                print("Error: ", e)
                            finally:
                                self.frame_processing = False  # Reset frame_processing flag to False after processing the frame

    def on_mousewheel(self, event):
        direction = event.delta // 120
        current_value = int(self.zoom_scale.get())
        if direction == 1 and current_value < 10:
            current_value += 1
        elif direction == -1 and current_value > 1:
            current_value -= 1
        self.zoom_scale.set(current_value)
        self.update_zoom()

    def on_press(self, event):
        self.start_x = self.canvas.canvasx(event.x)
        self.start_y = self.canvas.canvasy(event.y)
        self.bbox = None

    def on_drag(self, event):
```

```python
            cur_x = self.canvas.canvasx(event.x)
            cur_y = self.canvas.canvasy(event.y)
            if self.bbox_rect:
                self.canvas.delete(self.bbox_rect)
            self.bbox = (self.start_x, self.start_y, cur_x, cur_y)
            self.bbox_rect = self.canvas.create_rectangle(*self.bbox, outline='lightgreen', width=6)

    def prev_frame(self):
        if self.frame_index > 0:
            self.frame_index -= 1
            self.show_frame()

    def next_frame(self):
        if self.video and self.frame_index < len(self.video) - 1:
            self.show_frame()

    def clear_listbox(self):
        self.center_listbox.delete(0, tk.END)

    def set_window_title(self):
        if self.file_name:
            self.master.title(f"Object Tracking with GLOH (Gradient Location-Orientation Histogram) - {self.file_name}")
            self.master.title_font = ("Helvetica", 16, "bold")
        else:
            self.master.title("Object Tracking with GLOH (Gradient Location-Orientation Histogram)")

def main():
    root = tk.Tk()
    app = ObjectTracking_GLOH(root)
    root.mainloop()

if __name__ == "__main__":
    main()
```

RUNNING PROGRAM

OBJECT TRACKING WITH BOOSTING TRACKER

DESCRIPTION

The "boosting_tracker.py" project is a Python-based graphical application designed to facilitate object tracking in videos using a boosting tracker algorithm. The program employs the Tkinter library for its graphical user interface, allowing users to interact with video files and perform object tracking tasks through a visually intuitive setup. The application is named "Object Tracking with Boosting Tracker," and its primary functionalities include loading video files, navigating through frames, setting up tracking regions, applying various filters, and displaying histograms for selected regions.

Upon launching the application, the main window is initialized with the title "Object Tracking with Boosting Tracker." The window title is dynamically updated based on the loaded video file's name. The interface consists of multiple components, including a frame number label, a canvas for video display, a listbox for showing center coordinates of tracked objects, control buttons for video operations, and a combobox for selecting zoom scales and filters.

The core class of the application is the "BoostingTracker," which manages all functionalities related to video loading, playback control, object tracking, and filtering. The "create_widgets" method sets up the user interface elements, such as the video display canvas, control buttons, and other interactive components. The canvas is designed to handle user interactions like mouse wheel scrolling for zooming and mouse clicks for selecting tracking regions.

When a video file is loaded using the "open_video" method, the application reads the video frames using the "imageio" library and prepares them for display. The video playback can be controlled using buttons for play/pause, stop, previous frame, and next frame operations. Users can also adjust the zoom scale of the video display through the provided combobox.

Object tracking is initiated when a user selects a region on the video canvas. The selected region is represented as a bounding box, which is used to initialize the boosting tracker. The "track_object" method updates the bounding box's position in each frame, and the new coordinates are displayed in the listbox. The application ensures that the tracker is re-initialized whenever a new bounding box is selected.

The application supports various image filters that can be applied to the selected region of the video. Filters like Gaussian, Mean, Median, Bilateral Filtering, and more are available for selection. The chosen filter is applied to the cropped region of the video, enhancing or modifying its appearance based on the filter's characteristics.

In addition to object tracking and filtering, the application includes features for analyzing and displaying histograms of the selected video region. The histograms provide visual insights into the pixel value distribution of the selected region, which can be useful for further analysis and understanding of the video's content.

The "analyze_histogram" method is triggered when the user releases the mouse button after selecting a region. This method extracts the selected region from the current frame and applies the chosen filter. The filtered frame is then displayed in a popup window along with its histogram. Two types of histograms are generated: line histograms and bar histograms, providing different visual representations of the pixel value distribution.

The application also includes error handling mechanisms to ensure smooth operation. For instance, it checks for invalid inputs or conditions such as empty frames, invalid frame indices, and incorrect bounding box dimensions. Appropriate error messages are displayed, and the application continues to function without crashing.

Advanced filtering techniques like Haar Wavelet Transform and Daubechies Wavelet Transform are also supported, offering sophisticated methods for image enhancement and noise reduction. These transforms are applied to each color channel separately and then merged back to form the final filtered image.

The "apply_filter" method serves as the central point for applying the selected filter to the video frame. It checks the chosen filter's name and calls the corresponding method to process the frame. Filters like the Wiener Filter, Adaptive Thresholding, and Total Variation Denoising are implemented with specific parameters to achieve desired effects.

The application provides a user-friendly way to interact with video files, allowing for detailed analysis and manipulation of video frames. Users can navigate through the video, select regions for tracking, apply filters, and view histograms, all within a single integrated interface.

Overall, the "boosting_tracker.py" project combines object tracking, image filtering, and histogram analysis into a comprehensive tool for video analysis. Its graphical user interface, built with Tkinter, ensures accessibility and ease of use, making it suitable for various applications in video processing and analysis.

The project demonstrates the use of multiple libraries, including OpenCV for computer vision tasks, PIL for image processing, and Matplotlib for plotting histograms. It integrates these libraries seamlessly to provide a robust and versatile tool for users.

The design of the application emphasizes user interaction, providing clear and intuitive controls for navigating videos and applying tracking and filtering operations. The dynamic updating of the interface elements, such as the video display and listbox, enhances the user experience and ensures real-time feedback.

In summary, "boosting_tracker.py" is a feature-rich application that leverages Python's capabilities to deliver advanced video tracking and analysis functionalities. Its combination of object tracking, filtering, and histogram analysis, presented through a well-designed graphical interface, makes it a valuable tool for users working with video data.

SOURCE CODE

```python
# boosting_tracker.py
import tkinter as tk
from tkinter import ttk
from tkinter import filedialog
from PIL import Image, ImageTk
import imageio
import cv2
import numpy as np
import matplotlib.pyplot as plt
import pywt

class BoostingTracker:
    def __init__(self, master):
        self.master = master
        self.master.title("Object Tracking with Boosting Tracker")
        self.file_name = ""
        self.set_window_title()  # Set window title initially

        self.frame_number_label = tk.Label(master, text="Frame: 0")
        self.frame_number_label.pack()

        self.video = None
        self.video_path = None
        self.paused = False
        self.zoom_scale = tk.IntVar(value=1)
        self.frame_index = 0
        self.bbox = None
        self.bbox2 = None
        self.tracking_started = False  # Initialize tracking_started to False
        self.prev_frame_gray = None
        self.tracker = None
        self.initial_w = None
        self.initial_h = None
        self.bbox_rect = None  # Initialize bbox_rect attribute to None
        self.frame_processing = False  # Initialize frame_processing attribute to False

        # Available filters
        self.filters = ["None", "Gaussian", "Mean", "Median", "Bilateral Filtering",
                        "Non-local Means Denoising", "Anisotropic Diffusion",
                        "Total Variation Denoising", "Wiener Filter",
                        "Adaptive Thresholding", "Haar Wavelet Transform",
                        "Daubechies Wavelet Transform"]

        self.create_widgets()

    def create_widgets(self):
        # Panel for video display
        video_panel = tk.Frame(self.master)
        video_panel.pack(padx=10, pady=10)

        # Canvas to display the original video
        canvas_width = 800
        canvas_height = 500
```

```python
        self.canvas = tk.Canvas(video_panel, width=canvas_width, height=canvas_height)
        self.canvas.pack(side="left", fill="both", expand=True)
        self.canvas.bind("<MouseWheel>", self.on_mousewheel)
        self.canvas.bind("<ButtonPress-1>", self.on_press)
        self.canvas.bind("<B1-Motion>", self.on_drag)
        self.canvas.bind("<ButtonRelease-1>", self.on_release)  # Bind ButtonRelease event

        # List box to display center coordinates
        self.center_listbox = tk.Listbox(video_panel, width=30, height=20, font=("Helvetica", 14))
        self.center_listbox.pack(side="right", fill="y")
        # Scrollbar for the listbox
        scrollbar = tk.Scrollbar(video_panel, orient="vertical")
        scrollbar.pack(side="left", fill="y")
        scrollbar.config(command=self.center_listbox.yview)

        # Attach scrollbar to listbox
        self.center_listbox.config(yscrollcommand=scrollbar.set)

        # Panel for control buttons
        control_panel = tk.Frame(self.master)
        control_panel.pack(padx=10, pady=(0, 10), fill="x")

        # Button to open a video file
        self.open_button = tk.Button(control_panel, text="Open Video", command=self.open_video)
        self.open_button.grid(row=0, column=0, padx=10, pady=5)

        # Combobox for selecting zoom scale
        self.zoom_combobox = ttk.Combobox(control_panel, textvariable=self.zoom_scale, values=list(range(1, 11)))
        self.zoom_combobox.grid(row=0, column=1, padx=10, pady=5)
        self.zoom_combobox.bind("<<ComboboxSelected>>", self.update_zoom)

        # Button to play/pause the video
        self.play_button = tk.Button(control_panel, text="Play/Pause", command=self.toggle_play_pause)
        self.play_button.grid(row=0, column=2, padx=10, pady=5)

        # Button to stop the video
        self.stop_button = tk.Button(control_panel, text="Stop", command=self.stop_video)
        self.stop_button.grid(row=0, column=3, padx=10, pady=5)

        # Button to navigate to the previous frame
        self.prev_frame_button = tk.Button(control_panel, text="Previous Frame", command=self.prev_frame)
        self.prev_frame_button.grid(row=0, column=4, padx=10, pady=5)

        # Button to navigate to the next frame
        self.next_frame_button = tk.Button(control_panel, text="Next Frame", command=self.next_frame)
        self.next_frame_button.grid(row=0, column=5, padx=10, pady=5)

        # Button to clear the listbox
        self.clear_button = tk.Button(control_panel, text="Clear Listbox", command=self.clear_listbox)
        self.clear_button.grid(row=0, column=6, padx=10, pady=5)

        # Label and entry for specifying scale
        self.scale_label = tk.Label(control_panel, text="Scale:")
        self.scale_label.grid(row=0, column=7, padx=10, pady=5, sticky="e")
        self.scale_default = tk.StringVar(value="1")
        self.scale_entry = ttk.Entry(control_panel, textvariable=self.scale_default)
        self.scale_entry.grid(row=0, column=8, padx=10, pady=5, sticky="w")
        self.scale_entry.bind("<Return>", lambda event: self.toggle_play_pause())
```

```python
        # Combobox for selecting filters
        self.filter_combobox = ttk.Combobox(control_panel, values=self.filters)
        self.filter_combobox.grid(row=0, column=9, padx=10, pady=5)
        self.filter_combobox.current(0)  # Set default value

    def open_video(self):
        self.video_path = filedialog.askopenfilename(filetypes=[("Video files", 
"*.mp4;*.avi;*.mkv;*.wmv")])
        if self.video_path:
            self.video = imageio.get_reader(self.video_path)
            self.file_name = self.video_path.split('/')[-1]
            self.set_window_title()
            self.play_video()

    def play_video(self):
        if self.video:
            self.paused = False
            self.tracking_started = True
            self.show_frame()

    def stop_video(self):
        self.paused = True
        self.frame_index = 0
        self.bbox = None
        self.tracker = None  # Reset tracker
        self.initial_w = None  # Reset width
        self.initial_h = None  # Reset height
        self.show_frame()

    def toggle_play_pause(self):
        self.paused = not self.paused
        if not self.paused:
            if self.bbox is not None:
                self.tracking_started = True
            self.play_video()

    def update_zoom(self, event=None):
        self.show_frame()

    def initialize_tracker(self, frame, bbox, params=None):
        """Initialize the tracker with possible user-defined parameters."""
        if params:
            # Here you could adjust bbox based on params, if params affect size, etc.
            scale = int(self.scale_entry.get())  # Get threshold from entry
            bbox = (
                bbox[0], bbox[1],
                int(bbox[2] * scale), int(bbox[3] * scale)
            )

        # Initialize the tracker
        self.tracker = cv2.legacy.TrackerBoosting_create()
        self.tracker.init(frame, tuple(map(int, bbox)))
        self.initial_w, self.initial_h = bbox[2], bbox[3]

    def track_object(self, frame, bbox, user_params=None):
        """Track object using Boosting Tracker with optional user parameters."""
        if bbox:
            if self.tracker is None:
                self.initialize_tracker(frame, bbox, user_params)

            # Update the tracker and get the new bounding box
            success, bbox = self.tracker.update(frame)
            if success:
```

```python
            x1, y1, w, h = map(int, bbox)
            # Use stored initial dimensions
            w, h = self.initial_w, self.initial_h
            x2, y2 = x1 + w, y1 + h

            # Calculate and display the center of the bounding box
            center_x = (x1 + x2) // 2
            center_y = (y1 + y2) // 2
            self.center_listbox.insert(tk.END, f"(center_x = {center_x}, center_y = {center_y})")

            return x1, y1, x2, y2
        return None

    def update_bbox_rectangle(self, bbox):
        if bbox is not None:
            x1, y1, x2, y2 = map(int, bbox)
            if self.bbox_rect is not None:
                self.canvas.coords(self.bbox_rect, x1, y1, x2, y2)
                self.canvas.tag_raise(self.bbox_rect)  # Raise the bounding box to the front
            else:
                self.bbox_rect = self.canvas.create_rectangle(x1, y1, x2, y2, outline='#fc3d3d', width=8, tags="bbox")

    def show_frame(self):
        if self.video:
            if not self.paused:
                if 0 <= self.frame_index < len(self.video):
                    if not self.frame_processing:  # Check if the frame is already being processed
                        try:
                            self.frame_processing = True  # Set frame_processing flag to True to indicate frame processing

                            frame = self.video.get_data(self.frame_index)
                            frame = cv2.cvtColor(frame, cv2.COLOR_RGB2BGR)

                            if self.bbox is not None:
                                if not self.tracking_started:
                                    self.tracking_started = True

                                self.bbox = self.track_object(frame, self.bbox)
                                if self.bbox:
                                    frame = cv2.cvtColor(frame, cv2.COLOR_BGR2RGB)
                                    frame = Image.fromarray(frame)
                                    frame = frame.resize((frame.width * self.zoom_scale.get(), frame.height * self.zoom_scale.get()))
                                    photo = ImageTk.PhotoImage(frame)
                                    self.photo = photo
                                    self.canvas.delete("video")
                                    self.canvas.create_image(0, 0, anchor="nw", image=photo, tags="video")

                                    self.update_bbox_rectangle(self.bbox)

                            else:
                                frame = cv2.cvtColor(frame, cv2.COLOR_BGR2RGB)
                                frame = Image.fromarray(frame)
                                frame = frame.resize((frame.width * self.zoom_scale.get(), frame.height * self.zoom_scale.get()))
                                photo = ImageTk.PhotoImage(frame)
                                self.photo = photo
                                self.canvas.delete("video")
                                self.canvas.create_image(0, 0, anchor="nw", image=photo, tags="video")
```

```python
                            self.frame_number_label.config(text=f"Frame: {self.frame_index} / {self.video.count_frames()}", font=("Helvetica", 18))

                            self.frame_index += 1

                    except Exception as e:
                        print("Error: ", e)
                    finally:
                        self.frame_processing = False  # Reset frame_processing flag to False after processing the frame

    def on_mousewheel(self, event):
        direction = event.delta // 120
        current_value = int(self.zoom_scale.get())
        if direction == 1 and current_value < 10:
            current_value += 1
        elif direction == -1 and current_value > 1:
            current_value -= 1
        self.zoom_scale.set(current_value)
        self.update_zoom()

    def on_press(self, event):
        self.tracker = None
        self.start_x = self.canvas.canvasx(event.x)
        self.start_y = self.canvas.canvasy(event.y)
        # Clear the previous bounding box if it exists
        if self.bbox_rect:
            self.canvas.delete(self.bbox_rect)
            self.bbox_rect = None
        self.bbox = None
        self.bbox2 = None

    def on_drag(self, event):
        # Update the endpoint of the rectangle as the mouse moves
        cur_x = self.canvas.canvasx(event.x)
        cur_y = self.canvas.canvasy(event.y)

        # Define the coordinates correctly ensuring x1 < x2 and y1 < y2
        x1, y1 = min(self.start_x, cur_x), min(self.start_y, cur_y)
        x2, y2 = max(self.start_x, cur_x), max(self.start_y, cur_y)

        # Update dimensions for tracking
        self.initial_w = x2 - x1
        self.initial_h = y2 - y1
        self.bbox = (x1, y1, self.initial_w, self.initial_h)
        self.bbox2 = (self.start_x, self.start_y, cur_x, cur_y)

        # Update or create a rectangle on the canvas
        if self.bbox_rect:
            self.canvas.coords(self.bbox_rect, x1, y1, x2, y2)
        else:
            self.bbox_rect = self.canvas.create_rectangle(x1, y1, x2, y2, outline="cyan", width=6)

    def prev_frame(self):
        if self.frame_index > 0:
            self.frame_index -= 1
            self.show_frame()

    def next_frame(self):
        if self.video and self.frame_index < len(self.video) - 1:
            self.show_frame()
```

```python
    def clear_listbox(self):
        self.center_listbox.delete(0, tk.END)

    def set_window_title(self):
        if self.file_name:
            self.master.title(f"Object Tracking with Boosting Tracker - {self.file_name}")
            self.master.title_font = ("Helvetica", 16, "bold")
        else:
            self.master.title("Object Tracking with Boosting Tracker")

    def on_release(self, event):
        self.analyze_histogram()  # Call analyze_histogram() method when the mouse button is released

    def analyze_histogram(self):
        if self.bbox2 is not None and self.video:
            x1, y1, x2, y2 = map(int, self.bbox2)
            if x1 != x2 and y1 != y2:
                try:
                    frame = self.video.get_data(self.frame_index)
                    # Ensure the bounding box is within the frame boundaries
                    h, w, _ = frame.shape
                    x1, x2 = max(0, min(x1, w)), max(0, min(x2, w))
                    y1, y2 = max(0, min(y1, h)), max(0, min(y2, h))

                    # Ensure x1 < x2 and y1 < y2
                    x1, x2 = sorted([x1, x2])
                    y1, y2 = sorted([y1, y2])

                    cropped_frame = frame[y1:y2, x1:x2]
                    if cropped_frame.size > 0:
                        cropped_frame = cv2.cvtColor(cropped_frame, cv2.COLOR_BGR2RGB)

                        # Get selected filter from combobox
                        selected_filter = self.filter_combobox.get()
                        # Apply selected filter
                        filtered_frame = self.apply_filter(selected_filter, cropped_frame)

                        self.create_popup_window(filtered_frame)
                        self.display_cropped_image(filtered_frame)
                        self.display_histograms(filtered_frame)
                    else:
                        print("Cropped frame is empty.")
                except Exception as e:
                    print("Failed to process frame:", e)
            else:
                print("Bounding box dimensions are zero or negative.")

    def create_popup_window(self, cropped_frame):
        self.popup_window = tk.Toplevel(self.master)
        self.popup_window.title("Cropped Image and Its Histogram")
        self.popup_window.geometry("1500x700")

    def display_cropped_image(self, cropped_frame):
        cropped_frame_frame = tk.Frame(self.popup_window)
        cropped_frame_frame.pack(side="left")

        cropped_frame_rgb = cv2.cvtColor(cropped_frame, cv2.COLOR_BGR2RGB)
        cropped_img = Image.fromarray(cropped_frame_rgb)
        cropped_img = cropped_img.resize((600, 600))

        cropped_photo = ImageTk.PhotoImage(cropped_img)
        cropped_canvas = tk.Canvas(cropped_frame_frame, width=600, height=600)
        cropped_canvas.pack(side="left", anchor="nw")
```

```python
            cropped_canvas.create_image(0, 0, anchor="nw", image=cropped_photo)
            cropped_canvas.image = cropped_photo

    def display_histograms(self, cropped_frame):
        histograms_frame = tk.Frame(self.popup_window)
        histograms_frame.pack(side="right", padx=20)

        self.display_line_histogram(cropped_frame, histograms_frame)
        self.display_bar_histogram(cropped_frame, histograms_frame)

    def display_line_histogram(self, cropped_frame, histograms_frame):
        line_histogram_frame = tk.Frame(histograms_frame)
        line_histogram_frame.pack(side="top", pady=10)

        plt.figure(figsize=(12, 4))
        color = ('r', 'g', 'b')
        for i, col in enumerate(color):
            histr = cv2.calcHist([cropped_frame], [i], None, [256], [0, 256])
            plt.plot(histr, color=col, label=f'Channel {col.upper()}', linewidth=2)
            plt.xlim([0, 256])
        plt.title('Line Histogram')
        plt.xlabel('Pixel Value')
        plt.ylabel('Frequency')
        plt.tight_layout()
        plt.grid(True)
        plt.legend()

        line_histogram_img = self.plot_to_image(plt)
        self.display_histogram_image(line_histogram_frame, line_histogram_img)

    def display_bar_histogram(self, cropped_frame, histograms_frame):
        bar_histogram_frame = tk.Frame(histograms_frame)
        bar_histogram_frame.pack(side="bottom", pady=10)

        plt.figure(figsize=(12, 4))
        color = ('r', 'g', 'b')
        for i, col in enumerate(color):
            hist_range = (0, 256)
            hist_counts, _ = np.histogram(cropped_frame[:, :, i], bins=64, range=hist_range)
            plt.bar(np.arange(64), hist_counts, color=col, alpha=0.7, label=f'Channel {col.upper()}')
            for index, value in enumerate(hist_counts):
                plt.text(index, value + 10, str(int(value)), ha='center', va='bottom', fontsize=9)

        plt.title('Bar Histogram')
        plt.xlabel('Pixel Value')
        plt.ylabel('Frequency')
        plt.xticks(np.linspace(0, 63, num=5), np.linspace(0, 255, num=5, dtype=int))  # Adjust x-axis ticks
        plt.tight_layout()
        plt.grid(True)
        plt.legend()

        bar_histogram_img = self.plot_to_image(plt)
        self.display_histogram_image(bar_histogram_frame, bar_histogram_img)

    def display_histogram_image(self, parent_frame, img):
        histogram_photo = ImageTk.PhotoImage(image=img)
        histogram_canvas = tk.Canvas(parent_frame, width=900, height=300)
        histogram_canvas.pack(side="bottom", anchor="se")
        histogram_canvas.create_image(0, 0, anchor="nw", image=histogram_photo)
        histogram_canvas.image = histogram_photo
```

```python
    def plot_histogram_bar_to_image(self, image):
        # Calculate histogram for each channel
        histograms = []
        for i in range(3):
            hist_range = (0, 256)
            hist_counts, _ = np.histogram(image[:, :, i], bins=64, range=hist_range)  # Adjust bins to 64
            histograms.append(hist_counts)

        # Extracting only 64 bins from the histogram
        num_bins = 64  # Adjusted to 64 bins

        # Generating colors for each channel
        colors = ['red', 'green', 'blue']

        plt.figure()
        for i, histogram in enumerate(histograms):
            # Normalize the histogram counts for better visualization
            hist_counts = histogram / np.sum(histogram)
            # Setting the color for each channel
            plt.bar(np.arange(num_bins), hist_counts[:num_bins], color=colors[i], alpha=0.7, label=f'Channel {["Red", "Green", "Blue"][i]}')

        plt.xlabel('Pixel Value')
        plt.ylabel('Normalized Frequency')
        plt.title('RGB Channel Histograms')
        plt.grid(True)
        plt.tight_layout()
        plt.legend()

        # Convert the histogram bar graph to an image
        histogram_bar_img = self.plot_to_image(plt)
        histogram_bar_photo = ImageTk.PhotoImage(image=histogram_bar_img)

        return histogram_bar_photo

    def plot_to_image(self, plt):
        plt.savefig('temp_plot.png')
        img = Image.open('temp_plot.png')
        return img

    def apply_filter(self, filter_name, frame):
        if filter_name == "None":
            return frame
        elif filter_name == "Gaussian":
            return cv2.GaussianBlur(frame, (5, 5), 0)
        elif filter_name == "Mean":
            return cv2.blur(frame, (5, 5))
        elif filter_name == "Median":
            return cv2.medianBlur(frame, 5)
        elif filter_name == "Bilateral Filtering":
            return cv2.bilateralFilter(frame, 9, 75, 75)
        elif filter_name == "Non-local Means Denoising":
            return cv2.fastNlMeansDenoisingColored(frame, None, 10, 10, 7, 21)
        elif filter_name == "Anisotropic Diffusion":
            return self.anisotropic_diffusion(frame)
        elif filter_name == "Total Variation Denoising":
            return self.total_variation_denoising(frame)
        elif filter_name == "Wiener Filter":
            return self.wiener_filter(frame)
        elif filter_name == "Adaptive Thresholding":
            return self.adaptive_threshold_each_channel(frame)
        elif filter_name == "Haar Wavelet Transform":
            return self.haar_wavelet_transform(frame)
```

```python
            elif filter_name == "Daubechies Wavelet Transform":
                return self.daubechies_wavelet_transform(frame)
            else:
                return frame  # Default: return original frame if filter not found

    def wiener_filter(self, frame, kernel_size=(5, 5), noise_var=0.01):
        # Check if frame is None
        if frame is None:
            print("Error: Input frame is None.")
            return None

        # Check if frame is a valid numpy array
        if not isinstance(frame, np.ndarray):
            print("Error: Input frame is not a numpy array.")
            return None

        # Check if frame is an empty array
        if frame.size == 0:
            print("Error: Input frame is empty.")
            return None

        # Check if frame is in BGR color space
        if frame.shape[-1] != 3:
            print("Error: Input frame is not in BGR color space.")
            return None

        # Apply Wiener filter
        filtered_frame = cv2.medianBlur(frame, kernel_size[0])  # Use kernel_size[0] as the kernel size
        filtered_frame = cv2.fastNlMeansDenoising(filtered_frame, h=noise_var)
        return filtered_frame

    def adaptive_threshold_each_channel(self, frame):
        # Split the frame into individual channels
        b, g, r = cv2.split(frame)

        # Apply adaptive thresholding to each channel separately
        b_thresh = cv2.adaptiveThreshold(b, 255, cv2.ADAPTIVE_THRESH_GAUSSIAN_C, cv2.THRESH_BINARY, 11, 2)
        g_thresh = cv2.adaptiveThreshold(g, 255, cv2.ADAPTIVE_THRESH_GAUSSIAN_C, cv2.THRESH_BINARY, 11, 2)
        r_thresh = cv2.adaptiveThreshold(r, 255, cv2.ADAPTIVE_THRESH_GAUSSIAN_C, cv2.THRESH_BINARY, 11, 2)

        # Merge the thresholded channels back together
        return cv2.merge([b_thresh, g_thresh, r_thresh])

    def haar_wavelet_transform(self, frame):
        # Split the frame into its individual color channels
        b, g, r = cv2.split(frame)

        # Perform the wavelet transform on each channel separately
        b_coeffs = pywt.dwt2(b, 'haar')
        g_coeffs = pywt.dwt2(g, 'haar')
        r_coeffs = pywt.dwt2(r, 'haar')

        # Reconstruct the channels from the coefficients
        b_reconstructed = pywt.idwt2(b_coeffs, 'haar')
        g_reconstructed = pywt.idwt2(g_coeffs, 'haar')
        r_reconstructed = pywt.idwt2(r_coeffs, 'haar')

        # Clip the values to ensure they are within the valid range
        b_reconstructed = np.clip(b_reconstructed, 0, 255).astype(np.uint8)
        g_reconstructed = np.clip(g_reconstructed, 0, 255).astype(np.uint8)
```

```python
        r_reconstructed = np.clip(r_reconstructed, 0, 255).astype(np.uint8)

        # Merge the channels back together
        return cv2.merge([b_reconstructed, g_reconstructed, r_reconstructed])

    def daubechies_wavelet_transform(self, frame):
        # Split the frame into its individual color channels
        b, g, r = cv2.split(frame)

        # Choose the wavelet function (Daubechies 5)
        wavelet = 'db5'

        # Perform the wavelet transform on each channel separately
        b_coeffs = pywt.dwt2(b, wavelet)
        g_coeffs = pywt.dwt2(g, wavelet)
        r_coeffs = pywt.dwt2(r, wavelet)

        # Reconstruct the channels from the coefficients
        b_reconstructed = pywt.idwt2(b_coeffs, wavelet)
        g_reconstructed = pywt.idwt2(g_coeffs, wavelet)
        r_reconstructed = pywt.idwt2(r_coeffs, wavelet)

        # Clip the values to ensure they are within the valid range
        b_reconstructed = np.clip(b_reconstructed, 0, 255).astype(np.uint8)
        g_reconstructed = np.clip(g_reconstructed, 0, 255).astype(np.uint8)
        r_reconstructed = np.clip(r_reconstructed, 0, 255).astype(np.uint8)

        # Merge the channels back together
        return cv2.merge([b_reconstructed, g_reconstructed, r_reconstructed])

    def anisotropic_diffusion(self, img):
        return cv2.fastNlMeansDenoisingColored(img, None, 10, 10, 7, 21)

    def apply_total_variation_denoising_channel(self, channel, weight, iterations):
        # Initialize the result with the original channel
        result = channel.copy().astype(np.float64)  # Convert to float64

        # Perform total variation denoising
        for _ in range(iterations):
            # Compute the gradient of the channel
            dx = cv2.Sobel(result, cv2.CV_64F, 1, 0, ksize=3)
            dy = cv2.Sobel(result, cv2.CV_64F, 0, 1, ksize=3)

            # Update the channel using the gradient and the weight
            result -= weight * np.sqrt(dx**2 + dy**2)

        # Clip the values to ensure they are within the valid range
        result = np.clip(result, 0, 255).astype(np.uint8)

        return result

    def total_variation_denoising(self, img, weight=0.01, iterations=20):
        # Split the image into its individual color channels
        b, g, r = cv2.split(img)

        # Apply total variation denoising to each channel separately
        b_denoised = self.apply_total_variation_denoising_channel(b, weight, iterations)
        g_denoised = self.apply_total_variation_denoising_channel(g, weight, iterations)
        r_denoised = self.apply_total_variation_denoising_channel(r, weight, iterations)

        # Merge the denoised channels back together
        return cv2.merge([b_denoised, g_denoised, r_denoised])

def main():
```

```
    root = tk.Tk()
    app = BoostingTracker(root)
    root.mainloop()

if __name__ == "__main__":
    main()
```

RUNNING PROGRAM

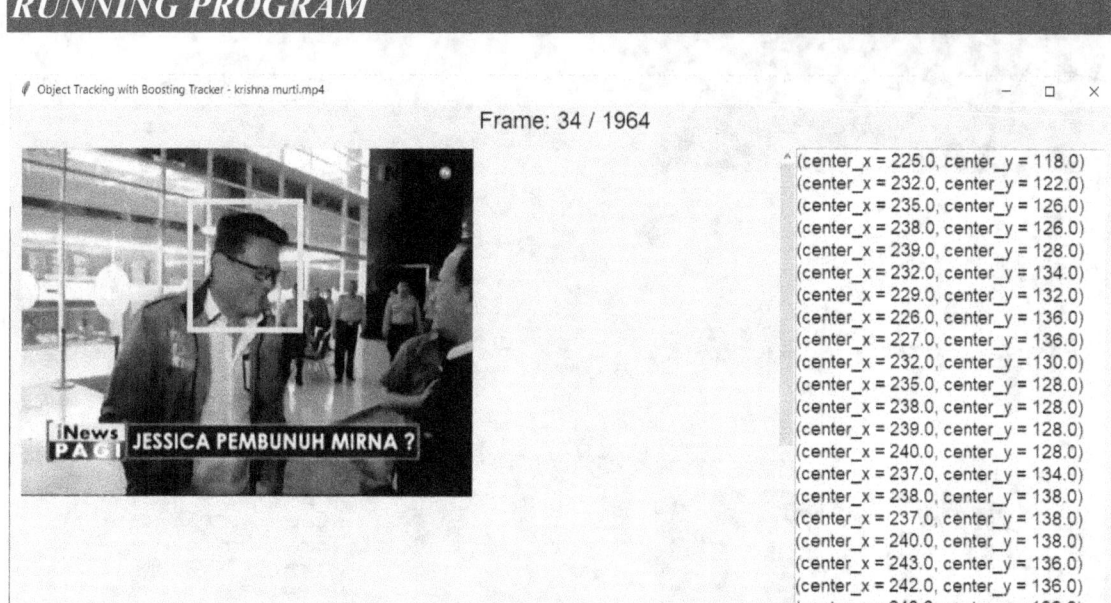

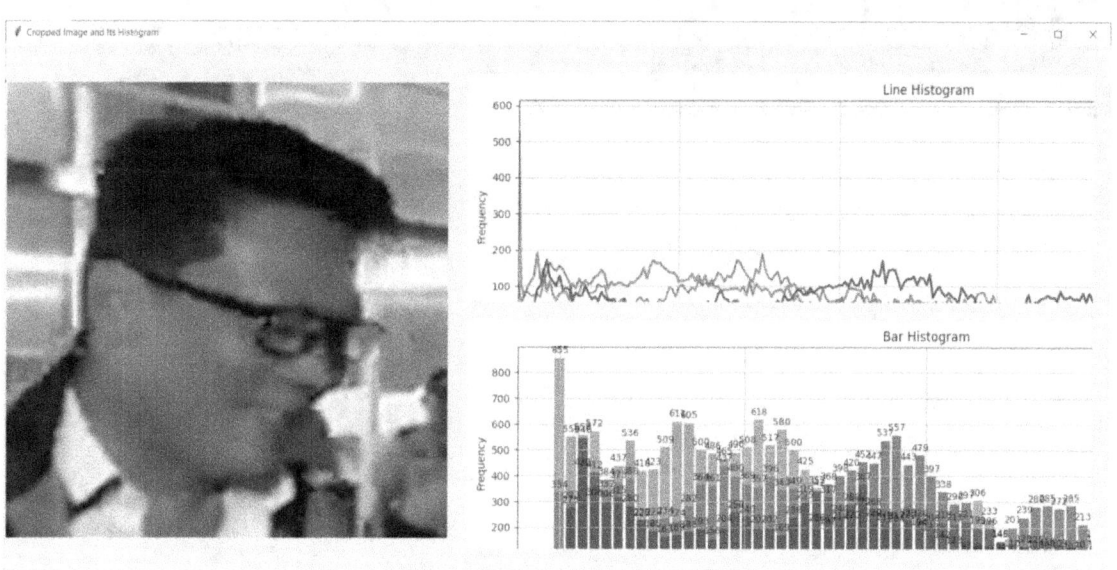

OBJECT TRACKING WITH CSRT (CHANNEL AND SPATIAL RELIABILITY TRACKER)

DESCRIPTION

The csrt_tracker.py script is a comprehensive implementation of a graphical user interface (GUI) for object tracking using the Channel and Spatial Reliability Tracker (CSRT). This Python project leverages several libraries such as tkinter for the GUI, imageio for video handling, cv2 from OpenCV for computer vision tasks, and PIL for image processing.

The script begins by importing necessary libraries, including tkinter for creating the GUI, PIL for handling image files, imageio for reading video files, cv2 for the CSRT tracker, and other supporting libraries like numpy, matplotlib, and pywt for wavelet transforms.

A class named CSRTTracker is defined to encapsulate the functionality of the object tracker. The constructor __init__ initializes various attributes and calls the method create_widgets to set up the GUI components. These components include a canvas for displaying the video, control buttons for video playback, a listbox to display center coordinates of the tracked object, and combo boxes for selecting zoom scale and filters.

The create_widgets method sets up the layout and interactive elements of the GUI. It creates panels for video display, control buttons, and a listbox with a scrollbar. Control buttons include options to open a video file, play/pause the video, stop the video, navigate frames, and clear the listbox. There are also combo boxes for selecting zoom levels and various image filters.

The open_video method allows users to select a video file using a file dialog. Once a video is selected, it is opened using imageio and the video filename is set. The play_video method starts video playback and initializes tracking if it hasn't started already.

The stop_video method pauses the video playback, resets the frame index to the beginning, and clears the tracking state. The toggle_play_pause method toggles between playing and pausing the video. The update_zoom method adjusts the zoom scale of the displayed video based on user input.

The initialize_tracker method sets up the CSRT tracker with an optional scaling parameter. It adjusts the bounding box based on the specified scale and initializes the CSRT tracker with the current frame and bounding box. The track_object method updates the tracker with the current frame and returns the new bounding box.

The update_bbox_rectangle method updates the graphical representation of the bounding box on the canvas. The show_frame method retrieves and displays the current frame from the video. It also updates the bounding box if tracking is active and adjusts the display according to the zoom scale.

Mouse event handlers on_mousewheel, on_press, on_drag, and on_release are defined to allow user interaction for zooming and selecting a region of interest (ROI) for tracking. The analyze_histogram method is called when the mouse button is released to analyze the selected ROI and display histograms of the cropped image.

The create_popup_window method creates a new window to display the cropped image and its histogram. The display_cropped_image method shows the cropped image in the popup window, while display_histograms generates and displays line and bar histograms of the cropped image's color channels.

The display_line_histogram and display_bar_histogram methods generate and display histograms for the cropped image. These histograms show the distribution of pixel values for each color channel. The display_histogram_image method displays these histograms as images on the canvas.

Several methods for image filtering are defined, such as apply_filter, wiener_filter, adaptive_threshold_each_channel, and haar_wavelet_transform. These methods apply different filters to the selected ROI, such as Gaussian blur, median filtering, bilateral filtering, and wavelet transforms.

The wiener_filter method applies a Wiener filter to the frame, while adaptive_threshold_each_channel performs adaptive thresholding on each color channel separately. The haar_wavelet_transform method performs a Haar wavelet transform on each color channel of the frame and reconstructs the image from the transformed coefficients.

The plot_histogram_bar_to_image method calculates histograms for each color channel and plots them as bar graphs. The plot_to_image method saves the current plot as an image and returns it for display in the GUI.

Overall, the csrt_tracker.py script provides a robust and interactive tool for object tracking in videos. It allows users to select and track objects, apply various image filters, and analyze the color distribution within the selected region. The use of tkinter for the GUI, imageio for video handling, cv2 for tracking, and PIL for image processing demonstrates a well-integrated approach to creating a functional and user-friendly application.

SOURCE CODE

```
#csrt_tracker.py
import tkinter as tk
from tkinter import ttk
from tkinter import filedialog
from PIL import Image, ImageTk
import imageio
import cv2
import numpy as np
import matplotlib.pyplot as plt
import pywt
```

```python
class CSRTTracker:
    def __init__(self, master):
        self.master = master
        self.master.title("Object Tracking with CSRT (Channel and Spatial Reliability Tracker)")
        self.file_name = ""
        self.set_window_title()  # Set window title initially

        self.frame_number_label = tk.Label(master, text="Frame: 0")
        self.frame_number_label.pack()

        self.video = None
        self.video_path = None
        self.paused = False
        self.zoom_scale = tk.IntVar(value=1)
        self.frame_index = 0
        self.bbox = None
        self.bbox2 = None
        self.tracking_started = False  # Initialize tracking_started to False
        self.prev_frame_gray = None
        self.tracker = None
        self.initial_w = None
        self.initial_h = None
        self.bbox_rect = None  # Initialize bbox_rect attribute to None
        self.frame_processing = False  # Initialize frame_processing attribute to False

        # Available filters
        self.filters = ["None", "Gaussian", "Mean", "Median", "Bilateral Filtering",
                        "Non-local Means Denoising", "Anisotropic Diffusion",
                        "Total Variation Denoising", "Wiener Filter",
                        "Adaptive Thresholding", "Haar Wavelet Transform",
                        "Daubechies Wavelet Transform"]

        self.create_widgets()

    def create_widgets(self):
        # Panel for video display
        video_panel = tk.Frame(self.master)
        video_panel.pack(padx=10, pady=10)

        # Canvas to display the original video
        canvas_width = 800
        canvas_height = 500
        self.canvas = tk.Canvas(video_panel, width=canvas_width, height=canvas_height)
        self.canvas.pack(side="left", fill="both", expand=True)
        self.canvas.bind("<MouseWheel>", self.on_mousewheel)
        self.canvas.bind("<ButtonPress-1>", self.on_press)
        self.canvas.bind("<B1-Motion>", self.on_drag)
        self.canvas.bind("<ButtonRelease-1>", self.on_release)  # Bind ButtonRelease event

        # List box to display center coordinates
        self.center_listbox = tk.Listbox(video_panel, width=30, height=20, font=("Helvetica", 14))
        self.center_listbox.pack(side="right", fill="y")
        # Scrollbar for the listbox
        scrollbar = tk.Scrollbar(video_panel, orient="vertical")
        scrollbar.pack(side="left", fill="y")
        scrollbar.config(command=self.center_listbox.yview)

        # Attach scrollbar to listbox
        self.center_listbox.config(yscrollcommand=scrollbar.set)

        # Panel for control buttons
        control_panel = tk.Frame(self.master)
```

```python
        control_panel.pack(padx=10, pady=(0, 10), fill="x")

        # Button to open a video file
        self.open_button = tk.Button(control_panel, text="Open Video", command=self.open_video)
        self.open_button.grid(row=0, column=0, padx=10, pady=5)

        # Combobox for selecting zoom scale
        self.zoom_combobox = ttk.Combobox(control_panel, textvariable=self.zoom_scale, values=list(range(1, 11)))
        self.zoom_combobox.grid(row=0, column=1, padx=10, pady=5)
        self.zoom_combobox.bind("<<ComboboxSelected>>", self.update_zoom)

        # Button to play/pause the video
        self.play_button = tk.Button(control_panel, text="Play/Pause", command=self.toggle_play_pause)
        self.play_button.grid(row=0, column=2, padx=10, pady=5)

        # Button to stop the video
        self.stop_button = tk.Button(control_panel, text="Stop", command=self.stop_video)
        self.stop_button.grid(row=0, column=3, padx=10, pady=5)

        # Button to navigate to the previous frame
        self.prev_frame_button = tk.Button(control_panel, text="Previous Frame", command=self.prev_frame)
        self.prev_frame_button.grid(row=0, column=4, padx=10, pady=5)

        # Button to navigate to the next frame
        self.next_frame_button = tk.Button(control_panel, text="Next Frame", command=self.next_frame)
        self.next_frame_button.grid(row=0, column=5, padx=10, pady=5)

        # Button to clear the listbox
        self.clear_button = tk.Button(control_panel, text="Clear Listbox", command=self.clear_listbox)
        self.clear_button.grid(row=0, column=6, padx=10, pady=5)

        # Label and entry for specifying scale
        self.scale_label = tk.Label(control_panel, text="Scale:")
        self.scale_label.grid(row=0, column=7, padx=10, pady=5, sticky="e")
        self.scale_default = tk.StringVar(value="1")
        self.scale_entry = ttk.Entry(control_panel, textvariable=self.scale_default)
        self.scale_entry.grid(row=0, column=8, padx=10, pady=5, sticky="w")
        self.scale_entry.bind("<Return>", lambda event: self.toggle_play_pause())

        # Combobox for selecting filters
        self.filter_combobox = ttk.Combobox(control_panel, values=self.filters)
        self.filter_combobox.grid(row=0, column=9, padx=10, pady=5)
        self.filter_combobox.current(0)  # Set default value

    def open_video(self):
        self.video_path = filedialog.askopenfilename(filetypes=[("Video files", "*.mp4;*.avi;*.mkv;*.wmv")])
        if self.video_path:
            self.video = imageio.get_reader(self.video_path)
            self.file_name = self.video_path.split('/')[-1]
            self.set_window_title()
            self.play_video()

    def play_video(self):
        if self.video:
            self.paused = False
            self.tracking_started = True
            self.show_frame()
```

```python
def stop_video(self):
    self.paused = True
    self.frame_index = 0
    self.bbox = None
    self.tracker = None  # Reset tracker
    self.initial_w = None  # Reset width
    self.initial_h = None  # Reset height
    self.show_frame()

def toggle_play_pause(self):
    self.paused = not self.paused
    if not self.paused:
        if self.bbox is not None:
            self.tracking_started = True
        self.play_video()

def update_zoom(self, event=None):
    self.show_frame()

def initialize_tracker(self, frame, bbox, params=None):
    """Initialize the CSRT tracker with possible user-defined parameters."""

    # Read scale factor from a GUI entry; ensure it is a float
    scale = float(self.scale_entry.get())

    # Adjust bbox based on the scaling parameter
    bbox = (
        int(bbox[0] + (1 - scale) * bbox[2] / 2),  # Center the scaling on the bbox
        int(bbox[1] + (1 - scale) * bbox[3] / 2),
        int(bbox[2] * scale),
        int(bbox[3] * scale)
    )

    # Initialize the CSRT tracker
    self.tracker = cv2.legacy.TrackerCSRT_create()

    # Initialize the tracker with the frame and adjusted bbox
    success = self.tracker.init(frame, tuple(map(int, bbox)))
    if not success:
        print("Tracker initialization failed.")
        return False

    self.initial_w, self.initial_h = bbox[2], bbox[3]
    return True

def track_object(self, frame, bbox, user_params=None):
    """Track object using CSRT Tracker with optional user parameters."""
    if not self.tracker:
        if not self.initialize_tracker(frame, bbox, user_params):
            return None

    # Update the tracker and get the new bounding box
    success, bbox = self.tracker.update(frame)
    if success:
        x1, y1, w, h = map(int, bbox)
        x2, y2 = x1 + w, y1 + h

        # Calculate and display the center of the bounding box
        center_x = (x1 + x2) // 2
        center_y = (y1 + y2) // 2
        if hasattr(self, 'center_listbox'):
            self.center_listbox.insert(tk.END, f"(center_x = {center_x}, center_y = {center_y})")
```

```python
            return (x1, y1, x2, y2)
        return None

    def update_bbox_rectangle(self, bbox):
        if bbox is not None:
            x1, y1, x2, y2 = map(int, bbox)
            if self.bbox_rect is not None:
                self.canvas.coords(self.bbox_rect, x1, y1, x2, y2)
                self.canvas.tag_raise(self.bbox_rect)  # Raise the bounding box to the front
            else:
                self.bbox_rect = self.canvas.create_rectangle(x1, y1, x2, y2, outline='#fc3d3d', width=8, tags="bbox")

    def show_frame(self):
        if self.video:
            if not self.paused:
                if 0 <= self.frame_index < len(self.video):
                    if not self.frame_processing:  # Check if the frame is already being processed
                        try:
                            self.frame_processing = True  # Set frame_processing flag to True to indicate frame processing

                            frame = self.video.get_data(self.frame_index)
                            frame = cv2.cvtColor(frame, cv2.COLOR_RGB2BGR)

                            if self.bbox is not None:
                                if not self.tracking_started:
                                    self.tracking_started = True

                                self.bbox = self.track_object(frame, self.bbox)
                                if self.bbox:
                                    frame = cv2.cvtColor(frame, cv2.COLOR_BGR2RGB)
                                    frame = Image.fromarray(frame)
                                    frame = frame.resize((frame.width * self.zoom_scale.get(), frame.height * self.zoom_scale.get()))
                                    photo = ImageTk.PhotoImage(frame)
                                    self.photo = photo
                                    self.canvas.delete("video")
                                    self.canvas.create_image(0, 0, anchor="nw", image=photo, tags="video")
                                    self.update_bbox_rectangle(self.bbox)

                            else:
                                frame = cv2.cvtColor(frame, cv2.COLOR_BGR2RGB)
                                frame = Image.fromarray(frame)
                                frame = frame.resize((frame.width * self.zoom_scale.get(), frame.height * self.zoom_scale.get()))
                                photo = ImageTk.PhotoImage(frame)
                                self.photo = photo
                                self.canvas.delete("video")
                                self.canvas.create_image(0, 0, anchor="nw", image=photo, tags="video")

                            self.frame_number_label.config(text=f"Frame: {self.frame_index} / {self.video.count_frames()}", font=("Helvetica", 18))

                            self.frame_index += 1

                        except Exception as e:
                            print("Error: ", e)
                        finally:
                            self.frame_processing = False  # Reset frame_processing flag to False after processing the frame
```

```python
    def on_mousewheel(self, event):
        direction = event.delta // 120
        current_value = int(self.zoom_scale.get())
        if direction == 1 and current_value < 10:
            current_value += 1
        elif direction == -1 and current_value > 1:
            current_value -= 1
        self.zoom_scale.set(current_value)
        self.update_zoom()

    def on_press(self, event):
        self.tracker = None
        self.start_x = self.canvas.canvasx(event.x)
        self.start_y = self.canvas.canvasy(event.y)
        # Clear the previous bounding box if it exists
        if self.bbox_rect:
            self.canvas.delete(self.bbox_rect)
            self.bbox_rect = None
        self.bbox = None
        self.bbox2 = None

    def on_drag(self, event):
        # Update the endpoint of the rectangle as the mouse moves
        cur_x = self.canvas.canvasx(event.x)
        cur_y = self.canvas.canvasy(event.y)

        # Define the coordinates correctly ensuring x1 < x2 and y1 < y2
        x1, y1 = min(self.start_x, cur_x), min(self.start_y, cur_y)
        x2, y2 = max(self.start_x, cur_x), max(self.start_y, cur_y)

        # Update dimensions for tracking
        self.initial_w = x2 - x1
        self.initial_h = y2 - y1
        self.bbox = (x1, y1, self.initial_w, self.initial_h)
        self.bbox2 = (self.start_x, self.start_y, cur_x, cur_y)

        # Update or create a rectangle on the canvas
        if self.bbox_rect:
            self.canvas.coords(self.bbox_rect, x1, y1, x2, y2)
        else:
            self.bbox_rect = self.canvas.create_rectangle(x1, y1, x2, y2, outline="cyan", width=6)

    def prev_frame(self):
        if self.frame_index > 0:
            self.frame_index -= 1
            self.show_frame()

    def next_frame(self):
        if self.video and self.frame_index < len(self.video) - 1:
            self.show_frame()

    def clear_listbox(self):
        self.center_listbox.delete(0, tk.END)

    def set_window_title(self):
        if self.file_name:
            self.master.title(f"Object Tracking with CSRT (Channel and Spatial Reliability Tracker) - {self.file_name}")
            self.master.title_font = ("Helvetica", 16, "bold")
        else:
```

```python
        self.master.title("Object Tracking with CSRT (Channel and Spatial Reliability 
Tracker)")

    def on_release(self, event):
        self.analyze_histogram()  # Call analyze_histogram() method when the mouse button is 
released

    def analyze_histogram(self):
        if self.bbox2 is not None and self.video:
            x1, y1, x2, y2 = map(int, self.bbox2)
            if x1 != x2 and y1 != y2:
                try:
                    frame = self.video.get_data(self.frame_index)
                    # Ensure the bounding box is within the frame boundaries
                    h, w, _ = frame.shape
                    x1, x2 = max(0, min(x1, w)), max(0, min(x2, w))
                    y1, y2 = max(0, min(y1, h)), max(0, min(y2, h))

                    # Ensure x1 < x2 and y1 < y2
                    x1, x2 = sorted([x1, x2])
                    y1, y2 = sorted([y1, y2])

                    cropped_frame = frame[y1:y2, x1:x2]
                    if cropped_frame.size > 0:
                        cropped_frame = cv2.cvtColor(cropped_frame, cv2.COLOR_BGR2RGB)

                        # Get selected filter from combobox
                        selected_filter = self.filter_combobox.get()
                        # Apply selected filter
                        filtered_frame = self.apply_filter(selected_filter, cropped_frame)

                        self.create_popup_window(filtered_frame)
                        self.display_cropped_image(filtered_frame)
                        self.display_histograms(filtered_frame)
                    else:
                        print("Cropped frame is empty.")
                except Exception as e:
                    print("Failed to process frame:", e)
            else:
                print("Bounding box dimensions are zero or negative.")

    def create_popup_window(self, cropped_frame):
        self.popup_window = tk.Toplevel(self.master)
        self.popup_window.title("Cropped Image and Its Histogram")
        self.popup_window.geometry("1500x700")

    def display_cropped_image(self, cropped_frame):
        cropped_frame_frame = tk.Frame(self.popup_window)
        cropped_frame_frame.pack(side="left")

        cropped_frame_rgb = cv2.cvtColor(cropped_frame, cv2.COLOR_BGR2RGB)
        cropped_img = Image.fromarray(cropped_frame_rgb)
        cropped_img = cropped_img.resize((600, 600))

        cropped_photo = ImageTk.PhotoImage(cropped_img)
        cropped_canvas = tk.Canvas(cropped_frame_frame, width=600, height=600)
        cropped_canvas.pack(side="left", anchor="nw")
        cropped_canvas.create_image(0, 0, anchor="nw", image=cropped_photo)
        cropped_canvas.image = cropped_photo

    def display_histograms(self, cropped_frame):
        histograms_frame = tk.Frame(self.popup_window)
```

```python
        histograms_frame.pack(side="right", padx=20)

        self.display_line_histogram(cropped_frame, histograms_frame)
        self.display_bar_histogram(cropped_frame, histograms_frame)

    def display_line_histogram(self, cropped_frame, histograms_frame):
        line_histogram_frame = tk.Frame(histograms_frame)
        line_histogram_frame.pack(side="top", pady=10)

        plt.figure(figsize=(12, 4))
        color = ('r', 'g', 'b')
        for i, col in enumerate(color):
            histr = cv2.calcHist([cropped_frame], [i], None, [256], [0, 256])
            plt.plot(histr, color=col, label=f'Channel {col.upper()}', linewidth=2)
            plt.xlim([0, 256])
        plt.title('Line Histogram')
        plt.xlabel('Pixel Value')
        plt.ylabel('Frequency')
        plt.tight_layout()
        plt.grid(True)
        plt.legend()

        line_histogram_img = self.plot_to_image(plt)
        self.display_histogram_image(line_histogram_frame, line_histogram_img)

    def display_bar_histogram(self, cropped_frame, histograms_frame):
        bar_histogram_frame = tk.Frame(histograms_frame)
        bar_histogram_frame.pack(side="bottom", pady=10)

        plt.figure(figsize=(12, 4))
        color = ('r', 'g', 'b')
        for i, col in enumerate(color):
            hist_range = (0, 256)
            hist_counts, _ = np.histogram(cropped_frame[:, :, i], bins=64, range=hist_range)
            plt.bar(np.arange(64), hist_counts, color=col, alpha=0.7, label=f'Channel {col.upper()}')
            for index, value in enumerate(hist_counts):
                plt.text(index, value + 10, str(int(value)), ha='center', va='bottom', fontsize=9)

        plt.title('Bar Histogram')
        plt.xlabel('Pixel Value')
        plt.ylabel('Frequency')
        plt.xticks(np.linspace(0, 63, num=5), np.linspace(0, 255, num=5, dtype=int))  # Adjust x-axis ticks
        plt.tight_layout()
        plt.grid(True)
        plt.legend()

        bar_histogram_img = self.plot_to_image(plt)
        self.display_histogram_image(bar_histogram_frame, bar_histogram_img)

    def display_histogram_image(self, parent_frame, img):
        histogram_photo = ImageTk.PhotoImage(image=img)
        histogram_canvas = tk.Canvas(parent_frame, width=900, height=300)
        histogram_canvas.pack(side="bottom", anchor="se")
        histogram_canvas.create_image(0, 0, anchor="nw", image=histogram_photo)
        histogram_canvas.image = histogram_photo

    def plot_histogram_bar_to_image(self, image):
        # Calculate histogram for each channel
        histograms = []
        for i in range(3):
            hist_range = (0, 256)
```

```python
            hist_counts, _ = np.histogram(image[:, :, i], bins=64, range=hist_range)  # Adjust bins to 64
            histograms.append(hist_counts)

        # Extracting only 64 bins from the histogram
        num_bins = 64  # Adjusted to 64 bins

        # Generating colors for each channel
        colors = ['red', 'green', 'blue']

        plt.figure()
        for i, histogram in enumerate(histograms):
            # Normalize the histogram counts for better visualization
            hist_counts = histogram / np.sum(histogram)
            # Setting the color for each channel
            plt.bar(np.arange(num_bins), hist_counts[:num_bins], color=colors[i], alpha=0.7, label=f'Channel {["Red", "Green", "Blue"][i]}')

        plt.xlabel('Pixel Value')
        plt.ylabel('Normalized Frequency')
        plt.title('RGB Channel Histograms')
        plt.grid(True)
        plt.tight_layout()
        plt.legend()

        # Convert the histogram bar graph to an image
        histogram_bar_img = self.plot_to_image(plt)
        histogram_bar_photo = ImageTk.PhotoImage(image=histogram_bar_img)

        return histogram_bar_photo

    def plot_to_image(self, plt):
        plt.savefig('temp_plot.png')
        img = Image.open('temp_plot.png')
        return img

    def apply_filter(self, filter_name, frame):
        if filter_name == "None":
            return frame
        elif filter_name == "Gaussian":
            return cv2.GaussianBlur(frame, (5, 5), 0)
        elif filter_name == "Mean":
            return cv2.blur(frame, (5, 5))
        elif filter_name == "Median":
            return cv2.medianBlur(frame, 5)
        elif filter_name == "Bilateral Filtering":
            return cv2.bilateralFilter(frame, 9, 75, 75)
        elif filter_name == "Non-local Means Denoising":
            return cv2.fastNlMeansDenoisingColored(frame, None, 10, 10, 7, 21)
        elif filter_name == "Anisotropic Diffusion":
            return self.anisotropic_diffusion(frame)
        elif filter_name == "Total Variation Denoising":
            return self.total_variation_denoising(frame)
        elif filter_name == "Wiener Filter":
            return self.wiener_filter(frame)
        elif filter_name == "Adaptive Thresholding":
            return self.adaptive_threshold_each_channel(frame)
        elif filter_name == "Haar Wavelet Transform":
            return self.haar_wavelet_transform(frame)
        elif filter_name == "Daubechies Wavelet Transform":
            return self.daubechies_wavelet_transform(frame)
        else:
            return frame  # Default: return original frame if filter not found
```

```python
    def wiener_filter(self, frame, kernel_size=(5, 5), noise_var=0.01):
        # Check if frame is None
        if frame is None:
            print("Error: Input frame is None.")
            return None

        # Check if frame is a valid numpy array
        if not isinstance(frame, np.ndarray):
            print("Error: Input frame is not a numpy array.")
            return None

        # Check if frame is an empty array
        if frame.size == 0:
            print("Error: Input frame is empty.")
            return None

        # Check if frame is in BGR color space
        if frame.shape[-1] != 3:
            print("Error: Input frame is not in BGR color space.")
            return None

        # Apply Wiener filter
        filtered_frame = cv2.medianBlur(frame, kernel_size[0])  # Use kernel_size[0] as the kernel size
        filtered_frame = cv2.fastNlMeansDenoising(filtered_frame, h=noise_var)
        return filtered_frame

    def adaptive_threshold_each_channel(self, frame):
        # Split the frame into individual channels
        b, g, r = cv2.split(frame)

        # Apply adaptive thresholding to each channel separately
        b_thresh = cv2.adaptiveThreshold(b, 255, cv2.ADAPTIVE_THRESH_GAUSSIAN_C, cv2.THRESH_BINARY, 11, 2)
        g_thresh = cv2.adaptiveThreshold(g, 255, cv2.ADAPTIVE_THRESH_GAUSSIAN_C, cv2.THRESH_BINARY, 11, 2)
        r_thresh = cv2.adaptiveThreshold(r, 255, cv2.ADAPTIVE_THRESH_GAUSSIAN_C, cv2.THRESH_BINARY, 11, 2)

        # Merge the thresholded channels back together
        return cv2.merge([b_thresh, g_thresh, r_thresh])

    def haar_wavelet_transform(self, frame):
        # Split the frame into its individual color channels
        b, g, r = cv2.split(frame)

        # Perform the wavelet transform on each channel separately
        b_coeffs = pywt.dwt2(b, 'haar')
        g_coeffs = pywt.dwt2(g, 'haar')
        r_coeffs = pywt.dwt2(r, 'haar')

        # Reconstruct the channels from the coefficients
        b_reconstructed = pywt.idwt2(b_coeffs, 'haar')
        g_reconstructed = pywt.idwt2(g_coeffs, 'haar')
        r_reconstructed = pywt.idwt2(r_coeffs, 'haar')

        # Clip the values to ensure they are within the valid range
        b_reconstructed = np.clip(b_reconstructed, 0, 255).astype(np.uint8)
        g_reconstructed = np.clip(g_reconstructed, 0, 255).astype(np.uint8)
        r_reconstructed = np.clip(r_reconstructed, 0, 255).astype(np.uint8)

        # Merge the channels back together
        return cv2.merge([b_reconstructed, g_reconstructed, r_reconstructed])
```

```python
    def daubechies_wavelet_transform(self, frame):
        # Split the frame into its individual color channels
        b, g, r = cv2.split(frame)

        # Choose the wavelet function (Daubechies 5)
        wavelet = 'db5'

        # Perform the wavelet transform on each channel separately
        b_coeffs = pywt.dwt2(b, wavelet)
        g_coeffs = pywt.dwt2(g, wavelet)
        r_coeffs = pywt.dwt2(r, wavelet)

        # Reconstruct the channels from the coefficients
        b_reconstructed = pywt.idwt2(b_coeffs, wavelet)
        g_reconstructed = pywt.idwt2(g_coeffs, wavelet)
        r_reconstructed = pywt.idwt2(r_coeffs, wavelet)

        # Clip the values to ensure they are within the valid range
        b_reconstructed = np.clip(b_reconstructed, 0, 255).astype(np.uint8)
        g_reconstructed = np.clip(g_reconstructed, 0, 255).astype(np.uint8)
        r_reconstructed = np.clip(r_reconstructed, 0, 255).astype(np.uint8)

        # Merge the channels back together
        return cv2.merge([b_reconstructed, g_reconstructed, r_reconstructed])

    def anisotropic_diffusion(self, img):
        return cv2.fastNlMeansDenoisingColored(img, None, 10, 10, 7, 21)

    def apply_total_variation_denoising_channel(self, channel, weight, iterations):
        # Initialize the result with the original channel
        result = channel.copy().astype(np.float64)  # Convert to float64

        # Perform total variation denoising
        for _ in range(iterations):
            # Compute the gradient of the channel
            dx = cv2.Sobel(result, cv2.CV_64F, 1, 0, ksize=3)
            dy = cv2.Sobel(result, cv2.CV_64F, 0, 1, ksize=3)

            # Update the channel using the gradient and the weight
            result -= weight * np.sqrt(dx**2 + dy**2)

        # Clip the values to ensure they are within the valid range
        result = np.clip(result, 0, 255).astype(np.uint8)

        return result

    def total_variation_denoising(self, img, weight=0.01, iterations=20):
        # Split the image into its individual color channels
        b, g, r = cv2.split(img)

        # Apply total variation denoising to each channel separately
        b_denoised = self.apply_total_variation_denoising_channel(b, weight, iterations)
        g_denoised = self.apply_total_variation_denoising_channel(g, weight, iterations)
        r_denoised = self.apply_total_variation_denoising_channel(r, weight, iterations)

        # Merge the denoised channels back together
        return cv2.merge([b_denoised, g_denoised, r_denoised])

def main():
    root = tk.Tk()
    app = CSRTTracker(root)
    root.mainloop()

if __name__ == "__main__":
```

        main()

RUNNING PROGRAM

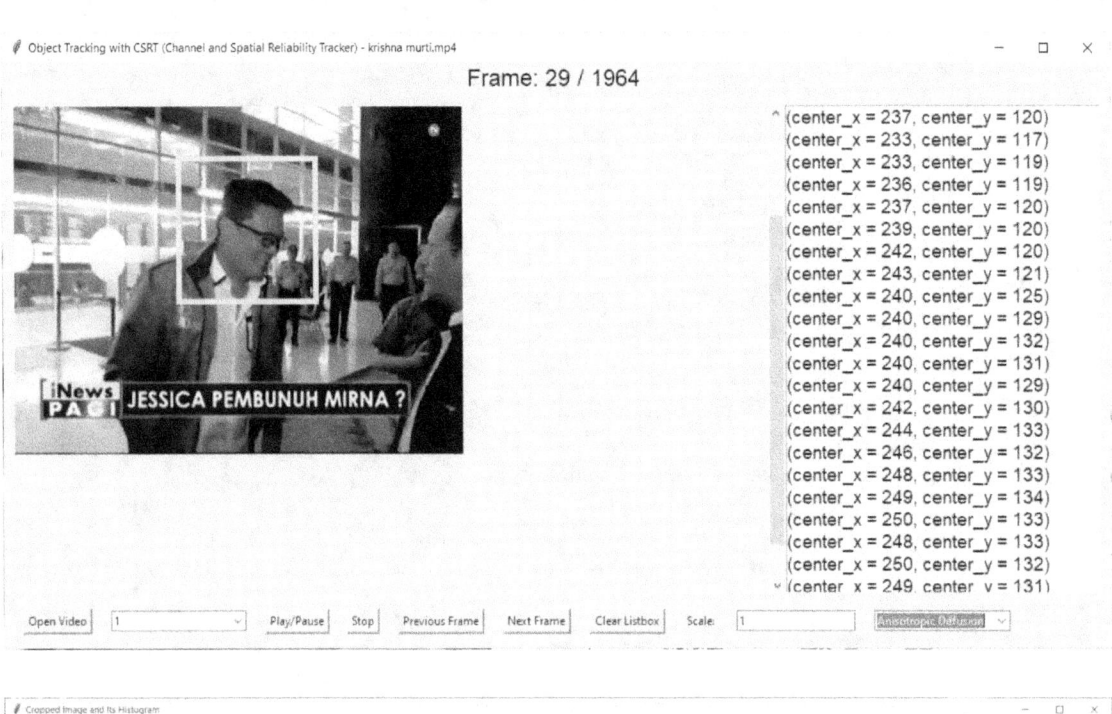

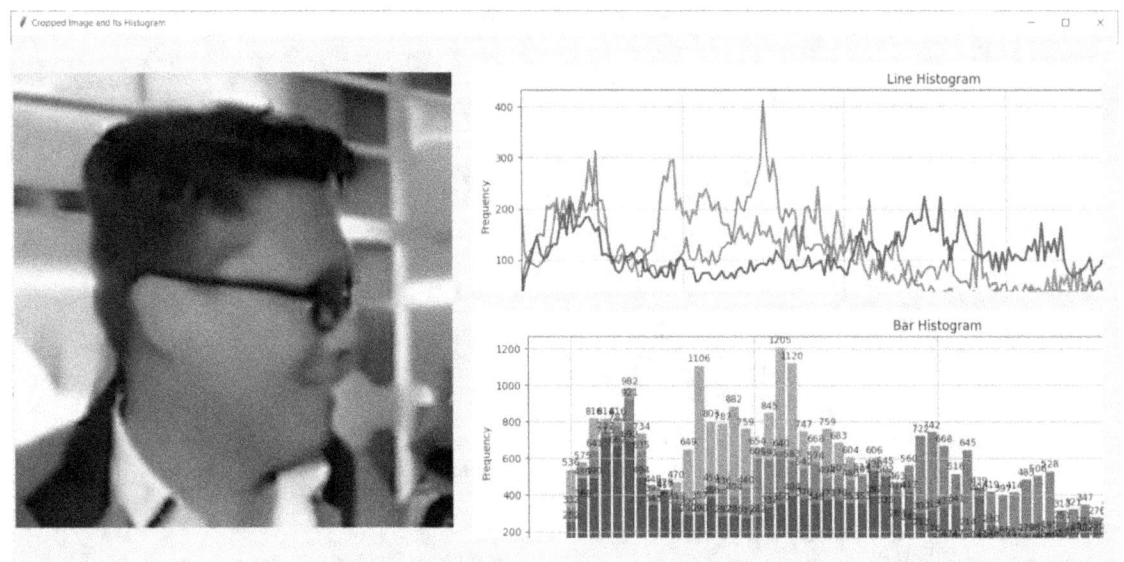

OBJECT TRACKING WITH KCF (KERNELIZED CORRELATION FILTERS) TRACKER

DESCRIPTION

The project outlined in the provided Python script is an object tracking application using the Kernelized Correlation Filters (KCF) method. This application is built with a graphical user interface (GUI) using the Tkinter library and offers a range of features for video processing and analysis.

The KCFTracker class is the core component of this application, managing all aspects of video handling, user interaction, and object tracking. Upon initialization, it sets up various attributes to manage the state of the video, such as whether it is paused, the current frame index, and the bounding box for tracking. It also defines a list of filters that can be applied to the video frames.

The create_widgets method is responsible for setting up the GUI elements. It creates a video display panel with a canvas for showing the video frames and a listbox for displaying the coordinates of the center of the tracked object. Control buttons are also added for opening videos, playing/pausing, stopping, navigating frames, and clearing the listbox. Additional input fields and comboboxes allow the user to specify parameters like zoom scale, threshold, and filters.

Opening a video file is handled by the open_video method, which uses the filedialog module to let the user select a video file. The selected video is then loaded using the imageio library, and the play_video method starts displaying the video frames.

The play_video method begins the video playback and sets the tracking_started flag to True, indicating that tracking can commence. The show_frame method is called to display each frame, handling both the video rendering and the tracking logic. It ensures the frame is processed correctly and updates the bounding box if tracking is active.

The toggle_play_pause method allows the user to pause and resume video playback. It also initiates tracking if a bounding box is defined and updates the frame display accordingly. The stop_video method stops the video playback, resets the frame index and bounding box, and clears the tracker.

Zoom functionality is managed by the update_zoom method, which is triggered when the user selects a different zoom level from the combobox. The on_mousewheel method allows the user to zoom in and out using the mouse wheel.

User interaction for defining the bounding box is handled by on_press, on_drag, and on_release methods. When the user clicks and drags on the canvas, these methods capture the coordinates and dimensions of the bounding box. The on_release method also triggers the analyze_histogram method to analyze the selected region.

The initialize_tracker and track_object methods handle the setup and updating of the KCF tracker. The tracker is initialized with default or user-defined parameters and updates the bounding box position as the video frames are processed. The track_object method also calculates the center of the bounding box and updates the listbox with these coordinates.

The show_frame method integrates the video display and tracking logic. It fetches the current frame from the video, processes it, and displays it on the canvas. If tracking is active, it updates the bounding box and its display.

The analyze_histogram method processes the selected bounding box region to generate and display histograms. It extracts the region from the current frame, applies any selected filters, and creates a popup window to display the cropped image and its histograms.

The create_popup_window method sets up a new window for displaying the cropped image and histograms. The display_cropped_image method shows the cropped image in the popup window, while the display_histograms method generates and displays both line and bar histograms for the cropped region.

Histograms are generated using the display_line_histogram and display_bar_histogram methods. These methods use matplotlib to plot the histograms and then convert these plots to images for display in the Tkinter canvas. The plot_to_image method handles the conversion of matplotlib plots to PIL images.

The apply_filter method applies various filters to the video frames, based on user selection. Available filters include Gaussian, Mean, Median, Bilateral Filtering, Non-local Means Denoising, and others. Each filter modifies the frame in a specific way to highlight different aspects of the image.

The prev_frame and next_frame methods allow the user to navigate through the video frames manually, updating the display accordingly. The clear_listbox method clears the list of tracked object centers, resetting the listbox.

The set_window_title method updates the window title with the current video file name, providing a clear context for the user. This method is called whenever a new video is opened or the window needs to be updated.

Overall, the KCFTracker project provides a comprehensive tool for object tracking and video analysis. It combines real-time video processing with interactive features, allowing users to define regions of interest, apply filters, and analyze the results through histograms. The use of KCF for object tracking ensures efficient and accurate tracking performance, making this application suitable for various video analysis tasks.

SOURCE CODE

```python
#kcf_tracker.py
import tkinter as tk
from tkinter import ttk
from tkinter import filedialog
from PIL import Image, ImageTk
import imageio
import cv2
import numpy as np
import matplotlib.pyplot as plt
import pywt

class KCFTracker:
    def __init__(self, master):
        self.master = master
        self.master.title("Object Tracking with KCF (Kernelized Correlation Filters) Tracker")
        self.file_name = ""
        self.set_window_title()  # Set window title initially

        self.frame_number_label = tk.Label(master, text="Frame: 0")
        self.frame_number_label.pack()

        self.video = None
        self.video_path = None
        self.paused = False
        self.zoom_scale = tk.IntVar(value=1)
        self.frame_index = 0
        self.bbox = None
        self.bbox2 = None
        self.tracking_started = False  # Initialize tracking_started to False
        self.prev_frame_gray = None
        self.tracker = None
        self.initial_w = None
        self.initial_h = None
        self.bbox_rect = None  # Initialize bbox_rect attribute to None
        self.frame_processing = False  # Initialize frame_processing attribute to False

        # Available filters
        self.filters = ["None", "Gaussian", "Mean", "Median", "Bilateral Filtering",
                        "Non-local Means Denoising", "Anisotropic Diffusion",
                        "Total Variation Denoising", "Wiener Filter",
                        "Adaptive Thresholding", "Haar Wavelet Transform",
                        "Daubechies Wavelet Transform"]

        self.create_widgets()

    def create_widgets(self):
        # Panel for video display
        video_panel = tk.Frame(self.master)
        video_panel.pack(padx=10, pady=10)

        # Canvas to display the original video
        canvas_width = 800
        canvas_height = 500
        self.canvas = tk.Canvas(video_panel, width=canvas_width, height=canvas_height)
        self.canvas.pack(side="left", fill="both", expand=True)
        self.canvas.bind("<MouseWheel>", self.on_mousewheel)
        self.canvas.bind("<ButtonPress-1>", self.on_press)
        self.canvas.bind("<B1-Motion>", self.on_drag)
        self.canvas.bind("<ButtonRelease-1>", self.on_release)  # Bind ButtonRelease event
```

```python
        # List box to display center coordinates
        self.center_listbox = tk.Listbox(video_panel, width=30, height=20, font=("Helvetica", 14))
        self.center_listbox.pack(side="right", fill="y")
        # Scrollbar for the listbox
        scrollbar = tk.Scrollbar(video_panel, orient="vertical")
        scrollbar.pack(side="left", fill="y")
        scrollbar.config(command=self.center_listbox.yview)

        # Attach scrollbar to listbox
        self.center_listbox.config(yscrollcommand=scrollbar.set)

        # Panel for control buttons
        control_panel = tk.Frame(self.master)
        control_panel.pack(padx=10, pady=(0, 10), fill="x")

        # Button to open a video file
        self.open_button = tk.Button(control_panel, text="Open Video", command=self.open_video)
        self.open_button.grid(row=0, column=0, padx=10, pady=5)

        # Combobox for selecting zoom scale
        self.zoom_combobox = ttk.Combobox(control_panel, textvariable=self.zoom_scale, values=list(range(1, 11)))
        self.zoom_combobox.grid(row=0, column=1, padx=10, pady=5)
        self.zoom_combobox.bind("<<ComboboxSelected>>", self.update_zoom)

        # Button to play/pause the video
        self.play_button = tk.Button(control_panel, text="Play/Pause", command=self.toggle_play_pause)
        self.play_button.grid(row=0, column=2, padx=10, pady=5)

        # Button to stop the video
        self.stop_button = tk.Button(control_panel, text="Stop", command=self.stop_video)
        self.stop_button.grid(row=0, column=3, padx=10, pady=5)

        # Button to navigate to the previous frame
        self.prev_frame_button = tk.Button(control_panel, text="Previous Frame", command=self.prev_frame)
        self.prev_frame_button.grid(row=0, column=4, padx=10, pady=5)

        # Button to navigate to the next frame
        self.next_frame_button = tk.Button(control_panel, text="Next Frame", command=self.next_frame)
        self.next_frame_button.grid(row=0, column=5, padx=10, pady=5)

        # Button to clear the listbox
        self.clear_button = tk.Button(control_panel, text="Clear Listbox", command=self.clear_listbox)
        self.clear_button.grid(row=0, column=6, padx=10, pady=5)

        # Label and entry for specifying scale
        self.scale_label = tk.Label(control_panel, text="Scale:")
        self.scale_label.grid(row=0, column=7, padx=10, pady=5, sticky="e")
        self.scale_default = tk.StringVar(value="1")
        self.scale_entry = ttk.Entry(control_panel, textvariable=self.scale_default)
        self.scale_entry.grid(row=0, column=8, padx=10, pady=5, sticky="w")
        self.scale_entry.bind("<Return>", lambda event: self.toggle_play_pause())

        # Combobox for selecting filters
        self.filter_combobox = ttk.Combobox(control_panel, values=self.filters)
        self.filter_combobox.grid(row=0, column=9, padx=10, pady=5)
        self.filter_combobox.current(0)  # Set default value

        # Label and entry for specifying threshold
```

```python
        self.thresh_label = tk.Label(control_panel, text="Threshold:")
        self.thresh_label.grid(row=1, column=0, padx=10, pady=5, sticky="e")
        self.thresh_default = tk.StringVar(value="0.4")
        self.thresh_entry = ttk.Entry(control_panel, textvariable=self.thresh_default)
        self.thresh_entry.grid(row=1, column=1, padx=10, pady=5, sticky="w")
        self.thresh_entry.bind("<Return>", lambda event: self.toggle_play_pause())

        # Label and entry for specifying lambda
        self.lambda_label = tk.Label(control_panel, text="Lambda:")
        self.lambda_label.grid(row=1, column=2, padx=10, pady=5, sticky="e")
        self.lambda_default = tk.StringVar(value="0.01")
        self.lambda_entry = ttk.Entry(control_panel, textvariable=self.lambda_default)
        self.lambda_entry.grid(row=1, column=3, padx=10, pady=5, sticky="w")
        self.lambda_entry.bind("<Return>", lambda event: self.toggle_play_pause())

        # Label and entry for specifying sigma
        self.sigma_label = tk.Label(control_panel, text="Lambda:")
        self.sigma_label.grid(row=1, column=4, padx=10, pady=5, sticky="e")
        self.sigma_default = tk.StringVar(value="0.5")
        self.sigma_entry = ttk.Entry(control_panel, textvariable=self.sigma_default)
        self.sigma_entry.grid(row=1, column=5, padx=10, pady=5, sticky="w")
        self.sigma_entry.bind("<Return>", lambda event: self.toggle_play_pause())

        # Label and entry for specifying max patch size
        self.patch_label = tk.Label(control_panel, text="Max. Patch Size:")
        self.patch_label.grid(row=1, column=6, padx=10, pady=5, sticky="e")
        self.patch_default = tk.StringVar(value="80")
        self.patch_entry = ttk.Entry(control_panel, textvariable=self.patch_default)
        self.patch_entry.grid(row=1, column=7, padx=10, pady=5, sticky="w")
        self.patch_entry.bind("<Return>", lambda event: self.toggle_play_pause())

        # Label and entry for specifying interpolation factor
        self.factor_label = tk.Label(control_panel, text="Max. Patch Size:")
        self.factor_label.grid(row=1, column=8, padx=10, pady=5, sticky="e")
        self.factor_default = tk.StringVar(value="0.075")
        self.factor_entry = ttk.Entry(control_panel, textvariable=self.factor_default)
        self.factor_entry.grid(row=1, column=9, padx=10, pady=5, sticky="w")
        self.factor_entry.bind("<Return>", lambda event: self.toggle_play_pause())

    def open_video(self):
        self.video_path = filedialog.askopenfilename(filetypes=[("Video files", 
"*.mp4;*.avi;*.mkv;*.wmv")])
        if self.video_path:
            self.video = imageio.get_reader(self.video_path)
            self.file_name = self.video_path.split('/')[-1]
            self.set_window_title()
            self.play_video()

    def play_video(self):
        if self.video:
            self.paused = False
            self.tracking_started = True
            self.show_frame()

    def stop_video(self):
        self.paused = True
        self.frame_index = 0
        self.bbox = None
        self.tracker = None   # Reset tracker
        self.initial_w = None  # Reset width
        self.initial_h = None  # Reset height
        self.show_frame()

    def toggle_play_pause(self):
```

```python
        self.paused = not self.paused
        if not self.paused:
            if self.bbox is not None:
                self.tracking_started = True
            self.play_video()

    def update_zoom(self, event=None):
        self.show_frame()

    def initialize_tracker(self, frame, bbox, params=None):
        """Initialize the KCF tracker with possible user-defined parameters."""

        # Default parameters for KCF Tracker
        default_params = {
            "detect_thresh": float(self.thresh_entry.get()),
            "sigma": float(self.sigma_entry.get()),
            "lambda": float(self.lambda_entry.get()),
            "interp_factor": float(self.factor_entry.get()),
            "output_sigma_factor": 0.1,
            "resize": True,
            "max_patch_size": int(self.patch_entry.get()),
            "split_coeff": True,
            "wrap_kernel": False,
            "desc_pca": 256,
            "desc_npca": 256
        }

        # If params are provided, update the default_params
        if params:
            default_params.update(params)

        # Adjust bbox based on parameters such as scaling
        scale = int(self.scale_entry.get())  #scale is provided through a GUI element
        bbox = (
            int(bbox[0] + (1 - scale) * bbox[2] / 2),  # Center the scaling on the bbox
            int(bbox[1] + (1 - scale) * bbox[3] / 2),
            int(bbox[2] * scale),
            int(bbox[3] * scale)
        )

        # Initialize the KCF tracker
        self.tracker = cv2.legacy.TrackerKCF_create()

        # Assuming a hypothetical method to set parameters (not available in the current OpenCV API)
        # This part is pseudo-code and will not work with standard OpenCV installations
        if hasattr(self.tracker, 'setParams'):
            self.tracker.setParams(default_params)

        self.tracker.init(frame, tuple(map(int, bbox)))
        self.initial_w, self.initial_h = bbox[2], bbox[3]

    def track_object(self, frame, bbox, user_params=None):
        """Track object using KCF Tracker with optional user parameters."""
        if bbox:
            if self.tracker is None:
                self.initialize_tracker(frame, bbox, user_params)

            # Update the tracker and get the new bounding box
            success, bbox = self.tracker.update(frame)
            if success:
                x1, y1, w, h = map(int, bbox)
                w, h = self.initial_w, self.initial_h  # Maintain initial dimensions if required
```

```python
                x2, y2 = x1 + w, y1 + h

                # Calculate and display the center of the bounding box
                center_x = (x1 + x2) // 2
                center_y = (y1 + y2) // 2
                self.center_listbox.insert(tk.END, f"(center_x = {center_x}, center_y = {center_y})")

                return x1, y1, x2, y2
        return None

    def update_bbox_rectangle(self, bbox):
        if bbox is not None:
            x1, y1, x2, y2 = map(int, bbox)
            if self.bbox_rect is not None:
                self.canvas.coords(self.bbox_rect, x1, y1, x2, y2)
                self.canvas.tag_raise(self.bbox_rect)  # Raise the bounding box to the front
            else:
                self.bbox_rect = self.canvas.create_rectangle(x1, y1, x2, y2, outline='#fc3d3d', width=8, tags="bbox")

    def show_frame(self):
        if self.video:
            if not self.paused:
                if 0 <= self.frame_index < len(self.video):
                    if not self.frame_processing:  # Check if the frame is already being processed
                        try:
                            self.frame_processing = True  # Set frame_processing flag to True to indicate frame processing

                            frame = self.video.get_data(self.frame_index)
                            frame = cv2.cvtColor(frame, cv2.COLOR_RGB2BGR)

                            if self.bbox is not None:
                                if not self.tracking_started:
                                    self.tracking_started = True

                                self.bbox = self.track_object(frame, self.bbox)
                                if self.bbox:
                                    frame = cv2.cvtColor(frame, cv2.COLOR_BGR2RGB)
                                    frame = Image.fromarray(frame)
                                    frame = frame.resize((frame.width * self.zoom_scale.get(), frame.height * self.zoom_scale.get()))
                                    photo = ImageTk.PhotoImage(frame)
                                    self.photo = photo
                                    self.canvas.delete("video")
                                    self.canvas.create_image(0, 0, anchor="nw", image=photo, tags="video")
                                    self.update_bbox_rectangle(self.bbox)

                            else:
                                frame = cv2.cvtColor(frame, cv2.COLOR_BGR2RGB)
                                frame = Image.fromarray(frame)
                                frame = frame.resize((frame.width * self.zoom_scale.get(), frame.height * self.zoom_scale.get()))
                                photo = ImageTk.PhotoImage(frame)
                                self.photo = photo
                                self.canvas.delete("video")
                                self.canvas.create_image(0, 0, anchor="nw", image=photo, tags="video")

                            self.frame_number_label.config(text=f"Frame: {self.frame_index} / {self.video.count_frames()}", font=("Helvetica", 18))
```

```python
                        self.frame_index += 1

            except Exception as e:
                print("Error: ", e)
            finally:
                self.frame_processing = False  # Reset frame_processing flag to
False after processing the frame

    def on_mousewheel(self, event):
        direction = event.delta // 120
        current_value = int(self.zoom_scale.get())
        if direction == 1 and current_value < 10:
            current_value += 1
        elif direction == -1 and current_value > 1:
            current_value -= 1
        self.zoom_scale.set(current_value)
        self.update_zoom()

    def on_press(self, event):
        self.tracker = None
        self.start_x = self.canvas.canvasx(event.x)
        self.start_y = self.canvas.canvasy(event.y)
        # Clear the previous bounding box if it exists
        if self.bbox_rect:
            self.canvas.delete(self.bbox_rect)
            self.bbox_rect = None
        self.bbox = None
        self.bbox2 = None

    def on_drag(self, event):
        # Update the endpoint of the rectangle as the mouse moves
        cur_x = self.canvas.canvasx(event.x)
        cur_y = self.canvas.canvasy(event.y)

        # Define the coordinates correctly ensuring x1 < x2 and y1 < y2
        x1, y1 = min(self.start_x, cur_x), min(self.start_y, cur_y)
        x2, y2 = max(self.start_x, cur_x), max(self.start_y, cur_y)

        # Update dimensions for tracking
        self.initial_w = x2 - x1
        self.initial_h = y2 - y1
        self.bbox = (x1, y1, self.initial_w, self.initial_h)
        self.bbox2 = (self.start_x, self.start_y, cur_x, cur_y)

        # Update or create a rectangle on the canvas
        if self.bbox_rect:
            self.canvas.coords(self.bbox_rect, x1, y1, x2, y2)
        else:
            self.bbox_rect = self.canvas.create_rectangle(x1, y1, x2, y2, outline="cyan",
width=6)

    def prev_frame(self):
        if self.frame_index > 0:
            self.frame_index -= 1
            self.show_frame()

    def next_frame(self):
        if self.video and self.frame_index < len(self.video) - 1:
            self.show_frame()

    def clear_listbox(self):
        self.center_listbox.delete(0, tk.END)
```

```python
    def set_window_title(self):
        if self.file_name:
            self.master.title(f"Object Tracking with KCF (Kernelized Correlation Filters) Tracker - {self.file_name}")
            self.master.title_font = ("Helvetica", 16, "bold")
        else:
            self.master.title("Object Tracking with KCF (Kernelized Correlation Filters) Tracker")

    def on_release(self, event):
        self.analyze_histogram()  # Call analyze_histogram() method when the mouse button is released

    def analyze_histogram(self):
        if self.bbox2 is not None and self.video:
            x1, y1, x2, y2 = map(int, self.bbox2)
            if x1 != x2 and y1 != y2:
                try:
                    frame = self.video.get_data(self.frame_index)
                    # Ensure the bounding box is within the frame boundaries
                    h, w, _ = frame.shape
                    x1, x2 = max(0, min(x1, w)), max(0, min(x2, w))
                    y1, y2 = max(0, min(y1, h)), max(0, min(y2, h))

                    # Ensure x1 < x2 and y1 < y2
                    x1, x2 = sorted([x1, x2])
                    y1, y2 = sorted([y1, y2])

                    cropped_frame = frame[y1:y2, x1:x2]
                    if cropped_frame.size > 0:
                        cropped_frame = cv2.cvtColor(cropped_frame, cv2.COLOR_BGR2RGB)

                        # Get selected filter from combobox
                        selected_filter = self.filter_combobox.get()
                        # Apply selected filter
                        filtered_frame = self.apply_filter(selected_filter, cropped_frame)

                        self.create_popup_window(filtered_frame)
                        self.display_cropped_image(filtered_frame)
                        self.display_histograms(filtered_frame)
                    else:
                        print("Cropped frame is empty.")
                except Exception as e:
                    print("Failed to process frame:", e)
            else:
                print("Bounding box dimensions are zero or negative.")

    def create_popup_window(self, cropped_frame):
        self.popup_window = tk.Toplevel(self.master)
        self.popup_window.title("Cropped Image and Its Histogram")
        self.popup_window.geometry("1500x700")

    def display_cropped_image(self, cropped_frame):
        cropped_frame_frame = tk.Frame(self.popup_window)
        cropped_frame_frame.pack(side="left")

        cropped_frame_rgb = cv2.cvtColor(cropped_frame, cv2.COLOR_BGR2RGB)
        cropped_img = Image.fromarray(cropped_frame_rgb)
        cropped_img = cropped_img.resize((600, 600))

        cropped_photo = ImageTk.PhotoImage(cropped_img)
```

```python
        cropped_canvas = tk.Canvas(cropped_frame_frame, width=600, height=600)
        cropped_canvas.pack(side="left", anchor="nw")
        cropped_canvas.create_image(0, 0, anchor="nw", image=cropped_photo)
        cropped_canvas.image = cropped_photo

    def display_histograms(self, cropped_frame):
        histograms_frame = tk.Frame(self.popup_window)
        histograms_frame.pack(side="right", padx=20)

        self.display_line_histogram(cropped_frame, histograms_frame)
        self.display_bar_histogram(cropped_frame, histograms_frame)

    def display_line_histogram(self, cropped_frame, histograms_frame):
        line_histogram_frame = tk.Frame(histograms_frame)
        line_histogram_frame.pack(side="top", pady=10)

        plt.figure(figsize=(12, 4))
        color = ('r', 'g', 'b')
        for i, col in enumerate(color):
            histr = cv2.calcHist([cropped_frame], [i], None, [256], [0, 256])
            plt.plot(histr, color=col, label=f'Channel {col.upper()}', linewidth=2)
            plt.xlim([0, 256])
        plt.title('Line Histogram')
        plt.xlabel('Pixel Value')
        plt.ylabel('Frequency')
        plt.tight_layout()
        plt.grid(True)
        plt.legend()

        line_histogram_img = self.plot_to_image(plt)
        self.display_histogram_image(line_histogram_frame, line_histogram_img)

    def display_bar_histogram(self, cropped_frame, histograms_frame):
        bar_histogram_frame = tk.Frame(histograms_frame)
        bar_histogram_frame.pack(side="bottom", pady=10)

        plt.figure(figsize=(12, 4))
        color = ('r', 'g', 'b')
        for i, col in enumerate(color):
            hist_range = (0, 256)
            hist_counts, _ = np.histogram(cropped_frame[:, :, i], bins=64, range=hist_range)
            plt.bar(np.arange(64), hist_counts, color=col, alpha=0.7, label=f'Channel {col.upper()}')
            for index, value in enumerate(hist_counts):
                plt.text(index, value + 10, str(int(value)), ha='center', va='bottom', fontsize=9)

        plt.title('Bar Histogram')
        plt.xlabel('Pixel Value')
        plt.ylabel('Frequency')
        plt.xticks(np.linspace(0, 63, num=5), np.linspace(0, 255, num=5, dtype=int))  # Adjust x-axis ticks
        plt.tight_layout()
        plt.grid(True)
        plt.legend()

        bar_histogram_img = self.plot_to_image(plt)
        self.display_histogram_image(bar_histogram_frame, bar_histogram_img)

    def display_histogram_image(self, parent_frame, img):
        histogram_photo = ImageTk.PhotoImage(image=img)
        histogram_canvas = tk.Canvas(parent_frame, width=900, height=300)
        histogram_canvas.pack(side="bottom", anchor="se")
        histogram_canvas.create_image(0, 0, anchor="nw", image=histogram_photo)
```

```python
        histogram_canvas.image = histogram_photo

    def plot_histogram_bar_to_image(self, image):
        # Calculate histogram for each channel
        histograms = []
        for i in range(3):
            hist_range = (0, 256)
            hist_counts, _ = np.histogram(image[:, :, i], bins=64, range=hist_range)  # Adjust bins to 64
            histograms.append(hist_counts)

        # Extracting only 64 bins from the histogram
        num_bins = 64  # Adjusted to 64 bins

        # Generating colors for each channel
        colors = ['red', 'green', 'blue']

        plt.figure()
        for i, histogram in enumerate(histograms):
            # Normalize the histogram counts for better visualization
            hist_counts = histogram / np.sum(histogram)
            # Setting the color for each channel
            plt.bar(np.arange(num_bins), hist_counts[:num_bins], color=colors[i], alpha=0.7, label=f'Channel {["Red", "Green", "Blue"][i]}')

        plt.xlabel('Pixel Value')
        plt.ylabel('Normalized Frequency')
        plt.title('RGB Channel Histograms')
        plt.grid(True)
        plt.tight_layout()
        plt.legend()

        # Convert the histogram bar graph to an image
        histogram_bar_img = self.plot_to_image(plt)
        histogram_bar_photo = ImageTk.PhotoImage(image=histogram_bar_img)

        return histogram_bar_photo

    def plot_to_image(self, plt):
        plt.savefig('temp_plot.png')
        img = Image.open('temp_plot.png')
        return img

    def apply_filter(self, filter_name, frame):
        if filter_name == "None":
            return frame
        elif filter_name == "Gaussian":
            return cv2.GaussianBlur(frame, (5, 5), 0)
        elif filter_name == "Mean":
            return cv2.blur(frame, (5, 5))
        elif filter_name == "Median":
            return cv2.medianBlur(frame, 5)
        elif filter_name == "Bilateral Filtering":
            return cv2.bilateralFilter(frame, 9, 75, 75)
        elif filter_name == "Non-local Means Denoising":
            return cv2.fastNlMeansDenoisingColored(frame, None, 10, 10, 7, 21)
        elif filter_name == "Anisotropic Diffusion":
            return self.anisotropic_diffusion(frame)
        elif filter_name == "Total Variation Denoising":
            return self.total_variation_denoising(frame)
        elif filter_name == "Wiener Filter":
            return self.wiener_filter(frame)
        elif filter_name == "Adaptive Thresholding":
            return self.adaptive_threshold_each_channel(frame)
```

```python
        elif filter_name == "Haar Wavelet Transform":
            return self.haar_wavelet_transform(frame)
        elif filter_name == "Daubechies Wavelet Transform":
            return self.daubechies_wavelet_transform(frame)
        else:
            return frame  # Default: return original frame if filter not found

    def wiener_filter(self, frame, kernel_size=(5, 5), noise_var=0.01):
        # Check if frame is None
        if frame is None:
            print("Error: Input frame is None.")
            return None

        # Check if frame is a valid numpy array
        if not isinstance(frame, np.ndarray):
            print("Error: Input frame is not a numpy array.")
            return None

        # Check if frame is an empty array
        if frame.size == 0:
            print("Error: Input frame is empty.")
            return None

        # Check if frame is in BGR color space
        if frame.shape[-1] != 3:
            print("Error: Input frame is not in BGR color space.")
            return None

        # Apply Wiener filter
        filtered_frame = cv2.medianBlur(frame, kernel_size[0])  # Use kernel_size[0] as the kernel size
        filtered_frame = cv2.fastNlMeansDenoising(filtered_frame, h=noise_var)
        return filtered_frame

    def adaptive_threshold_each_channel(self, frame):
        # Split the frame into individual channels
        b, g, r = cv2.split(frame)

        # Apply adaptive thresholding to each channel separately
        b_thresh = cv2.adaptiveThreshold(b, 255, cv2.ADAPTIVE_THRESH_GAUSSIAN_C, cv2.THRESH_BINARY, 11, 2)
        g_thresh = cv2.adaptiveThreshold(g, 255, cv2.ADAPTIVE_THRESH_GAUSSIAN_C, cv2.THRESH_BINARY, 11, 2)
        r_thresh = cv2.adaptiveThreshold(r, 255, cv2.ADAPTIVE_THRESH_GAUSSIAN_C, cv2.THRESH_BINARY, 11, 2)

        # Merge the thresholded channels back together
        return cv2.merge([b_thresh, g_thresh, r_thresh])

    def haar_wavelet_transform(self, frame):
        # Split the frame into its individual color channels
        b, g, r = cv2.split(frame)

        # Perform the wavelet transform on each channel separately
        b_coeffs = pywt.dwt2(b, 'haar')
        g_coeffs = pywt.dwt2(g, 'haar')
        r_coeffs = pywt.dwt2(r, 'haar')

        # Reconstruct the channels from the coefficients
        b_reconstructed = pywt.idwt2(b_coeffs, 'haar')
        g_reconstructed = pywt.idwt2(g_coeffs, 'haar')
        r_reconstructed = pywt.idwt2(r_coeffs, 'haar')

        # Clip the values to ensure they are within the valid range
```

```python
        b_reconstructed = np.clip(b_reconstructed, 0, 255).astype(np.uint8)
        g_reconstructed = np.clip(g_reconstructed, 0, 255).astype(np.uint8)
        r_reconstructed = np.clip(r_reconstructed, 0, 255).astype(np.uint8)

        # Merge the channels back together
        return cv2.merge([b_reconstructed, g_reconstructed, r_reconstructed])

    def daubechies_wavelet_transform(self, frame):
        # Split the frame into its individual color channels
        b, g, r = cv2.split(frame)

        # Choose the wavelet function (Daubechies 5)
        wavelet = 'db5'

        # Perform the wavelet transform on each channel separately
        b_coeffs = pywt.dwt2(b, wavelet)
        g_coeffs = pywt.dwt2(g, wavelet)
        r_coeffs = pywt.dwt2(r, wavelet)

        # Reconstruct the channels from the coefficients
        b_reconstructed = pywt.idwt2(b_coeffs, wavelet)
        g_reconstructed = pywt.idwt2(g_coeffs, wavelet)
        r_reconstructed = pywt.idwt2(r_coeffs, wavelet)

        # Clip the values to ensure they are within the valid range
        b_reconstructed = np.clip(b_reconstructed, 0, 255).astype(np.uint8)
        g_reconstructed = np.clip(g_reconstructed, 0, 255).astype(np.uint8)
        r_reconstructed = np.clip(r_reconstructed, 0, 255).astype(np.uint8)

        # Merge the channels back together
        return cv2.merge([b_reconstructed, g_reconstructed, r_reconstructed])

    def anisotropic_diffusion(self, img):
        return cv2.fastNlMeansDenoisingColored(img, None, 10, 10, 7, 21)

    def apply_total_variation_denoising_channel(self, channel, weight, iterations):
        # Initialize the result with the original channel
        result = channel.copy().astype(np.float64)  # Convert to float64

        # Perform total variation denoising
        for _ in range(iterations):
            # Compute the gradient of the channel
            dx = cv2.Sobel(result, cv2.CV_64F, 1, 0, ksize=3)
            dy = cv2.Sobel(result, cv2.CV_64F, 0, 1, ksize=3)

            # Update the channel using the gradient and the weight
            result -= weight * np.sqrt(dx**2 + dy**2)

        # Clip the values to ensure they are within the valid range
        result = np.clip(result, 0, 255).astype(np.uint8)

        return result

    def total_variation_denoising(self, img, weight=0.01, iterations=20):
        # Split the image into its individual color channels
        b, g, r = cv2.split(img)

        # Apply total variation denoising to each channel separately
        b_denoised = self.apply_total_variation_denoising_channel(b, weight, iterations)
        g_denoised = self.apply_total_variation_denoising_channel(g, weight, iterations)
        r_denoised = self.apply_total_variation_denoising_channel(r, weight, iterations)

        # Merge the denoised channels back together
        return cv2.merge([b_denoised, g_denoised, r_denoised])
```

```python
def main():
    root = tk.Tk()
    app = KCFTracker(root)
    root.mainloop()

if __name__ == "__main__":
    main()
```

RUNNING PROGRAM

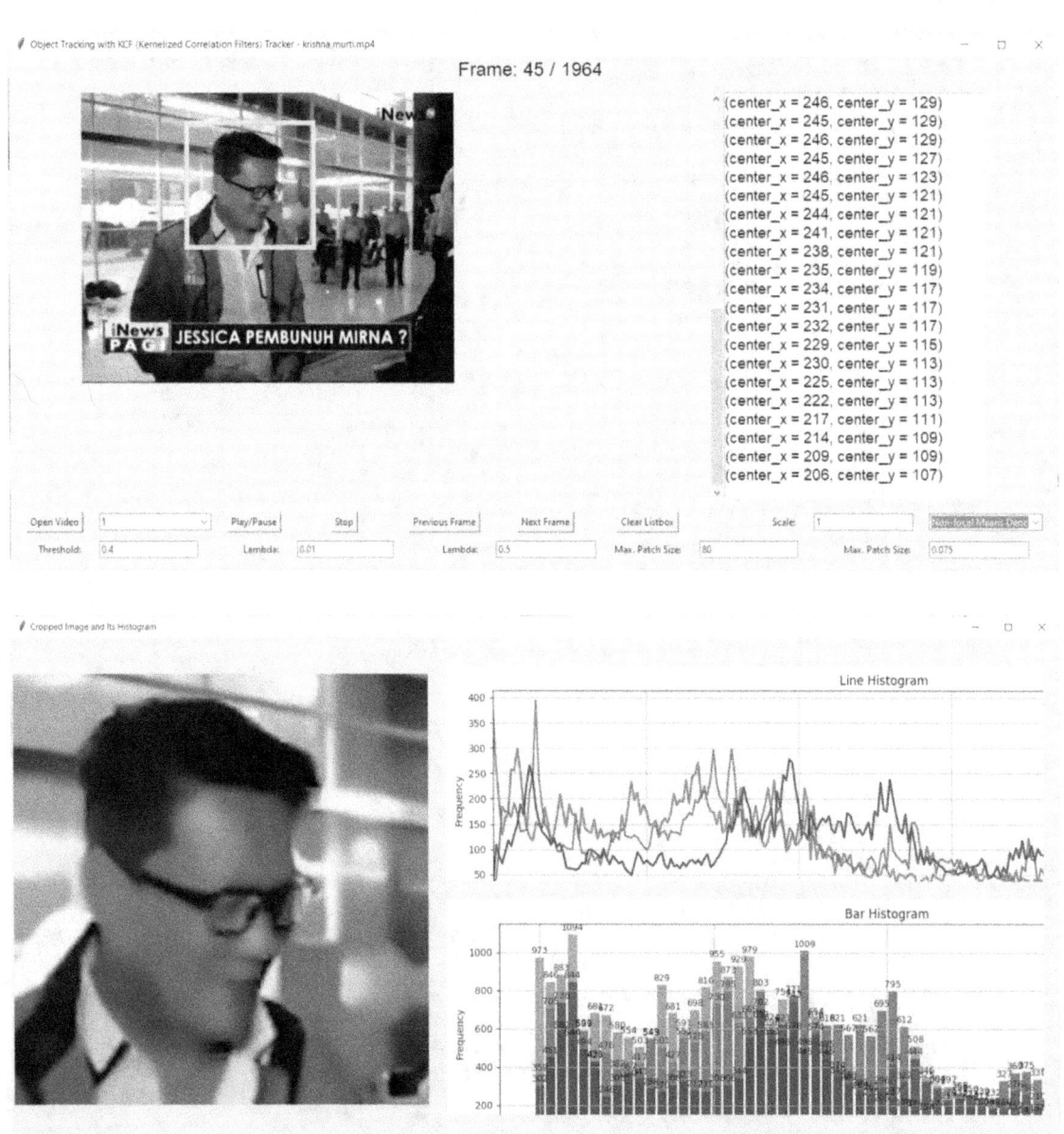

OBJECT TRACKING WITH MEDIAN FLOW TRACKER

DESCRIPTION

The MedianFlow Tracker project is a Python application that utilizes various libraries to provide an interactive tool for video object tracking and histogram analysis. The project is implemented using Tkinter for the graphical user interface, OpenCV for the tracking algorithm, and other libraries for additional image processing tasks. The main class, MedianFlowTracker, initializes the interface and sets up the necessary components for video manipulation and object tracking.

Upon launching the application, the user is presented with a window titled "Object Tracking with MedianFlow Tracker". The user can open a video file, which is then read and displayed frame by frame on a canvas within the Tkinter window. The video can be played, paused, or stopped using the control buttons provided. A listbox on the right side of the window displays the center coordinates of the tracked object, updating in real-time as the video plays.

The tracking mechanism is powered by OpenCV's MedianFlow tracker, which requires a user-defined bounding box to initialize. Users can draw this bounding box directly on the video canvas using mouse events. The bounding box is dynamically updated as the user drags the mouse, and the dimensions are displayed and adjusted in real-time. Once the bounding box is set, the tracker can follow the object through subsequent frames, updating its position and recalculating the center coordinates.

Additionally, the project includes several image processing filters that can be applied to the cropped area of the frame where the object is being tracked. These filters include Gaussian Blur, Median Blur, Bilateral Filtering, and more. The filters are selectable via a combobox, and the selected filter is applied to the cropped image before displaying the results.

The application also features advanced controls for tweaking the tracking parameters, such as window size, maximum levels, points in the grid, maximum iterations, and epsilon threshold. These parameters can be adjusted through entry fields in the control panel, allowing for fine-tuning of the tracking algorithm's performance.

When the user releases the mouse button after drawing the bounding box, the application analyzes the histogram of the cropped image area. It computes and displays both line and bar histograms for the RGB channels, providing a detailed view of the color distribution within the selected region. This analysis is shown in a separate popup window, which also displays the cropped image.

The histogram analysis includes line histograms, where the frequency of each pixel value is plotted for the red, green, and blue channels, and bar histograms, where the frequency of pixel values is represented as bars. Both types of histograms are generated using Matplotlib and displayed in the popup window alongside the cropped image.

The project employs several helper methods to facilitate the histogram analysis and display. For instance, analyze_histogram is responsible for extracting the cropped frame and applying the selected filter before computing the histograms. The method create_popup_window initializes the popup window where the histograms are displayed, and display_histograms manages the creation and arrangement of histogram plots.

The apply_filter method applies the selected filter to the cropped frame. Each filter type, from Gaussian Blur to Adaptive Thresholding, is implemented with specific parameters to demonstrate various image processing techniques. For example, the Anisotropic Diffusion and Total Variation Denoising filters provide more advanced noise reduction methods, enhancing the quality of the cropped image before histogram analysis.

The zoom functionality is another key feature, allowing users to adjust the zoom level of the video canvas using a combobox or mouse wheel. The on_mousewheel method handles the zoom adjustments, updating the display accordingly to provide a closer look at the tracked object or a broader view of the entire frame.

Error handling is incorporated throughout the project to ensure robustness. For instance, the show_frame method includes a try-except block to catch and print errors that may occur during frame processing. This ensures that the application continues to run smoothly even if an unexpected issue arises with a specific frame or video file.

Overall, the MedianFlow Tracker project combines various technologies and techniques to create a comprehensive tool for video analysis. It provides an interactive and user-friendly interface for object tracking, frame-by-frame navigation, and detailed histogram analysis. The integration of multiple image processing filters and advanced tracking parameter controls further enhances its utility and flexibility.

The project's use of Tkinter for the GUI, OpenCV for tracking, and other libraries for additional processing tasks exemplifies a well-rounded approach to software development. It showcases the power and versatility of Python in handling complex multimedia applications and offers a practical solution for real-time video analysis and object tracking.

SOURCE CODE

```
#medianflow_tracker.py
import tkinter as tk
from tkinter import ttk
from tkinter import filedialog
from PIL import Image, ImageTk
import imageio
import cv2
import numpy as np
import matplotlib.pyplot as plt
import pywt

class MedianFlowTracker:
    def __init__(self, master):
```

```python
        self.master = master
        self.master.title("Object Tracking with MedianFlow Tracker")
        self.file_name = ""
        self.set_window_title()  # Set window title initially
        
        self.frame_number_label = tk.Label(master, text="Frame: 0")
        self.frame_number_label.pack()
        
        self.video = None
        self.video_path = None
        self.paused = False
        self.zoom_scale = tk.IntVar(value=1)
        self.frame_index = 0
        self.bbox = None
        self.bbox2 = None
        self.tracking_started = False  # Initialize tracking_started to False
        self.prev_frame_gray = None
        self.tracker = None
        self.initial_w = None
        self.initial_h = None
        self.bbox_rect = None  # Initialize bbox_rect attribute to None
        self.frame_processing = False  # Initialize frame_processing attribute to False
        
        # Available filters
        self.filters = ["None", "Gaussian", "Mean", "Median", "Bilateral Filtering",
                        "Non-local Means Denoising", "Anisotropic Diffusion",
                        "Total Variation Denoising", "Wiener Filter",
                        "Adaptive Thresholding", "Haar Wavelet Transform",
                        "Daubechies Wavelet Transform"]
        
        self.create_widgets()

    def create_widgets(self):
        # Panel for video display
        video_panel = tk.Frame(self.master)
        video_panel.pack(padx=10, pady=10)
        
        # Canvas to display the original video
        canvas_width = 800
        canvas_height = 500
        self.canvas = tk.Canvas(video_panel, width=canvas_width, height=canvas_height)
        self.canvas.pack(side="left", fill="both", expand=True)
        self.canvas.bind("<MouseWheel>", self.on_mousewheel)
        self.canvas.bind("<ButtonPress-1>", self.on_press)
        self.canvas.bind("<B1-Motion>", self.on_drag)
        self.canvas.bind("<ButtonRelease-1>", self.on_release)  # Bind ButtonRelease event
        
        # List box to display center coordinates
        self.center_listbox = tk.Listbox(video_panel, width=30, height=20, font=("Helvetica", 14))
        self.center_listbox.pack(side="right", fill="y")
        # Scrollbar for the listbox
        scrollbar = tk.Scrollbar(video_panel, orient="vertical")
        scrollbar.pack(side="left", fill="y")
        scrollbar.config(command=self.center_listbox.yview)
        
        # Attach scrollbar to listbox
        self.center_listbox.config(yscrollcommand=scrollbar.set)
        
        # Panel for control buttons
        control_panel = tk.Frame(self.master)
        control_panel.pack(padx=10, pady=(0, 10), fill="x")
        
        # Button to open a video file
```

```python
        self.open_button = tk.Button(control_panel, text="Open Video", command=self.open_video)
        self.open_button.grid(row=0, column=0, padx=10, pady=5)

        # Combobox for selecting zoom scale
        self.zoom_combobox = ttk.Combobox(control_panel, textvariable=self.zoom_scale, values=list(range(1, 11)))
        self.zoom_combobox.grid(row=0, column=1, padx=10, pady=5)
        self.zoom_combobox.bind("<<ComboboxSelected>>", self.update_zoom)

        # Button to play/pause the video
        self.play_button = tk.Button(control_panel, text="Play/Pause", command=self.toggle_play_pause)
        self.play_button.grid(row=0, column=2, padx=10, pady=5)

        # Button to stop the video
        self.stop_button = tk.Button(control_panel, text="Stop", command=self.stop_video)
        self.stop_button.grid(row=0, column=3, padx=10, pady=5)

        # Button to navigate to the previous frame
        self.prev_frame_button = tk.Button(control_panel, text="Previous Frame", command=self.prev_frame)
        self.prev_frame_button.grid(row=0, column=4, padx=10, pady=5)

        # Button to navigate to the next frame
        self.next_frame_button = tk.Button(control_panel, text="Next Frame", command=self.next_frame)
        self.next_frame_button.grid(row=0, column=5, padx=10, pady=5)

        # Button to clear the listbox
        self.clear_button = tk.Button(control_panel, text="Clear Listbox", command=self.clear_listbox)
        self.clear_button.grid(row=0, column=6, padx=10, pady=5)

        # Label and entry for specifying scale
        self.scale_label = tk.Label(control_panel, text="Scale:")
        self.scale_label.grid(row=0, column=7, padx=10, pady=5, sticky="e")
        self.scale_default = tk.StringVar(value="1")
        self.scale_entry = ttk.Entry(control_panel, textvariable=self.scale_default)
        self.scale_entry.grid(row=0, column=8, padx=10, pady=5, sticky="w")
        self.scale_entry.bind("<Return>", lambda event: self.toggle_play_pause())

        # Combobox for selecting filters
        self.filter_combobox = ttk.Combobox(control_panel, values=self.filters)
        self.filter_combobox.grid(row=0, column=9, padx=10, pady=5)
        self.filter_combobox.current(0)  # Set default value

        # Label and entry for specifying Window Size
        self.win_label = tk.Label(control_panel, text="Window Size:")
        self.win_label.grid(row=1, column=0, padx=10, pady=5, sticky="e")
        self.win_default = tk.StringVar(value="15")
        self.win_entry = ttk.Entry(control_panel, textvariable=self.win_default)
        self.win_entry.grid(row=1, column=1, padx=10, pady=5, sticky="w")
        self.win_entry.bind("<Return>", lambda event: self.toggle_play_pause())

        # Label and entry for specifying max level
        self.level_label = tk.Label(control_panel, text="Max. Level:")
        self.level_label.grid(row=1, column=2, padx=10, pady=5, sticky="e")
        self.level_default = tk.StringVar(value="3")
        self.level_entry = ttk.Entry(control_panel, textvariable=self.level_default)
        self.level_entry.grid(row=1, column=3, padx=10, pady=5, sticky="w")
        self.level_entry.bind("<Return>", lambda event: self.toggle_play_pause())

        # Label and entry for specifying points in grid
        self.point_label = tk.Label(control_panel, text="Points In Grid:")
```

```python
        self.point_label.grid(row=1, column=4, padx=10, pady=5, sticky="e")
        self.point_default = tk.StringVar(value="10")
        self.point_entry = ttk.Entry(control_panel, textvariable=self.point_default)
        self.point_entry.grid(row=1, column=5, padx=10, pady=5, sticky="w")
        self.point_entry.bind("<Return>", lambda event: self.toggle_play_pause())

        # Label and entry for specifying max iteration
        self.iter_label = tk.Label(control_panel, text="Max. Iteration:")
        self.iter_label.grid(row=1, column=6, padx=10, pady=5, sticky="e")
        self.iter_default = tk.StringVar(value="20")
        self.iter_entry = ttk.Entry(control_panel, textvariable=self.iter_default)
        self.iter_entry.grid(row=1, column=7, padx=10, pady=5, sticky="w")
        self.iter_entry.bind("<Return>", lambda event: self.toggle_play_pause())

        # Label and entry for specifying threshold
        self.thresh_label = tk.Label(control_panel, text="Epsilon:")
        self.thresh_label.grid(row=1, column=8, padx=10, pady=5, sticky="e")
        self.thresh_default = tk.StringVar(value="0.03")
        self.thresh_entry = ttk.Entry(control_panel, textvariable=self.thresh_default)
        self.thresh_entry.grid(row=1, column=9, padx=10, pady=5, sticky="w")
        self.thresh_entry.bind("<Return>", lambda event: self.toggle_play_pause())

    def open_video(self):
        self.video_path = filedialog.askopenfilename(filetypes=[("Video files", "*.mp4;*.avi;*.mkv;*.wmv")])
        if self.video_path:
            self.video = imageio.get_reader(self.video_path)
            self.file_name = self.video_path.split('/')[-1]
            self.set_window_title()
            self.play_video()

    def play_video(self):
        if self.video:
            self.paused = False
            self.tracking_started = True
            self.show_frame()

    def stop_video(self):
        self.paused = True
        self.frame_index = 0
        self.bbox = None
        self.tracker = None  # Reset tracker
        self.initial_w = None  # Reset width
        self.initial_h = None  # Reset height
        self.show_frame()

    def toggle_play_pause(self):
        self.paused = not self.paused
        if not self.paused:
            if self.bbox is not None:
                self.tracking_started = True
            self.play_video()

    def update_zoom(self, event=None):
        self.show_frame()

    def initialize_tracker(self, frame, bbox, params=None):
        """Initialize the MedianFlow tracker with possible user-defined parameters."""

        # Default parameters for MedianFlow Tracker
        default_params = {
            'winSize': (int(self.win_entry.get()), int(self.win_entry.get())),
            'maxLevel': int(self.level_entry.get()),
            'pointsInGrid': int(self.point_entry.get()),
```

```python
            'termCriteria': (cv2.TERM_CRITERIA_COUNT + cv2.TERM_CRITERIA_EPS,
int(self.iter_entry.get()), float(self.thresh_entry.get()))
        }

        # If params are provided, update the default_params
        if params:
            default_params.update(params)

        # Adjust bbox based on parameters such as scaling
        scale = int(self.scale_entry.get()) #scale is provided through a GUI element
        bbox = (
            int(bbox[0] + (1 - scale) * bbox[2] / 2),  # Center the scaling on the bbox
            int(bbox[1] + (1 - scale) * bbox[3] / 2),
            int(bbox[2] * scale),
            int(bbox[3] * scale)
        )

        # Initialize the Median Flow tracker
        self.tracker = cv2.legacy.TrackerMedianFlow_create()

        # Assuming a hypothetical method to set parameters (not available in the current OpenCV API)
        # This part is pseudo-code and will not work with standard OpenCV installations
        if hasattr(self.tracker, 'setParams'):
            self.tracker.setParams(default_params)

        self.tracker.init(frame, tuple(map(int, bbox)))
        self.initial_w, self.initial_h = bbox[2], bbox[3]

    def track_object(self, frame, bbox, user_params=None):
        """Track object using MedianFlow Tracker with optional user parameters."""
        if bbox:
            if self.tracker is None:
                self.initialize_tracker(frame, bbox, user_params)

            # Update the tracker and get the new bounding box
            success, bbox = self.tracker.update(frame)
            if success:
                x1, y1, w, h = map(int, bbox)
                # Use the dimensions as tracked, no adjustment to maintain initial dimensions
                x2, y2 = x1 + w, y1 + h

                # Calculate and display the center of the bounding box
                center_x = (x1 + x2) // 2
                center_y = (y1 + y2) // 2
                self.center_listbox.insert(tk.END, f"(center_x = {center_x}, center_y = {center_y})")

                return x1, y1, x2, y2
        return None

    def update_bbox_rectangle(self, bbox):
        if bbox is not None:
            x1, y1, x2, y2 = map(int, bbox)
            if self.bbox_rect is not None:
                self.canvas.coords(self.bbox_rect, x1, y1, x2, y2)
                self.canvas.tag_raise(self.bbox_rect)  # Raise the bounding box to the front
            else:
                self.bbox_rect = self.canvas.create_rectangle(x1, y1, x2, y2, outline='#fc3d3d', width=8, tags="bbox")

    def show_frame(self):
        if self.video:
            if not self.paused:
```

```python
            if 0 <= self.frame_index < len(self.video):
                if not self.frame_processing:  # Check if the frame is already being processed
                    try:
                        self.frame_processing = True  # Set frame_processing flag to True to indicate frame processing

                        frame = self.video.get_data(self.frame_index)
                        frame = cv2.cvtColor(frame, cv2.COLOR_RGB2BGR)

                        if self.bbox is not None:
                            if not self.tracking_started:
                                self.tracking_started = True

                            self.bbox = self.track_object(frame, self.bbox)
                            if self.bbox:
                                frame = cv2.cvtColor(frame, cv2.COLOR_BGR2RGB)
                                frame = Image.fromarray(frame)
                                frame = frame.resize((frame.width * self.zoom_scale.get(), frame.height * self.zoom_scale.get()))
                                photo = ImageTk.PhotoImage(frame)
                                self.photo = photo
                                self.canvas.delete("video")
                                self.canvas.create_image(0, 0, anchor="nw", image=photo, tags="video")

                                self.update_bbox_rectangle(self.bbox)

                        else:
                            frame = cv2.cvtColor(frame, cv2.COLOR_BGR2RGB)
                            frame = Image.fromarray(frame)
                            frame = frame.resize((frame.width * self.zoom_scale.get(), frame.height * self.zoom_scale.get()))
                            photo = ImageTk.PhotoImage(frame)
                            self.photo = photo
                            self.canvas.delete("video")
                            self.canvas.create_image(0, 0, anchor="nw", image=photo, tags="video")

                        self.frame_number_label.config(text=f"Frame: {self.frame_index} / {self.video.count_frames()}", font=("Helvetica", 18))

                        self.frame_index += 1

                    except Exception as e:
                        print("Error: ", e)
                    finally:
                        self.frame_processing = False  # Reset frame_processing flag to False after processing the frame

    def on_mousewheel(self, event):
        direction = event.delta // 120
        current_value = int(self.zoom_scale.get())
        if direction == 1 and current_value < 10:
            current_value += 1
        elif direction == -1 and current_value > 1:
            current_value -= 1
        self.zoom_scale.set(current_value)
        self.update_zoom()

    def on_press(self, event):
        self.tracker = None
        self.start_x = self.canvas.canvasx(event.x)
        self.start_y = self.canvas.canvasy(event.y)
        # Clear the previous bounding box if it exists
```

```python
            if self.bbox_rect:
                self.canvas.delete(self.bbox_rect)
                self.bbox_rect = None
            self.bbox = None
            self.bbox2 = None

    def on_drag(self, event):
        # Update the endpoint of the rectangle as the mouse moves
        cur_x = self.canvas.canvasx(event.x)
        cur_y = self.canvas.canvasy(event.y)

        # Define the coordinates correctly ensuring x1 < x2 and y1 < y2
        x1, y1 = min(self.start_x, cur_x), min(self.start_y, cur_y)
        x2, y2 = max(self.start_x, cur_x), max(self.start_y, cur_y)

        # Update dimensions for tracking
        self.initial_w = x2 - x1
        self.initial_h = y2 - y1
        self.bbox = (x1, y1, self.initial_w, self.initial_h)
        self.bbox2 = (self.start_x, self.start_y, cur_x, cur_y)

        # Update or create a rectangle on the canvas
        if self.bbox_rect:
            self.canvas.coords(self.bbox_rect, x1, y1, x2, y2)
        else:
            self.bbox_rect = self.canvas.create_rectangle(x1, y1, x2, y2, outline="cyan", width=6)

    def prev_frame(self):
        if self.frame_index > 0:
            self.frame_index -= 1
            self.show_frame()

    def next_frame(self):
        if self.video and self.frame_index < len(self.video) - 1:
            self.show_frame()

    def clear_listbox(self):
        self.center_listbox.delete(0, tk.END)

    def set_window_title(self):
        if self.file_name:
            self.master.title(f"Object Tracking with MedianFlow Tracker - {self.file_name}")
            self.master.title_font = ("Helvetica", 16, "bold")
        else:
            self.master.title("Object Tracking with MedianFlow Tracker")

    def on_release(self, event):
        self.analyze_histogram()  # Call analyze_histogram() method when the mouse button is released

    def analyze_histogram(self):
        if self.bbox2 is not None and self.video:
            x1, y1, x2, y2 = map(int, self.bbox2)
            if x1 != x2 and y1 != y2:
                try:
                    frame = self.video.get_data(self.frame_index)
                    # Ensure the bounding box is within the frame boundaries
                    h, w, _ = frame.shape
                    x1, x2 = max(0, min(x1, w)), max(0, min(x2, w))
                    y1, y2 = max(0, min(y1, h)), max(0, min(y2, h))

                    # Ensure x1 < x2 and y1 < y2
```

```python
                    x1, x2 = sorted([x1, x2])
                    y1, y2 = sorted([y1, y2])

                    cropped_frame = frame[y1:y2, x1:x2]
                    if cropped_frame.size > 0:
                        cropped_frame = cv2.cvtColor(cropped_frame, cv2.COLOR_BGR2RGB)

                        # Get selected filter from combobox
                        selected_filter = self.filter_combobox.get()
                        # Apply selected filter
                        filtered_frame = self.apply_filter(selected_filter, cropped_frame)

                        self.create_popup_window(filtered_frame)
                        self.display_cropped_image(filtered_frame)
                        self.display_histograms(filtered_frame)
                    else:
                        print("Cropped frame is empty.")
                except Exception as e:
                    print("Failed to process frame:", e)
            else:
                print("Bounding box dimensions are zero or negative.")

    def create_popup_window(self, cropped_frame):
        self.popup_window = tk.Toplevel(self.master)
        self.popup_window.title("Cropped Image and Its Histogram")
        self.popup_window.geometry("1500x700")

    def display_cropped_image(self, cropped_frame):
        cropped_frame_frame = tk.Frame(self.popup_window)
        cropped_frame_frame.pack(side="left")

        cropped_frame_rgb = cv2.cvtColor(cropped_frame, cv2.COLOR_BGR2RGB)
        cropped_img = Image.fromarray(cropped_frame_rgb)
        cropped_img = cropped_img.resize((600, 600))

        cropped_photo = ImageTk.PhotoImage(cropped_img)
        cropped_canvas = tk.Canvas(cropped_frame_frame, width=600, height=600)
        cropped_canvas.pack(side="left", anchor="nw")
        cropped_canvas.create_image(0, 0, anchor="nw", image=cropped_photo)
        cropped_canvas.image = cropped_photo

    def display_histograms(self, cropped_frame):
        histograms_frame = tk.Frame(self.popup_window)
        histograms_frame.pack(side="right", padx=20)

        self.display_line_histogram(cropped_frame, histograms_frame)
        self.display_bar_histogram(cropped_frame, histograms_frame)

    def display_line_histogram(self, cropped_frame, histograms_frame):
        line_histogram_frame = tk.Frame(histograms_frame)
        line_histogram_frame.pack(side="top", pady=10)

        plt.figure(figsize=(12, 4))
        color = ('r', 'g', 'b')
        for i, col in enumerate(color):
            histr = cv2.calcHist([cropped_frame], [i], None, [256], [0, 256])
            plt.plot(histr, color=col, label=f'Channel {col.upper()}', linewidth=2)
            plt.xlim([0, 256])
        plt.title('Line Histogram')
        plt.xlabel('Pixel Value')
        plt.ylabel('Frequency')
        plt.tight_layout()
```

```python
        plt.grid(True)
        plt.legend()

        line_histogram_img = self.plot_to_image(plt)
        self.display_histogram_image(line_histogram_frame, line_histogram_img)

    def display_bar_histogram(self, cropped_frame, histograms_frame):
        bar_histogram_frame = tk.Frame(histograms_frame)
        bar_histogram_frame.pack(side="bottom", pady=10)

        plt.figure(figsize=(12, 4))
        color = ('r', 'g', 'b')
        for i, col in enumerate(color):
            hist_range = (0, 256)
            hist_counts, _ = np.histogram(cropped_frame[:, :, i], bins=64, range=hist_range)
            plt.bar(np.arange(64), hist_counts, color=col, alpha=0.7, label=f'Channel {col.upper()}')
            for index, value in enumerate(hist_counts):
                plt.text(index, value + 10, str(int(value)), ha='center', va='bottom', fontsize=9)

        plt.title('Bar Histogram')
        plt.xlabel('Pixel Value')
        plt.ylabel('Frequency')
        plt.xticks(np.linspace(0, 63, num=5), np.linspace(0, 255, num=5, dtype=int))  # Adjust x-axis ticks
        plt.tight_layout()
        plt.grid(True)
        plt.legend()

        bar_histogram_img = self.plot_to_image(plt)
        self.display_histogram_image(bar_histogram_frame, bar_histogram_img)

    def display_histogram_image(self, parent_frame, img):
        histogram_photo = ImageTk.PhotoImage(image=img)
        histogram_canvas = tk.Canvas(parent_frame, width=900, height=300)
        histogram_canvas.pack(side="bottom", anchor="se")
        histogram_canvas.create_image(0, 0, anchor="nw", image=histogram_photo)
        histogram_canvas.image = histogram_photo

    def plot_histogram_bar_to_image(self, image):
        # Calculate histogram for each channel
        histograms = []
        for i in range(3):
            hist_range = (0, 256)
            hist_counts, _ = np.histogram(image[:, :, i], bins=64, range=hist_range)  # Adjust bins to 64
            histograms.append(hist_counts)

        # Extracting only 64 bins from the histogram
        num_bins = 64  # Adjusted to 64 bins

        # Generating colors for each channel
        colors = ['red', 'green', 'blue']

        plt.figure()
        for i, histogram in enumerate(histograms):
            # Normalize the histogram counts for better visualization
            hist_counts = histogram / np.sum(histogram)
            # Setting the color for each channel
            plt.bar(np.arange(num_bins), hist_counts[:num_bins], color=colors[i], alpha=0.7, label=f'Channel {["Red", "Green", "Blue"][i]}')

        plt.xlabel('Pixel Value')
```

```python
        plt.ylabel('Normalized Frequency')
        plt.title('RGB Channel Histograms')
        plt.grid(True)
        plt.tight_layout()
        plt.legend()

        # Convert the histogram bar graph to an image
        histogram_bar_img = self.plot_to_image(plt)
        histogram_bar_photo = ImageTk.PhotoImage(image=histogram_bar_img)

        return histogram_bar_photo

    def plot_to_image(self, plt):
        plt.savefig('temp_plot.png')
        img = Image.open('temp_plot.png')
        return img

    def apply_filter(self, filter_name, frame):
        if filter_name == "None":
            return frame
        elif filter_name == "Gaussian":
            return cv2.GaussianBlur(frame, (5, 5), 0)
        elif filter_name == "Mean":
            return cv2.blur(frame, (5, 5))
        elif filter_name == "Median":
            return cv2.medianBlur(frame, 5)
        elif filter_name == "Bilateral Filtering":
            return cv2.bilateralFilter(frame, 9, 75, 75)
        elif filter_name == "Non-local Means Denoising":
            return cv2.fastNlMeansDenoisingColored(frame, None, 10, 10, 7, 21)
        elif filter_name == "Anisotropic Diffusion":
            return self.anisotropic_diffusion(frame)
        elif filter_name == "Total Variation Denoising":
            return self.total_variation_denoising(frame)
        elif filter_name == "Wiener Filter":
            return self.wiener_filter(frame)
        elif filter_name == "Adaptive Thresholding":
            return self.adaptive_threshold_each_channel(frame)
        elif filter_name == "Haar Wavelet Transform":
            return self.haar_wavelet_transform(frame)
        elif filter_name == "Daubechies Wavelet Transform":
            return self.daubechies_wavelet_transform(frame)
        else:
            return frame  # Default: return original frame if filter not found

    def wiener_filter(self, frame, kernel_size=(5, 5), noise_var=0.01):
        # Check if frame is None
        if frame is None:
            print("Error: Input frame is None.")
            return None

        # Check if frame is a valid numpy array
        if not isinstance(frame, np.ndarray):
            print("Error: Input frame is not a numpy array.")
            return None

        # Check if frame is an empty array
        if frame.size == 0:
            print("Error: Input frame is empty.")
            return None

        # Check if frame is in BGR color space
        if frame.shape[-1] != 3:
            print("Error: Input frame is not in BGR color space.")
```

```python
        return None

        # Apply Wiener filter
        filtered_frame = cv2.medianBlur(frame, kernel_size[0])  # Use kernel_size[0] as the kernel size
        filtered_frame = cv2.fastNlMeansDenoising(filtered_frame, h=noise_var)
        return filtered_frame

    def adaptive_threshold_each_channel(self, frame):
        # Split the frame into individual channels
        b, g, r = cv2.split(frame)

        # Apply adaptive thresholding to each channel separately
        b_thresh = cv2.adaptiveThreshold(b, 255, cv2.ADAPTIVE_THRESH_GAUSSIAN_C, cv2.THRESH_BINARY, 11, 2)
        g_thresh = cv2.adaptiveThreshold(g, 255, cv2.ADAPTIVE_THRESH_GAUSSIAN_C, cv2.THRESH_BINARY, 11, 2)
        r_thresh = cv2.adaptiveThreshold(r, 255, cv2.ADAPTIVE_THRESH_GAUSSIAN_C, cv2.THRESH_BINARY, 11, 2)

        # Merge the thresholded channels back together
        return cv2.merge([b_thresh, g_thresh, r_thresh])

    def haar_wavelet_transform(self, frame):
        # Split the frame into its individual color channels
        b, g, r = cv2.split(frame)

        # Perform the wavelet transform on each channel separately
        b_coeffs = pywt.dwt2(b, 'haar')
        g_coeffs = pywt.dwt2(g, 'haar')
        r_coeffs = pywt.dwt2(r, 'haar')

        # Reconstruct the channels from the coefficients
        b_reconstructed = pywt.idwt2(b_coeffs, 'haar')
        g_reconstructed = pywt.idwt2(g_coeffs, 'haar')
        r_reconstructed = pywt.idwt2(r_coeffs, 'haar')

        # Clip the values to ensure they are within the valid range
        b_reconstructed = np.clip(b_reconstructed, 0, 255).astype(np.uint8)
        g_reconstructed = np.clip(g_reconstructed, 0, 255).astype(np.uint8)
        r_reconstructed = np.clip(r_reconstructed, 0, 255).astype(np.uint8)

        # Merge the channels back together
        return cv2.merge([b_reconstructed, g_reconstructed, r_reconstructed])

    def daubechies_wavelet_transform(self, frame):
        # Split the frame into its individual color channels
        b, g, r = cv2.split(frame)

        # Choose the wavelet function (Daubechies 5)
        wavelet = 'db5'

        # Perform the wavelet transform on each channel separately
        b_coeffs = pywt.dwt2(b, wavelet)
        g_coeffs = pywt.dwt2(g, wavelet)
        r_coeffs = pywt.dwt2(r, wavelet)

        # Reconstruct the channels from the coefficients
        b_reconstructed = pywt.idwt2(b_coeffs, wavelet)
        g_reconstructed = pywt.idwt2(g_coeffs, wavelet)
        r_reconstructed = pywt.idwt2(r_coeffs, wavelet)

        # Clip the values to ensure they are within the valid range
        b_reconstructed = np.clip(b_reconstructed, 0, 255).astype(np.uint8)
```

```python
            g_reconstructed = np.clip(g_reconstructed, 0, 255).astype(np.uint8)
            r_reconstructed = np.clip(r_reconstructed, 0, 255).astype(np.uint8)

            # Merge the channels back together
            return cv2.merge([b_reconstructed, g_reconstructed, r_reconstructed])

    def anisotropic_diffusion(self, img):
        return cv2.fastNlMeansDenoisingColored(img, None, 10, 10, 7, 21)

    def apply_total_variation_denoising_channel(self, channel, weight, iterations):
        # Initialize the result with the original channel
        result = channel.copy().astype(np.float64)  # Convert to float64

        # Perform total variation denoising
        for _ in range(iterations):
            # Compute the gradient of the channel
            dx = cv2.Sobel(result, cv2.CV_64F, 1, 0, ksize=3)
            dy = cv2.Sobel(result, cv2.CV_64F, 0, 1, ksize=3)

            # Update the channel using the gradient and the weight
            result -= weight * np.sqrt(dx**2 + dy**2)

        # Clip the values to ensure they are within the valid range
        result = np.clip(result, 0, 255).astype(np.uint8)

        return result

    def total_variation_denoising(self, img, weight=0.01, iterations=20):
        # Split the image into its individual color channels
        b, g, r = cv2.split(img)

        # Apply total variation denoising to each channel separately
        b_denoised = self.apply_total_variation_denoising_channel(b, weight, iterations)
        g_denoised = self.apply_total_variation_denoising_channel(g, weight, iterations)
        r_denoised = self.apply_total_variation_denoising_channel(r, weight, iterations)

        # Merge the denoised channels back together
        return cv2.merge([b_denoised, g_denoised, r_denoised])

def main():
    root = tk.Tk()
    app = MedianFlowTracker(root)
    root.mainloop()

if __name__ == "__main__":
    main()
```

RUNNING PROGRAM

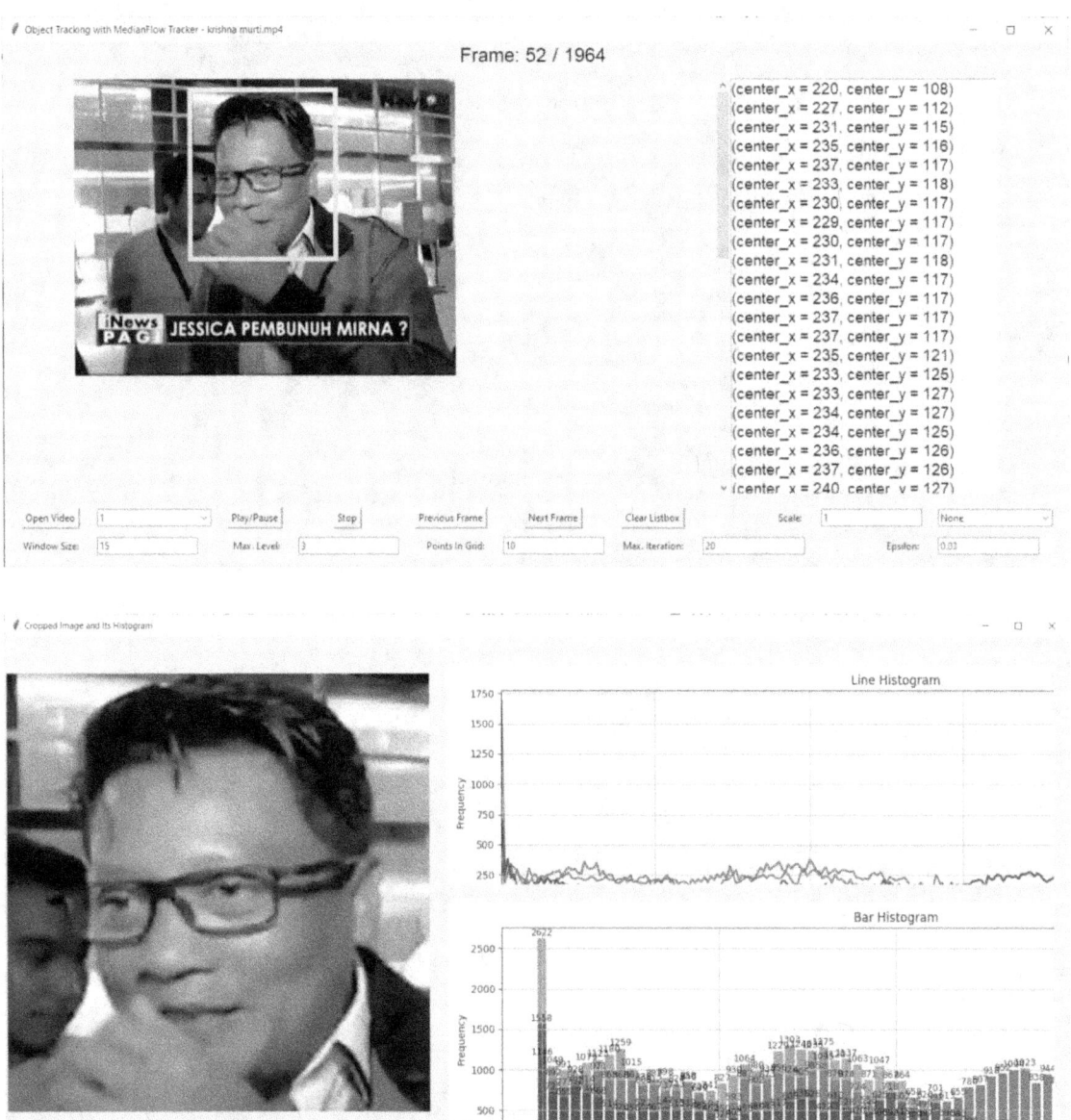

OBJECT TRACKING WITH MIL (MULTIPLE INSTANCE LEARNING) TRACKER

DESCRIPTION

The MILTracker project is a Python application that implements an object tracking system using the Multiple Instance Learning (MIL) algorithm. It leverages the Tkinter library for the graphical user interface (GUI), OpenCV for video processing and tracking, and other libraries like imageio, PIL, matplotlib, and pywt for additional image and video manipulations. The core functionality of the application is to allow users to open video files, select regions of interest (ROI) for tracking, and apply various filters to enhance the tracking process.

When the application starts, it creates the main window with a title indicating that it is an object tracking application using MIL. The initial GUI elements include a frame number label, buttons for video controls, a list box for displaying coordinates, and a canvas for displaying the video. The user can load video files of different formats such as MP4, AVI,

MKV, and WMV using a file dialog, and the selected file's name is displayed in the window title.

The primary components of the GUI include a canvas for displaying the video frames, a list box for displaying the center coordinates of the tracked object, and control buttons for opening videos, playing/pausing, stopping, and navigating through frames. The canvas also supports mouse interactions for selecting the ROI for tracking by dragging the mouse to draw a bounding box.

The video processing begins when a video file is opened. The video frames are read using the imageio library, and the application supports playing and pausing the video, as well as navigating through individual frames. The MIL tracker from the legacy OpenCV API is used to track the selected ROI. The tracker is initialized with the first frame and the selected bounding box, and then it continuously updates the bounding box as the video plays.

The application also provides a zoom functionality, allowing users to zoom in and out of the video frames using a combobox. The zoom level can be adjusted from 1 to 10, and the video frame is resized accordingly. The zoom functionality is controlled through the mouse wheel and combobox selection events.

One of the advanced features of the application is the ability to apply various image filters to the selected ROI. Filters such as Gaussian blur, mean filter, median filter, bilateral filtering, non-local means denoising, anisotropic diffusion, total variation denoising, Wiener filter, adaptive thresholding, and wavelet transforms (Haar and Daubechies) can be applied to enhance the tracking performance or for analysis purposes.

The tracking functionality is robust, allowing the tracker to handle the changes in the object's position and appearance. The tracked object's bounding box is updated in each frame, and the center coordinates of the bounding box are displayed in the list box. The application supports both automatic and manual tracking, where users can manually adjust the bounding box if needed.

The application provides histogram analysis of the selected ROI. When the bounding box is released after selection, the application analyzes the histogram of the ROI. The histogram is displayed in a popup window, showing both line and bar histograms for the red, green, and blue channels. The histograms provide a visual representation of the color distribution within the selected ROI.

The application includes error handling to ensure smooth operation. For instance, it checks for valid input frames and handles scenarios where the bounding box might be outside the frame boundaries or when the frame is empty. The filters and transformations are applied only if the input frame is valid.

Additionally, the project supports saving the histograms as images. The histograms generated by matplotlib are converted to images using PIL, and these images are displayed in the popup window. This allows users to analyze the histograms visually and understand the color distribution in the selected ROI.

The code also includes utility functions for handling mouse events on the canvas. These functions allow users to interactively select the ROI by clicking and dragging the mouse. The on_press, on_drag, and on_release methods manage the selection process, updating the bounding box as the mouse is dragged and finalizing it when the mouse button is released.

The apply_filter method applies the selected filter to the ROI. Each filter is implemented as a separate method, and the selected filter is applied to the ROI before displaying the filtered image and its histograms. The filters enhance the tracking performance by reducing noise or highlighting certain features of the ROI.

The update_zoom method is called whenever the zoom level is changed. This method rescales the current frame based on the selected zoom level and updates the canvas accordingly. The zoom functionality helps users to closely inspect the ROI and make precise adjustments to the bounding box.

The show_frame method is responsible for displaying the current video frame on the canvas. It handles the frame processing, updating the bounding box, and displaying the frame with the applied zoom level. This method ensures that the video playback and tracking are smooth and responsive.

In summary, the MILTracker project is a comprehensive tool for object tracking in videos. It combines advanced tracking algorithms with a user-friendly interface, allowing users to interactively select and track objects in videos. The application supports various image filters and histogram analysis, making it a versatile tool for video analysis and tracking tasks. The use of Tkinter for the GUI, OpenCV for tracking, and other libraries for image processing demonstrates the integration of different technologies to achieve a functional and interactive application.

SOURCE CODE

```python
#mil_tracker.py
import tkinter as tk
from tkinter import ttk
from tkinter import filedialog
from PIL import Image, ImageTk
import imageio
import cv2
import numpy as np
import matplotlib.pyplot as plt
import pywt

class MILTracker:
    def __init__(self, master):
        self.master = master
        self.master.title("Object Tracking with MIL (Multiple Instance Learning) Tracker")
        self.file_name = ""
        self.set_window_title()  # Set window title initially

        self.frame_number_label = tk.Label(master, text="Frame: 0")
        self.frame_number_label.pack()

        self.video = None
        self.video_path = None
        self.paused = False
        self.zoom_scale = tk.IntVar(value=1)
        self.frame_index = 0
        self.bbox = None
        self.bbox2 = None
        self.tracking_started = False  # Initialize tracking_started to False
        self.prev_frame_gray = None
        self.tracker = None
        self.initial_w = None
        self.initial_h = None
        self.bbox_rect = None  # Initialize bbox_rect attribute to None
        self.frame_processing = False  # Initialize frame_processing attribute to False

        # Available filters
        self.filters = ["None", "Gaussian", "Mean", "Median", "Bilateral Filtering",
                        "Non-local Means Denoising", "Anisotropic Diffusion",
                        "Total Variation Denoising", "Wiener Filter",
                        "Adaptive Thresholding", "Haar Wavelet Transform",
                        "Daubechies Wavelet Transform"]

        self.create_widgets()

    def create_widgets(self):
        # Panel for video display
        video_panel = tk.Frame(self.master)
        video_panel.pack(padx=10, pady=10)
```

```python
        # Canvas to display the original video
        canvas_width = 800
        canvas_height = 500
        self.canvas = tk.Canvas(video_panel, width=canvas_width, height=canvas_height)
        self.canvas.pack(side="left", fill="both", expand=True)
        self.canvas.bind("<MouseWheel>", self.on_mousewheel)
        self.canvas.bind("<ButtonPress-1>", self.on_press)
        self.canvas.bind("<B1-Motion>", self.on_drag)
        self.canvas.bind("<ButtonRelease-1>", self.on_release)  # Bind ButtonRelease event

        # List box to display center coordinates
        self.center_listbox = tk.Listbox(video_panel, width=30, height=20, font=("Helvetica", 14))
        self.center_listbox.pack(side="right", fill="y")
        # Scrollbar for the listbox
        scrollbar = tk.Scrollbar(video_panel, orient="vertical")
        scrollbar.pack(side="left", fill="y")
        scrollbar.config(command=self.center_listbox.yview)

        # Attach scrollbar to listbox
        self.center_listbox.config(yscrollcommand=scrollbar.set)

        # Panel for control buttons
        control_panel = tk.Frame(self.master)
        control_panel.pack(padx=10, pady=(0, 10), fill="x")

        # Button to open a video file
        self.open_button = tk.Button(control_panel, text="Open Video", command=self.open_video)
        self.open_button.grid(row=0, column=0, padx=10, pady=5)

        # Combobox for selecting zoom scale
        self.zoom_combobox = ttk.Combobox(control_panel, textvariable=self.zoom_scale, values=list(range(1, 11)))
        self.zoom_combobox.grid(row=0, column=1, padx=10, pady=5)
        self.zoom_combobox.bind("<<ComboboxSelected>>", self.update_zoom)

        # Button to play/pause the video
        self.play_button = tk.Button(control_panel, text="Play/Pause", command=self.toggle_play_pause)
        self.play_button.grid(row=0, column=2, padx=10, pady=5)

        # Button to stop the video
        self.stop_button = tk.Button(control_panel, text="Stop", command=self.stop_video)
        self.stop_button.grid(row=0, column=3, padx=10, pady=5)

        # Button to navigate to the previous frame
        self.prev_frame_button = tk.Button(control_panel, text="Previous Frame", command=self.prev_frame)
        self.prev_frame_button.grid(row=0, column=4, padx=10, pady=5)

        # Button to navigate to the next frame
        self.next_frame_button = tk.Button(control_panel, text="Next Frame", command=self.next_frame)
        self.next_frame_button.grid(row=0, column=5, padx=10, pady=5)

        # Button to clear the listbox
        self.clear_button = tk.Button(control_panel, text="Clear Listbox", command=self.clear_listbox)
        self.clear_button.grid(row=0, column=6, padx=10, pady=5)

        # Label and entry for specifying scale
        self.scale_label = tk.Label(control_panel, text="Scale:")
        self.scale_label.grid(row=0, column=7, padx=10, pady=5, sticky="e")
        self.scale_default = tk.StringVar(value="1")
```

```python
        self.scale_entry = ttk.Entry(control_panel, textvariable=self.scale_default)
        self.scale_entry.grid(row=0, column=8, padx=10, pady=5, sticky="w")
        self.scale_entry.bind("<Return>", lambda event: self.toggle_play_pause())

        # Combobox for selecting filters
        self.filter_combobox = ttk.Combobox(control_panel, values=self.filters)
        self.filter_combobox.grid(row=0, column=9, padx=10, pady=5)
        self.filter_combobox.current(0)  # Set default value

    def open_video(self):
        self.video_path = filedialog.askopenfilename(filetypes=[("Video files", "*.mp4;*.avi;*.mkv;*.wmv")])
        if self.video_path:
            self.video = imageio.get_reader(self.video_path)
            self.file_name = self.video_path.split('/')[-1]
            self.set_window_title()
            self.play_video()

    def play_video(self):
        if self.video:
            self.paused = False
            self.tracking_started = True
            self.show_frame()

    def stop_video(self):
        self.paused = True
        self.frame_index = 0
        self.bbox = None
        self.tracker = None  # Reset tracker
        self.initial_w = None  # Reset width
        self.initial_h = None  # Reset height
        self.show_frame()

    def toggle_play_pause(self):
        self.paused = not self.paused
        if not self.paused:
            if self.bbox is not None:
                self.tracking_started = True
            self.play_video()

    def update_zoom(self, event=None):
        self.show_frame()

    def initialize_tracker(self, frame, bbox, params=None):
        """Initialize the tracker with possible user-defined parameters."""
        if params:
            # Adjust bbox based on parameters such as scaling
            scale = int(self.scale_entry.get())  #scale is provided through a GUI element
            bbox = (
                bbox[0], bbox[1],
                int(bbox[2] * scale), int(bbox[3] * scale)
            )

        # Initialize the MIL tracker instead of Boosting
        self.tracker = cv2.legacy.TrackerMIL_create()  # Using legacy API as per the original setup
        self.tracker.init(frame, tuple(map(int, bbox)))
        self.initial_w, self.initial_h = bbox[2], bbox[3]

    def track_object(self, frame, bbox, user_params=None):
        """Track object using MIL Tracker with optional user parameters."""
        if bbox:
            if self.tracker is None:
                self.initialize_tracker(frame, bbox, user_params)
```

```python
            # Update the tracker and get the new bounding box
            success, bbox = self.tracker.update(frame)
            if success:
                x1, y1, w, h = map(int, bbox)
                # Use stored initial dimensions (if this logic is required, otherwise adjust as needed)
                w, h = self.initial_w, self.initial_h
                x2, y2 = x1 + w, y1 + h

                # Calculate and display the center of the bounding box
                center_x = (x1 + x2) // 2
                center_y = (y1 + y2) // 2
                self.center_listbox.insert(tk.END, f"(center_x = {center_x}, center_y = {center_y})")

                return x1, y1, x2, y2
        return None

    def update_bbox_rectangle(self, bbox):
        if bbox is not None:
            x1, y1, x2, y2 = map(int, bbox)
            if self.bbox_rect is not None:
                self.canvas.coords(self.bbox_rect, x1, y1, x2, y2)
                self.canvas.tag_raise(self.bbox_rect)  # Raise the bounding box to the front
            else:
                self.bbox_rect = self.canvas.create_rectangle(x1, y1, x2, y2, outline='#fc3d3d', width=8, tags="bbox")

    def show_frame(self):
        if self.video:
            if not self.paused:
                if 0 <= self.frame_index < len(self.video):
                    if not self.frame_processing:  # Check if the frame is already being processed
                        try:
                            self.frame_processing = True  # Set frame_processing flag to True to indicate frame processing

                            frame = self.video.get_data(self.frame_index)
                            frame = cv2.cvtColor(frame, cv2.COLOR_RGB2BGR)

                            if self.bbox is not None:
                                if not self.tracking_started:
                                    self.tracking_started = True

                                self.bbox = self.track_object(frame, self.bbox)
                                if self.bbox:
                                    frame = cv2.cvtColor(frame, cv2.COLOR_BGR2RGB)
                                    frame = Image.fromarray(frame)
                                    frame = frame.resize((frame.width * self.zoom_scale.get(), frame.height * self.zoom_scale.get()))
                                    photo = ImageTk.PhotoImage(frame)
                                    self.photo = photo
                                    self.canvas.delete("video")
                                    self.canvas.create_image(0, 0, anchor="nw", image=photo, tags="video")
                                    self.update_bbox_rectangle(self.bbox)

                            else:
                                frame = cv2.cvtColor(frame, cv2.COLOR_BGR2RGB)
                                frame = Image.fromarray(frame)
                                frame = frame.resize((frame.width * self.zoom_scale.get(), frame.height * self.zoom_scale.get()))
```

```python
                            photo = ImageTk.PhotoImage(frame)
                            self.photo = photo
                            self.canvas.delete("video")
                            self.canvas.create_image(0, 0, anchor="nw", image=photo, tags="video")

                        self.frame_number_label.config(text=f"Frame: {self.frame_index} / {self.video.count_frames()}", font=("Helvetica", 18))
                                              
                        self.frame_index += 1

                except Exception as e:
                    print("Error: ", e)
                finally:
                    self.frame_processing = False  # Reset frame_processing flag to False after processing the frame

    def on_mousewheel(self, event):
        direction = event.delta // 120
        current_value = int(self.zoom_scale.get())
        if direction == 1 and current_value < 10:
            current_value += 1
        elif direction == -1 and current_value > 1:
            current_value -= 1
        self.zoom_scale.set(current_value)
        self.update_zoom()

    def on_press(self, event):
        self.tracker = None
        self.start_x = self.canvas.canvasx(event.x)
        self.start_y = self.canvas.canvasy(event.y)
        # Clear the previous bounding box if it exists
        if self.bbox_rect:
            self.canvas.delete(self.bbox_rect)
            self.bbox_rect = None
        self.bbox = None
        self.bbox2 = None

    def on_drag(self, event):
        # Update the endpoint of the rectangle as the mouse moves
        cur_x = self.canvas.canvasx(event.x)
        cur_y = self.canvas.canvasy(event.y)

        # Define the coordinates correctly ensuring x1 < x2 and y1 < y2
        x1, y1 = min(self.start_x, cur_x), min(self.start_y, cur_y)
        x2, y2 = max(self.start_x, cur_x), max(self.start_y, cur_y)

        # Update dimensions for tracking
        self.initial_w = x2 - x1
        self.initial_h = y2 - y1
        self.bbox = (x1, y1, self.initial_w, self.initial_h)
        self.bbox2 = (self.start_x, self.start_y, cur_x, cur_y)

        # Update or create a rectangle on the canvas
        if self.bbox_rect:
            self.canvas.coords(self.bbox_rect, x1, y1, x2, y2)
        else:
            self.bbox_rect = self.canvas.create_rectangle(x1, y1, x2, y2, outline="cyan", width=6)

    def prev_frame(self):
        if self.frame_index > 0:
            self.frame_index -= 1
```

```python
            self.show_frame()

    def next_frame(self):
        if self.video and self.frame_index < len(self.video) - 1:
            self.show_frame()

    def clear_listbox(self):
        self.center_listbox.delete(0, tk.END)

    def set_window_title(self):
        if self.file_name:
            self.master.title(f"Object Tracking with MIL (Multiple Instance Learning) Tracker - {self.file_name}")
            self.master.title_font = ("Helvetica", 16, "bold")
        else:
            self.master.title("Object Tracking with MIL (Multiple Instance Learning) Tracker")

    def on_release(self, event):
        self.analyze_histogram()  # Call analyze_histogram() method when the mouse button is released

    def analyze_histogram(self):
        if self.bbox2 is not None and self.video:
            x1, y1, x2, y2 = map(int, self.bbox2)
            if x1 != x2 and y1 != y2:
                try:
                    frame = self.video.get_data(self.frame_index)
                    # Ensure the bounding box is within the frame boundaries
                    h, w, _ = frame.shape
                    x1, x2 = max(0, min(x1, w)), max(0, min(x2, w))
                    y1, y2 = max(0, min(y1, h)), max(0, min(y2, h))

                    # Ensure x1 < x2 and y1 < y2
                    x1, x2 = sorted([x1, x2])
                    y1, y2 = sorted([y1, y2])

                    cropped_frame = frame[y1:y2, x1:x2]
                    if cropped_frame.size > 0:
                        cropped_frame = cv2.cvtColor(cropped_frame, cv2.COLOR_BGR2RGB)

                        # Get selected filter from combobox
                        selected_filter = self.filter_combobox.get()
                        # Apply selected filter
                        filtered_frame = self.apply_filter(selected_filter, cropped_frame)

                        self.create_popup_window(filtered_frame)
                        self.display_cropped_image(filtered_frame)
                        self.display_histograms(filtered_frame)
                    else:
                        print("Cropped frame is empty.")
                except Exception as e:
                    print("Failed to process frame:", e)
            else:
                print("Bounding box dimensions are zero or negative.")

    def create_popup_window(self, cropped_frame):
        self.popup_window = tk.Toplevel(self.master)
        self.popup_window.title("Cropped Image and Its Histogram")
        self.popup_window.geometry("1500x700")


    def display_cropped_image(self, cropped_frame):
        cropped_frame_frame = tk.Frame(self.popup_window)
```

```python
            cropped_frame_frame.pack(side="left")

            cropped_frame_rgb = cv2.cvtColor(cropped_frame, cv2.COLOR_BGR2RGB)
            cropped_img = Image.fromarray(cropped_frame_rgb)
            cropped_img = cropped_img.resize((600, 600))

            cropped_photo = ImageTk.PhotoImage(cropped_img)
            cropped_canvas = tk.Canvas(cropped_frame_frame, width=600, height=600)
            cropped_canvas.pack(side="left", anchor="nw")
            cropped_canvas.create_image(0, 0, anchor="nw", image=cropped_photo)
            cropped_canvas.image = cropped_photo

    def display_histograms(self, cropped_frame):
        histograms_frame = tk.Frame(self.popup_window)
        histograms_frame.pack(side="right", padx=20)

        self.display_line_histogram(cropped_frame, histograms_frame)
        self.display_bar_histogram(cropped_frame, histograms_frame)

    def display_line_histogram(self, cropped_frame, histograms_frame):
        line_histogram_frame = tk.Frame(histograms_frame)
        line_histogram_frame.pack(side="top", pady=10)

        plt.figure(figsize=(12, 4))
        color = ('r', 'g', 'b')
        for i, col in enumerate(color):
            histr = cv2.calcHist([cropped_frame], [i], None, [256], [0, 256])
            plt.plot(histr, color=col, label=f'Channel {col.upper()}', linewidth=2)
            plt.xlim([0, 256])
        plt.title('Line Histogram')
        plt.xlabel('Pixel Value')
        plt.ylabel('Frequency')
        plt.tight_layout()
        plt.grid(True)
        plt.legend()

        line_histogram_img = self.plot_to_image(plt)
        self.display_histogram_image(line_histogram_frame, line_histogram_img)

    def display_bar_histogram(self, cropped_frame, histograms_frame):
        bar_histogram_frame = tk.Frame(histograms_frame)
        bar_histogram_frame.pack(side="bottom", pady=10)

        plt.figure(figsize=(12, 4))
        color = ('r', 'g', 'b')
        for i, col in enumerate(color):
            hist_range = (0, 256)
            hist_counts, _ = np.histogram(cropped_frame[:, :, i], bins=64, range=hist_range)
            plt.bar(np.arange(64), hist_counts, color=col, alpha=0.7, label=f'Channel {col.upper()}')
            for index, value in enumerate(hist_counts):
                plt.text(index, value + 10, str(int(value)), ha='center', va='bottom', fontsize=9)

        plt.title('Bar Histogram')
        plt.xlabel('Pixel Value')
        plt.ylabel('Frequency')
        plt.xticks(np.linspace(0, 63, num=5), np.linspace(0, 255, num=5, dtype=int))  # Adjust x-axis ticks
        plt.tight_layout()
        plt.grid(True)
        plt.legend()

        bar_histogram_img = self.plot_to_image(plt)
```

```python
            self.display_histogram_image(bar_histogram_frame, bar_histogram_img)

    def display_histogram_image(self, parent_frame, img):
        histogram_photo = ImageTk.PhotoImage(image=img)
        histogram_canvas = tk.Canvas(parent_frame, width=900, height=300)
        histogram_canvas.pack(side="bottom", anchor="se")
        histogram_canvas.create_image(0, 0, anchor="nw", image=histogram_photo)
        histogram_canvas.image = histogram_photo

    def plot_histogram_bar_to_image(self, image):
        # Calculate histogram for each channel
        histograms = []
        for i in range(3):
            hist_range = (0, 256)
            hist_counts, _ = np.histogram(image[:, :, i], bins=64, range=hist_range)  # Adjust bins to 64
            histograms.append(hist_counts)

        # Extracting only 64 bins from the histogram
        num_bins = 64  # Adjusted to 64 bins

        # Generating colors for each channel
        colors = ['red', 'green', 'blue']

        plt.figure()
        for i, histogram in enumerate(histograms):
            # Normalize the histogram counts for better visualization
            hist_counts = histogram / np.sum(histogram)
            # Setting the color for each channel
            plt.bar(np.arange(num_bins), hist_counts[:num_bins], color=colors[i], alpha=0.7, label=f'Channel {["Red", "Green", "Blue"][i]}')

        plt.xlabel('Pixel Value')
        plt.ylabel('Normalized Frequency')
        plt.title('RGB Channel Histograms')
        plt.grid(True)
        plt.tight_layout()
        plt.legend()

        # Convert the histogram bar graph to an image
        histogram_bar_img = self.plot_to_image(plt)
        histogram_bar_photo = ImageTk.PhotoImage(image=histogram_bar_img)

        return histogram_bar_photo

    def plot_to_image(self, plt):
        plt.savefig('temp_plot.png')
        img = Image.open('temp_plot.png')
        return img

    def apply_filter(self, filter_name, frame):
        if filter_name == "None":
            return frame
        elif filter_name == "Gaussian":
            return cv2.GaussianBlur(frame, (5, 5), 0)
        elif filter_name == "Mean":
            return cv2.blur(frame, (5, 5))
        elif filter_name == "Median":
            return cv2.medianBlur(frame, 5)
        elif filter_name == "Bilateral Filtering":
            return cv2.bilateralFilter(frame, 9, 75, 75)
        elif filter_name == "Non-local Means Denoising":
            return cv2.fastNlMeansDenoisingColored(frame, None, 10, 10, 7, 21)
        elif filter_name == "Anisotropic Diffusion":
```

```python
            return self.anisotropic_diffusion(frame)
        elif filter_name == "Total Variation Denoising":
            return self.total_variation_denoising(frame)
        elif filter_name == "Wiener Filter":
            return self.wiener_filter(frame)
        elif filter_name == "Adaptive Thresholding":
            return self.adaptive_threshold_each_channel(frame)
        elif filter_name == "Haar Wavelet Transform":
            return self.haar_wavelet_transform(frame)
        elif filter_name == "Daubechies Wavelet Transform":
            return self.daubechies_wavelet_transform(frame)
        else:
            return frame  # Default: return original frame if filter not found

    def wiener_filter(self, frame, kernel_size=(5, 5), noise_var=0.01):
        # Check if frame is None
        if frame is None:
            print("Error: Input frame is None.")
            return None

        # Check if frame is a valid numpy array
        if not isinstance(frame, np.ndarray):
            print("Error: Input frame is not a numpy array.")
            return None

        # Check if frame is an empty array
        if frame.size == 0:
            print("Error: Input frame is empty.")
            return None

        # Check if frame is in BGR color space
        if frame.shape[-1] != 3:
            print("Error: Input frame is not in BGR color space.")
            return None

        # Apply Wiener filter
        filtered_frame = cv2.medianBlur(frame, kernel_size[0])  # Use kernel_size[0] as the kernel size
        filtered_frame = cv2.fastNlMeansDenoising(filtered_frame, h=noise_var)
        return filtered_frame

    def adaptive_threshold_each_channel(self, frame):
        # Split the frame into individual channels
        b, g, r = cv2.split(frame)

        # Apply adaptive thresholding to each channel separately
        b_thresh = cv2.adaptiveThreshold(b, 255, cv2.ADAPTIVE_THRESH_GAUSSIAN_C, cv2.THRESH_BINARY, 11, 2)
        g_thresh = cv2.adaptiveThreshold(g, 255, cv2.ADAPTIVE_THRESH_GAUSSIAN_C, cv2.THRESH_BINARY, 11, 2)
        r_thresh = cv2.adaptiveThreshold(r, 255, cv2.ADAPTIVE_THRESH_GAUSSIAN_C, cv2.THRESH_BINARY, 11, 2)

        # Merge the thresholded channels back together
        return cv2.merge([b_thresh, g_thresh, r_thresh])

    def haar_wavelet_transform(self, frame):
        # Split the frame into its individual color channels
        b, g, r = cv2.split(frame)

        # Perform the wavelet transform on each channel separately
        b_coeffs = pywt.dwt2(b, 'haar')
        g_coeffs = pywt.dwt2(g, 'haar')
        r_coeffs = pywt.dwt2(r, 'haar')
```

```python
        # Reconstruct the channels from the coefficients
        b_reconstructed = pywt.idwt2(b_coeffs, 'haar')
        g_reconstructed = pywt.idwt2(g_coeffs, 'haar')
        r_reconstructed = pywt.idwt2(r_coeffs, 'haar')

        # Clip the values to ensure they are within the valid range
        b_reconstructed = np.clip(b_reconstructed, 0, 255).astype(np.uint8)
        g_reconstructed = np.clip(g_reconstructed, 0, 255).astype(np.uint8)
        r_reconstructed = np.clip(r_reconstructed, 0, 255).astype(np.uint8)

        # Merge the channels back together
        return cv2.merge([b_reconstructed, g_reconstructed, r_reconstructed])

    def daubechies_wavelet_transform(self, frame):
        # Split the frame into its individual color channels
        b, g, r = cv2.split(frame)

        # Choose the wavelet function (Daubechies 5)
        wavelet = 'db5'

        # Perform the wavelet transform on each channel separately
        b_coeffs = pywt.dwt2(b, wavelet)
        g_coeffs = pywt.dwt2(g, wavelet)
        r_coeffs = pywt.dwt2(r, wavelet)

        # Reconstruct the channels from the coefficients
        b_reconstructed = pywt.idwt2(b_coeffs, wavelet)
        g_reconstructed = pywt.idwt2(g_coeffs, wavelet)
        r_reconstructed = pywt.idwt2(r_coeffs, wavelet)

        # Clip the values to ensure they are within the valid range
        b_reconstructed = np.clip(b_reconstructed, 0, 255).astype(np.uint8)
        g_reconstructed = np.clip(g_reconstructed, 0, 255).astype(np.uint8)
        r_reconstructed = np.clip(r_reconstructed, 0, 255).astype(np.uint8)

        # Merge the channels back together
        return cv2.merge([b_reconstructed, g_reconstructed, r_reconstructed])

    def anisotropic_diffusion(self, img):
        return cv2.fastNlMeansDenoisingColored(img, None, 10, 10, 7, 21)

    def apply_total_variation_denoising_channel(self, channel, weight, iterations):
        # Initialize the result with the original channel
        result = channel.copy().astype(np.float64)  # Convert to float64

        # Perform total variation denoising
        for _ in range(iterations):
            # Compute the gradient of the channel
            dx = cv2.Sobel(result, cv2.CV_64F, 1, 0, ksize=3)
            dy = cv2.Sobel(result, cv2.CV_64F, 0, 1, ksize=3)

            # Update the channel using the gradient and the weight
            result -= weight * np.sqrt(dx**2 + dy**2)

        # Clip the values to ensure they are within the valid range
        result = np.clip(result, 0, 255).astype(np.uint8)

        return result

    def total_variation_denoising(self, img, weight=0.01, iterations=20):
        # Split the image into its individual color channels
        b, g, r = cv2.split(img)
```

```python
        # Apply total variation denoising to each channel separately
        b_denoised = self.apply_total_variation_denoising_channel(b, weight, iterations)
        g_denoised = self.apply_total_variation_denoising_channel(g, weight, iterations)
        r_denoised = self.apply_total_variation_denoising_channel(r, weight, iterations)

        # Merge the denoised channels back together
        return cv2.merge([b_denoised, g_denoised, r_denoised])

def main():
    root = tk.Tk()
    app = MILTracker(root)
    root.mainloop()

if __name__ == "__main__":
    main()
```

RUNNING PROGRAM

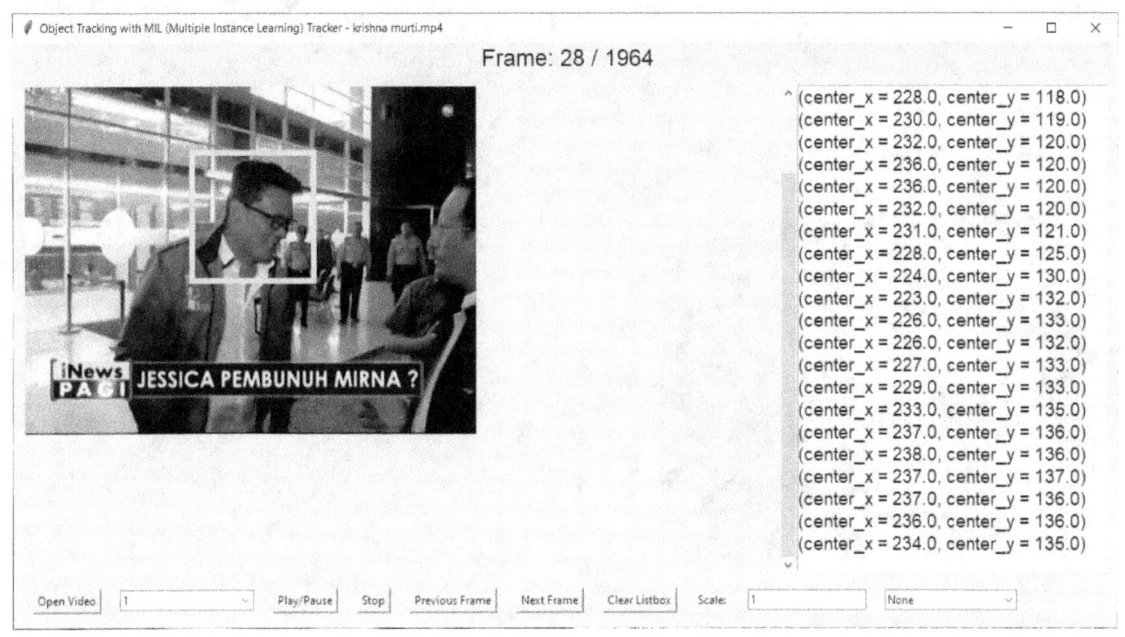

OBJECT TRACKING WITH MOSSE (MINIMUM OUTPUT SUM OF SQUARED ERROR) TRACKER

DESCRIPTION

The MOSSE (Minimum Output Sum of Squared Error) Tracker project, implemented in the mosse_tracker.py script, is a sophisticated application designed for object tracking within video files. It leverages the capabilities of the Tkinter library for its graphical user interface (GUI) and utilizes the OpenCV library for video processing and object tracking.

The application begins by setting up the main window and initializing essential variables. It includes a frame number label to keep track of the current frame in the video and several control variables like the video path, paused state, and the zoom scale. The tracker-specific variables include the bounding box (bbox) for the object being tracked, previous frame data, and the tracker object itself.

The GUI is constructed with several components: a video display panel with a canvas for showing the video frames, a list box to display center coordinates of the tracked object, and a control panel with various buttons and comboboxes for user interaction. Users can open video files, control playback, navigate through frames, and apply different filters to the video.

Opening a video file is handled by the open_video method, which utilizes the filedialog module to select a video file. Once a video is selected, it is read using the imageio library, and the file name is updated in the window title. The play_video method then begins the video playback by displaying frames on the canvas.

The stop_video method halts the playback, resets the frame index, and clears the tracker and bounding box data. The toggle_play_pause method allows the user to pause and resume the video playback, toggling the paused state accordingly. The update_zoom method updates the display when the zoom scale is changed.

To initialize the MOSSE tracker, the initialize_tracker method sets up the tracker with the first frame and the specified bounding box. It also adjusts the bounding box based on a scaling factor and ensures the tracker is ready for subsequent frames. The track_object method updates the tracker's bounding box on each frame, calculates the center coordinates, and displays these in the list box.

The update_bbox_rectangle method updates or creates a rectangle on the canvas to visually represent the bounding box. The show_frame method is responsible for displaying each frame of the video on the canvas, applying the selected zoom scale, and updating the bounding box if tracking is active.

User interactions with the mouse are managed through several event handlers. The on_mousewheel method adjusts the zoom scale when the mouse wheel is used. The on_press, on_drag, and on_release methods manage the drawing of the bounding box on the canvas by capturing mouse movements and updating the box dimensions.

The application includes methods for navigating through frames (prev_frame and next_frame), clearing the list box (clear_listbox), and updating the window title (set_window_title). When the mouse button is released, the analyze_histogram method is called to process the selected bounding box area.

The analyze_histogram method extracts the region within the bounding box, applies the selected filter, and displays the processed image and its histograms in a popup window. The histograms are shown in both line and bar formats, providing visual insights into the color distribution within the selected area.

Various filters can be applied to the video frames, including Gaussian, Mean, Median, Bilateral Filtering, Non-local Means Denoising, Anisotropic Diffusion, Total Variation Denoising, Wiener Filter, Adaptive Thresholding, Haar Wavelet Transform, and Daubechies Wavelet Transform. Each filter has a corresponding method to process the frame accordingly.

For instance, the wiener_filter method applies Wiener filtering to reduce noise in the frame. The adaptive_threshold_each_channel method applies adaptive thresholding to each color channel separately. Wavelet transforms are handled by the haar_wavelet_transform and daubechies_wavelet_transform methods, which perform discrete wavelet transforms and reconstruct the image.

The display_cropped_image method shows the filtered cropped image in the popup window, and the display_histograms method visualizes the histograms of the cropped image. The histograms are generated and displayed using Matplotlib, and the plot_to_image method converts the plots into images that can be displayed on the Tkinter canvas.

Overall, the MOSSE Tracker project is a comprehensive application that combines video processing, object tracking, and image analysis within an interactive GUI. It allows users to open video files, select regions for tracking, apply various filters, and visualize the results with detailed histograms, making it a powerful tool for analyzing video content and tracking objects within frames.

SOURCE CODE

```python
#mosse_tracker.py
import tkinter as tk
from tkinter import ttk
from tkinter import filedialog
from PIL import Image, ImageTk
import imageio
import cv2
import numpy as np
import matplotlib.pyplot as plt
import pywt

class MOSSETracker:
    def __init__(self, master):
        self.master = master
        self.master.title("Object Tracking with MOSSE (Minimum Output Sum of Squared Error) Tracker")
        self.file_name = ""
        self.set_window_title()  # Set window title initially

        self.frame_number_label = tk.Label(master, text="Frame: 0")
        self.frame_number_label.pack()

        self.video = None
```

```python
        self.video_path = None
        self.paused = False
        self.zoom_scale = tk.IntVar(value=1)
        self.frame_index = 0
        self.bbox = None
        self.bbox2 = None
        self.tracking_started = False  # Initialize tracking_started to False
        self.prev_frame_gray = None
        self.tracker = None
        self.initial_w = None
        self.initial_h = None
        self.bbox_rect = None  # Initialize bbox_rect attribute to None
        self.frame_processing = False  # Initialize frame_processing attribute to False

        # Available filters
        self.filters = ["None", "Gaussian", "Mean", "Median", "Bilateral Filtering",
                    "Non-local Means Denoising", "Anisotropic Diffusion",
                    "Total Variation Denoising", "Wiener Filter",
                    "Adaptive Thresholding", "Haar Wavelet Transform",
                    "Daubechies Wavelet Transform"]

        self.create_widgets()

    def create_widgets(self):
        # Panel for video display
        video_panel = tk.Frame(self.master)
        video_panel.pack(padx=10, pady=10)

        # Canvas to display the original video
        canvas_width = 800
        canvas_height = 500
        self.canvas = tk.Canvas(video_panel, width=canvas_width, height=canvas_height)
        self.canvas.pack(side="left", fill="both", expand=True)
        self.canvas.bind("<MouseWheel>", self.on_mousewheel)
        self.canvas.bind("<ButtonPress-1>", self.on_press)
        self.canvas.bind("<B1-Motion>", self.on_drag)
        self.canvas.bind("<ButtonRelease-1>", self.on_release)  # Bind ButtonRelease event

        # List box to display center coordinates
        self.center_listbox = tk.Listbox(video_panel, width=30, height=20, font=("Helvetica", 14))
        self.center_listbox.pack(side="right", fill="y")
        # Scrollbar for the listbox
        scrollbar = tk.Scrollbar(video_panel, orient="vertical")
        scrollbar.pack(side="left", fill="y")
        scrollbar.config(command=self.center_listbox.yview)

        # Attach scrollbar to listbox
        self.center_listbox.config(yscrollcommand=scrollbar.set)

        # Panel for control buttons
        control_panel = tk.Frame(self.master)
        control_panel.pack(padx=10, pady=(0, 10), fill="x")

        # Button to open a video file
        self.open_button = tk.Button(control_panel, text="Open Video", command=self.open_video)
        self.open_button.grid(row=0, column=0, padx=10, pady=5)

        # Combobox for selecting zoom scale
        self.zoom_combobox = ttk.Combobox(control_panel, textvariable=self.zoom_scale, values=list(range(1, 11)))
        self.zoom_combobox.grid(row=0, column=1, padx=10, pady=5)
        self.zoom_combobox.bind("<<ComboboxSelected>>", self.update_zoom)
```

```python
        # Button to play/pause the video
        self.play_button = tk.Button(control_panel, text="Play/Pause", command=self.toggle_play_pause)
        self.play_button.grid(row=0, column=2, padx=10, pady=5)

        # Button to stop the video
        self.stop_button = tk.Button(control_panel, text="Stop", command=self.stop_video)
        self.stop_button.grid(row=0, column=3, padx=10, pady=5)

        # Button to navigate to the previous frame
        self.prev_frame_button = tk.Button(control_panel, text="Previous Frame", command=self.prev_frame)
        self.prev_frame_button.grid(row=0, column=4, padx=10, pady=5)

        # Button to navigate to the next frame
        self.next_frame_button = tk.Button(control_panel, text="Next Frame", command=self.next_frame)
        self.next_frame_button.grid(row=0, column=5, padx=10, pady=5)

        # Button to clear the listbox
        self.clear_button = tk.Button(control_panel, text="Clear Listbox", command=self.clear_listbox)
        self.clear_button.grid(row=0, column=6, padx=10, pady=5)

        # Label and entry for specifying scale
        self.scale_label = tk.Label(control_panel, text="Scale:")
        self.scale_label.grid(row=0, column=7, padx=10, pady=5, sticky="e")
        self.scale_default = tk.StringVar(value="1")
        self.scale_entry = ttk.Entry(control_panel, textvariable=self.scale_default)
        self.scale_entry.grid(row=0, column=8, padx=10, pady=5, sticky="w")
        self.scale_entry.bind("<Return>", lambda event: self.toggle_play_pause())

        # Combobox for selecting filters
        self.filter_combobox = ttk.Combobox(control_panel, values=self.filters)
        self.filter_combobox.grid(row=0, column=9, padx=10, pady=5)
        self.filter_combobox.current(0)  # Set default value

    def open_video(self):
        self.video_path = filedialog.askopenfilename(filetypes=[("Video files", "*.mp4;*.avi;*.mkv;*.wmv")])
        if self.video_path:
            self.video = imageio.get_reader(self.video_path)
            self.file_name = self.video_path.split('/')[-1]
            self.set_window_title()
            self.play_video()

    def play_video(self):
        if self.video:
            self.paused = False
            self.tracking_started = True
            self.show_frame()

    def stop_video(self):
        self.paused = True
        self.frame_index = 0
        self.bbox = None
        self.tracker = None  # Reset tracker
        self.initial_w = None  # Reset width
        self.initial_h = None  # Reset height
        self.show_frame()

    def toggle_play_pause(self):
        self.paused = not self.paused
        if not self.paused:
```

```python
            if self.bbox is not None:
                self.tracking_started = True
            self.play_video()

    def update_zoom(self, event=None):
        self.show_frame()

    def initialize_tracker(self, frame, bbox, params=None):
        """Initialize the MOSSE tracker with possible user-defined parameters."""

        # Read scale factor from a GUI entry; ensure it is a float
        scale = float(self.scale_entry.get())

        # Adjust bbox based on the scaling parameter
        bbox = (
            int(bbox[0] + (1 - scale) * bbox[2] / 2),  # Center the scaling on the bbox
            int(bbox[1] + (1 - scale) * bbox[3] / 2),
            int(bbox[2] * scale),
            int(bbox[3] * scale)
        )

        # Initialize the MOSSE tracker
        self.tracker = cv2.legacy.TrackerMOSSE_create()

        # Initialize the tracker with the frame and adjusted bbox
        success = self.tracker.init(frame, tuple(map(int, bbox)))
        if not success:
            print("Tracker initialization failed.")
            return False

        self.initial_w, self.initial_h = bbox[2], bbox[3]
        return True

    def track_object(self, frame, bbox, user_params=None):
        """Track object using MOSSE Tracker with optional user parameters."""
        if not self.tracker:
            if not self.initialize_tracker(frame, bbox, user_params):
                return None

        # Update the tracker and get the new bounding box
        success, bbox = self.tracker.update(frame)
        if success:
            x1, y1, w, h = map(int, bbox)
            x2, y2 = x1 + w, y1 + h

            # Calculate and display the center of the bounding box
            center_x = (x1 + x2) // 2
            center_y = (y1 + y2) // 2
            if hasattr(self, 'center_listbox'):
                self.center_listbox.insert(tk.END, f"(center_x = {center_x}, center_y = {center_y})")

            return (x1, y1, x2, y2)
        return None

    def update_bbox_rectangle(self, bbox):
        if bbox is not None:
            x1, y1, x2, y2 = map(int, bbox)
            if self.bbox_rect is not None:
                self.canvas.coords(self.bbox_rect, x1, y1, x2, y2)
                self.canvas.tag_raise(self.bbox_rect)  # Raise the bounding box to the front
            else:
                self.bbox_rect = self.canvas.create_rectangle(x1, y1, x2, y2, outline='#fc3d3d', width=8, tags="bbox")
```

```python
def show_frame(self):
    if self.video:
        if not self.paused:
            if 0 <= self.frame_index < len(self.video):
                if not self.frame_processing:  # Check if the frame is already being processed
                    try:
                        self.frame_processing = True  # Set frame_processing flag to True to indicate frame processing

                        frame = self.video.get_data(self.frame_index)
                        frame = cv2.cvtColor(frame, cv2.COLOR_RGB2BGR)

                        if self.bbox is not None:
                            if not self.tracking_started:
                                self.tracking_started = True

                            self.bbox = self.track_object(frame, self.bbox)
                            if self.bbox:
                                frame = cv2.cvtColor(frame, cv2.COLOR_BGR2RGB)
                                frame = Image.fromarray(frame)
                                frame = frame.resize((frame.width * self.zoom_scale.get(), frame.height * self.zoom_scale.get()))
                                photo = ImageTk.PhotoImage(frame)
                                self.photo = photo
                                self.canvas.delete("video")
                                self.canvas.create_image(0, 0, anchor="nw", image=photo, tags="video")
                                self.update_bbox_rectangle(self.bbox)

                        else:
                            frame = cv2.cvtColor(frame, cv2.COLOR_BGR2RGB)
                            frame = Image.fromarray(frame)
                            frame = frame.resize((frame.width * self.zoom_scale.get(), frame.height * self.zoom_scale.get()))
                            photo = ImageTk.PhotoImage(frame)
                            self.photo = photo
                            self.canvas.delete("video")
                            self.canvas.create_image(0, 0, anchor="nw", image=photo, tags="video")

                        self.frame_number_label.config(text=f"Frame: {self.frame_index} / {self.video.count_frames()}", font=("Helvetica", 18))

                        self.frame_index += 1

                    except Exception as e:
                        print("Error: ", e)
                    finally:
                        self.frame_processing = False  # Reset frame_processing flag to False after processing the frame

def on_mousewheel(self, event):
    direction = event.delta // 120
    current_value = int(self.zoom_scale.get())
    if direction == 1 and current_value < 10:
        current_value += 1
    elif direction == -1 and current_value > 1:
        current_value -= 1
    self.zoom_scale.set(current_value)
    self.update_zoom()

def on_press(self, event):
```

```python
        self.tracker = None
        self.start_x = self.canvas.canvasx(event.x)
        self.start_y = self.canvas.canvasy(event.y)
        # Clear the previous bounding box if it exists
        if self.bbox_rect:
            self.canvas.delete(self.bbox_rect)
            self.bbox_rect = None
        self.bbox = None
        self.bbox2 = None

    def on_drag(self, event):
        # Update the endpoint of the rectangle as the mouse moves
        cur_x = self.canvas.canvasx(event.x)
        cur_y = self.canvas.canvasy(event.y)

        # Define the coordinates correctly ensuring x1 < x2 and y1 < y2
        x1, y1 = min(self.start_x, cur_x), min(self.start_y, cur_y)
        x2, y2 = max(self.start_x, cur_x), max(self.start_y, cur_y)

        # Update dimensions for tracking
        self.initial_w = x2 - x1
        self.initial_h = y2 - y1
        self.bbox = (x1, y1, self.initial_w, self.initial_h)
        self.bbox2 = (self.start_x, self.start_y, cur_x, cur_y)

        # Update or create a rectangle on the canvas
        if self.bbox_rect:
            self.canvas.coords(self.bbox_rect, x1, y1, x2, y2)
        else:
            self.bbox_rect = self.canvas.create_rectangle(x1, y1, x2, y2, outline="cyan", width=6)

    def prev_frame(self):
        if self.frame_index > 0:
            self.frame_index -= 1
            self.show_frame()

    def next_frame(self):
        if self.video and self.frame_index < len(self.video) - 1:
            self.show_frame()

    def clear_listbox(self):
        self.center_listbox.delete(0, tk.END)

    def set_window_title(self):
        if self.file_name:
            self.master.title(f"Object Tracking with MOSSE (Minimum Output Sum of Squared Error) Tracker - {self.file_name}")
            self.master.title_font = ("Helvetica", 16, "bold")
        else:
            self.master.title("Object Tracking with MOSSE (Minimum Output Sum of Squared Error) Tracker")

    def on_release(self, event):
        self.analyze_histogram()  # Call analyze_histogram() method when the mouse button is released

    def analyze_histogram(self):
        if self.bbox2 is not None and self.video:
            x1, y1, x2, y2 = map(int, self.bbox2)
            if x1 != x2 and y1 != y2:
                try:
                    frame = self.video.get_data(self.frame_index)
```

```python
                    # Ensure the bounding box is within the frame boundaries
                    h, w, _ = frame.shape
                    x1, x2 = max(0, min(x1, w)), max(0, min(x2, w))
                    y1, y2 = max(0, min(y1, h)), max(0, min(y2, h))

                    # Ensure x1 < x2 and y1 < y2
                    x1, x2 = sorted([x1, x2])
                    y1, y2 = sorted([y1, y2])

                    cropped_frame = frame[y1:y2, x1:x2]
                    if cropped_frame.size > 0:
                        cropped_frame = cv2.cvtColor(cropped_frame, cv2.COLOR_BGR2RGB)

                        # Get selected filter from combobox
                        selected_filter = self.filter_combobox.get()
                        # Apply selected filter
                        filtered_frame = self.apply_filter(selected_filter, cropped_frame)

                        self.create_popup_window(filtered_frame)
                        self.display_cropped_image(filtered_frame)
                        self.display_histograms(filtered_frame)
                    else:
                        print("Cropped frame is empty.")
                except Exception as e:
                    print("Failed to process frame:", e)
        else:
            print("Bounding box dimensions are zero or negative.")

def create_popup_window(self, cropped_frame):
    self.popup_window = tk.Toplevel(self.master)
    self.popup_window.title("Cropped Image and Its Histogram")
    self.popup_window.geometry("1500x700")


def display_cropped_image(self, cropped_frame):
    cropped_frame_frame = tk.Frame(self.popup_window)
    cropped_frame_frame.pack(side="left")

    cropped_frame_rgb = cv2.cvtColor(cropped_frame, cv2.COLOR_BGR2RGB)
    cropped_img = Image.fromarray(cropped_frame_rgb)
    cropped_img = cropped_img.resize((600, 600))

    cropped_photo = ImageTk.PhotoImage(cropped_img)
    cropped_canvas = tk.Canvas(cropped_frame_frame, width=600, height=600)
    cropped_canvas.pack(side="left", anchor="nw")
    cropped_canvas.create_image(0, 0, anchor="nw", image=cropped_photo)
    cropped_canvas.image = cropped_photo

def display_histograms(self, cropped_frame):
    histograms_frame = tk.Frame(self.popup_window)
    histograms_frame.pack(side="right", padx=20)

    self.display_line_histogram(cropped_frame, histograms_frame)
    self.display_bar_histogram(cropped_frame, histograms_frame)

def display_line_histogram(self, cropped_frame, histograms_frame):
    line_histogram_frame = tk.Frame(histograms_frame)
    line_histogram_frame.pack(side="top", pady=10)

    plt.figure(figsize=(12, 4))
    color = ('r', 'g', 'b')
    for i, col in enumerate(color):
        histr = cv2.calcHist([cropped_frame], [i], None, [256], [0, 256])
```

```python
                plt.plot(histr, color=col, label=f'Channel {col.upper()}', linewidth=2)
                plt.xlim([0, 256])
            plt.title('Line Histogram')
            plt.xlabel('Pixel Value')
            plt.ylabel('Frequency')
            plt.tight_layout()
            plt.grid(True)
            plt.legend()

            line_histogram_img = self.plot_to_image(plt)
            self.display_histogram_image(line_histogram_frame, line_histogram_img)

    def display_bar_histogram(self, cropped_frame, histograms_frame):
        bar_histogram_frame = tk.Frame(histograms_frame)
        bar_histogram_frame.pack(side="bottom", pady=10)

        plt.figure(figsize=(12, 4))
        color = ('r', 'g', 'b')
        for i, col in enumerate(color):
            hist_range = (0, 256)
            hist_counts, _ = np.histogram(cropped_frame[:, :, i], bins=64, range=hist_range)
            plt.bar(np.arange(64), hist_counts, color=col, alpha=0.7, label=f'Channel {col.upper()}')
            for index, value in enumerate(hist_counts):
                plt.text(index, value + 10, str(int(value)), ha='center', va='bottom', fontsize=9)

        plt.title('Bar Histogram')
        plt.xlabel('Pixel Value')
        plt.ylabel('Frequency')
        plt.xticks(np.linspace(0, 63, num=5), np.linspace(0, 255, num=5, dtype=int))  # Adjust x-axis ticks
        plt.tight_layout()
        plt.grid(True)
        plt.legend()

        bar_histogram_img = self.plot_to_image(plt)
        self.display_histogram_image(bar_histogram_frame, bar_histogram_img)

    def display_histogram_image(self, parent_frame, img):
        histogram_photo = ImageTk.PhotoImage(image=img)
        histogram_canvas = tk.Canvas(parent_frame, width=900, height=300)
        histogram_canvas.pack(side="bottom", anchor="se")
        histogram_canvas.create_image(0, 0, anchor="nw", image=histogram_photo)
        histogram_canvas.image = histogram_photo

    def plot_histogram_bar_to_image(self, image):
        # Calculate histogram for each channel
        histograms = []
        for i in range(3):
            hist_range = (0, 256)
            hist_counts, _ = np.histogram(image[:, :, i], bins=64, range=hist_range)  # Adjust bins to 64
            histograms.append(hist_counts)

        # Extracting only 64 bins from the histogram
        num_bins = 64  # Adjusted to 64 bins

        # Generating colors for each channel
        colors = ['red', 'green', 'blue']

        plt.figure()
        for i, histogram in enumerate(histograms):
            # Normalize the histogram counts for better visualization
```

```python
            hist_counts = histogram / np.sum(histogram)
            # Setting the color for each channel
            plt.bar(np.arange(num_bins), hist_counts[:num_bins], color=colors[i], alpha=0.7, 
label=f'Channel {["Red", "Green", "Blue"][i]}')
        
        plt.xlabel('Pixel Value')
        plt.ylabel('Normalized Frequency')
        plt.title('RGB Channel Histograms')
        plt.grid(True)
        plt.tight_layout()
        plt.legend()

        # Convert the histogram bar graph to an image
        histogram_bar_img = self.plot_to_image(plt)
        histogram_bar_photo = ImageTk.PhotoImage(image=histogram_bar_img)

        return histogram_bar_photo

    def plot_to_image(self, plt):
        plt.savefig('temp_plot.png')
        img = Image.open('temp_plot.png')
        return img

    def apply_filter(self, filter_name, frame):
        if filter_name == "None":
            return frame
        elif filter_name == "Gaussian":
            return cv2.GaussianBlur(frame, (5, 5), 0)
        elif filter_name == "Mean":
            return cv2.blur(frame, (5, 5))
        elif filter_name == "Median":
            return cv2.medianBlur(frame, 5)
        elif filter_name == "Bilateral Filtering":
            return cv2.bilateralFilter(frame, 9, 75, 75)
        elif filter_name == "Non-local Means Denoising":
            return cv2.fastNlMeansDenoisingColored(frame, None, 10, 10, 7, 21)
        elif filter_name == "Anisotropic Diffusion":
            return self.anisotropic_diffusion(frame)
        elif filter_name == "Total Variation Denoising":
            return self.total_variation_denoising(frame)
        elif filter_name == "Wiener Filter":
            return self.wiener_filter(frame)
        elif filter_name == "Adaptive Thresholding":
            return self.adaptive_threshold_each_channel(frame)
        elif filter_name == "Haar Wavelet Transform":
            return self.haar_wavelet_transform(frame)
        elif filter_name == "Daubechies Wavelet Transform":
            return self.daubechies_wavelet_transform(frame)
        else:
            return frame  # Default: return original frame if filter not found

    def wiener_filter(self, frame, kernel_size=(5, 5), noise_var=0.01):
        # Check if frame is None
        if frame is None:
            print("Error: Input frame is None.")
            return None

        # Check if frame is a valid numpy array
        if not isinstance(frame, np.ndarray):
            print("Error: Input frame is not a numpy array.")
            return None

        # Check if frame is an empty array
        if frame.size == 0:
```

```python
            print("Error: Input frame is empty.")
            return None

        # Check if frame is in BGR color space
        if frame.shape[-1] != 3:
            print("Error: Input frame is not in BGR color space.")
            return None

        # Apply Wiener filter
        filtered_frame = cv2.medianBlur(frame, kernel_size[0])  # Use kernel_size[0] as the kernel size
        filtered_frame = cv2.fastNlMeansDenoising(filtered_frame, h=noise_var)
        return filtered_frame

    def adaptive_threshold_each_channel(self, frame):
        # Split the frame into individual channels
        b, g, r = cv2.split(frame)

        # Apply adaptive thresholding to each channel separately
        b_thresh = cv2.adaptiveThreshold(b, 255, cv2.ADAPTIVE_THRESH_GAUSSIAN_C, cv2.THRESH_BINARY, 11, 2)
        g_thresh = cv2.adaptiveThreshold(g, 255, cv2.ADAPTIVE_THRESH_GAUSSIAN_C, cv2.THRESH_BINARY, 11, 2)
        r_thresh = cv2.adaptiveThreshold(r, 255, cv2.ADAPTIVE_THRESH_GAUSSIAN_C, cv2.THRESH_BINARY, 11, 2)

        # Merge the thresholded channels back together
        return cv2.merge([b_thresh, g_thresh, r_thresh])

    def haar_wavelet_transform(self, frame):
        # Split the frame into its individual color channels
        b, g, r = cv2.split(frame)

        # Perform the wavelet transform on each channel separately
        b_coeffs = pywt.dwt2(b, 'haar')
        g_coeffs = pywt.dwt2(g, 'haar')
        r_coeffs = pywt.dwt2(r, 'haar')

        # Reconstruct the channels from the coefficients
        b_reconstructed = pywt.idwt2(b_coeffs, 'haar')
        g_reconstructed = pywt.idwt2(g_coeffs, 'haar')
        r_reconstructed = pywt.idwt2(r_coeffs, 'haar')

        # Clip the values to ensure they are within the valid range
        b_reconstructed = np.clip(b_reconstructed, 0, 255).astype(np.uint8)
        g_reconstructed = np.clip(g_reconstructed, 0, 255).astype(np.uint8)
        r_reconstructed = np.clip(r_reconstructed, 0, 255).astype(np.uint8)

        # Merge the channels back together
        return cv2.merge([b_reconstructed, g_reconstructed, r_reconstructed])

    def daubechies_wavelet_transform(self, frame):
        # Split the frame into its individual color channels
        b, g, r = cv2.split(frame)

        # Choose the wavelet function (Daubechies 5)
        wavelet = 'db5'

        # Perform the wavelet transform on each channel separately
        b_coeffs = pywt.dwt2(b, wavelet)
        g_coeffs = pywt.dwt2(g, wavelet)
        r_coeffs = pywt.dwt2(r, wavelet)

        # Reconstruct the channels from the coefficients
```

```python
            b_reconstructed = pywt.idwt2(b_coeffs, wavelet)
            g_reconstructed = pywt.idwt2(g_coeffs, wavelet)
            r_reconstructed = pywt.idwt2(r_coeffs, wavelet)

            # Clip the values to ensure they are within the valid range
            b_reconstructed = np.clip(b_reconstructed, 0, 255).astype(np.uint8)
            g_reconstructed = np.clip(g_reconstructed, 0, 255).astype(np.uint8)
            r_reconstructed = np.clip(r_reconstructed, 0, 255).astype(np.uint8)

            # Merge the channels back together
            return cv2.merge([b_reconstructed, g_reconstructed, r_reconstructed])

        def anisotropic_diffusion(self, img):
            return cv2.fastNlMeansDenoisingColored(img, None, 10, 10, 7, 21)

        def apply_total_variation_denoising_channel(self, channel, weight, iterations):
            # Initialize the result with the original channel
            result = channel.copy().astype(np.float64)  # Convert to float64

            # Perform total variation denoising
            for _ in range(iterations):
                # Compute the gradient of the channel
                dx = cv2.Sobel(result, cv2.CV_64F, 1, 0, ksize=3)
                dy = cv2.Sobel(result, cv2.CV_64F, 0, 1, ksize=3)

                # Update the channel using the gradient and the weight
                result -= weight * np.sqrt(dx**2 + dy**2)

            # Clip the values to ensure they are within the valid range
            result = np.clip(result, 0, 255).astype(np.uint8)

            return result

        def total_variation_denoising(self, img, weight=0.01, iterations=20):
            # Split the image into its individual color channels
            b, g, r = cv2.split(img)

            # Apply total variation denoising to each channel separately
            b_denoised = self.apply_total_variation_denoising_channel(b, weight, iterations)
            g_denoised = self.apply_total_variation_denoising_channel(g, weight, iterations)
            r_denoised = self.apply_total_variation_denoising_channel(r, weight, iterations)

            # Merge the denoised channels back together
            return cv2.merge([b_denoised, g_denoised, r_denoised])

def main():
    root = tk.Tk()
    app = MOSSETracker(root)
    root.mainloop()

if __name__ == "__main__":
    main()
```

RUNNING PROGRAM

OBJECT TRACKING WITH TLD (TRACKING, LEARNING, AND DETECTION) TRACKER

DESCRIPTION

The TLDTracker project is a comprehensive tool for object tracking using the TLD (Tracking, Learning, and Detection) algorithm. The primary interface of the application is built using Tkinter, a popular GUI library in Python. The main window of the application allows users to interact with the tracking system through various controls and displays. The tool is designed to handle video input, allowing users to open and play video files from their local system.

The interface features a frame number label to display the current frame number of the video being played. Users can control video playback using buttons for playing, pausing, stopping, and navigating through frames. Additionally, there is a listbox to display the coordinates of the tracked object's center, providing a clear visual indication of the tracking process.

A key aspect of the TLDTracker is the ability to zoom into the video, which is controlled by a combobox allowing users to select a zoom scale from 1 to 10. This feature is particularly useful for closely examining the tracked object's behavior. The canvas element in the Tkinter interface is used to display the video frames, and it is interactive, allowing users to draw bounding boxes around objects they wish to track.

The tracking process starts with the user selecting a region of interest by clicking and dragging on the video canvas. This initializes the tracker with the specified bounding box, which is then used to track the object across subsequent frames. The tracker uses the OpenCV library's TLD tracker implementation, providing robust tracking capabilities.

An innovative feature of the TLDTracker is the ability to apply various filters to the video frames. Users can choose from a range of filters, such as Gaussian, Mean, Median, Bilateral Filtering, and more, using a combobox in the control panel. These filters can enhance the video frames and improve the tracking accuracy under different conditions.

When a bounding box is selected, the application can analyze the histogram of the selected region. This involves extracting the frame data within the bounding box, applying the selected filter, and then displaying the filtered frame along with its histograms. Histograms are displayed in both line and bar formats, providing detailed insights into the pixel value distributions across the RGB channels.

The TLDTracker includes functionality for saving the histograms as images. This is achieved by converting the plotted histograms into images using the Matplotlib library and then displaying these images in a popup window. The popup window shows both the cropped frame and the corresponding histograms, facilitating a detailed analysis of the selected region.

One of the advanced features of the TLDTracker is the implementation of various wavelet transforms, such as the Haar and Daubechies wavelet transforms. These transforms are applied to the individual color channels of the video frames, allowing for sophisticated image processing techniques that can enhance the tracking capabilities.

The application ensures that the tracking and filtering operations are performed efficiently, with safeguards to prevent processing when frames are already being handled. This ensures smooth and responsive user interactions, even with computationally intensive tasks like video processing and filtering.

The TLDTracker also includes error handling mechanisms to manage potential issues during frame processing. For example, it checks for the validity of the input frames and ensures that the bounding box coordinates are within the frame boundaries. This robustness makes the tool reliable for real-world applications.

To enhance the usability, the TLDTracker provides a clear and concise user interface, with labeled buttons and entries for setting parameters like scale and filter types. The zoom functionality is particularly user-friendly, with mouse wheel events bound to adjust the zoom scale interactively.

The use of image processing libraries such as OpenCV and PIL (Python Imaging Library) ensures that the TLDTracker can handle a wide range of video formats and perform complex image manipulations. The integration of these libraries into the Tkinter interface provides a powerful and flexible tool for object tracking and analysis.

The TLDTracker is designed to be extensible, allowing for future enhancements and additional features. The current implementation provides a solid foundation for tracking and analyzing objects in video streams, but it can be further developed to include more advanced tracking algorithms and additional image processing techniques.

In summary, the TLDTracker project is a versatile and powerful tool for object tracking using the TLD algorithm. Its user-friendly interface, combined with advanced image processing capabilities, makes it suitable for a wide range of applications, from academic research to practical video analysis tasks. The tool's ability to handle various filters and display detailed histograms further enhances its utility for in-depth analysis of video content.

The integration of wavelet transforms and other advanced filtering techniques showcases the project's potential for sophisticated image processing applications. The robust error handling and efficient frame processing ensure that the TLDTracker is reliable and responsive, providing a smooth user experience even with demanding tasks.

Overall, the TLDTracker project represents a significant contribution to the field of object tracking and video analysis, combining the power of Python's image processing libraries with a user-friendly GUI to create a comprehensive and effective tool.

SOURCE CODE

```python
#tld_tracker.py
import tkinter as tk
from tkinter import ttk
from tkinter import filedialog
from PIL import Image, ImageTk
import imageio
import cv2
import numpy as np
import matplotlib.pyplot as plt
import pywt

class TLDTracker:
    def __init__(self, master):
        self.master = master
        self.master.title("Object Tracking with TLD (Tracking, Learning, and Detection) Tracker")
        self.file_name = ""
        self.set_window_title()  # Set window title initially

        self.frame_number_label = tk.Label(master, text="Frame: 0")
        self.frame_number_label.pack()

        self.video = None
        self.video_path = None
        self.paused = False
        self.zoom_scale = tk.IntVar(value=1)
        self.frame_index = 0
        self.bbox = None
        self.bbox2 = None
        self.tracking_started = False  # Initialize tracking_started to False
        self.prev_frame_gray = None
        self.tracker = None
        self.initial_w = None
        self.initial_h = None
        self.bbox_rect = None  # Initialize bbox_rect attribute to None
        self.frame_processing = False  # Initialize frame_processing attribute to False

        # Available filters
        self.filters = ["None", "Gaussian", "Mean", "Median", "Bilateral Filtering",
                        "Non-local Means Denoising", "Anisotropic Diffusion",
                        "Total Variation Denoising", "Wiener Filter",
                        "Adaptive Thresholding", "Haar Wavelet Transform",
                        "Daubechies Wavelet Transform"]

        self.create_widgets()

    def create_widgets(self):
        # Panel for video display
        video_panel = tk.Frame(self.master)
        video_panel.pack(padx=10, pady=10)
```

```python
        # Canvas to display the original video
        canvas_width = 800
        canvas_height = 500
        self.canvas = tk.Canvas(video_panel, width=canvas_width, height=canvas_height)
        self.canvas.pack(side="left", fill="both", expand=True)
        self.canvas.bind("<MouseWheel>", self.on_mousewheel)
        self.canvas.bind("<ButtonPress-1>", self.on_press)
        self.canvas.bind("<B1-Motion>", self.on_drag)
        self.canvas.bind("<ButtonRelease-1>", self.on_release)  # Bind ButtonRelease event

        # List box to display center coordinates
        self.center_listbox = tk.Listbox(video_panel, width=30, height=20, font=("Helvetica", 14))
        self.center_listbox.pack(side="right", fill="y")
        # Scrollbar for the listbox
        scrollbar = tk.Scrollbar(video_panel, orient="vertical")
        scrollbar.pack(side="left", fill="y")
        scrollbar.config(command=self.center_listbox.yview)

        # Attach scrollbar to listbox
        self.center_listbox.config(yscrollcommand=scrollbar.set)

        # Panel for control buttons
        control_panel = tk.Frame(self.master)
        control_panel.pack(padx=10, pady=(0, 10), fill="x")

        # Button to open a video file
        self.open_button = tk.Button(control_panel, text="Open Video", command=self.open_video)
        self.open_button.grid(row=0, column=0, padx=10, pady=5)

        # Combobox for selecting zoom scale
        self.zoom_combobox = ttk.Combobox(control_panel, textvariable=self.zoom_scale, values=list(range(1, 11)))
        self.zoom_combobox.grid(row=0, column=1, padx=10, pady=5)
        self.zoom_combobox.bind("<<ComboboxSelected>>", self.update_zoom)

        # Button to play/pause the video
        self.play_button = tk.Button(control_panel, text="Play/Pause", command=self.toggle_play_pause)
        self.play_button.grid(row=0, column=2, padx=10, pady=5)

        # Button to stop the video
        self.stop_button = tk.Button(control_panel, text="Stop", command=self.stop_video)
        self.stop_button.grid(row=0, column=3, padx=10, pady=5)

        # Button to navigate to the previous frame
        self.prev_frame_button = tk.Button(control_panel, text="Previous Frame", command=self.prev_frame)
        self.prev_frame_button.grid(row=0, column=4, padx=10, pady=5)

        # Button to navigate to the next frame
        self.next_frame_button = tk.Button(control_panel, text="Next Frame", command=self.next_frame)
        self.next_frame_button.grid(row=0, column=5, padx=10, pady=5)

        # Button to clear the listbox
        self.clear_button = tk.Button(control_panel, text="Clear Listbox", command=self.clear_listbox)
        self.clear_button.grid(row=0, column=6, padx=10, pady=5)

        # Label and entry for specifying scale
        self.scale_label = tk.Label(control_panel, text="Scale:")
        self.scale_label.grid(row=0, column=7, padx=10, pady=5, sticky="e")
        self.scale_default = tk.StringVar(value="1")
```

```python
        self.scale_entry = ttk.Entry(control_panel, textvariable=self.scale_default)
        self.scale_entry.grid(row=0, column=8, padx=10, pady=5, sticky="w")
        self.scale_entry.bind("<Return>", lambda event: self.toggle_play_pause())

        # Combobox for selecting filters
        self.filter_combobox = ttk.Combobox(control_panel, values=self.filters)
        self.filter_combobox.grid(row=0, column=9, padx=10, pady=5)
        self.filter_combobox.current(0)  # Set default value

    def open_video(self):
        self.video_path = filedialog.askopenfilename(filetypes=[("Video files", "*.mp4;*.avi;*.mkv;*.wmv")])
        if self.video_path:
            self.video = imageio.get_reader(self.video_path)
            self.file_name = self.video_path.split('/')[-1]
            self.set_window_title()
            self.play_video()

    def play_video(self):
        if self.video:
            self.paused = False
            self.tracking_started = True
            self.show_frame()

    def stop_video(self):
        self.paused = True
        self.frame_index = 0
        self.bbox = None
        self.tracker = None  # Reset tracker
        self.initial_w = None  # Reset width
        self.initial_h = None  # Reset height
        self.show_frame()

    def toggle_play_pause(self):
        self.paused = not self.paused
        if not self.paused:
            if self.bbox is not None:
                self.tracking_started = True
            self.play_video()

    def update_zoom(self, event=None):
        self.show_frame()

    def initialize_tracker(self, frame, bbox, params=None):
        """Initialize the TLD tracker with possible user-defined parameters."""

        # Adjust bbox based on parameters such as scaling
        scale = float(self.scale_entry.get())  # Ensure scale is a float
        bbox = (
            int(bbox[0] + (1 - scale) * bbox[2] / 2),  # Center the scaling on the bbox
            int(bbox[1] + (1 - scale) * bbox[3] / 2),
            int(bbox[2] * scale),
            int(bbox[3] * scale)
        )

        # Initialize the TLD tracker
        self.tracker = cv2.legacy.TrackerTLD_create()

        self.tracker.init(frame, tuple(map(int, bbox)))
        self.initial_w, self.initial_h = bbox[2], bbox[3]

    def track_object(self, frame, bbox, user_params=None):
        """Track object using TLD Tracker with optional user parameters."""
        if bbox:
```

```python
            if self.tracker is None:
                self.initialize_tracker(frame, bbox, user_params)

            # Update the tracker and get the new bounding box
            success, bbox = self.tracker.update(frame)
            if success:
                x1, y1, w, h = map(int, bbox)
                # Use initial dimensions if required, or directly use the tracked dimensions
                x2, y2 = x1 + w, y1 + h

                # Calculate and display the center of the bounding box
                center_x = (x1 + x2) // 2
                center_y = (y1 + y2) // 2
                self.center_listbox.insert(tk.END, f"(center_x = {center_x}, center_y = {center_y})")

                return x1, y1, x2, y2
        return None

    def update_bbox_rectangle(self, bbox):
        if bbox is not None:
            x1, y1, x2, y2 = map(int, bbox)
            if self.bbox_rect is not None:
                self.canvas.coords(self.bbox_rect, x1, y1, x2, y2)
                self.canvas.tag_raise(self.bbox_rect)  # Raise the bounding box to the front
            else:
                self.bbox_rect = self.canvas.create_rectangle(x1, y1, x2, y2, outline='#fc3d3d', width=8, tags="bbox")

    def show_frame(self):
        if self.video:
            if not self.paused:
                if 0 <= self.frame_index < len(self.video):
                    if not self.frame_processing:  # Check if the frame is already being processed
                        try:
                            self.frame_processing = True  # Set frame_processing flag to True to indicate frame processing

                            frame = self.video.get_data(self.frame_index)
                            frame = cv2.cvtColor(frame, cv2.COLOR_RGB2BGR)

                            if self.bbox is not None:
                                if not self.tracking_started:
                                    self.tracking_started = True

                                self.bbox = self.track_object(frame, self.bbox)
                                if self.bbox:
                                    frame = cv2.cvtColor(frame, cv2.COLOR_BGR2RGB)
                                    frame = Image.fromarray(frame)
                                    frame = frame.resize((frame.width * self.zoom_scale.get(), frame.height * self.zoom_scale.get()))
                                    photo = ImageTk.PhotoImage(frame)
                                    self.photo = photo
                                    self.canvas.delete("video")
                                    self.canvas.create_image(0, 0, anchor="nw", image=photo, tags="video")

                                    self.update_bbox_rectangle(self.bbox)

                            else:
                                frame = cv2.cvtColor(frame, cv2.COLOR_BGR2RGB)
                                frame = Image.fromarray(frame)
                                frame = frame.resize((frame.width * self.zoom_scale.get(), frame.height * self.zoom_scale.get()))
```

```python
                                photo = ImageTk.PhotoImage(frame)
                                self.photo = photo
                                self.canvas.delete("video")
                                self.canvas.create_image(0, 0, anchor="nw", image=photo, tags="video")

                                self.frame_number_label.config(text=f"Frame: {self.frame_index} / {self.video.count_frames()}", font=("Helvetica", 18))

                                self.frame_index += 1

                except Exception as e:
                        print("Error: ", e)
                finally:
                        self.frame_processing = False  # Reset frame_processing flag to False after processing the frame

    def on_mousewheel(self, event):
        direction = event.delta // 120
        current_value = int(self.zoom_scale.get())
        if direction == 1 and current_value < 10:
            current_value += 1
        elif direction == -1 and current_value > 1:
            current_value -= 1
        self.zoom_scale.set(current_value)
        self.update_zoom()

    def on_press(self, event):
        self.tracker = None
        self.start_x = self.canvas.canvasx(event.x)
        self.start_y = self.canvas.canvasy(event.y)
        # Clear the previous bounding box if it exists
        if self.bbox_rect:
            self.canvas.delete(self.bbox_rect)
            self.bbox_rect = None
        self.bbox = None
        self.bbox2 = None

    def on_drag(self, event):
        # Update the endpoint of the rectangle as the mouse moves
        cur_x = self.canvas.canvasx(event.x)
        cur_y = self.canvas.canvasy(event.y)

        # Define the coordinates correctly ensuring x1 < x2 and y1 < y2
        x1, y1 = min(self.start_x, cur_x), min(self.start_y, cur_y)
        x2, y2 = max(self.start_x, cur_x), max(self.start_y, cur_y)

        # Update dimensions for tracking
        self.initial_w = x2 - x1
        self.initial_h = y2 - y1
        self.bbox = (x1, y1, self.initial_w, self.initial_h)
        self.bbox2 = (self.start_x, self.start_y, cur_x, cur_y)

        # Update or create a rectangle on the canvas
        if self.bbox_rect:
            self.canvas.coords(self.bbox_rect, x1, y1, x2, y2)
        else:
            self.bbox_rect = self.canvas.create_rectangle(x1, y1, x2, y2, outline="cyan", width=6)

    def prev_frame(self):
        if self.frame_index > 0:
            self.frame_index -= 1
```

```python
            self.show_frame()

    def next_frame(self):
        if self.video and self.frame_index < len(self.video) - 1:
            self.show_frame()

    def clear_listbox(self):
        self.center_listbox.delete(0, tk.END)

    def set_window_title(self):
        if self.file_name:
            self.master.title(f"Object Tracking with TLD (Tracking, Learning, and Detection) Tracker - {self.file_name}")
            self.master.title_font = ("Helvetica", 16, "bold")
        else:
            self.master.title("Object Tracking with TLD (Tracking, Learning, and Detection) Tracker")

    def on_release(self, event):
        self.analyze_histogram()  # Call analyze_histogram() method when the mouse button is released

    def analyze_histogram(self):
        if self.bbox2 is not None and self.video:
            x1, y1, x2, y2 = map(int, self.bbox2)
            if x1 != x2 and y1 != y2:
                try:
                    frame = self.video.get_data(self.frame_index)
                    # Ensure the bounding box is within the frame boundaries
                    h, w, _ = frame.shape
                    x1, x2 = max(0, min(x1, w)), max(0, min(x2, w))
                    y1, y2 = max(0, min(y1, h)), max(0, min(y2, h))

                    # Ensure x1 < x2 and y1 < y2
                    x1, x2 = sorted([x1, x2])
                    y1, y2 = sorted([y1, y2])

                    cropped_frame = frame[y1:y2, x1:x2]
                    if cropped_frame.size > 0:
                        cropped_frame = cv2.cvtColor(cropped_frame, cv2.COLOR_BGR2RGB)

                        # Get selected filter from combobox
                        selected_filter = self.filter_combobox.get()
                        # Apply selected filter
                        filtered_frame = self.apply_filter(selected_filter, cropped_frame)

                        self.create_popup_window(filtered_frame)
                        self.display_cropped_image(filtered_frame)
                        self.display_histograms(filtered_frame)
                    else:
                        print("Cropped frame is empty.")
                except Exception as e:
                    print("Failed to process frame:", e)
            else:
                print("Bounding box dimensions are zero or negative.")

    def create_popup_window(self, cropped_frame):
        self.popup_window = tk.Toplevel(self.master)
        self.popup_window.title("Cropped Image and Its Histogram")
        self.popup_window.geometry("1500x700")


    def display_cropped_image(self, cropped_frame):
```

```
            cropped_frame_frame = tk.Frame(self.popup_window)
            cropped_frame_frame.pack(side="left")

            cropped_frame_rgb = cv2.cvtColor(cropped_frame, cv2.COLOR_BGR2RGB)
            cropped_img = Image.fromarray(cropped_frame_rgb)
            cropped_img = cropped_img.resize((600, 600))

            cropped_photo = ImageTk.PhotoImage(cropped_img)
            cropped_canvas = tk.Canvas(cropped_frame_frame, width=600, height=600)
            cropped_canvas.pack(side="left", anchor="nw")
            cropped_canvas.create_image(0, 0, anchor="nw", image=cropped_photo)
            cropped_canvas.image = cropped_photo

    def display_histograms(self, cropped_frame):
        histograms_frame = tk.Frame(self.popup_window)
        histograms_frame.pack(side="right", padx=20)

        self.display_line_histogram(cropped_frame, histograms_frame)
        self.display_bar_histogram(cropped_frame, histograms_frame)

    def display_line_histogram(self, cropped_frame, histograms_frame):
        line_histogram_frame = tk.Frame(histograms_frame)
        line_histogram_frame.pack(side="top", pady=10)

        plt.figure(figsize=(12, 4))
        color = ('r', 'g', 'b')
        for i, col in enumerate(color):
            histr = cv2.calcHist([cropped_frame], [i], None, [256], [0, 256])
            plt.plot(histr, color=col, label=f'Channel {col.upper()}', linewidth=2)
            plt.xlim([0, 256])
        plt.title('Line Histogram')
        plt.xlabel('Pixel Value')
        plt.ylabel('Frequency')
        plt.tight_layout()
        plt.grid(True)
        plt.legend()

        line_histogram_img = self.plot_to_image(plt)
        self.display_histogram_image(line_histogram_frame, line_histogram_img)

    def display_bar_histogram(self, cropped_frame, histograms_frame):
        bar_histogram_frame = tk.Frame(histograms_frame)
        bar_histogram_frame.pack(side="bottom", pady=10)

        plt.figure(figsize=(12, 4))
        color = ('r', 'g', 'b')
        for i, col in enumerate(color):
            hist_range = (0, 256)
            hist_counts, _ = np.histogram(cropped_frame[:, :, i], bins=64, range=hist_range)
            plt.bar(np.arange(64), hist_counts, color=col, alpha=0.7, label=f'Channel {col.upper()}')
            for index, value in enumerate(hist_counts):
                plt.text(index, value + 10, str(int(value)), ha='center', va='bottom', fontsize=9)

        plt.title('Bar Histogram')
        plt.xlabel('Pixel Value')
        plt.ylabel('Frequency')
        plt.xticks(np.linspace(0, 63, num=5), np.linspace(0, 255, num=5, dtype=int))  # Adjust x-axis ticks
        plt.tight_layout()
        plt.grid(True)
        plt.legend()
```

```python
        bar_histogram_img = self.plot_to_image(plt)
        self.display_histogram_image(bar_histogram_frame, bar_histogram_img)

    def display_histogram_image(self, parent_frame, img):
        histogram_photo = ImageTk.PhotoImage(image=img)
        histogram_canvas = tk.Canvas(parent_frame, width=900, height=300)
        histogram_canvas.pack(side="bottom", anchor="se")
        histogram_canvas.create_image(0, 0, anchor="nw", image=histogram_photo)
        histogram_canvas.image = histogram_photo

    def plot_histogram_bar_to_image(self, image):
        # Calculate histogram for each channel
        histograms = []
        for i in range(3):
            hist_range = (0, 256)
            hist_counts, _ = np.histogram(image[:, :, i], bins=64, range=hist_range)  # Adjust bins to 64
            histograms.append(hist_counts)

        # Extracting only 64 bins from the histogram
        num_bins = 64  # Adjusted to 64 bins

        # Generating colors for each channel
        colors = ['red', 'green', 'blue']

        plt.figure()
        for i, histogram in enumerate(histograms):
            # Normalize the histogram counts for better visualization
            hist_counts = histogram / np.sum(histogram)
            # Setting the color for each channel
            plt.bar(np.arange(num_bins), hist_counts[:num_bins], color=colors[i], alpha=0.7, label=f'Channel {["Red", "Green", "Blue"][i]}')

        plt.xlabel('Pixel Value')
        plt.ylabel('Normalized Frequency')
        plt.title('RGB Channel Histograms')
        plt.grid(True)
        plt.tight_layout()
        plt.legend()

        # Convert the histogram bar graph to an image
        histogram_bar_img = self.plot_to_image(plt)
        histogram_bar_photo = ImageTk.PhotoImage(image=histogram_bar_img)

        return histogram_bar_photo

    def plot_to_image(self, plt):
        plt.savefig('temp_plot.png')
        img = Image.open('temp_plot.png')
        return img

    def apply_filter(self, filter_name, frame):
        if filter_name == "None":
            return frame
        elif filter_name == "Gaussian":
            return cv2.GaussianBlur(frame, (5, 5), 0)
        elif filter_name == "Mean":
            return cv2.blur(frame, (5, 5))
        elif filter_name == "Median":
            return cv2.medianBlur(frame, 5)
        elif filter_name == "Bilateral Filtering":
            return cv2.bilateralFilter(frame, 9, 75, 75)
        elif filter_name == "Non-local Means Denoising":
            return cv2.fastNlMeansDenoisingColored(frame, None, 10, 10, 7, 21)
```

```python
        elif filter_name == "Anisotropic Diffusion":
            return self.anisotropic_diffusion(frame)
        elif filter_name == "Total Variation Denoising":
            return self.total_variation_denoising(frame)
        elif filter_name == "Wiener Filter":
            return self.wiener_filter(frame)
        elif filter_name == "Adaptive Thresholding":
            return self.adaptive_threshold_each_channel(frame)
        elif filter_name == "Haar Wavelet Transform":
            return self.haar_wavelet_transform(frame)
        elif filter_name == "Daubechies Wavelet Transform":
            return self.daubechies_wavelet_transform(frame)
        else:
            return frame  # Default: return original frame if filter not found

    def wiener_filter(self, frame, kernel_size=(5, 5), noise_var=0.01):
        # Check if frame is None
        if frame is None:
            print("Error: Input frame is None.")
            return None

        # Check if frame is a valid numpy array
        if not isinstance(frame, np.ndarray):
            print("Error: Input frame is not a numpy array.")
            return None

        # Check if frame is an empty array
        if frame.size == 0:
            print("Error: Input frame is empty.")
            return None

        # Check if frame is in BGR color space
        if frame.shape[-1] != 3:
            print("Error: Input frame is not in BGR color space.")
            return None

        # Apply Wiener filter
        filtered_frame = cv2.medianBlur(frame, kernel_size[0])  # Use kernel_size[0] as the kernel size
        filtered_frame = cv2.fastNlMeansDenoising(filtered_frame, h=noise_var)
        return filtered_frame

    def adaptive_threshold_each_channel(self, frame):
        # Split the frame into individual channels
        b, g, r = cv2.split(frame)

        # Apply adaptive thresholding to each channel separately
        b_thresh = cv2.adaptiveThreshold(b, 255, cv2.ADAPTIVE_THRESH_GAUSSIAN_C, cv2.THRESH_BINARY, 11, 2)
        g_thresh = cv2.adaptiveThreshold(g, 255, cv2.ADAPTIVE_THRESH_GAUSSIAN_C, cv2.THRESH_BINARY, 11, 2)
        r_thresh = cv2.adaptiveThreshold(r, 255, cv2.ADAPTIVE_THRESH_GAUSSIAN_C, cv2.THRESH_BINARY, 11, 2)

        # Merge the thresholded channels back together
        return cv2.merge([b_thresh, g_thresh, r_thresh])

    def haar_wavelet_transform(self, frame):
        # Split the frame into its individual color channels
        b, g, r = cv2.split(frame)

        # Perform the wavelet transform on each channel separately
        b_coeffs = pywt.dwt2(b, 'haar')
        g_coeffs = pywt.dwt2(g, 'haar')
```

```python
        r_coeffs = pywt.dwt2(r, 'haar')

        # Reconstruct the channels from the coefficients
        b_reconstructed = pywt.idwt2(b_coeffs, 'haar')
        g_reconstructed = pywt.idwt2(g_coeffs, 'haar')
        r_reconstructed = pywt.idwt2(r_coeffs, 'haar')

        # Clip the values to ensure they are within the valid range
        b_reconstructed = np.clip(b_reconstructed, 0, 255).astype(np.uint8)
        g_reconstructed = np.clip(g_reconstructed, 0, 255).astype(np.uint8)
        r_reconstructed = np.clip(r_reconstructed, 0, 255).astype(np.uint8)

        # Merge the channels back together
        return cv2.merge([b_reconstructed, g_reconstructed, r_reconstructed])

    def daubechies_wavelet_transform(self, frame):
        # Split the frame into its individual color channels
        b, g, r = cv2.split(frame)

        # Choose the wavelet function (Daubechies 5)
        wavelet = 'db5'

        # Perform the wavelet transform on each channel separately
        b_coeffs = pywt.dwt2(b, wavelet)
        g_coeffs = pywt.dwt2(g, wavelet)
        r_coeffs = pywt.dwt2(r, wavelet)

        # Reconstruct the channels from the coefficients
        b_reconstructed = pywt.idwt2(b_coeffs, wavelet)
        g_reconstructed = pywt.idwt2(g_coeffs, wavelet)
        r_reconstructed = pywt.idwt2(r_coeffs, wavelet)

        # Clip the values to ensure they are within the valid range
        b_reconstructed = np.clip(b_reconstructed, 0, 255).astype(np.uint8)
        g_reconstructed = np.clip(g_reconstructed, 0, 255).astype(np.uint8)
        r_reconstructed = np.clip(r_reconstructed, 0, 255).astype(np.uint8)

        # Merge the channels back together
        return cv2.merge([b_reconstructed, g_reconstructed, r_reconstructed])

    def anisotropic_diffusion(self, img):
        return cv2.fastNlMeansDenoisingColored(img, None, 10, 10, 7, 21)

    def apply_total_variation_denoising_channel(self, channel, weight, iterations):
        # Initialize the result with the original channel
        result = channel.copy().astype(np.float64)  # Convert to float64

        # Perform total variation denoising
        for _ in range(iterations):
            # Compute the gradient of the channel
            dx = cv2.Sobel(result, cv2.CV_64F, 1, 0, ksize=3)
            dy = cv2.Sobel(result, cv2.CV_64F, 0, 1, ksize=3)

            # Update the channel using the gradient and the weight
            result -= weight * np.sqrt(dx**2 + dy**2)

        # Clip the values to ensure they are within the valid range
        result = np.clip(result, 0, 255).astype(np.uint8)

        return result

    def total_variation_denoising(self, img, weight=0.01, iterations=20):
        # Split the image into its individual color channels
        b, g, r = cv2.split(img)
```

```python
        # Apply total variation denoising to each channel separately
        b_denoised = self.apply_total_variation_denoising_channel(b, weight, iterations)
        g_denoised = self.apply_total_variation_denoising_channel(g, weight, iterations)
        r_denoised = self.apply_total_variation_denoising_channel(r, weight, iterations)

        # Merge the denoised channels back together
        return cv2.merge([b_denoised, g_denoised, r_denoised])

def main():
    root = tk.Tk()
    app = TLDTracker(root)
    root.mainloop()

if __name__ == "__main__":
    main()
```

RUNNING PROGRAM

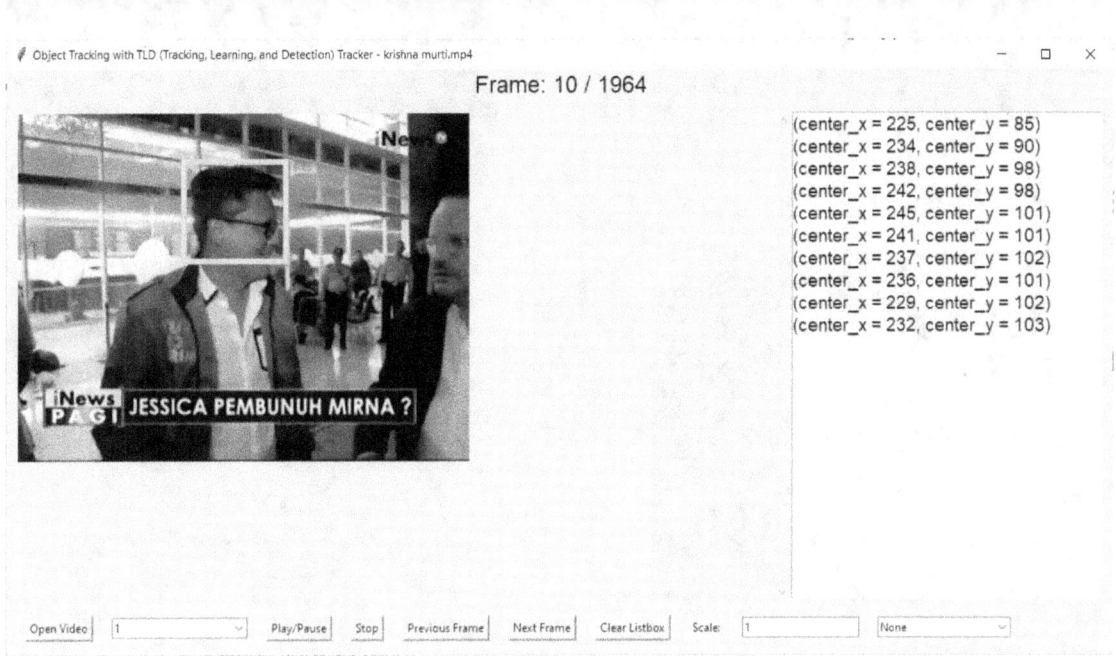

MOTION DETECTION WITH K-NEAREST NEIGHBORS (KNN)

DESCRIPTION

The given code defines a Tkinter-based application for motion detection using the K-Nearest Neighbors (KNN) background subtraction method. It also incorporates a variety of image filtering techniques for enhanced image processing and analysis. The project is structured around a MixtureofGaussiansWithFilter class that encapsulates all the functionality required for loading, playing, processing, and displaying video frames.

The application's user interface includes a main window where the video is displayed, and a control panel with buttons for opening videos, playing/pausing, stopping, and navigating through the frames. Additionally, there is a listbox for displaying detected object centers and a combobox for selecting different image filters. The canvas widget is used to draw and display the video frames, as well as any bounding boxes for detected objects.

Upon initialization, the MixtureofGaussiansWithFilter class sets up the KNN background subtractor and other necessary attributes for handling video playback and processing. The create_widgets method sets up the user interface components, including the canvas, listbox, and control panel buttons. The canvas is configured to respond to mouse events for interaction.

The open_video method allows users to load a video file using a file dialog. Once a video is selected, it is read using the imageio library, and video playback can be controlled using the play/pause, stop, and frame navigation buttons. The current frame number is displayed and updated as the video plays or when frames are navigated manually.

The play_video method manages the video playback, continuously processing and displaying frames as long as the video is not paused and there are frames left to process. Frames are processed using the process_frame method, which applies Gaussian blur, KNN background subtraction, thresholding, and contour detection to identify moving objects in the frame.

Detected objects are highlighted with bounding boxes, and their centers are displayed in the listbox. The process_frame method also handles the drawing of these bounding boxes and updating the listbox with the centers of the detected objects. The display_frame method ensures the processed frame is rendered on the canvas.

The process_and_display_frame, next_frame, and prev_frame methods provide functionality for manually navigating through the frames. This is particularly useful for frame-by-frame analysis and ensures the correct frame is displayed based on the current frame index.

The application allows users to interact with the video frames by zooming in and out using the mouse wheel and selecting regions of interest (ROIs) by drawing bounding boxes with the mouse. These ROIs can be analyzed further to extract histograms and apply various image filtering techniques.

When a bounding box is drawn, the on_release event triggers the analyze_histogram method, which processes the cropped region within the bounding box. This method ensures that the selected region is within the frame boundaries and then extracts the corresponding region from the frame.

The create_popup_window method generates a new pop-up window where the cropped image and its associated histograms will be displayed. This window provides a dedicated space for analyzing the selected region without cluttering the main interface.

Within the pop-up window, the display_cropped_image method displays the cropped region on the left side of the window, allowing users to visually inspect the selected area. The display_histograms method presents histograms of the cropped region on the right side of the window, providing insights into the pixel intensity distribution across different color channels.

The histograms are plotted using both line graphs and bar graphs, showing the frequency distribution of pixel values. These histograms aid in understanding the characteristics of the selected region and can be used for further analysis or comparison.

The image filtering functionality is integrated into the application, allowing users to apply various filters to the cropped region. Filters such as Gaussian blur, mean blur, median blur, bilateral filtering, non-local means denoising, anisotropic diffusion, total variation denoising, Wiener filter, adaptive thresholding, and wavelet transforms can be selected from a dropdown menu.

The apply_filter method applies the selected filter to the cropped region, enhancing its quality or extracting specific features. Each filter has its own implementation based on OpenCV or other image processing libraries, ensuring versatility and flexibility in image enhancement.

Overall, the application provides a comprehensive environment for motion detection, object tracking, and image analysis. It combines advanced algorithms with intuitive user interface design, empowering users to explore and understand video data effectively. Additionally, the modular structure of the code allows for easy extension and customization to suit specific research or application requirements.

SOURCE CODE

```python
#knn_with_filtering.py
import tkinter as tk
from tkinter import ttk
from tkinter import filedialog
from PIL import Image, ImageTk
import cv2
import imageio
import matplotlib.pyplot as plt
import pywt
import numpy as np

class MixtureofGaussiansWithFilter:
    def __init__(self, master):
        self.master = master
        self.master.title("Motion Detection with K-Nearest Neighbors (KNN)")
        self.bbox_rect = None  # Initialize bbox_rect attribute to None

        # Initialize the KNN background subtractor
        self.knn_subtractor = cv2.createBackgroundSubtractorKNN(detectShadows=True)

        # Video related variables
        self.video = None
        self.previous_frame = None
        self.frame_index = 0
        self.paused = True
        self.threshold = 5  # Default threshold for frame differencing

        # Creates widgets
        self.create_widgets(master)

    def create_widgets(self, master):
        # Create a frame for the canvas and listbox
        display_frame = tk.Frame(master)
        display_frame.pack(fill=tk.BOTH, expand=True)

        # Set up the canvas
        self.canvas = tk.Canvas(display_frame, width=1200, height=700)
        self.canvas.pack(side=tk.LEFT, fill=tk.BOTH, expand=True)
        self.canvas.bind("<MouseWheel>", self.on_mousewheel)
        self.canvas.bind("<ButtonPress-1>", self.on_press)
        self.canvas.bind("<B1-Motion>", self.on_drag)
        self.canvas.bind("<ButtonRelease-1>", self.on_release)  # Bind ButtonRelease event

        # Set up the listbox for displaying centers
        self.listbox = tk.Listbox(display_frame, width=40, height=20)
        self.listbox.pack(side=tk.RIGHT, fill=tk.Y)

        # Add scrollbar to the listbox
        scrollbar = tk.Scrollbar(display_frame, orient="vertical", command=self.listbox.yview)
        scrollbar.pack(side=tk.RIGHT, fill=tk.Y)
        self.listbox.config(yscrollcommand=scrollbar.set)

        # Control Panel below the display frame
        control_panel = tk.Frame(master)
        control_panel.pack(fill=tk.X)

        self.open_button = tk.Button(control_panel, text="Open Video", command=self.open_video)
        self.open_button.pack(side=tk.LEFT)
```

```python
        self.play_button = tk.Button(control_panel, text="Play/Pause", command=self.toggle_play_pause)
        self.play_button.pack(side=tk.LEFT)

        self.stop_button = tk.Button(control_panel, text="Stop", command=self.stop_video)
        self.stop_button.pack(side=tk.LEFT)

        self.prev_button = tk.Button(control_panel, text="Previous Frame", command=self.prev_frame)
        self.prev_button.pack(side=tk.LEFT)

        self.next_button = tk.Button(control_panel, text="Next Frame", command=self.next_frame)
        self.next_button.pack(side=tk.LEFT)

        # Frame number label
        self.frame_label = tk.Label(master, text="Frame: 0", font=('Helvetica', 18))
        self.frame_label.pack()

        # Threshold Control
        self.threshold_label = tk.Label(control_panel, text="Threshold:")
        self.threshold_label.pack(side=tk.LEFT)

        self.threshold_entry = tk.Entry(control_panel, width=5)
        self.threshold_entry.pack(side=tk.LEFT)
        self.threshold_entry.insert(0, '1')  # Default threshold value
        self.threshold_entry.bind("<Return>", self.update_threshold)

        # Available filters
        self.filters = ["None", "Gaussian", "Mean", "Median", "Bilateral Filtering",
                        "Non-local Means Denoising", "Anisotropic Diffusion",
                        "Total Variation Denoising", "Wiener Filter",
                        "Adaptive Thresholding", "Haar Wavelet Transform",
                        "Daubechies Wavelet Transform"]

        # Subframe for complex controls such as combobox
        filter_frame = tk.Frame(control_panel)
        filter_frame.pack(side=tk.LEFT, fill=tk.X, expand=True)

        # Combobox for Selecting Filters
        self.filter_combobox = ttk.Combobox(filter_frame, values=self.filters)
        self.filter_combobox.pack(side=tk.LEFT, padx=10, pady=5)
        self.filter_combobox.current(0)  # Set default value

    def update_threshold(self, event):
        try:
            self.threshold = int(self.threshold_entry.get())
            print(f"Threshold updated to {self.threshold}")
        except ValueError:
            print("Invalid input for threshold. Please enter an integer.")

    def open_video(self):
        video_path = filedialog.askopenfilename(filetypes=[("Video files", "*.mp4;*.avi;*.mkv;*.wmv")])
        if video_path:
            self.video = imageio.get_reader(video_path)
            self.frame_index = 0
            self.previous_frame = None
            self.paused = False
            self.play_video()
            self.update_frame_label()

    def toggle_play_pause(self):
        self.paused = not self.paused
        if not self.paused:
```

```python
            self.play_video()

    def stop_video(self):
        self.paused = True
        self.frame_index = 0
        self.previous_frame = None
        self.update_frame_label()
        self.display_frame(None)  # Clear the canvas

    def play_video(self):
        if not self.paused and self.video:
            if self.frame_index < len(self.video):
                try:
                    frame_data = self.video.get_data(self.frame_index)
                    frame = cv2.cvtColor(frame_data, cv2.COLOR_RGB2BGR)
                    self.process_frame(frame)
                    self.frame_index += 1
                    self.master.after(42, self.play_video)  # Schedule next frame
                except IndexError:
                    print("Reached the end of the video.")
                    self.paused = True  # Stop the video playback
                self.update_frame_label()

    def process_frame(self, frame):
        gray = cv2.cvtColor(frame, cv2.COLOR_BGR2GRAY)
        gray = cv2.GaussianBlur(gray, (11, 11), 0)  # Blur to reduce noise

        # Apply the KNN model to get the foreground mask
        fg_mask = self.knn_subtractor.apply(gray)

        # Optional: apply additional threshold to clean up the foreground mask
        _, fg_mask = cv2.threshold(fg_mask, self.threshold, 255, cv2.THRESH_BINARY)

        # Dilate the thresholded image to fill in holes, helping in better contour detection
        fg_mask = cv2.dilate(fg_mask, None, iterations=2)

        # Find contours on the thresholded image to detect moving objects
        contours, _ = cv2.findContours(fg_mask, cv2.RETR_EXTERNAL, cv2.CHAIN_APPROX_SIMPLE)

        self.listbox.delete(0, tk.END)  # Clear existing entries in the listbox
        box_number = 0  # Initialize box number

        # Loop over the contours
        for contour in contours:
            if cv2.contourArea(contour) < 500:
                continue  # Ignore small contours
            box_number += 1  # Increment the box number for each contour
            (x, y, w, h) = cv2.boundingRect(contour)
            center_x, center_y = x + w // 2, y + h // 2
            cv2.rectangle(frame, (x, y), (x+w, y+h), (50, 0, 255), 2)
            self.listbox.insert(tk.END, f"Box {box_number}: Center ({center_x}, {center_y})")
            cv2.putText(frame, f"{box_number}", (x + 5, y + 20), cv2.FONT_HERSHEY_SIMPLEX, 0.6, (0, 255, 0), 2)

        self.display_frame(frame)

    def display_frame(self, frame):
        if frame is not None:
            image = cv2.cvtColor(frame, cv2.COLOR_BGR2RGB)
            image = Image.fromarray(image)
            photo = ImageTk.PhotoImage(image=image)
            self.canvas.create_image(0, 0, anchor=tk.NW, image=photo)
            self.canvas.image = photo  # Keep the reference
        else:
```

```python
            self.canvas.delete("all")

    def process_and_display_frame(self):
        if self.video and self.frame_index >= 0 and self.frame_index < len(self.video):
            try:
                frame_data = self.video.get_data(self.frame_index)
                frame = cv2.cvtColor(frame_data, cv2.COLOR_RGB2BGR)
                self.process_frame(frame)
            except IndexError:
                print(f"Frame index {self.frame_index} is out of range.")
                self.paused = True  # Pause to prevent further errors
            except Exception as e:
                print(f"Error processing frame: {e}")
                self.paused = True
        self.update_frame_label()

    def next_frame(self):
        if self.video and self.frame_index < len(self.video) - 1:  # Check if next frame exists
            self.frame_index += 1
            self.process_and_display_frame()
        else:
            print("No more frames to display.")
            self.paused = True

    def prev_frame(self):
        if self.video and self.frame_index > 0:
            self.frame_index -= 1
            self.process_and_display_frame()
        else:
            print("Already at the first frame.")
            self.paused = True


    def update_frame_label(self):
        self.frame_label.config(text=f"Frame: {self.frame_index}")

    def on_mousewheel(self, event):
        direction = event.delta // 120
        current_value = int(self.zoom_scale.get())
        if direction == 1 and current_value < 10:
            current_value += 1
        elif direction == -1 and current_value > 1:
            current_value -= 1
        self.zoom_scale.set(current_value)
        self.update_zoom()

    def on_press(self, event):
        self.tracker = None
        self.start_x = self.canvas.canvasx(event.x)
        self.start_y = self.canvas.canvasy(event.y)
        # Clear the previous bounding box if it exists
        if self.bbox_rect:
            self.canvas.delete(self.bbox_rect)
            self.bbox_rect = None
        self.bbox = None
        self.bbox2 = None

    def on_drag(self, event):
        # Update the endpoint of the rectangle as the mouse moves
        cur_x = self.canvas.canvasx(event.x)
        cur_y = self.canvas.canvasy(event.y)

        # Define the coordinates correctly ensuring x1 < x2 and y1 < y2
```

```python
            x1, y1 = min(self.start_x, cur_x), min(self.start_y, cur_y)
            x2, y2 = max(self.start_x, cur_x), max(self.start_y, cur_y)

            # Update dimensions for tracking
            self.initial_w = x2 - x1
            self.initial_h = y2 - y1
            self.bbox = (x1, y1, self.initial_w, self.initial_h)
            self.bbox2 = (self.start_x, self.start_y, cur_x, cur_y)

            # Update or create a rectangle on the canvas
            if self.bbox_rect:
                self.canvas.coords(self.bbox_rect, x1, y1, x2, y2)
            else:
                self.bbox_rect = self.canvas.create_rectangle(x1, y1, x2, y2, outline="cyan", width=6)

    def on_release(self, event):
        self.analyze_histogram()  # Call analyze_histogram() method when the mouse button is released

    def analyze_histogram(self):
        if self.bbox2 is not None and self.video:
            x1, y1, x2, y2 = map(int, self.bbox2)
            if x1 != x2 and y1 != y2:
                try:
                    frame = self.video.get_data(self.frame_index)
                    # Ensure the bounding box is within the frame boundaries
                    h, w, _ = frame.shape
                    x1, x2 = max(0, min(x1, w)), max(0, min(x2, w))
                    y1, y2 = max(0, min(y1, h)), max(0, min(y2, h))

                    # Ensure x1 < x2 and y1 < y2
                    x1, x2 = sorted([x1, x2])
                    y1, y2 = sorted([y1, y2])

                    cropped_frame = frame[y1:y2, x1:x2]
                    if cropped_frame.size > 0:
                        cropped_frame = cv2.cvtColor(cropped_frame, cv2.COLOR_BGR2RGB)

                        # Get selected filter from combobox
                        selected_filter = self.filter_combobox.get()
                        # Apply selected filter
                        filtered_frame = self.apply_filter(selected_filter, cropped_frame)

                        self.create_popup_window(filtered_frame)
                        self.display_cropped_image(filtered_frame)
                        self.display_histograms(filtered_frame)
                    else:
                        print("Cropped frame is empty.")
                except Exception as e:
                    print("Failed to process frame:", e)
            else:
                print("Bounding box dimensions are zero or negative.")

    def create_popup_window(self, cropped_frame):
        self.popup_window = tk.Toplevel(self.master)
        self.popup_window.title("Cropped Image and Its Histogram")
        self.popup_window.geometry("1500x700")


    def display_cropped_image(self, cropped_frame):
        cropped_frame_frame = tk.Frame(self.popup_window)
        cropped_frame_frame.pack(side="left")
```

```python
            cropped_frame_rgb = cv2.cvtColor(cropped_frame, cv2.COLOR_BGR2RGB)
            cropped_img = Image.fromarray(cropped_frame_rgb)
            cropped_img = cropped_img.resize((600, 600))

            cropped_photo = ImageTk.PhotoImage(cropped_img)
            cropped_canvas = tk.Canvas(cropped_frame_frame, width=600, height=600)
            cropped_canvas.pack(side="left", anchor="nw")
            cropped_canvas.create_image(0, 0, anchor="nw", image=cropped_photo)
            cropped_canvas.image = cropped_photo

    def display_histograms(self, cropped_frame):
        histograms_frame = tk.Frame(self.popup_window)
        histograms_frame.pack(side="right", padx=20)

        self.display_line_histogram(cropped_frame, histograms_frame)
        self.display_bar_histogram(cropped_frame, histograms_frame)

    def display_line_histogram(self, cropped_frame, histograms_frame):
        line_histogram_frame = tk.Frame(histograms_frame)
        line_histogram_frame.pack(side="top", pady=10)

        plt.figure(figsize=(12, 4))
        color = ('r', 'g', 'b')
        for i, col in enumerate(color):
            histr = cv2.calcHist([cropped_frame], [i], None, [256], [0, 256])
            plt.plot(histr, color=col, label=f'Channel {col.upper()}', linewidth=2)
            plt.xlim([0, 256])
        plt.title('Line Histogram')
        plt.xlabel('Pixel Value')
        plt.ylabel('Frequency')
        plt.tight_layout()
        plt.grid(True)
        plt.legend()

        line_histogram_img = self.plot_to_image(plt)
        self.display_histogram_image(line_histogram_frame, line_histogram_img)

    def display_bar_histogram(self, cropped_frame, histograms_frame):
        bar_histogram_frame = tk.Frame(histograms_frame)
        bar_histogram_frame.pack(side="bottom", pady=10)

        plt.figure(figsize=(12, 4))
        color = ('r', 'g', 'b')
        for i, col in enumerate(color):
            hist_range = (0, 256)
            hist_counts, _ = np.histogram(cropped_frame[:, :, i], bins=64, range=hist_range)
            plt.bar(np.arange(64), hist_counts, color=col, alpha=0.7, label=f'Channel {col.upper()}')
            for index, value in enumerate(hist_counts):
                plt.text(index, value + 10, str(int(value)), ha='center', va='bottom', fontsize=9)

        plt.title('Bar Histogram')
        plt.xlabel('Pixel Value')
        plt.ylabel('Frequency')
        plt.xticks(np.linspace(0, 63, num=5), np.linspace(0, 255, num=5, dtype=int))  # Adjust x-axis ticks
        plt.tight_layout()
        plt.grid(True)
        plt.legend()

        bar_histogram_img = self.plot_to_image(plt)
        self.display_histogram_image(bar_histogram_frame, bar_histogram_img)
```

```python
    def display_histogram_image(self, parent_frame, img):
        histogram_photo = ImageTk.PhotoImage(image=img)
        histogram_canvas = tk.Canvas(parent_frame, width=900, height=300)
        histogram_canvas.pack(side="bottom", anchor="se")
        histogram_canvas.create_image(0, 0, anchor="nw", image=histogram_photo)
        histogram_canvas.image = histogram_photo

    def plot_histogram_bar_to_image(self, image):
        # Calculate histogram for each channel
        histograms = []
        for i in range(3):
            hist_range = (0, 256)
            hist_counts, _ = np.histogram(image[:, :, i], bins=64, range=hist_range)  # Adjust bins to 64
            histograms.append(hist_counts)

        # Extracting only 64 bins from the histogram
        num_bins = 64  # Adjusted to 64 bins

        # Generating colors for each channel
        colors = ['red', 'green', 'blue']

        plt.figure()
        for i, histogram in enumerate(histograms):
            # Normalize the histogram counts for better visualization
            hist_counts = histogram / np.sum(histogram)
            # Setting the color for each channel
            plt.bar(np.arange(num_bins), hist_counts[:num_bins], color=colors[i], alpha=0.7, label=f'Channel {["Red", "Green", "Blue"][i]}')

        plt.xlabel('Pixel Value')
        plt.ylabel('Normalized Frequency')
        plt.title('RGB Channel Histograms')
        plt.grid(True)
        plt.tight_layout()
        plt.legend()

        # Convert the histogram bar graph to an image
        histogram_bar_img = self.plot_to_image(plt)
        histogram_bar_photo = ImageTk.PhotoImage(image=histogram_bar_img)

        return histogram_bar_photo

    def plot_to_image(self, plt):
        plt.savefig('temp_plot.png')
        img = Image.open('temp_plot.png')
        return img

    def apply_filter(self, filter_name, frame):
        if filter_name == "None":
            return frame
        elif filter_name == "Gaussian":
            return cv2.GaussianBlur(frame, (5, 5), 0)
        elif filter_name == "Mean":
            return cv2.blur(frame, (5, 5))
        elif filter_name == "Median":
            return cv2.medianBlur(frame, 5)
        elif filter_name == "Bilateral Filtering":
            return cv2.bilateralFilter(frame, 9, 75, 75)
        elif filter_name == "Non-local Means Denoising":
            return cv2.fastNlMeansDenoisingColored(frame, None, 10, 10, 7, 21)
        elif filter_name == "Anisotropic Diffusion":
            return self.anisotropic_diffusion(frame)
```

```python
        elif filter_name == "Total Variation Denoising":
            return self.total_variation_denoising(frame)
        elif filter_name == "Wiener Filter":
            return self.wiener_filter(frame)
        elif filter_name == "Adaptive Thresholding":
            return self.adaptive_threshold_each_channel(frame)
        elif filter_name == "Haar Wavelet Transform":
            return self.haar_wavelet_transform(frame)
        elif filter_name == "Daubechies Wavelet Transform":
            return self.daubechies_wavelet_transform(frame)
        else:
            return frame  # Default: return original frame if filter not found

    def wiener_filter(self, frame, kernel_size=(5, 5), noise_var=0.01):
        # Check if frame is None
        if frame is None:
            print("Error: Input frame is None.")
            return None

        # Check if frame is a valid numpy array
        if not isinstance(frame, np.ndarray):
            print("Error: Input frame is not a numpy array.")
            return None

        # Check if frame is an empty array
        if frame.size == 0:
            print("Error: Input frame is empty.")
            return None

        # Check if frame is in BGR color space
        if frame.shape[-1] != 3:
            print("Error: Input frame is not in BGR color space.")
            return None

        # Apply Wiener filter
        filtered_frame = cv2.medianBlur(frame, kernel_size[0])  # Use kernel_size[0] as the kernel size
        filtered_frame = cv2.fastNlMeansDenoising(filtered_frame, h=noise_var)
        return filtered_frame

    def adaptive_threshold_each_channel(self, frame):
        frame = self.total_variation_denoising(frame)
        # Split the frame into individual channels
        b, g, r = cv2.split(frame)

        # Apply adaptive thresholding to each channel separately
        b_thresh = cv2.adaptiveThreshold(b, 255, cv2.ADAPTIVE_THRESH_GAUSSIAN_C, cv2.THRESH_BINARY, 199, 2)
        g_thresh = cv2.adaptiveThreshold(g, 255, cv2.ADAPTIVE_THRESH_GAUSSIAN_C, cv2.THRESH_BINARY, 199, 2)
        r_thresh = cv2.adaptiveThreshold(r, 255, cv2.ADAPTIVE_THRESH_GAUSSIAN_C, cv2.THRESH_BINARY, 199, 2)

        # Merge the thresholded channels back together
        return cv2.merge([b_thresh, g_thresh, r_thresh])

    def haar_wavelet_transform(self, frame):
        # Split the frame into its individual color channels
        b, g, r = cv2.split(frame)

        # Perform the wavelet transform on each channel separately
        b_coeffs = pywt.dwt2(b, 'haar')
        g_coeffs = pywt.dwt2(g, 'haar')
        r_coeffs = pywt.dwt2(r, 'haar')
```

```python
        # Reconstruct the channels from the coefficients
        b_reconstructed = pywt.idwt2(b_coeffs, 'haar')
        g_reconstructed = pywt.idwt2(g_coeffs, 'haar')
        r_reconstructed = pywt.idwt2(r_coeffs, 'haar')

        # Clip the values to ensure they are within the valid range
        b_reconstructed = np.clip(b_reconstructed, 0, 255).astype(np.uint8)
        g_reconstructed = np.clip(g_reconstructed, 0, 255).astype(np.uint8)
        r_reconstructed = np.clip(r_reconstructed, 0, 255).astype(np.uint8)

        # Merge the channels back together
        return cv2.merge([b_reconstructed, g_reconstructed, r_reconstructed])

    def daubechies_wavelet_transform(self, frame):
        # Split the frame into its individual color channels
        b, g, r = cv2.split(frame)

        # Choose the wavelet function (Daubechies 5)
        wavelet = 'db5'

        # Perform the wavelet transform on each channel separately
        b_coeffs = pywt.dwt2(b, wavelet)
        g_coeffs = pywt.dwt2(g, wavelet)
        r_coeffs = pywt.dwt2(r, wavelet)

        # Reconstruct the channels from the coefficients
        b_reconstructed = pywt.idwt2(b_coeffs, wavelet)
        g_reconstructed = pywt.idwt2(g_coeffs, wavelet)
        r_reconstructed = pywt.idwt2(r_coeffs, wavelet)

        # Clip the values to ensure they are within the valid range
        b_reconstructed = np.clip(b_reconstructed, 0, 255).astype(np.uint8)
        g_reconstructed = np.clip(g_reconstructed, 0, 255).astype(np.uint8)
        r_reconstructed = np.clip(r_reconstructed, 0, 255).astype(np.uint8)

        # Merge the channels back together
        return cv2.merge([b_reconstructed, g_reconstructed, r_reconstructed])

    def anisotropic_diffusion(self, img):
        return cv2.fastNlMeansDenoisingColored(img, None, 10, 10, 7, 21)

    def apply_total_variation_denoising_channel(self, channel, weight, iterations):
        # Initialize the result with the original channel
        result = channel.copy().astype(np.float64)  # Convert to float64

        # Perform total variation denoising
        for _ in range(iterations):
            # Compute the gradient of the channel
            dx = cv2.Sobel(result, cv2.CV_64F, 1, 0, ksize=3)
            dy = cv2.Sobel(result, cv2.CV_64F, 0, 1, ksize=3)

            # Update the channel using the gradient and the weight
            result -= weight * np.sqrt(dx**2 + dy**2)

        # Clip the values to ensure they are within the valid range
        result = np.clip(result, 0, 255).astype(np.uint8)

        return result

    def total_variation_denoising(self, img, weight=0.01, iterations=20):
        # Split the image into its individual color channels
        b, g, r = cv2.split(img)
```

```python
        # Apply total variation denoising to each channel separately
        b_denoised = self.apply_total_variation_denoising_channel(b, weight, iterations)
        g_denoised = self.apply_total_variation_denoising_channel(g, weight, iterations)
        r_denoised = self.apply_total_variation_denoising_channel(r, weight, iterations)

        # Merge the denoised channels back together
        return cv2.merge([b_denoised, g_denoised, r_denoised])
def main():
    root = tk.Tk()
    app = MixtureofGaussiansWithFilter(root)
    root.mainloop()

if __name__ == "__main__":
    main()
```

RUNNING PROGRAM

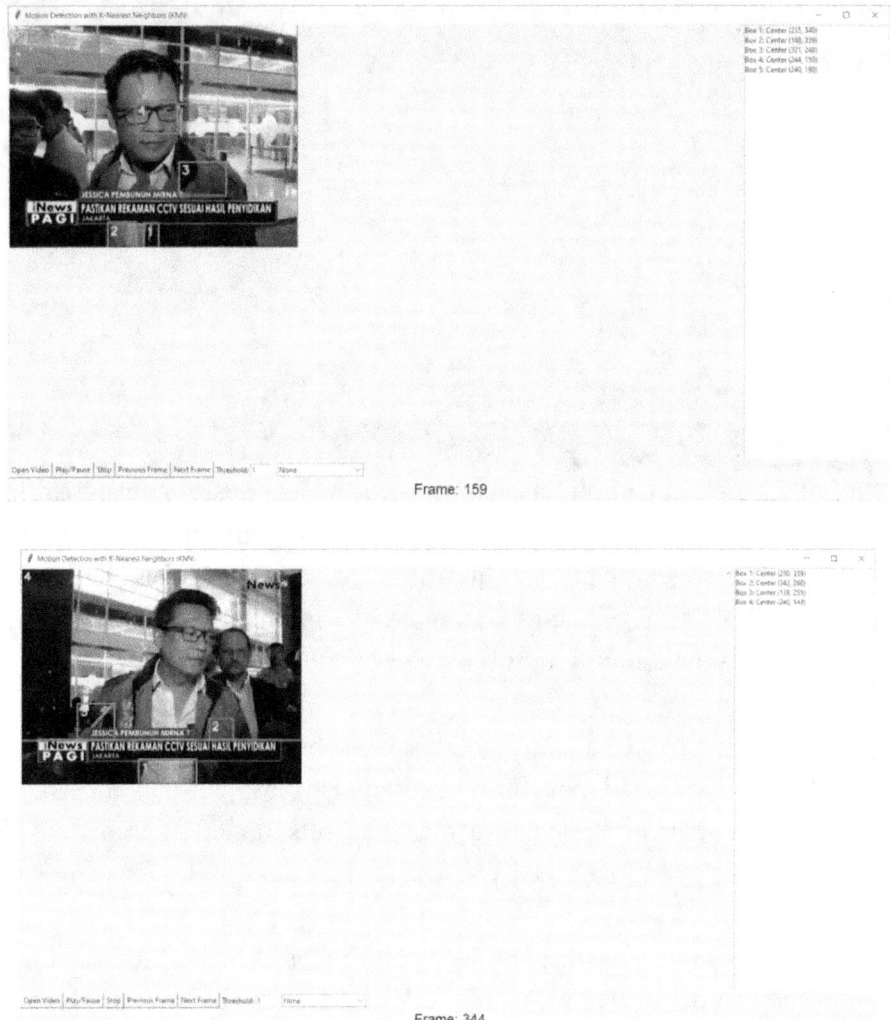

MOTION DETECTION WITH MIXTURE OF GAUSSIANS (MOG)

DESCRIPTION

The "Mixture of Gaussians with Filtering" project is a Python script designed for motion detection in videos using the Mixture of Gaussians (MOG) algorithm along with various filtering techniques. The script utilizes libraries such as tkinter for GUI, OpenCV for image processing, PIL for image manipulation, imageio for reading video files, matplotlib for plotting histograms, and numpy for numerical operations.

The script defines a class named MixtureofGaussiansWithFilter, which serves as the main controller for the application. Upon initialization, the class sets up the GUI window, initializes the MOG2 background subtractor, and sets default parameters for video processing.

The GUI consists of a canvas for displaying video frames, a listbox for displaying object centers, and control buttons for video playback and frame navigation. Users can open video files, play/pause video playback, stop video, and navigate through frames using the provided buttons.

Additionally, users can adjust the threshold for motion detection and select various filtering techniques from a dropdown menu (combobox). Available filters include Gaussian blur, mean blur, median blur, bilateral filtering, non-local means denoising, anisotropic diffusion, total variation denoising, Wiener filter, adaptive thresholding, Haar wavelet transform, and Daubechies wavelet transform.

The script utilizes the MOG2 background subtractor to detect motion in video frames. After background subtraction, additional thresholding and contour detection are applied to identify moving objects. Detected objects are outlined on the video frame, and their centers are displayed in the listbox.

Furthermore, users can draw bounding boxes on the video frame to analyze histograms of selected regions. Histograms are displayed in a separate popup window, showing both line and bar representations of pixel intensities for the selected region.

The script provides implementations for various filtering techniques, including Gaussian blur, mean blur, median blur, bilateral filtering, non-local means denoising, anisotropic diffusion, total variation denoising, Wiener filter, adaptive thresholding, Haar wavelet transform, and Daubechies wavelet transform. These filters can be applied to the selected region within the bounding box to visualize their effects on the image and histogram.

Overall, the "Mixture of Gaussians with Filtering" project offers a comprehensive toolset for motion detection and analysis in videos, allowing users to explore different filtering techniques for noise reduction and image enhancement.

SOURCE CODE

```
#mixture_of_gaussian_with_filtering.py
import tkinter as tk
from tkinter import ttk
from tkinter import filedialog
from PIL import Image, ImageTk
import cv2
import imageio
import matplotlib.pyplot as plt
import pywt
import numpy as np
```

```python
class MixtureofGaussiansWithFilter:
    def __init__(self, master):
        self.master = master
        self.master.title("Motion Detection with Mixture of Gaussians (MOG)")
        self.bbox_rect = None  # Initialize bbox_rect attribute to None

        # Initialize the MOG2 background subtractor
        self.mog2 = cv2.createBackgroundSubtractorMOG2(history=500, varThreshold=25, detectShadows=True)

        # Video related variables
        self.video = None
        self.previous_frame = None
        self.frame_index = 0
        self.paused = True
        self.threshold = 5  # Default threshold for frame differencing

        # Creates widgets
        self.create_widgets(master)

    def create_widgets(self, master):
        # Create a frame for the canvas and listbox
        display_frame = tk.Frame(master)
        display_frame.pack(fill=tk.BOTH, expand=True)

        # Set up the canvas
        self.canvas = tk.Canvas(display_frame, width=800, height=600)
        self.canvas.pack(side=tk.LEFT, fill=tk.BOTH, expand=True)
        self.canvas.bind("<MouseWheel>", self.on_mousewheel)
        self.canvas.bind("<ButtonPress-1>", self.on_press)
        self.canvas.bind("<B1-Motion>", self.on_drag)
        self.canvas.bind("<ButtonRelease-1>", self.on_release)  # Bind ButtonRelease event

        # Set up the listbox for displaying centers
        self.listbox = tk.Listbox(display_frame, width=40, height=20)
        self.listbox.pack(side=tk.RIGHT, fill=tk.Y)

        # Add scrollbar to the listbox
        scrollbar = tk.Scrollbar(display_frame, orient="vertical", command=self.listbox.yview)
        scrollbar.pack(side=tk.RIGHT, fill=tk.Y)
        self.listbox.config(yscrollcommand=scrollbar.set)

        # Control Panel below the display frame
        control_panel = tk.Frame(master)
        control_panel.pack(fill=tk.X)

        self.open_button = tk.Button(control_panel, text="Open Video", command=self.open_video)
        self.open_button.pack(side=tk.LEFT)

        self.play_button = tk.Button(control_panel, text="Play/Pause", command=self.toggle_play_pause)
        self.play_button.pack(side=tk.LEFT)

        self.stop_button = tk.Button(control_panel, text="Stop", command=self.stop_video)
        self.stop_button.pack(side=tk.LEFT)

        self.prev_button = tk.Button(control_panel, text="Previous Frame", command=self.prev_frame)
        self.prev_button.pack(side=tk.LEFT)

        self.next_button = tk.Button(control_panel, text="Next Frame", command=self.next_frame)
        self.next_button.pack(side=tk.LEFT)
```

```python
        # Frame number label
        self.frame_label = tk.Label(master, text="Frame: 0", font=('Helvetica', 18))
        self.frame_label.pack()

        # Threshold Control
        self.threshold_label = tk.Label(control_panel, text="Threshold:")
        self.threshold_label.pack(side=tk.LEFT)

        self.threshold_entry = tk.Entry(control_panel, width=5)
        self.threshold_entry.pack(side=tk.LEFT)
        self.threshold_entry.insert(0, '5')  # Default threshold value
        self.threshold_entry.bind("<Return>", self.update_threshold)

        # Available filters
        self.filters = ["None", "Gaussian", "Mean", "Median", "Bilateral Filtering",
                    "Non-local Means Denoising", "Anisotropic Diffusion",
                    "Total Variation Denoising", "Wiener Filter",
                    "Adaptive Thresholding", "Haar Wavelet Transform",
                    "Daubechies Wavelet Transform"]

        # Subframe for complex controls such as combobox
        filter_frame = tk.Frame(control_panel)
        filter_frame.pack(side=tk.LEFT, fill=tk.X, expand=True)

        # Combobox for Selecting Filters
        self.filter_combobox = ttk.Combobox(filter_frame, values=self.filters)
        self.filter_combobox.pack(side=tk.LEFT, padx=10, pady=5)
        self.filter_combobox.current(0)  # Set default value

    def update_threshold(self, event):
        try:
            self.threshold = int(self.threshold_entry.get())
            print(f"Threshold updated to {self.threshold}")
        except ValueError:
            print("Invalid input for threshold. Please enter an integer.")

    def open_video(self):
        video_path = filedialog.askopenfilename(filetypes=[("Video files",
"*.mp4;*.avi;*.mkv;*.wmv")])
        if video_path:
            self.video = imageio.get_reader(video_path)
            self.frame_index = 0
            self.previous_frame = None
            self.paused = False
            self.play_video()
            self.update_frame_label()

    def toggle_play_pause(self):
        self.paused = not self.paused
        if not self.paused:
            self.play_video()

    def stop_video(self):
        self.paused = True
        self.frame_index = 0
        self.previous_frame = None
        self.update_frame_label()
        self.display_frame(None)  # Clear the canvas

    def play_video(self):
        if not self.paused and self.video:
            if self.frame_index < len(self.video):
                try:
                    frame_data = self.video.get_data(self.frame_index)
```

```python
                frame = cv2.cvtColor(frame_data, cv2.COLOR_RGB2BGR)
                self.process_frame(frame)
                self.frame_index += 1
                self.master.after(42, self.play_video)  # Schedule next frame
            except IndexError:
                print("Reached the end of the video.")
                self.paused = True  # Stop the video playback
        self.update_frame_label()

    def process_frame(self, frame):
        # Convert the frame to grayscale (optional based on approach)
        gray = cv2.cvtColor(frame, cv2.COLOR_BGR2GRAY)
        gray = cv2.GaussianBlur(gray, (21, 21), 0)  # Blur to reduce noise

        # Apply the MOG2 model to get the foreground mask
        fg_mask = self.mog2.apply(gray)

        # Optional: apply additional threshold to clean up the foreground mask
        _, fg_mask = cv2.threshold(fg_mask, self.threshold, 255, cv2.THRESH_BINARY)

        # Find contours on the thresholded image to detect moving objects
        contours, _ = cv2.findContours(fg_mask, cv2.RETR_EXTERNAL, cv2.CHAIN_APPROX_SIMPLE)

        self.listbox.delete(0, tk.END)  # Clear existing entries in the listbox
        box_number = 0  # Initialize box number

        # Loop over the contours
        for contour in contours:
            if cv2.contourArea(contour) < 500:
                continue  # Ignore small contours
            box_number += 1  # Increment the box number for each contour
            (x, y, w, h) = cv2.boundingRect(contour)
            center_x, center_y = x + w // 2, y + h // 2
            cv2.rectangle(frame, (x, y), (x+w, y+h), (50, 0, 255), 2)
            self.listbox.insert(tk.END, f"Box {box_number}: Center ({center_x}, {center_y})")
            cv2.rectangle(frame, (x, y), (x+w, y+h), (50, 0, 255), 2)
            cv2.putText(frame, f"{box_number}", (x + 5, y + 20), cv2.FONT_HERSHEY_SIMPLEX,
0.6, (0, 255, 0), 2)
        self.display_frame(frame)

    def display_frame(self, frame):
        if frame is not None:
            image = cv2.cvtColor(frame, cv2.COLOR_BGR2RGB)
            image = Image.fromarray(image)
            photo = ImageTk.PhotoImage(image=image)
            self.canvas.create_image(0, 0, anchor=tk.NW, image=photo)
            self.canvas.image = photo  # Keep the reference
        else:
            self.canvas.delete("all")

    def process_and_display_frame(self):
        if self.video and self.frame_index >= 0 and self.frame_index < len(self.video):
            try:
                frame_data = self.video.get_data(self.frame_index)
                frame = cv2.cvtColor(frame_data, cv2.COLOR_RGB2BGR)
                self.process_frame(frame)
            except IndexError:
                print(f"Frame index {self.frame_index} is out of range.")
                self.paused = True  # Pause to prevent further errors
            except Exception as e:
                print(f"Error processing frame: {e}")
                self.paused = True
        self.update_frame_label()
```

```python
    def next_frame(self):
        if self.video and self.frame_index < len(self.video) - 1:  # Check if next frame exists
            self.frame_index += 1
            self.process_and_display_frame()
        else:
            print("No more frames to display.")
            self.paused = True

    def prev_frame(self):
        if self.video and self.frame_index > 0:
            self.frame_index -= 1
            self.process_and_display_frame()
        else:
            print("Already at the first frame.")
            self.paused = True


    def update_frame_label(self):
        self.frame_label.config(text=f"Frame: {self.frame_index}")

    def on_mousewheel(self, event):
        direction = event.delta // 120
        current_value = int(self.zoom_scale.get())
        if direction == 1 and current_value < 10:
            current_value += 1
        elif direction == -1 and current_value > 1:
            current_value -= 1
        self.zoom_scale.set(current_value)
        self.update_zoom()

    def on_press(self, event):
        self.tracker = None
        self.start_x = self.canvas.canvasx(event.x)
        self.start_y = self.canvas.canvasy(event.y)
        # Clear the previous bounding box if it exists
        if self.bbox_rect:
            self.canvas.delete(self.bbox_rect)
            self.bbox_rect = None
        self.bbox = None
        self.bbox2 = None

    def on_drag(self, event):
        # Update the endpoint of the rectangle as the mouse moves
        cur_x = self.canvas.canvasx(event.x)
        cur_y = self.canvas.canvasy(event.y)

        # Define the coordinates correctly ensuring x1 < x2 and y1 < y2
        x1, y1 = min(self.start_x, cur_x), min(self.start_y, cur_y)
        x2, y2 = max(self.start_x, cur_x), max(self.start_y, cur_y)

        # Update dimensions for tracking
        self.initial_w = x2 - x1
        self.initial_h = y2 - y1
        self.bbox = (x1, y1, self.initial_w, self.initial_h)
        self.bbox2 = (self.start_x, self.start_y, cur_x, cur_y)

        # Update or create a rectangle on the canvas
        if self.bbox_rect:
            self.canvas.coords(self.bbox_rect, x1, y1, x2, y2)
        else:
            self.bbox_rect = self.canvas.create_rectangle(x1, y1, x2, y2, outline="cyan", width=6)
```

```python
    def on_release(self, event):
        self.analyze_histogram()  # Call analyze_histogram() method when the mouse button is released

    def analyze_histogram(self):
        if self.bbox2 is not None and self.video:
            x1, y1, x2, y2 = map(int, self.bbox2)
            if x1 != x2 and y1 != y2:
                try:
                    frame = self.video.get_data(self.frame_index)
                    # Ensure the bounding box is within the frame boundaries
                    h, w, _ = frame.shape
                    x1, x2 = max(0, min(x1, w)), max(0, min(x2, w))
                    y1, y2 = max(0, min(y1, h)), max(0, min(y2, h))

                    # Ensure x1 < x2 and y1 < y2
                    x1, x2 = sorted([x1, x2])
                    y1, y2 = sorted([y1, y2])

                    cropped_frame = frame[y1:y2, x1:x2]
                    if cropped_frame.size > 0:
                        cropped_frame = cv2.cvtColor(cropped_frame, cv2.COLOR_BGR2RGB)

                        # Get selected filter from combobox
                        selected_filter = self.filter_combobox.get()
                        # Apply selected filter
                        filtered_frame = self.apply_filter(selected_filter, cropped_frame)

                        self.create_popup_window(filtered_frame)
                        self.display_cropped_image(filtered_frame)
                        self.display_histograms(filtered_frame)
                    else:
                        print("Cropped frame is empty.")
                except Exception as e:
                    print("Failed to process frame:", e)
            else:
                print("Bounding box dimensions are zero or negative.")

    def create_popup_window(self, cropped_frame):
        self.popup_window = tk.Toplevel(self.master)
        self.popup_window.title("Cropped Image and Its Histogram")
        self.popup_window.geometry("1500x700")


    def display_cropped_image(self, cropped_frame):
        cropped_frame_frame = tk.Frame(self.popup_window)
        cropped_frame_frame.pack(side="left")

        cropped_frame_rgb = cv2.cvtColor(cropped_frame, cv2.COLOR_BGR2RGB)
        cropped_img = Image.fromarray(cropped_frame_rgb)
        cropped_img = cropped_img.resize((600, 600))

        cropped_photo = ImageTk.PhotoImage(cropped_img)
        cropped_canvas = tk.Canvas(cropped_frame_frame, width=600, height=600)
        cropped_canvas.pack(side="left", anchor="nw")
        cropped_canvas.create_image(0, 0, anchor="nw", image=cropped_photo)
        cropped_canvas.image = cropped_photo

    def display_histograms(self, cropped_frame):
        histograms_frame = tk.Frame(self.popup_window)
        histograms_frame.pack(side="right", padx=20)

        self.display_line_histogram(cropped_frame, histograms_frame)
```

```python
        self.display_bar_histogram(cropped_frame, histograms_frame)

    def display_line_histogram(self, cropped_frame, histograms_frame):
        line_histogram_frame = tk.Frame(histograms_frame)
        line_histogram_frame.pack(side="top", pady=10)

        plt.figure(figsize=(12, 4))
        color = ('r', 'g', 'b')
        for i, col in enumerate(color):
            histr = cv2.calcHist([cropped_frame], [i], None, [256], [0, 256])
            plt.plot(histr, color=col, label=f'Channel {col.upper()}', linewidth=2)
            plt.xlim([0, 256])
        plt.title('Line Histogram')
        plt.xlabel('Pixel Value')
        plt.ylabel('Frequency')
        plt.tight_layout()
        plt.grid(True)
        plt.legend()

        line_histogram_img = self.plot_to_image(plt)
        self.display_histogram_image(line_histogram_frame, line_histogram_img)

    def display_bar_histogram(self, cropped_frame, histograms_frame):
        bar_histogram_frame = tk.Frame(histograms_frame)
        bar_histogram_frame.pack(side="bottom", pady=10)

        plt.figure(figsize=(12, 4))
        color = ('r', 'g', 'b')
        for i, col in enumerate(color):
            hist_range = (0, 256)
            hist_counts, _ = np.histogram(cropped_frame[:, :, i], bins=64, range=hist_range)
            plt.bar(np.arange(64), hist_counts, color=col, alpha=0.7, label=f'Channel {col.upper()}')
            for index, value in enumerate(hist_counts):
                plt.text(index, value + 10, str(int(value)), ha='center', va='bottom', fontsize=9)

        plt.title('Bar Histogram')
        plt.xlabel('Pixel Value')
        plt.ylabel('Frequency')
        plt.xticks(np.linspace(0, 63, num=5), np.linspace(0, 255, num=5, dtype=int))  # Adjust x-axis ticks
        plt.tight_layout()
        plt.grid(True)
        plt.legend()

        bar_histogram_img = self.plot_to_image(plt)
        self.display_histogram_image(bar_histogram_frame, bar_histogram_img)

    def display_histogram_image(self, parent_frame, img):
        histogram_photo = ImageTk.PhotoImage(image=img)
        histogram_canvas = tk.Canvas(parent_frame, width=900, height=300)
        histogram_canvas.pack(side="bottom", anchor="se")
        histogram_canvas.create_image(0, 0, anchor="nw", image=histogram_photo)
        histogram_canvas.image = histogram_photo

    def plot_histogram_bar_to_image(self, image):
        # Calculate histogram for each channel
        histograms = []
        for i in range(3):
            hist_range = (0, 256)
            hist_counts, _ = np.histogram(image[:, :, i], bins=64, range=hist_range)  # Adjust bins to 64
            histograms.append(hist_counts)
```

```python
        # Extracting only 64 bins from the histogram
        num_bins = 64  # Adjusted to 64 bins

        # Generating colors for each channel
        colors = ['red', 'green', 'blue']

        plt.figure()
        for i, histogram in enumerate(histograms):
            # Normalize the histogram counts for better visualization
            hist_counts = histogram / np.sum(histogram)
            # Setting the color for each channel
            plt.bar(np.arange(num_bins), hist_counts[:num_bins], color=colors[i], alpha=0.7,
label=f'Channel {["Red", "Green", "Blue"][i]}')

        plt.xlabel('Pixel Value')
        plt.ylabel('Normalized Frequency')
        plt.title('RGB Channel Histograms')
        plt.grid(True)
        plt.tight_layout()
        plt.legend()

        # Convert the histogram bar graph to an image
        histogram_bar_img = self.plot_to_image(plt)
        histogram_bar_photo = ImageTk.PhotoImage(image=histogram_bar_img)

        return histogram_bar_photo

    def plot_to_image(self, plt):
        plt.savefig('temp_plot.png')
        img = Image.open('temp_plot.png')
        return img

    def apply_filter(self, filter_name, frame):
        if filter_name == "None":
            return frame
        elif filter_name == "Gaussian":
            return cv2.GaussianBlur(frame, (5, 5), 0)
        elif filter_name == "Mean":
            return cv2.blur(frame, (5, 5))
        elif filter_name == "Median":
            return cv2.medianBlur(frame, 5)
        elif filter_name == "Bilateral Filtering":
            return cv2.bilateralFilter(frame, 9, 75, 75)
        elif filter_name == "Non-local Means Denoising":
            return cv2.fastNlMeansDenoisingColored(frame, None, 10, 10, 7, 21)
        elif filter_name == "Anisotropic Diffusion":
            return self.anisotropic_diffusion(frame)
        elif filter_name == "Total Variation Denoising":
            return self.total_variation_denoising(frame)
        elif filter_name == "Wiener Filter":
            return self.wiener_filter(frame)
        elif filter_name == "Adaptive Thresholding":
            return self.adaptive_threshold_each_channel(frame)
        elif filter_name == "Haar Wavelet Transform":
            return self.haar_wavelet_transform(frame)
        elif filter_name == "Daubechies Wavelet Transform":
            return self.daubechies_wavelet_transform(frame)
        else:
            return frame  # Default: return original frame if filter not found

    def wiener_filter(self, frame, kernel_size=(5, 5), noise_var=0.01):
        # Check if frame is None
        if frame is None:
```

```python
            print("Error: Input frame is None.")
            return None

        # Check if frame is a valid numpy array
        if not isinstance(frame, np.ndarray):
            print("Error: Input frame is not a numpy array.")
            return None

        # Check if frame is an empty array
        if frame.size == 0:
            print("Error: Input frame is empty.")
            return None

        # Check if frame is in BGR color space
        if frame.shape[-1] != 3:
            print("Error: Input frame is not in BGR color space.")
            return None

        # Apply Wiener filter
        filtered_frame = cv2.medianBlur(frame, kernel_size[0])  # Use kernel_size[0] as the kernel size
        filtered_frame = cv2.fastNlMeansDenoising(filtered_frame, h=noise_var)
        return filtered_frame

    def adaptive_threshold_each_channel(self, frame):
        # Split the frame into individual channels
        b, g, r = cv2.split(frame)

        # Apply adaptive thresholding to each channel separately
        b_thresh = cv2.adaptiveThreshold(b, 255, cv2.ADAPTIVE_THRESH_GAUSSIAN_C, cv2.THRESH_BINARY, 11, 2)
        g_thresh = cv2.adaptiveThreshold(g, 255, cv2.ADAPTIVE_THRESH_GAUSSIAN_C, cv2.THRESH_BINARY, 11, 2)
        r_thresh = cv2.adaptiveThreshold(r, 255, cv2.ADAPTIVE_THRESH_GAUSSIAN_C, cv2.THRESH_BINARY, 11, 2)

        # Merge the thresholded channels back together
        return cv2.merge([b_thresh, g_thresh, r_thresh])

    def haar_wavelet_transform(self, frame):
        # Split the frame into its individual color channels
        b, g, r = cv2.split(frame)

        # Perform the wavelet transform on each channel separately
        b_coeffs = pywt.dwt2(b, 'haar')
        g_coeffs = pywt.dwt2(g, 'haar')
        r_coeffs = pywt.dwt2(r, 'haar')

        # Reconstruct the channels from the coefficients
        b_reconstructed = pywt.idwt2(b_coeffs, 'haar')
        g_reconstructed = pywt.idwt2(g_coeffs, 'haar')
        r_reconstructed = pywt.idwt2(r_coeffs, 'haar')

        # Clip the values to ensure they are within the valid range
        b_reconstructed = np.clip(b_reconstructed, 0, 255).astype(np.uint8)
        g_reconstructed = np.clip(g_reconstructed, 0, 255).astype(np.uint8)
        r_reconstructed = np.clip(r_reconstructed, 0, 255).astype(np.uint8)

        # Merge the channels back together
        return cv2.merge([b_reconstructed, g_reconstructed, r_reconstructed])

    def daubechies_wavelet_transform(self, frame):
        # Split the frame into its individual color channels
        b, g, r = cv2.split(frame)
```

```python
        # Choose the wavelet function (Daubechies 5)
        wavelet = 'db5'

        # Perform the wavelet transform on each channel separately
        b_coeffs = pywt.dwt2(b, wavelet)
        g_coeffs = pywt.dwt2(g, wavelet)
        r_coeffs = pywt.dwt2(r, wavelet)

        # Reconstruct the channels from the coefficients
        b_reconstructed = pywt.idwt2(b_coeffs, wavelet)
        g_reconstructed = pywt.idwt2(g_coeffs, wavelet)
        r_reconstructed = pywt.idwt2(r_coeffs, wavelet)

        # Clip the values to ensure they are within the valid range
        b_reconstructed = np.clip(b_reconstructed, 0, 255).astype(np.uint8)
        g_reconstructed = np.clip(g_reconstructed, 0, 255).astype(np.uint8)
        r_reconstructed = np.clip(r_reconstructed, 0, 255).astype(np.uint8)

        # Merge the channels back together
        return cv2.merge([b_reconstructed, g_reconstructed, r_reconstructed])

    def anisotropic_diffusion(self, img):
        return cv2.fastNlMeansDenoisingColored(img, None, 10, 10, 7, 21)

    def apply_total_variation_denoising_channel(self, channel, weight, iterations):
        # Initialize the result with the original channel
        result = channel.copy().astype(np.float64)  # Convert to float64

        # Perform total variation denoising
        for _ in range(iterations):
            # Compute the gradient of the channel
            dx = cv2.Sobel(result, cv2.CV_64F, 1, 0, ksize=3)
            dy = cv2.Sobel(result, cv2.CV_64F, 0, 1, ksize=3)

            # Update the channel using the gradient and the weight
            result -= weight * np.sqrt(dx**2 + dy**2)

        # Clip the values to ensure they are within the valid range
        result = np.clip(result, 0, 255).astype(np.uint8)

        return result

    def total_variation_denoising(self, img, weight=0.01, iterations=20):
        # Split the image into its individual color channels
        b, g, r = cv2.split(img)

        # Apply total variation denoising to each channel separately
        b_denoised = self.apply_total_variation_denoising_channel(b, weight, iterations)
        g_denoised = self.apply_total_variation_denoising_channel(g, weight, iterations)
        r_denoised = self.apply_total_variation_denoising_channel(r, weight, iterations)

        # Merge the denoised channels back together
        return cv2.merge([b_denoised, g_denoised, r_denoised])
def main():
    root = tk.Tk()
    app = MixtureofGaussiansWithFilter(root)
    root.mainloop()

if __name__ == "__main__":
    main()
```

RUNNING PROGRAM

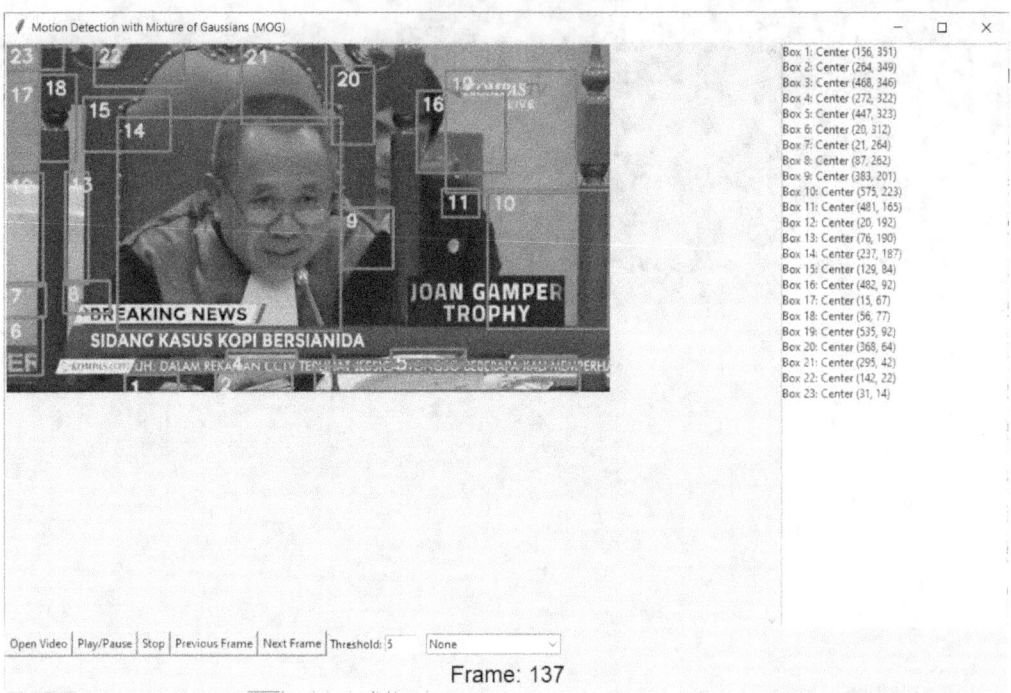

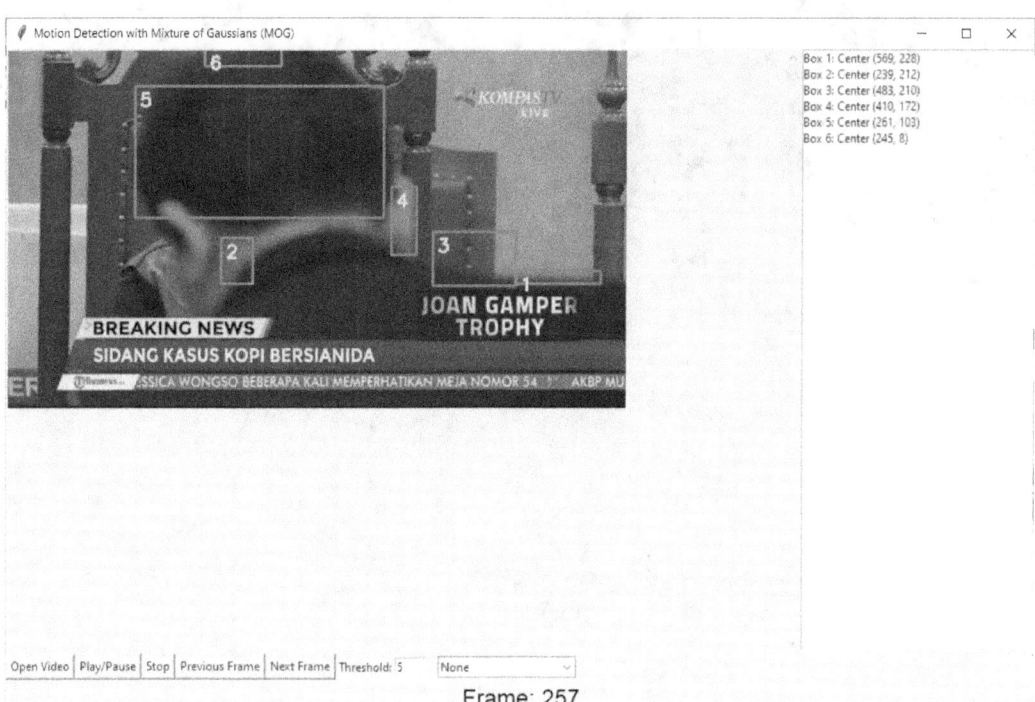

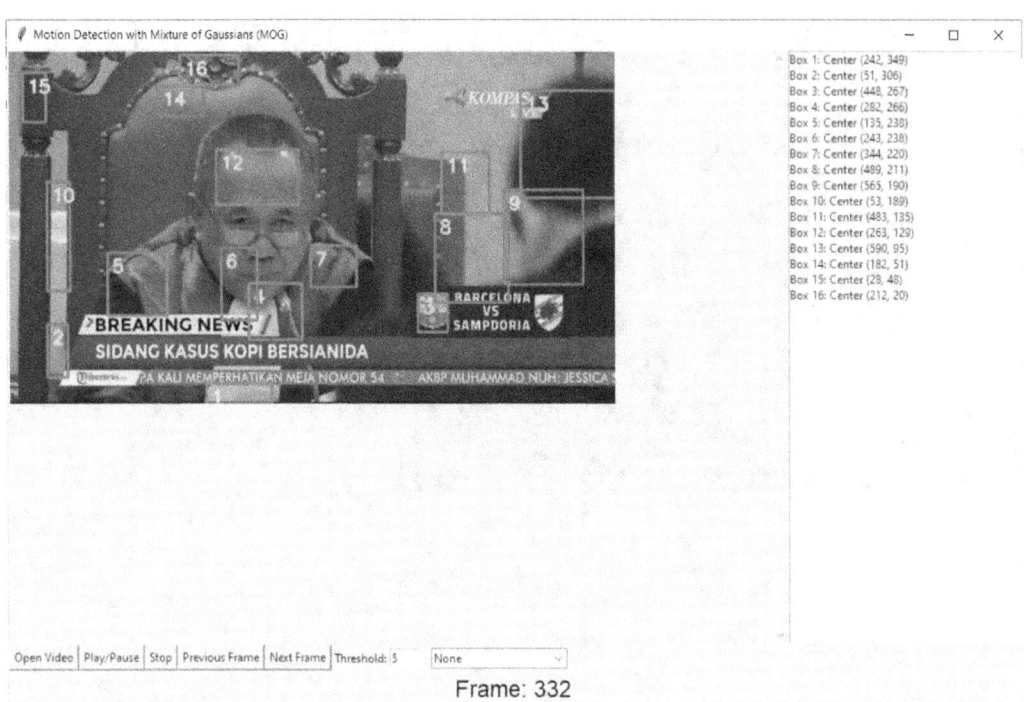

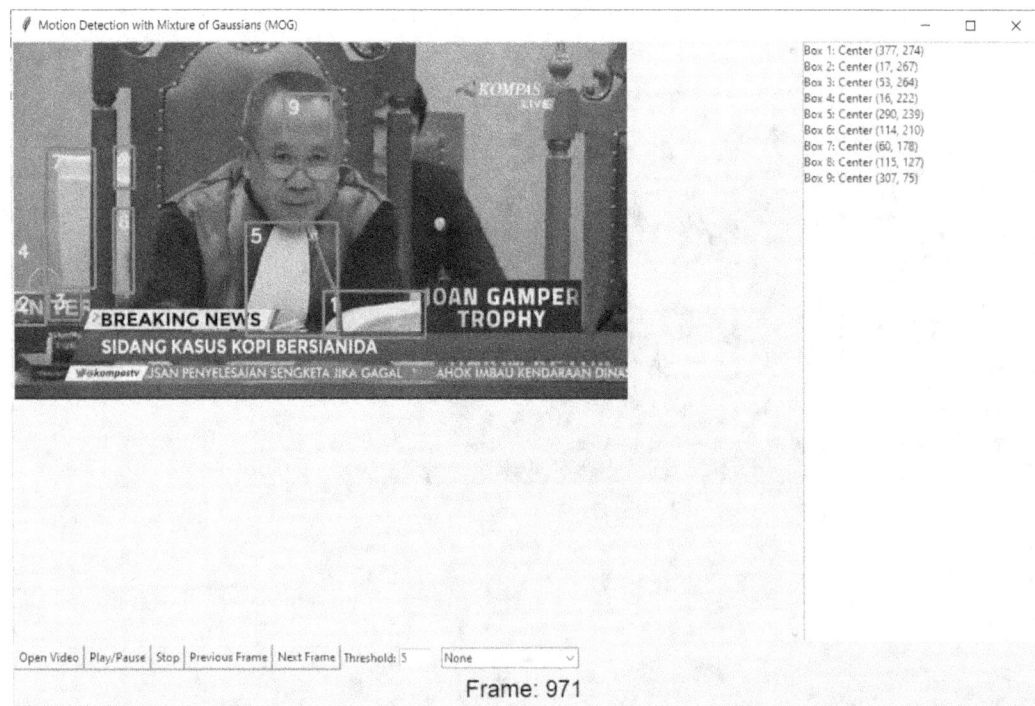

MOTION DETECTION WITH RUNNING GAUSSIAN AVERAGE

DESCRIPTION

The project running_gaussian_average_with_filtering.py is a Python script that implements motion detection using the Running Gaussian Average algorithm along with various filtering techniques. Here's an overview of the script:

The script utilizes the Tkinter library for creating a graphical user interface (GUI) to interact with video files. It also imports necessary modules such as OpenCV, PIL (Python Imaging Library), imageio, matplotlib, pywt (PyWavelets), and numpy.

The RunningGaussianAverage class serves as the main component of the application. It handles the initialization of the GUI, video processing, frame differencing, contour detection, and filtering.

The GUI consists of a canvas for displaying video frames, a listbox for showing detected object centers, and control buttons for video playback, frame navigation, and threshold adjustment.

The create_widgets method sets up the layout of the GUI components, including buttons, listbox, and threshold entry.

The open_video method allows users to select a video file and initializes the video reader object for further processing.

The toggle_play_pause method toggles the video playback state between play and pause.

The stop_video method stops the video playback and resets the frame index.

The play_video method continuously reads frames from the video file, processes them, and updates the display.

The process_frame method performs frame differencing, thresholding, contour detection, and object tracking.

The display_frame method updates the canvas with the processed video frame.

The on_mousewheel, on_press, on_drag, and on_release methods handle mouse events for zooming and object selection.

The analyze_histogram, create_popup_window, display_cropped_image, and display_histograms methods manage histogram analysis and visualization for selected regions of interest.

The apply_filter method applies various image filtering techniques based on user selection.

The main function initializes the Tkinter application and runs the GUI loop.

Overall, the script provides a user-friendly interface for motion detection and object tracking in video files, with options for applying different image filtering methods for enhanced analysis.

SOURCE CODE

```python
#running_gaussian_average_with_filtering.py
import tkinter as tk
from tkinter import ttk
from tkinter import filedialog
from PIL import Image, ImageTk
import cv2
import imageio
import matplotlib.pyplot as plt
import pywt
import numpy as np

class RunningGaussianAverage:
    def __init__(self, master):
        self.master = master
        self.master.title("Motion Detection with Running Gaussian Average")
        self.bbox_rect = None  # Initialize bbox_rect attribute to None
        self.running_average = None  # Stores the running average of frames

        # Video related variables
        self.video = None
        self.previous_frame = None
        self.frame_index = 0
        self.paused = True
        self.threshold = 5  # Default threshold for frame differencing

        # Creates widgets
        self.create_widgets(master)

    def create_widgets(self, master):
        # Create a frame for the canvas and listbox
        display_frame = tk.Frame(master)
        display_frame.pack(fill=tk.BOTH, expand=True)

        # Set up the canvas
        self.canvas = tk.Canvas(display_frame, width=800, height=600)
        self.canvas.pack(side=tk.LEFT, fill=tk.BOTH, expand=True)
        self.canvas.bind("<MouseWheel>", self.on_mousewheel)
        self.canvas.bind("<ButtonPress-1>", self.on_press)
        self.canvas.bind("<B1-Motion>", self.on_drag)
        self.canvas.bind("<ButtonRelease-1>", self.on_release)  # Bind ButtonRelease event

        # Set up the listbox for displaying centers
        self.listbox = tk.Listbox(display_frame, width=40, height=20)
        self.listbox.pack(side=tk.RIGHT, fill=tk.Y)

        # Add scrollbar to the listbox
        scrollbar = tk.Scrollbar(display_frame, orient="vertical", command=self.listbox.yview)
        scrollbar.pack(side=tk.RIGHT, fill=tk.Y)
        self.listbox.config(yscrollcommand=scrollbar.set)

        # Control Panel below the display frame
        control_panel = tk.Frame(master)
        control_panel.pack(fill=tk.X)

        self.open_button = tk.Button(control_panel, text="Open Video", command=self.open_video)
        self.open_button.pack(side=tk.LEFT)

        self.play_button = tk.Button(control_panel, text="Play/Pause", command=self.toggle_play_pause)
        self.play_button.pack(side=tk.LEFT)
```

```python
        self.stop_button = tk.Button(control_panel, text="Stop", command=self.stop_video)
        self.stop_button.pack(side=tk.LEFT)

        self.prev_button = tk.Button(control_panel, text="Previous Frame", command=self.prev_frame)
        self.prev_button.pack(side=tk.LEFT)

        self.next_button = tk.Button(control_panel, text="Next Frame", command=self.next_frame)
        self.next_button.pack(side=tk.LEFT)

        # Threshold Control
        self.threshold_label = tk.Label(control_panel, text="Threshold:")
        self.threshold_label.pack(side=tk.LEFT)

        self.threshold_entry = tk.Entry(control_panel, width=5)
        self.threshold_entry.pack(side=tk.LEFT)
        self.threshold_entry.insert(0, '5')  # Default threshold value
        self.threshold_entry.bind("<Return>", self.update_threshold)

        # Available filters
        self.filters = ["None", "Gaussian", "Mean", "Median", "Bilateral Filtering",
                        "Non-local Means Denoising", "Anisotropic Diffusion",
                        "Total Variation Denoising", "Wiener Filter",
                        "Adaptive Thresholding", "Haar Wavelet Transform",
                        "Daubechies Wavelet Transform"]

        # Subframe for complex controls such as combobox
        filter_frame = tk.Frame(control_panel)
        filter_frame.pack(side=tk.LEFT, fill=tk.X, expand=True)

        # Combobox for Selecting Filters
        self.filter_combobox = ttk.Combobox(filter_frame, values=self.filters)
        self.filter_combobox.pack(side=tk.LEFT, padx=10, pady=5)
        self.filter_combobox.current(0)  # Set default value

    def update_threshold(self, event):
        try:
            self.threshold = int(self.threshold_entry.get())
            print(f"Threshold updated to {self.threshold}")
        except ValueError:
            print("Invalid input for threshold. Please enter an integer.")

    def open_video(self):
        video_path = filedialog.askopenfilename(filetypes=[("Video files",
"*.mp4;*.avi;*.mkv;*.wmv")])
        if video_path:
            self.video = imageio.get_reader(video_path)
            self.frame_index = 0
            self.previous_frame = None
            self.paused = False
            self.play_video()
            self.update_frame_label()

    def toggle_play_pause(self):
        self.paused = not self.paused
        if not self.paused:
            self.play_video()

    def stop_video(self):
        self.paused = True
        self.frame_index = 0
        self.previous_frame = None
        self.update_frame_label()
```

```python
            self.display_frame(None)  # Clear the canvas

    def play_video(self):
        if not self.paused and self.video:
            if self.frame_index < len(self.video):
                try:
                    frame_data = self.video.get_data(self.frame_index)
                    frame = cv2.cvtColor(frame_data, cv2.COLOR_RGB2BGR)
                    self.process_frame(frame)
                    self.frame_index += 1
                    self.master.after(42, self.play_video)  # Schedule next frame
                except IndexError:
                    print("Reached the end of the video.")
                    self.paused = True  # Stop the video playback
                self.update_frame_label()

    def process_frame(self, frame):
        gray = cv2.cvtColor(frame, cv2.COLOR_BGR2GRAY)
        gray = cv2.GaussianBlur(gray, (21, 21), 0)  # Blur to reduce noise

        if self.running_average is None:
            self.running_average = gray.astype("float")
            return  # Skip the rest until the running average is initialized

        # Update the running average
        cv2.accumulateWeighted(gray, self.running_average, 0.05)

        # Compute the difference between the current frame and the running average
        frame_delta = cv2.absdiff(gray, cv2.convertScaleAbs(self.running_average))

        # Threshold the delta image
        thresh = cv2.threshold(frame_delta, self.threshold, 255, cv2.THRESH_BINARY)[1]
        thresh = cv2.dilate(thresh, None, iterations=2)  # Dilate the thresholded image to fill in holes

        # Find contours on the thresholded image
        contours, _ = cv2.findContours(thresh.copy(), cv2.RETR_EXTERNAL, cv2.CHAIN_APPROX_SIMPLE)

        self.listbox.delete(0, tk.END)  # Clear existing entries in the listbox
        box_number = 0  # Initialize box number

        # Loop over the contours
        for contour in contours:
            if cv2.contourArea(contour) < 500:
                continue  # Ignore small contours
            box_number += 1  # Increment the box number for each contour
            (x, y, w, h) = cv2.boundingRect(contour)
            center_x, center_y = x + w // 2, y + h // 2
            cv2.rectangle(frame, (x, y), (x+w, y+h), (50, 0, 255), 2)
            self.listbox.insert(tk.END, f"Box {box_number}: Center ({center_x}, {center_y})")
            cv2.rectangle(frame, (x, y), (x+w, y+h), (50, 0, 255), 2)
            cv2.putText(frame, f"{box_number}", (x + 5, y + 20), cv2.FONT_HERSHEY_SIMPLEX, 0.6, (0, 255, 0), 2)
        self.display_frame(frame)

    def display_frame(self, frame):
        if frame is not None:
            image = cv2.cvtColor(frame, cv2.COLOR_BGR2RGB)
            image = Image.fromarray(image)
            photo = ImageTk.PhotoImage(image=image)
            self.canvas.create_image(0, 0, anchor=tk.NW, image=photo)
            self.canvas.image = photo  # Keep the reference
        else:
```

```python
            self.canvas.delete("all")

    def process_and_display_frame(self):
        if self.video and self.frame_index >= 0 and self.frame_index < len(self.video):
            try:
                frame_data = self.video.get_data(self.frame_index)
                frame = cv2.cvtColor(frame_data, cv2.COLOR_RGB2BGR)
                self.process_frame(frame)
            except IndexError:
                print(f"Frame index {self.frame_index} is out of range.")
                self.paused = True  # Pause to prevent further errors
            except Exception as e:
                print(f"Error processing frame: {e}")
                self.paused = True
        self.update_frame_label()

    def next_frame(self):
        if self.video and self.frame_index < len(self.video) - 1:  # Check if next frame exists
            self.frame_index += 1
            self.process_and_display_frame()
        else:
            print("No more frames to display.")
            self.paused = True

    def prev_frame(self):
        if self.video and self.frame_index > 0:
            self.frame_index -= 1
            self.process_and_display_frame()
        else:
            print("Already at the first frame.")
            self.paused = True


    def update_frame_label(self):
        self.frame_label.config(text=f"Frame: {self.frame_index}")

    def on_mousewheel(self, event):
        direction = event.delta // 120
        current_value = int(self.zoom_scale.get())
        if direction == 1 and current_value < 10:
            current_value += 1
        elif direction == -1 and current_value > 1:
            current_value -= 1
        self.zoom_scale.set(current_value)
        self.update_zoom()

    def on_press(self, event):
        self.tracker = None
        self.start_x = self.canvas.canvasx(event.x)
        self.start_y = self.canvas.canvasy(event.y)
        # Clear the previous bounding box if it exists
        if self.bbox_rect:
            self.canvas.delete(self.bbox_rect)
            self.bbox_rect = None
        self.bbox = None
        self.bbox2 = None

    def on_drag(self, event):
        # Update the endpoint of the rectangle as the mouse moves
        cur_x = self.canvas.canvasx(event.x)
        cur_y = self.canvas.canvasy(event.y)

        # Define the coordinates correctly ensuring x1 < x2 and y1 < y2
```

```python
            x1, y1 = min(self.start_x, cur_x), min(self.start_y, cur_y)
            x2, y2 = max(self.start_x, cur_x), max(self.start_y, cur_y)

            # Update dimensions for tracking
            self.initial_w = x2 - x1
            self.initial_h = y2 - y1
            self.bbox = (x1, y1, self.initial_w, self.initial_h)
            self.bbox2 = (self.start_x, self.start_y, cur_x, cur_y)

            # Update or create a rectangle on the canvas
            if self.bbox_rect:
                self.canvas.coords(self.bbox_rect, x1, y1, x2, y2)
            else:
                self.bbox_rect = self.canvas.create_rectangle(x1, y1, x2, y2, outline="cyan", width=6)

    def on_release(self, event):
        self.analyze_histogram()   # Call analyze_histogram() method when the mouse button is released

    def analyze_histogram(self):
        if self.bbox2 is not None and self.video:
            x1, y1, x2, y2 = map(int, self.bbox2)
            if x1 != x2 and y1 != y2:
                try:
                    frame = self.video.get_data(self.frame_index)
                    # Ensure the bounding box is within the frame boundaries
                    h, w, _ = frame.shape
                    x1, x2 = max(0, min(x1, w)), max(0, min(x2, w))
                    y1, y2 = max(0, min(y1, h)), max(0, min(y2, h))

                    # Ensure x1 < x2 and y1 < y2
                    x1, x2 = sorted([x1, x2])
                    y1, y2 = sorted([y1, y2])

                    cropped_frame = frame[y1:y2, x1:x2]
                    if cropped_frame.size > 0:
                        cropped_frame = cv2.cvtColor(cropped_frame, cv2.COLOR_BGR2RGB)

                        # Get selected filter from combobox
                        selected_filter = self.filter_combobox.get()
                        # Apply selected filter
                        filtered_frame = self.apply_filter(selected_filter, cropped_frame)

                        self.create_popup_window(filtered_frame)
                        self.display_cropped_image(filtered_frame)
                        self.display_histograms(filtered_frame)
                    else:
                        print("Cropped frame is empty.")
                except Exception as e:
                    print("Failed to process frame:", e)
            else:
                print("Bounding box dimensions are zero or negative.")

    def create_popup_window(self, cropped_frame):
        self.popup_window = tk.Toplevel(self.master)
        self.popup_window.title("Cropped Image and Its Histogram")
        self.popup_window.geometry("1500x700")


    def display_cropped_image(self, cropped_frame):
        cropped_frame_frame = tk.Frame(self.popup_window)
        cropped_frame_frame.pack(side="left")
```

```python
            cropped_frame_rgb = cv2.cvtColor(cropped_frame, cv2.COLOR_BGR2RGB)
            cropped_img = Image.fromarray(cropped_frame_rgb)
            cropped_img = cropped_img.resize((600, 600))

            cropped_photo = ImageTk.PhotoImage(cropped_img)
            cropped_canvas = tk.Canvas(cropped_frame_frame, width=600, height=600)
            cropped_canvas.pack(side="left", anchor="nw")
            cropped_canvas.create_image(0, 0, anchor="nw", image=cropped_photo)
            cropped_canvas.image = cropped_photo

    def display_histograms(self, cropped_frame):
        histograms_frame = tk.Frame(self.popup_window)
        histograms_frame.pack(side="right", padx=20)

        self.display_line_histogram(cropped_frame, histograms_frame)
        self.display_bar_histogram(cropped_frame, histograms_frame)

    def display_line_histogram(self, cropped_frame, histograms_frame):
        line_histogram_frame = tk.Frame(histograms_frame)
        line_histogram_frame.pack(side="top", pady=10)

        plt.figure(figsize=(12, 4))
        color = ('r', 'g', 'b')
        for i, col in enumerate(color):
            histr = cv2.calcHist([cropped_frame], [i], None, [256], [0, 256])
            plt.plot(histr, color=col, label=f'Channel {col.upper()}', linewidth=2)
            plt.xlim([0, 256])
        plt.title('Line Histogram')
        plt.xlabel('Pixel Value')
        plt.ylabel('Frequency')
        plt.tight_layout()
        plt.grid(True)
        plt.legend()

        line_histogram_img = self.plot_to_image(plt)
        self.display_histogram_image(line_histogram_frame, line_histogram_img)

    def display_bar_histogram(self, cropped_frame, histograms_frame):
        bar_histogram_frame = tk.Frame(histograms_frame)
        bar_histogram_frame.pack(side="bottom", pady=10)

        plt.figure(figsize=(12, 4))
        color = ('r', 'g', 'b')
        for i, col in enumerate(color):
            hist_range = (0, 256)
            hist_counts, _ = np.histogram(cropped_frame[:, :, i], bins=64, range=hist_range)
            plt.bar(np.arange(64), hist_counts, color=col, alpha=0.7, label=f'Channel {col.upper()}')
            for index, value in enumerate(hist_counts):
                plt.text(index, value + 10, str(int(value)), ha='center', va='bottom', fontsize=9)

        plt.title('Bar Histogram')
        plt.xlabel('Pixel Value')
        plt.ylabel('Frequency')
        plt.xticks(np.linspace(0, 63, num=5), np.linspace(0, 255, num=5, dtype=int))  # Adjust x-axis ticks
        plt.tight_layout()
        plt.grid(True)
        plt.legend()

        bar_histogram_img = self.plot_to_image(plt)
        self.display_histogram_image(bar_histogram_frame, bar_histogram_img)
```

```python
    def display_histogram_image(self, parent_frame, img):
        histogram_photo = ImageTk.PhotoImage(image=img)
        histogram_canvas = tk.Canvas(parent_frame, width=900, height=300)
        histogram_canvas.pack(side="bottom", anchor="se")
        histogram_canvas.create_image(0, 0, anchor="nw", image=histogram_photo)
        histogram_canvas.image = histogram_photo

    def plot_histogram_bar_to_image(self, image):
        # Calculate histogram for each channel
        histograms = []
        for i in range(3):
            hist_range = (0, 256)
            hist_counts, _ = np.histogram(image[:, :, i], bins=64, range=hist_range)  # Adjust bins to 64
            histograms.append(hist_counts)

        # Extracting only 64 bins from the histogram
        num_bins = 64  # Adjusted to 64 bins

        # Generating colors for each channel
        colors = ['red', 'green', 'blue']

        plt.figure()
        for i, histogram in enumerate(histograms):
            # Normalize the histogram counts for better visualization
            hist_counts = histogram / np.sum(histogram)
            # Setting the color for each channel
            plt.bar(np.arange(num_bins), hist_counts[:num_bins], color=colors[i], alpha=0.7, label=f'Channel {["Red", "Green", "Blue"][i]}')

        plt.xlabel('Pixel Value')
        plt.ylabel('Normalized Frequency')
        plt.title('RGB Channel Histograms')
        plt.grid(True)
        plt.tight_layout()
        plt.legend()

        # Convert the histogram bar graph to an image
        histogram_bar_img = self.plot_to_image(plt)
        histogram_bar_photo = ImageTk.PhotoImage(image=histogram_bar_img)

        return histogram_bar_photo

    def plot_to_image(self, plt):
        plt.savefig('temp_plot.png')
        img = Image.open('temp_plot.png')
        return img

    def apply_filter(self, filter_name, frame):
        if filter_name == "None":
            return frame
        elif filter_name == "Gaussian":
            return cv2.GaussianBlur(frame, (5, 5), 0)
        elif filter_name == "Mean":
            return cv2.blur(frame, (5, 5))
        elif filter_name == "Median":
            return cv2.medianBlur(frame, 5)
        elif filter_name == "Bilateral Filtering":
            return cv2.bilateralFilter(frame, 9, 75, 75)
        elif filter_name == "Non-local Means Denoising":
            return cv2.fastNlMeansDenoisingColored(frame, None, 10, 10, 7, 21)
        elif filter_name == "Anisotropic Diffusion":
            return self.anisotropic_diffusion(frame)
```

```python
        elif filter_name == "Total Variation Denoising":
            return self.total_variation_denoising(frame)
        elif filter_name == "Wiener Filter":
            return self.wiener_filter(frame)
        elif filter_name == "Adaptive Thresholding":
            return self.adaptive_threshold_each_channel(frame)
        elif filter_name == "Haar Wavelet Transform":
            return self.haar_wavelet_transform(frame)
        elif filter_name == "Daubechies Wavelet Transform":
            return self.daubechies_wavelet_transform(frame)
        else:
            return frame  # Default: return original frame if filter not found

    def wiener_filter(self, frame, kernel_size=(5, 5), noise_var=0.01):
        # Check if frame is None
        if frame is None:
            print("Error: Input frame is None.")
            return None

        # Check if frame is a valid numpy array
        if not isinstance(frame, np.ndarray):
            print("Error: Input frame is not a numpy array.")
            return None

        # Check if frame is an empty array
        if frame.size == 0:
            print("Error: Input frame is empty.")
            return None

        # Check if frame is in BGR color space
        if frame.shape[-1] != 3:
            print("Error: Input frame is not in BGR color space.")
            return None

        # Apply Wiener filter
        filtered_frame = cv2.medianBlur(frame, kernel_size[0])  # Use kernel_size[0] as the kernel size
        filtered_frame = cv2.fastNlMeansDenoising(filtered_frame, h=noise_var)
        return filtered_frame

    def adaptive_threshold_each_channel(self, frame):
        # Split the frame into individual channels
        b, g, r = cv2.split(frame)

        # Apply adaptive thresholding to each channel separately
        b_thresh = cv2.adaptiveThreshold(b, 255, cv2.ADAPTIVE_THRESH_GAUSSIAN_C, cv2.THRESH_BINARY, 11, 2)
        g_thresh = cv2.adaptiveThreshold(g, 255, cv2.ADAPTIVE_THRESH_GAUSSIAN_C, cv2.THRESH_BINARY, 11, 2)
        r_thresh = cv2.adaptiveThreshold(r, 255, cv2.ADAPTIVE_THRESH_GAUSSIAN_C, cv2.THRESH_BINARY, 11, 2)

        # Merge the thresholded channels back together
        return cv2.merge([b_thresh, g_thresh, r_thresh])

    def haar_wavelet_transform(self, frame):
        # Split the frame into its individual color channels
        b, g, r = cv2.split(frame)

        # Perform the wavelet transform on each channel separately
        b_coeffs = pywt.dwt2(b, 'haar')
        g_coeffs = pywt.dwt2(g, 'haar')
        r_coeffs = pywt.dwt2(r, 'haar')
```

```python
        # Reconstruct the channels from the coefficients
        b_reconstructed = pywt.idwt2(b_coeffs, 'haar')
        g_reconstructed = pywt.idwt2(g_coeffs, 'haar')
        r_reconstructed = pywt.idwt2(r_coeffs, 'haar')

        # Clip the values to ensure they are within the valid range
        b_reconstructed = np.clip(b_reconstructed, 0, 255).astype(np.uint8)
        g_reconstructed = np.clip(g_reconstructed, 0, 255).astype(np.uint8)
        r_reconstructed = np.clip(r_reconstructed, 0, 255).astype(np.uint8)

        # Merge the channels back together
        return cv2.merge([b_reconstructed, g_reconstructed, r_reconstructed])

    def daubechies_wavelet_transform(self, frame):
        # Split the frame into its individual color channels
        b, g, r = cv2.split(frame)

        # Choose the wavelet function (Daubechies 5)
        wavelet = 'db5'

        # Perform the wavelet transform on each channel separately
        b_coeffs = pywt.dwt2(b, wavelet)
        g_coeffs = pywt.dwt2(g, wavelet)
        r_coeffs = pywt.dwt2(r, wavelet)

        # Reconstruct the channels from the coefficients
        b_reconstructed = pywt.idwt2(b_coeffs, wavelet)
        g_reconstructed = pywt.idwt2(g_coeffs, wavelet)
        r_reconstructed = pywt.idwt2(r_coeffs, wavelet)

        # Clip the values to ensure they are within the valid range
        b_reconstructed = np.clip(b_reconstructed, 0, 255).astype(np.uint8)
        g_reconstructed = np.clip(g_reconstructed, 0, 255).astype(np.uint8)
        r_reconstructed = np.clip(r_reconstructed, 0, 255).astype(np.uint8)

        # Merge the channels back together
        return cv2.merge([b_reconstructed, g_reconstructed, r_reconstructed])

    def anisotropic_diffusion(self, img):
        return cv2.fastNlMeansDenoisingColored(img, None, 10, 10, 7, 21)

    def apply_total_variation_denoising_channel(self, channel, weight, iterations):
        # Initialize the result with the original channel
        result = channel.copy().astype(np.float64)  # Convert to float64

        # Perform total variation denoising
        for _ in range(iterations):
            # Compute the gradient of the channel
            dx = cv2.Sobel(result, cv2.CV_64F, 1, 0, ksize=3)
            dy = cv2.Sobel(result, cv2.CV_64F, 0, 1, ksize=3)

            # Update the channel using the gradient and the weight
            result -= weight * np.sqrt(dx**2 + dy**2)

        # Clip the values to ensure they are within the valid range
        result = np.clip(result, 0, 255).astype(np.uint8)

        return result

    def total_variation_denoising(self, img, weight=0.01, iterations=20):
        # Split the image into its individual color channels
        b, g, r = cv2.split(img)

        # Apply total variation denoising to each channel separately
```

```
            b_denoised = self.apply_total_variation_denoising_channel(b, weight, iterations)
            g_denoised = self.apply_total_variation_denoising_channel(g, weight, iterations)
            r_denoised = self.apply_total_variation_denoising_channel(r, weight, iterations)

            # Merge the denoised channels back together
            return cv2.merge([b_denoised, g_denoised, r_denoised])
def main():
    root = tk.Tk()
    app = RunningGaussianAverage(root)
    root.mainloop()

if __name__ == "__main__":
    main()
```

RUNNING PROGRAM

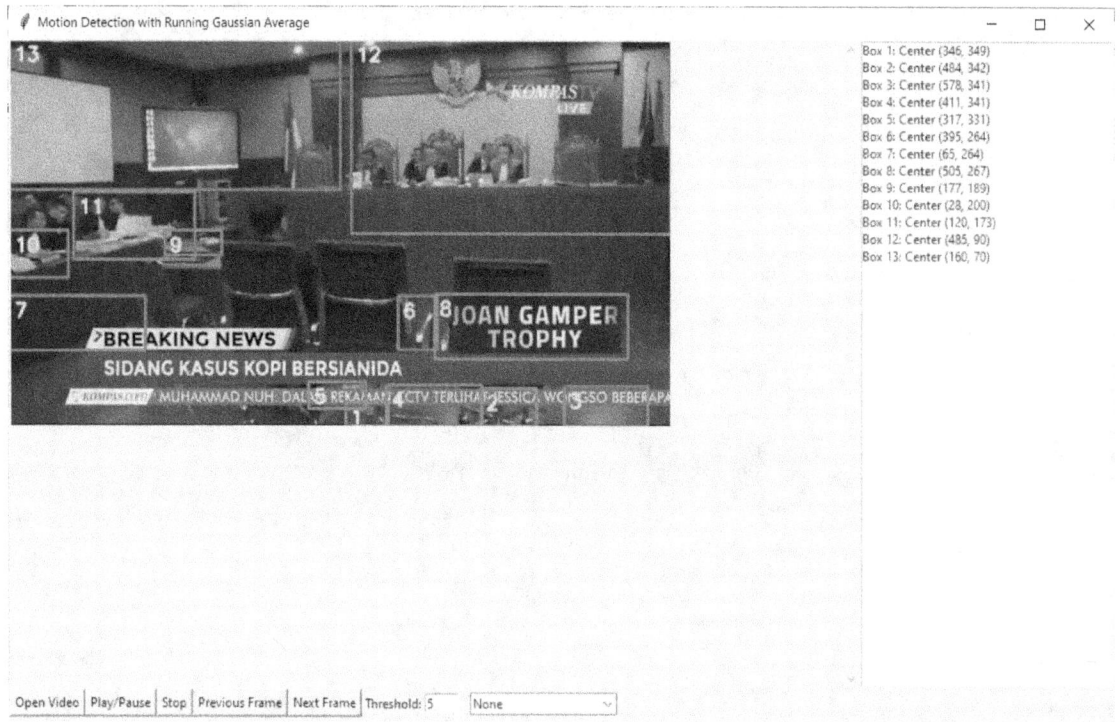

MOTION DETECTION WITH KERNEL DENSITY ESTIMATION

DESCRIPTION

This project, named kernel_density_estimation_with_filtering.py, is a Python script that implements motion detection using Kernel Density Estimation (KDE) and various filtering techniques. The script utilizes the Tkinter library for creating a graphical user interface (GUI) to interact with video files and visualize motion detection results.

The main class defined in the script is KDEWithFilter, which manages the GUI and the processing of video frames. Upon initialization, the class sets up the GUI elements including buttons, canvas for displaying video frames, listbox for showing detected objects, and a control panel for adjusting parameters.

The script relies on several libraries such as OpenCV (cv2), imageio, Matplotlib, PyWavelets (pywt), and NumPy for various tasks including video file I/O, image processing, contour detection, and filtering operations.

The KDEWithFilter class defines methods for opening video files, playing/pausing/stopping video playback, navigating through frames, updating threshold values, and applying filters to video frames.

The motion detection algorithm involves background subtraction using the MOG2 (Mixture of Gaussians) method, followed by contour detection to identify moving objects. The detected objects are then displayed on the canvas along with their bounding boxes and center coordinates.

Additionally, the script provides functionality for selecting regions of interest (ROI) within video frames using mouse events. Users can draw bounding boxes around objects to analyze their histograms and apply various filters such as Gaussian blur, mean filter, median filter, bilateral filtering, and more.

The script also includes methods for displaying cropped images, generating and displaying histograms (both line histograms and bar histograms) for the selected regions, and applying wavelet transforms for denoising.

Furthermore, the GUI allows users to interactively adjust parameters such as threshold values and filter types using sliders and comboboxes.

Overall, this project offers a comprehensive tool for motion detection and image filtering, providing both visual feedback through the GUI and numerical analysis of image features. The combination of KDE-based motion detection and filtering techniques makes it a versatile tool for various computer vision applications.

SOURCE CODE

```
#kernel_density_estimation_with_filtering.py
import tkinter as tk
from tkinter import ttk
from tkinter import filedialog
from PIL import Image, ImageTk
import cv2
```

```python
import imageio
import matplotlib.pyplot as plt
import pywt
import numpy as np

class KDEWithFilter:
    def __init__(self, master):
        self.master = master
        self.master.title("Motion Detection with Kernel Density Estimation")
        self.bbox_rect = None  # Initialize bbox_rect attribute to None

        # Initialize the MOG2 background subtractor
        self.mog2 = cv2.createBackgroundSubtractorMOG2(history=500, varThreshold=25, detectShadows=True)
        self.motion_density = None  # Initialize the motion density map

        # Video related variables
        self.video = None
        self.previous_frame = None
        self.frame_index = 0
        self.paused = True
        self.threshold = 5  # Default threshold for frame differencing

        # Creates widgets
        self.create_widgets(master)

    def create_widgets(self, master):
        # Create a frame for the canvas and listbox
        display_frame = tk.Frame(master)
        display_frame.pack(fill=tk.BOTH, expand=True)

        # Set up the canvas
        self.canvas = tk.Canvas(display_frame, width=800, height=600)
        self.canvas.pack(side=tk.LEFT, fill=tk.BOTH, expand=True)
        self.canvas.bind("<MouseWheel>", self.on_mousewheel)
        self.canvas.bind("<ButtonPress-1>", self.on_press)
        self.canvas.bind("<B1-Motion>", self.on_drag)
        self.canvas.bind("<ButtonRelease-1>", self.on_release)  # Bind ButtonRelease event

        # Set up the listbox for displaying centers
        self.listbox = tk.Listbox(display_frame, width=40, height=20)
        self.listbox.pack(side=tk.RIGHT, fill=tk.Y)

        # Add scrollbar to the listbox
        scrollbar = tk.Scrollbar(display_frame, orient="vertical", command=self.listbox.yview)
        scrollbar.pack(side=tk.RIGHT, fill=tk.Y)
        self.listbox.config(yscrollcommand=scrollbar.set)

        # Control Panel below the display frame
        control_panel = tk.Frame(master)
        control_panel.pack(fill=tk.X)

        self.open_button = tk.Button(control_panel, text="Open Video", command=self.open_video)
        self.open_button.pack(side=tk.LEFT)

        self.play_button = tk.Button(control_panel, text="Play/Pause", command=self.toggle_play_pause)
        self.play_button.pack(side=tk.LEFT)

        self.stop_button = tk.Button(control_panel, text="Stop", command=self.stop_video)
        self.stop_button.pack(side=tk.LEFT)

        self.prev_button = tk.Button(control_panel, text="Previous Frame", command=self.prev_frame)
```

```python
        self.prev_button.pack(side=tk.LEFT)
        
        self.next_button = tk.Button(control_panel, text="Next Frame", command=self.next_frame)
        self.next_button.pack(side=tk.LEFT)
        
        # Frame number label
        self.frame_label = tk.Label(master, text="Frame: 0", font=('Helvetica', 18))
        self.frame_label.pack()
        
        # Threshold Control
        self.threshold_label = tk.Label(control_panel, text="Threshold:")
        self.threshold_label.pack(side=tk.LEFT)
        
        self.threshold_entry = tk.Entry(control_panel, width=5)
        self.threshold_entry.pack(side=tk.LEFT)
        self.threshold_entry.insert(0, '5')  # Default threshold value
        self.threshold_entry.bind("<Return>", self.update_threshold)
        
        # Available filters
        self.filters = ["None", "Gaussian", "Mean", "Median", "Bilateral Filtering",
                        "Non-local Means Denoising", "Anisotropic Diffusion",
                        "Total Variation Denoising", "Wiener Filter",
                        "Adaptive Thresholding", "Haar Wavelet Transform",
                        "Daubechies Wavelet Transform"]
        
        # Subframe for complex controls such as combobox
        filter_frame = tk.Frame(control_panel)
        filter_frame.pack(side=tk.LEFT, fill=tk.X, expand=True)
        
        # Combobox for Selecting Filters
        self.filter_combobox = ttk.Combobox(filter_frame, values=self.filters)
        self.filter_combobox.pack(side=tk.LEFT, padx=10, pady=5)
        self.filter_combobox.current(0)  # Set default value
    
    def update_threshold(self, event):
        try:
            self.threshold = int(self.threshold_entry.get())
            print(f"Threshold updated to {self.threshold}")
        except ValueError:
            print("Invalid input for threshold. Please enter an integer.")
    
    def open_video(self):
        video_path = filedialog.askopenfilename(filetypes=[("Video files",
"*.mp4;*.avi;*.mkv;*.wmv")])
        if video_path:
            self.video = imageio.get_reader(video_path)
            self.frame_index = 0
            self.previous_frame = None
            self.paused = False
            self.play_video()
            self.update_frame_label()
    
    def toggle_play_pause(self):
        self.paused = not self.paused
        if not self.paused:
            self.play_video()
    
    def stop_video(self):
        self.paused = True
        self.frame_index = 0
        self.previous_frame = None
        self.update_frame_label()
        self.display_frame(None)  # Clear the canvas
```

```python
    def play_video(self):
        if not self.paused and self.video:
            if self.frame_index < len(self.video):
                try:
                    frame_data = self.video.get_data(self.frame_index)
                    frame = cv2.cvtColor(frame_data, cv2.COLOR_RGB2BGR)
                    self.process_frame(frame)
                    self.frame_index += 1
                    self.master.after(42, self.play_video)  # Schedule next frame
                except IndexError:
                    print("Reached the end of the video.")
                    self.paused = True  # Stop the video playback
                self.update_frame_label()

    def process_frame(self, frame):
        gray = cv2.cvtColor(frame, cv2.COLOR_BGR2GRAY)
        gray = cv2.GaussianBlur(gray, (21, 21), 0)

        # Apply the MOG2 model to get the foreground mask
        fg_mask = self.mog2.apply(gray)
        _, fg_mask = cv2.threshold(fg_mask, self.threshold, 255, cv2.THRESH_BINARY)

        # Update the motion density map
        if self.motion_density is None:
            self.motion_density = np.zeros_like(gray, dtype=float)
        # Accumulate the motion information
        self.motion_density += fg_mask.astype(float)

        # Optionally apply Gaussian blur to simulate KDE smoothing
        density_smoothed = cv2.GaussianBlur(self.motion_density, (21, 21), 0)
        density_normalized = np.clip((density_smoothed / density_smoothed.max()) * 255, 0, 255).astype(np.uint8)

        # Find contours on the thresholded image to detect moving objects
        contours, _ = cv2.findContours(fg_mask, cv2.RETR_EXTERNAL, cv2.CHAIN_APPROX_SIMPLE)

        self.listbox.delete(0, tk.END)
        box_number = 0

        # First, display the density map to set it as background
        background_image = cv2.applyColorMap(density_normalized, cv2.COLORMAP_JET)

        for contour in contours:
            if cv2.contourArea(contour) < 500:
                continue
            box_number += 1
            (x, y, w, h) = cv2.boundingRect(contour)
            center_x, center_y = x + w // 2, y + h // 2

            # Draw rectangle and text over the background image
            cv2.rectangle(background_image, (x, y), (x+w, y+h), (255, 255, 255), 2)
            cv2.putText(background_image, f"{box_number}", (x + 5, y + 20), cv2.FONT_HERSHEY_SIMPLEX, 0.6, (0, 0, 0), 2)
            self.listbox.insert(tk.END, f"Box {box_number}: Center ({center_x}, {center_y})")

        # Display the final image (density map + bounding boxes)
        self.display_frame(background_image)

    def display_frame(self, frame):
        if frame is not None:
            image = cv2.cvtColor(frame, cv2.COLOR_BGR2RGB)
            image = Image.fromarray(image)
            photo = ImageTk.PhotoImage(image=image)
            self.canvas.create_image(0, 0, anchor=tk.NW, image=photo)
```

```python
                self.canvas.image = photo  # Keep the reference
        else:
            self.canvas.delete("all")

    def process_and_display_frame(self):
        if self.video and self.frame_index >= 0 and self.frame_index < len(self.video):
            try:
                frame_data = self.video.get_data(self.frame_index)
                frame = cv2.cvtColor(frame_data, cv2.COLOR_RGB2BGR)
                self.process_frame(frame)
            except IndexError:
                print(f"Frame index {self.frame_index} is out of range.")
                self.paused = True  # Pause to prevent further errors
            except Exception as e:
                print(f"Error processing frame: {e}")
                self.paused = True
            self.update_frame_label()

    def next_frame(self):
        if self.video and self.frame_index < len(self.video) - 1:  # Check if next frame exists
            self.frame_index += 1
            self.process_and_display_frame()
        else:
            print("No more frames to display.")
            self.paused = True

    def prev_frame(self):
        if self.video and self.frame_index > 0:
            self.frame_index -= 1
            self.process_and_display_frame()
        else:
            print("Already at the first frame.")
            self.paused = True

    def update_frame_label(self):
        self.frame_label.config(text=f"Frame: {self.frame_index}")

    def on_mousewheel(self, event):
        direction = event.delta // 120
        current_value = int(self.zoom_scale.get())
        if direction == 1 and current_value < 10:
            current_value += 1
        elif direction == -1 and current_value > 1:
            current_value -= 1
        self.zoom_scale.set(current_value)
        self.update_zoom()

    def on_press(self, event):
        self.tracker = None
        self.start_x = self.canvas.canvasx(event.x)
        self.start_y = self.canvas.canvasy(event.y)
        # Clear the previous bounding box if it exists
        if self.bbox_rect:
            self.canvas.delete(self.bbox_rect)
            self.bbox_rect = None
        self.bbox = None
        self.bbox2 = None

    def on_drag(self, event):
        # Update the endpoint of the rectangle as the mouse moves
        cur_x = self.canvas.canvasx(event.x)
        cur_y = self.canvas.canvasy(event.y)
```

```python
        # Define the coordinates correctly ensuring x1 < x2 and y1 < y2
        x1, y1 = min(self.start_x, cur_x), min(self.start_y, cur_y)
        x2, y2 = max(self.start_x, cur_x), max(self.start_y, cur_y)

        # Update dimensions for tracking
        self.initial_w = x2 - x1
        self.initial_h = y2 - y1
        self.bbox = (x1, y1, self.initial_w, self.initial_h)
        self.bbox2 = (self.start_x, self.start_y, cur_x, cur_y)

        # Update or create a rectangle on the canvas
        if self.bbox_rect:
            self.canvas.coords(self.bbox_rect, x1, y1, x2, y2)
        else:
            self.bbox_rect = self.canvas.create_rectangle(x1, y1, x2, y2, outline="red", width=6)

    def on_release(self, event):
        self.analyze_histogram()  # Call analyze_histogram() method when the mouse button is released

    def analyze_histogram(self):
        if self.bbox2 is not None and self.video:
            x1, y1, x2, y2 = map(int, self.bbox2)
            if x1 != x2 and y1 != y2:
                try:
                    frame = self.video.get_data(self.frame_index)
                    # Ensure the bounding box is within the frame boundaries
                    h, w, _ = frame.shape
                    x1, x2 = max(0, min(x1, w)), max(0, min(x2, w))
                    y1, y2 = max(0, min(y1, h)), max(0, min(y2, h))

                    # Ensure x1 < x2 and y1 < y2
                    x1, x2 = sorted([x1, x2])
                    y1, y2 = sorted([y1, y2])

                    cropped_frame = frame[y1:y2, x1:x2]
                    if cropped_frame.size > 0:
                        cropped_frame = cv2.cvtColor(cropped_frame, cv2.COLOR_BGR2RGB)

                        # Get selected filter from combobox
                        selected_filter = self.filter_combobox.get()
                        # Apply selected filter
                        filtered_frame = self.apply_filter(selected_filter, cropped_frame)

                        self.create_popup_window(filtered_frame)
                        self.display_cropped_image(filtered_frame)
                        self.display_histograms(filtered_frame)
                    else:
                        print("Cropped frame is empty.")
                except Exception as e:
                    print("Failed to process frame:", e)
            else:
                print("Bounding box dimensions are zero or negative.")

    def create_popup_window(self, cropped_frame):
        self.popup_window = tk.Toplevel(self.master)
        self.popup_window.title("Cropped Image and Its Histogram")
        self.popup_window.geometry("1500x700")

    def display_cropped_image(self, cropped_frame):
        cropped_frame_frame = tk.Frame(self.popup_window)
```

```python
        cropped_frame_frame.pack(side="left")

        cropped_frame_rgb = cv2.cvtColor(cropped_frame, cv2.COLOR_BGR2RGB)
        cropped_img = Image.fromarray(cropped_frame_rgb)
        cropped_img = cropped_img.resize((600, 600))

        cropped_photo = ImageTk.PhotoImage(cropped_img)
        cropped_canvas = tk.Canvas(cropped_frame_frame, width=600, height=600)
        cropped_canvas.pack(side="left", anchor="nw")
        cropped_canvas.create_image(0, 0, anchor="nw", image=cropped_photo)
        cropped_canvas.image = cropped_photo

    def display_histograms(self, cropped_frame):
        histograms_frame = tk.Frame(self.popup_window)
        histograms_frame.pack(side="right", padx=20)

        self.display_line_histogram(cropped_frame, histograms_frame)
        self.display_bar_histogram(cropped_frame, histograms_frame)

    def display_line_histogram(self, cropped_frame, histograms_frame):
        line_histogram_frame = tk.Frame(histograms_frame)
        line_histogram_frame.pack(side="top", pady=10)

        plt.figure(figsize=(12, 4))
        color = ('r', 'g', 'b')
        for i, col in enumerate(color):
            histr = cv2.calcHist([cropped_frame], [i], None, [256], [0, 256])
            plt.plot(histr, color=col, label=f'Channel {col.upper()}', linewidth=2)
            plt.xlim([0, 256])
        plt.title('Line Histogram')
        plt.xlabel('Pixel Value')
        plt.ylabel('Frequency')
        plt.tight_layout()
        plt.grid(True)
        plt.legend()

        line_histogram_img = self.plot_to_image(plt)
        self.display_histogram_image(line_histogram_frame, line_histogram_img)

    def display_bar_histogram(self, cropped_frame, histograms_frame):
        bar_histogram_frame = tk.Frame(histograms_frame)
        bar_histogram_frame.pack(side="bottom", pady=10)

        plt.figure(figsize=(12, 4))
        color = ('r', 'g', 'b')
        for i, col in enumerate(color):
            hist_range = (0, 256)
            hist_counts, _ = np.histogram(cropped_frame[:, :, i], bins=64, range=hist_range)
            plt.bar(np.arange(64), hist_counts, color=col, alpha=0.7, label=f'Channel {col.upper()}')
            for index, value in enumerate(hist_counts):
                plt.text(index, value + 10, str(int(value)), ha='center', va='bottom', fontsize=9)

        plt.title('Bar Histogram')
        plt.xlabel('Pixel Value')
        plt.ylabel('Frequency')
        plt.xticks(np.linspace(0, 63, num=5), np.linspace(0, 255, num=5, dtype=int))  # Adjust x-axis ticks
        plt.tight_layout()
        plt.grid(True)
        plt.legend()

        bar_histogram_img = self.plot_to_image(plt)
```

```python
            self.display_histogram_image(bar_histogram_frame, bar_histogram_img)

    def display_histogram_image(self, parent_frame, img):
        histogram_photo = ImageTk.PhotoImage(image=img)
        histogram_canvas = tk.Canvas(parent_frame, width=900, height=300)
        histogram_canvas.pack(side="bottom", anchor="se")
        histogram_canvas.create_image(0, 0, anchor="nw", image=histogram_photo)
        histogram_canvas.image = histogram_photo

    def plot_histogram_bar_to_image(self, image):
        # Calculate histogram for each channel
        histograms = []
        for i in range(3):
            hist_range = (0, 256)
            hist_counts, _ = np.histogram(image[:, :, i], bins=64, range=hist_range)  # Adjust bins to 64
            histograms.append(hist_counts)

        # Extracting only 64 bins from the histogram
        num_bins = 64  # Adjusted to 64 bins

        # Generating colors for each channel
        colors = ['red', 'green', 'blue']

        plt.figure()
        for i, histogram in enumerate(histograms):
            # Normalize the histogram counts for better visualization
            hist_counts = histogram / np.sum(histogram)
            # Setting the color for each channel
            plt.bar(np.arange(num_bins), hist_counts[:num_bins], color=colors[i], alpha=0.7, label=f'Channel {["Red", "Green", "Blue"][i]}')

        plt.xlabel('Pixel Value')
        plt.ylabel('Normalized Frequency')
        plt.title('RGB Channel Histograms')
        plt.grid(True)
        plt.tight_layout()
        plt.legend()

        # Convert the histogram bar graph to an image
        histogram_bar_img = self.plot_to_image(plt)
        histogram_bar_photo = ImageTk.PhotoImage(image=histogram_bar_img)

        return histogram_bar_photo

    def plot_to_image(self, plt):
        plt.savefig('temp_plot.png')
        img = Image.open('temp_plot.png')
        return img

    def apply_filter(self, filter_name, frame):
        if filter_name == "None":
            return frame
        elif filter_name == "Gaussian":
            return cv2.GaussianBlur(frame, (5, 5), 0)
        elif filter_name == "Mean":
            return cv2.blur(frame, (5, 5))
        elif filter_name == "Median":
            return cv2.medianBlur(frame, 5)
        elif filter_name == "Bilateral Filtering":
            return cv2.bilateralFilter(frame, 9, 75, 75)
        elif filter_name == "Non-local Means Denoising":
            return cv2.fastNlMeansDenoisingColored(frame, None, 10, 10, 7, 21)
        elif filter_name == "Anisotropic Diffusion":
```

```python
            return self.anisotropic_diffusion(frame)
        elif filter_name == "Total Variation Denoising":
            return self.total_variation_denoising(frame)
        elif filter_name == "Wiener Filter":
            return self.wiener_filter(frame)
        elif filter_name == "Adaptive Thresholding":
            return self.adaptive_threshold_each_channel(frame)
        elif filter_name == "Haar Wavelet Transform":
            return self.haar_wavelet_transform(frame)
        elif filter_name == "Daubechies Wavelet Transform":
            return self.daubechies_wavelet_transform(frame)
        else:
            return frame  # Default: return original frame if filter not found

    def wiener_filter(self, frame, kernel_size=(5, 5), noise_var=0.01):
        # Check if frame is None
        if frame is None:
            print("Error: Input frame is None.")
            return None

        # Check if frame is a valid numpy array
        if not isinstance(frame, np.ndarray):
            print("Error: Input frame is not a numpy array.")
            return None

        # Check if frame is an empty array
        if frame.size == 0:
            print("Error: Input frame is empty.")
            return None

        # Check if frame is in BGR color space
        if frame.shape[-1] != 3:
            print("Error: Input frame is not in BGR color space.")
            return None

        # Apply Wiener filter
        filtered_frame = cv2.medianBlur(frame, kernel_size[0])  # Use kernel_size[0] as the kernel size
        filtered_frame = cv2.fastNlMeansDenoising(filtered_frame, h=noise_var)
        return filtered_frame

    def adaptive_threshold_each_channel(self, frame):
        # Split the frame into individual channels
        b, g, r = cv2.split(frame)

        # Apply adaptive thresholding to each channel separately
        b_thresh = cv2.adaptiveThreshold(b, 255, cv2.ADAPTIVE_THRESH_GAUSSIAN_C, cv2.THRESH_BINARY, 11, 2)
        g_thresh = cv2.adaptiveThreshold(g, 255, cv2.ADAPTIVE_THRESH_GAUSSIAN_C, cv2.THRESH_BINARY, 11, 2)
        r_thresh = cv2.adaptiveThreshold(r, 255, cv2.ADAPTIVE_THRESH_GAUSSIAN_C, cv2.THRESH_BINARY, 11, 2)

        # Merge the thresholded channels back together
        return cv2.merge([b_thresh, g_thresh, r_thresh])

    def haar_wavelet_transform(self, frame):
        # Split the frame into its individual color channels
        b, g, r = cv2.split(frame)

        # Perform the wavelet transform on each channel separately
        b_coeffs = pywt.dwt2(b, 'haar')
        g_coeffs = pywt.dwt2(g, 'haar')
        r_coeffs = pywt.dwt2(r, 'haar')
```

```python
        # Reconstruct the channels from the coefficients
        b_reconstructed = pywt.idwt2(b_coeffs, 'haar')
        g_reconstructed = pywt.idwt2(g_coeffs, 'haar')
        r_reconstructed = pywt.idwt2(r_coeffs, 'haar')

        # Clip the values to ensure they are within the valid range
        b_reconstructed = np.clip(b_reconstructed, 0, 255).astype(np.uint8)
        g_reconstructed = np.clip(g_reconstructed, 0, 255).astype(np.uint8)
        r_reconstructed = np.clip(r_reconstructed, 0, 255).astype(np.uint8)

        # Merge the channels back together
        return cv2.merge([b_reconstructed, g_reconstructed, r_reconstructed])

    def daubechies_wavelet_transform(self, frame):
        # Split the frame into its individual color channels
        b, g, r = cv2.split(frame)

        # Choose the wavelet function (Daubechies 5)
        wavelet = 'db5'

        # Perform the wavelet transform on each channel separately
        b_coeffs = pywt.dwt2(b, wavelet)
        g_coeffs = pywt.dwt2(g, wavelet)
        r_coeffs = pywt.dwt2(r, wavelet)

        # Reconstruct the channels from the coefficients
        b_reconstructed = pywt.idwt2(b_coeffs, wavelet)
        g_reconstructed = pywt.idwt2(g_coeffs, wavelet)
        r_reconstructed = pywt.idwt2(r_coeffs, wavelet)

        # Clip the values to ensure they are within the valid range
        b_reconstructed = np.clip(b_reconstructed, 0, 255).astype(np.uint8)
        g_reconstructed = np.clip(g_reconstructed, 0, 255).astype(np.uint8)
        r_reconstructed = np.clip(r_reconstructed, 0, 255).astype(np.uint8)

        # Merge the channels back together
        return cv2.merge([b_reconstructed, g_reconstructed, r_reconstructed])

    def anisotropic_diffusion(self, img):
        return cv2.fastNlMeansDenoisingColored(img, None, 10, 10, 7, 21)

    def apply_total_variation_denoising_channel(self, channel, weight, iterations):
        # Initialize the result with the original channel
        result = channel.copy().astype(np.float64)  # Convert to float64

        # Perform total variation denoising
        for _ in range(iterations):
            # Compute the gradient of the channel
            dx = cv2.Sobel(result, cv2.CV_64F, 1, 0, ksize=3)
            dy = cv2.Sobel(result, cv2.CV_64F, 0, 1, ksize=3)

            # Update the channel using the gradient and the weight
            result -= weight * np.sqrt(dx**2 + dy**2)

        # Clip the values to ensure they are within the valid range
        result = np.clip(result, 0, 255).astype(np.uint8)

        return result

    def total_variation_denoising(self, img, weight=0.01, iterations=20):
        # Split the image into its individual color channels
        b, g, r = cv2.split(img)
```

```
        # Apply total variation denoising to each channel separately
        b_denoised = self.apply_total_variation_denoising_channel(b, weight, iterations)
        g_denoised = self.apply_total_variation_denoising_channel(g, weight, iterations)
        r_denoised = self.apply_total_variation_denoising_channel(r, weight, iterations)

        # Merge the denoised channels back together
        return cv2.merge([b_denoised, g_denoised, r_denoised])
def main():
    root = tk.Tk()
    app = KDEWithFilter(root)
    root.mainloop()

if __name__ == "__main__":
    main()
```

RUNNING PROGRAM

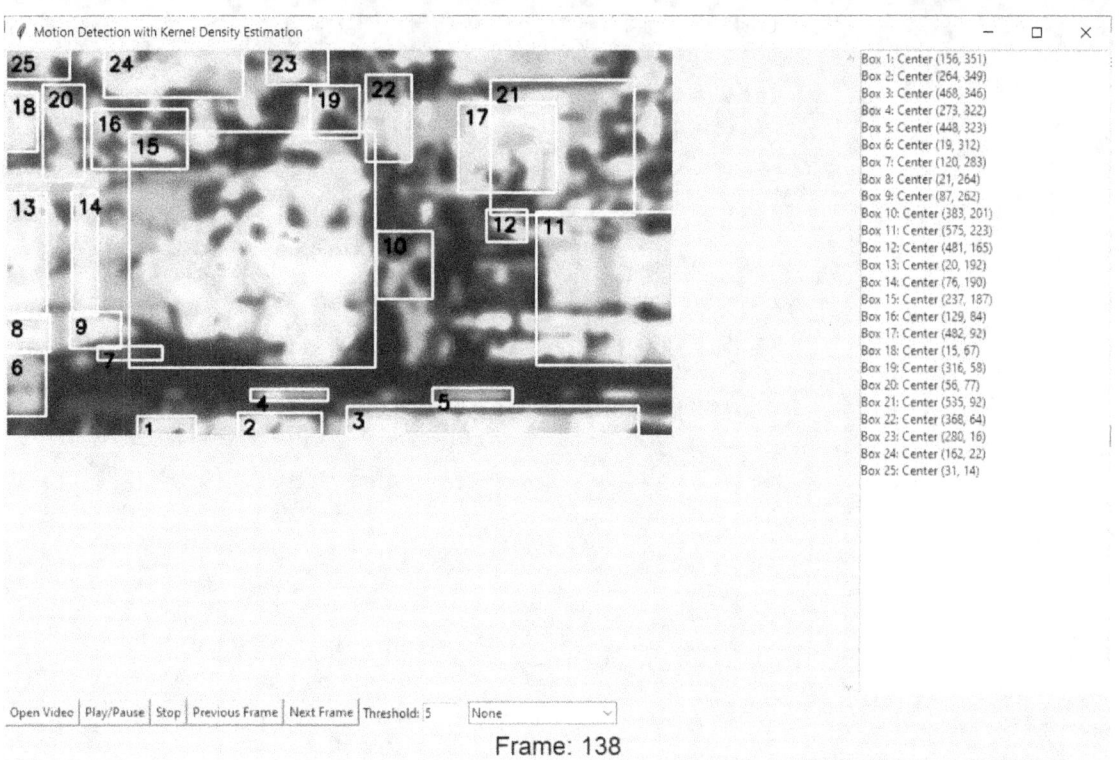

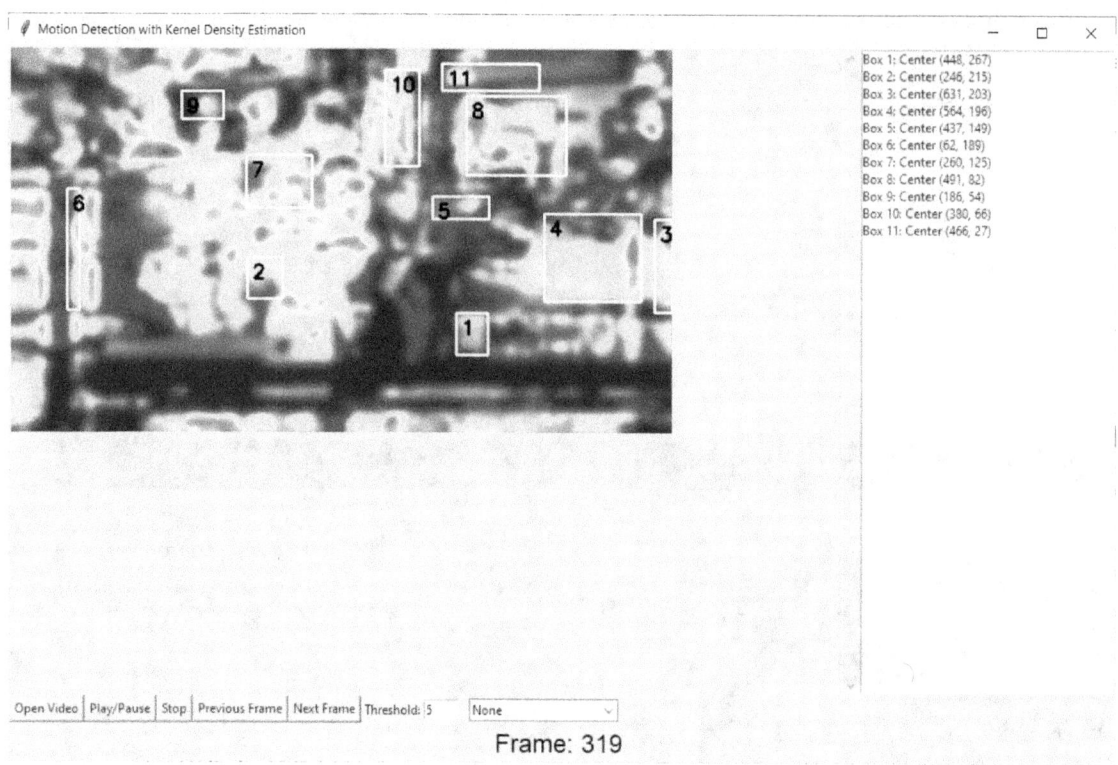

Bibliography

Vivian Siahaan and Rismon Hasiholan Sianipar. *TKINTER, DATA SCIENCE, AND MACHINE LEARNING*. North Sumatera: Balige Publishing, 2023.

Vivian Siahaan and Rismon Hasiholan Sianipar. *DATA VISUALIZATION, TIME-SERIES FORECASTING, AND PREDICTION USING MACHINE LEARNING WITH TKINTER*. North Sumatera: Balige Publishing, 2023.

Vivian Siahaan and Rismon Hasiholan Sianipar. *TIME-SERIES WEATHER FORECASTING AND PREDICTION USING MACHINE LEARNING WITH TKINTER*. North Sumatera: Balige Publishing, 2023.

Vivian Siahaan and Rismon Hasiholan Sianipar. DATA VISUALIZATION, TIME-SERIES FORECASTING, AND PREDICTION USING MACHINE LEARNING WITH TKINTER. North Sumatera: Balige Publishing, 2023.

Vivian Siahaan and Rismon Hasiholan Sianipar. START FROM SCRATCH DIGITAL SIGNAL PROCESSING WITH TKINTER. North Sumatera: Balige Publishing, 2023.

Vivian Siahaan and Rismon Hasiholan Sianipar. START FROM SCRATCH DIGITAL IMAGE PROCESSING WITH TKINTER. North Sumatera: Balige Publishing, 2023.

Vivian Siahaan and Rismon Hasiholan Sianipar. START FROM SCRATCH DIGITAL IMAGE PROCESSING WITH TKINTER. North Sumatera: Balige Publishing, 2023.

Vivian Siahaan and Rismon Hasiholan Sianipar. IMAGE DENOISING, EDGE DETECTION, AND SEGMENTATION WITH TKINTER. North Sumatera: Balige Publishing, 2023.

Vivian Siahaan and Rismon Hasiholan Sianipar. DIGITAL VIDEO PROCESSING PROJECTS USING PYTHON AND TKINTER. North Sumatera: Balige Publishing, 2024.

Vivian Siahaan and Rismon Hasiholan Sianipar. FRAME ANALYSIS AND PROCESSING IN DIGITAL VIDEO USING PYTHON AND TKINTER. North Sumatera: Balige Publishing, 2024.

Vivian Siahaan and Rismon Hasiholan Sianipar. MOTION ANALYSIS AND OBJECT TRACKING USING PYTHON AND TKINTER. North Sumatera: Balige Publishing, 2024.

Vivian Siahaan and Rismon Hasiholan Sianipar. FRAME FILTERING AND EDGES-DETECTION USING PYTHON AND TKINTER. North Sumatera: Balige Publishing, 2024.

Vivian Siahaan and Rismon Hasiholan Sianipar. OPTICAL FLOW ANALYSIS AND MOTION ESTIMATION IN DIGITAL VIDEO WITH PYTHON AND TKINTER. North Sumatera: Balige Publishing, 2024.

Vivian Siahaan and Rismon Hasiholan Sianipar. GRADIENT-BASED BLOCK MATCHING MOTION ESTIMATION AND OBJECT TRACKING WITH PYTHON AND TKINTER. North Sumatera: Balige Publishing, 2024.

Vivian Siahaan and Rismon Hasiholan Sianipar. FEATURES-BASED MOTION ESTIMATION AND OBJECT TRACKING WITH PYTHON AND TKINTER. North Sumatera: Balige Publishing, 2024.